The
NAPA & SONOMA
Book
A Complete Guide

A sure sign of spring: brilliant yellow mustard blooming.

THE
NAPA & SONOMA
BOOK
A Complete Guide

SIXTH EDITION

TIM FISH and PEG MELNIK

Berkshire House Publishers
Lee, Massachusetts

THE NAPA & SONOMA BOOK: A COMPLETE GUIDE
SIXTH EDITION — 2002

ISBN: 1-58157-054-6
ISSN: 1056-7968 (series)

Editor: Dale Evva Gelfand. Managing Editor: Philip Rich. Text design and typography: Dianne Pinkowitz. Cover design and typography: Jane McWhorter. Index by Diane Brenner. Maps by Maps.com.

Berkshire House books are available at substantial discounts for bulk purchases by corporations and other organizations for promotions and premiums. Special personalized editions can also be produced in large quantities. For more information, contact:

Berkshire House Publishers
480 Pleasant St., Suite 5, Lee, MA 01238
800-321-8526
E-mail: info@berkshirehouse.com
Website: www.berkshirehouse.com

Manufactured in the United States of America

10 9 8 7 6 5 4 3 2 1

No complimentary meals or lodgings were accepted by the author and reviewers in gathering information for this work.

Berkshire House Publishers'
Great Destinations™ travel guidebook series

Recommended by NATIONAL GEOGRAPHIC TRAVELER and TRAVEL & LEISURE magazines.

[A] crisp and critical approach, for travelers who want to live like locals.

USA TODAY

Great Destinations™ guidebooks are known for their comprehensive, critical coverage of regions of extraordinary cultural interest and natural beauty. The authors in this series are professional travel writers who have lived for many years in the regions they describe. Each title in this series is continuously updated with each printing, in order to insure accurate and timely information. All of the books contain over 100 photographs and maps.

Neither the publisher, the authors, the reviewers, nor other contributors accept complimentary lodgings, meals, or any other consideration (such as advertising) while gathering information for any book in this series.

Current titles available:
The Adirondack Book
The Berkshire Book
The Charleston, Savannah & Coastal Islands Book
The Chesapeake Bay Book
The Coast of Maine Book
The Finger Lakes Book
The Hamptons Book
The Monterey Bay, Big Sur & Gold Coast Wine Country Book
The Nantucket Book
The Newport & Narragansett Bay Book
The Napa & Sonoma Book
The Santa Fe & Taos Book
The Sarasota, Sanibel Island & Naples Book
The Texas Hill Country Book
Wineries of the Eastern States

If you are traveling to, moving to, residing in, or just interested in any (or all!) of these enchanting regions, a **Great Destinations™** guidebook is a superior companion. Honest and painstakingly critical, full of information only a local can provide, **Great Destinations™** guidebooks provide you with all the practical knowledge you need to enjoy the best of each region. Why not own them all?

Acknowledgments

The fingerprints of many people are all over this book.

Particular thanks to Christina Markell and Caitlin Woodbury for helping us update the book. Christina helped with the Shopping chapter, while both updated the Recreation chapter. We appreciate their precision and enthusiasm. We also had the good fortune to work with Thomas Hallstein, our meticulous chief photographer, a man of true vision. And where would we be without our team of restaurant and lodging reviewers? Researchers included John Holdredge and Carri O'Loughlin, Leslie Mancillas, Dan Kosta, Diane Holt and Michele D. McFarland, and Sarah Goan.

Numerous organizations proved to be great resources. The Napa County Historical Society and Sonoma County Museum supplied many of our priceless historic photographs. The chambers of commerce of Calistoga, St. Helena, and Napa as well as the Sonoma County Convention and Visitors Bureau and the Sonoma Valley Visitors Bureau provided detailed and valuable information.

And a very special thanks to Jean Rousseau, Philip Rich and Carol Bosco Baumann of Berkshire House Publishers.

Finally, the authors would like to hear from you. What do you like and dislike about this book? Also, let them know about your experiences in Wine Country — both good and bad. They hope the inns, restaurants, wineries, and other businesses that are mentioned live up to their recommendations. If they don't, let them know. Contact Fish and Melnik directly via e-mail at TimFish@ saber.net.

Contents

CHAPTER ONE
Wine Country Chronicles
HISTORY
1

CHAPTER TWO
Getting There
TRANSPORTATION
14

CHAPTER THREE
A Place to Call Your Own
LODGING
24

CHAPTER FOUR
Life is Sweet!
CULTURE
78

CHAPTER FIVE
Bon Appetit!
RESTAURANTS & FOOD PURVEYORS
110

CHAPTER SIX
Poetry in a Bottle
WINERIES & SPECIALTY BREWERS
162

CHAPTER SEVEN
The Great Outdoors
RECREATION
233

CHAPTER EIGHT
For the Sport of It
SHOPPING
271

CHAPTER NINE
Facts on File
INFORMATION
287

Introduction

This book is for tourists and natives alike who not only appreciate opinionated authors like us - but welcome our advice. We feel strongly that we want you to spend your time wisely. You shouldn't be wasting your time on tourist traps or even second-rate restaurants. After all, your time in Wine Country is precious, prime time.

Putting together the sixth edition of *The Napa and Sonoma Book* was quite a challenge. How do you improve a book that has already been called the best Wine Country guide by *The New York Times, The Los Angeles Times, Wine & Spirits, San Francisco Focus* magazine, the *Orange County Register* and *The California Grapevine*? But we gave it a shot and believe you'll be pleased with the results.

One thing has not changed since the first edition, of course. Napa and Sonoma counties are remarkable places. After a few days of sampling the cabernet sauvignons, zinfandels, and chardonnays, you may never go home. But as you read this book you'll see that there's far more to Napa and Sonoma than wine. We are continually amazed at the beauty of this place. Merely driving to work remains a treat. There is a sense of mystery and strength in the surrounding mountains. The vineyards and fields take on a vibrant yellow in the spring as the wild mustard arrives with the fog and rain. In the summer, the vines grow bushy and green, weighed down with grapes, and in the

fall they take on the delicate reds and yellows of autumn leaves. The hills rolling to the coast assume a shimmering green in the spring, reminding us unmistakably of Ireland. With its cliffs and pounding shore, the coastline is dramatic and jagged. It rivals even the famed Big Sur to the south.

With this Great Outdoors comes a whirl of recreational activities, everything from tennis to tide pooling. For those who prefer pampering to a strenuous hike among redwoods, Napa and Sonoma will indulge. Health spas soothe the body and soul. The restaurants of Wine Country insist that you can be healthy and luxurious at the same time, marrying the best of local meats and produce with just the right wine. The inns and bed-and-breakfasts appeal to every style, from easy country pleasure to posh extravagance.

How can you possibly know where to begin? That's where we come in. We've created a book to guide you through Wine Country with a minimum of fuss and a maximum of pleasure. We wish you a congenial and happy stay. Read on and enjoy.

Tim Fish and Peg Melnik
Santa Rosa, California

THE WAY THIS BOOK WORKS

This book is divided into nine chapters. Entries within each chapter are first divided into "Napa County" and "Sonoma County," and then each county is broken down geographically, according to the names of towns, moving generally from south to north.

Some entries include specific information, telephone numbers, addresses, business hours and the like, organized for easy reference in blocks in the left-hand column. All information was checked as close to the publication date as possible. Even so, since details can change without warning, it is always wise to call ahead.

For the same reason we have routinely avoided listing specific prices, indicating instead a range. Lodging price codes are based on a per-room rate, double occupancy during summer months. Off-season rates are often cheaper. Restaurant price ratings indicate the cost of an individual meal including appetizer, entrée, and dessert but not cocktails, wine, tax, or tip.

PRICE CODES

Lodging	Dining	
Inexpensive	Up to $100	Up to $10
Moderate	$100 to $150	$10 to $22
Expensive	$150 to $250	$22 to $35
Very Expensive	Over $250	$35 or more

Credit cards are abbreviated as follows:

AE — American Express   DC — Diner's Club
CB —Carte Blanche   MC — Master Card
D — Discover Card   V — Visa

TOWNS IN NAPA AND SONOMA COUNTIES

Napa and Sonoma Counties, you'll discover, resist being broken down into neat geographic areas. Easier to categorize is Napa Valley, with its strip of small towns and villages beginning in the south with the population center, the city of Napa. North from there is Yountville, a popular tourist mecca with shops and restaurants. The vineyard villages of Oakville and Rutherford come next, followed by St. Helena with its lovely downtown storefronts. Finally, at the county's warm northern end is the resort town of Calistoga. Sonoma County is larger and more varied. Sonoma Valley, narrow and somehow separate, is home to the historical city of Sonoma and to the vineyard communities of Kenwood and Glen Ellen. In south-central Sonoma County is the river town of Petaluma, bordered on the north by the village of Cotati and the ever-growing bedroom community of Rohnert Park.. Santa Rosa is Sonoma County's largest city as well as its business and cultural hub. To the north, surrounded by vineyards, is the quiet community of Healdsburg. "West County," as locals call it, has a personality of its own. Its wild terrain makes it part "rugged individualist," but its popularity as an immigration spot for San Francisco's counterculturalists during the 1960s makes it part "earth child," as well.

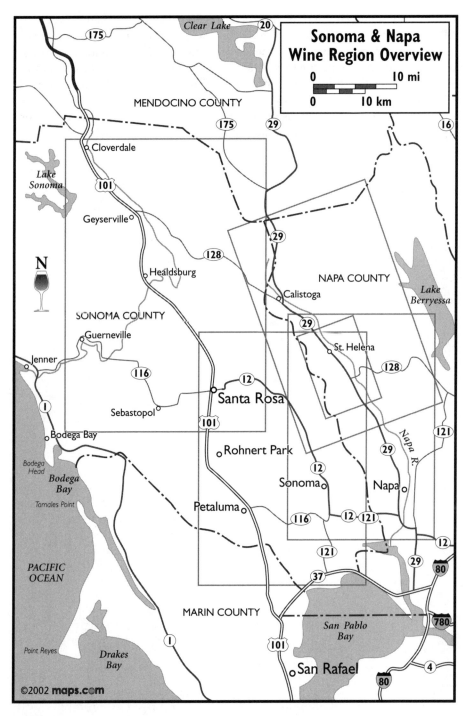

Detailed maps for areas marked by boxes can be found on pages 330–339.

CHAPTER ONE
Wine Country Chronicles
HISTORY

History repeats itself; that's the one thing that's wrong with history.
— Clarence Darrow

At Fort Ross State Historic park, the cannon and chapel at the Russian settlement await history buffs.

Thomas Hallstein/Outsight

Why was it, back in school, that the worst, most monotonous teachers taught history? It didn't take long before all those dates and wars and proclamations made your brain glaze over like an Easter ham. Well, that history won't repeat itself here. It helps, of course, that Napa and Sonoma Counties have a lively past, busy with fascinating people and places — and, yes, dates and wars and proclamations, too. From the thunderous tremors that raised the land out of a prehistoric sea to the chic winery life of today, Napa and Sonoma Counties have been twins — not identical but fraternal. They share similar origins but have grown into distinctly different siblings.

NATURAL HISTORY

A vast inland sea once spanned Napa and Sonoma Counties, the salt water over the millennia nourishing the soil. The Mayacamas Mountains, as well as coastal and other mountain ranges, attest to the land's violent origins. Continental plates have fought for elbow room here for millions of years, colliding and complaining, creating a tectonic furnace of magma and spewing forth volcanoes and towering mountain spines that now divide and surround the two counties.

The rolling hills of the Carneros mark the southern borders, where Napa and Sonoma Counties meet San Pablo Bay. Between them looms the Mayacamas range with the peaks of Mt. Veeder and Diamond Mountain. Low coastal hills border Sonoma on the west, and the Blue Ridge shoulders Napa on the east. On the northern edge begins a vast stairstep of ranges that lead to the California border and beyond.

At 4,344 feet, Mount St. Helena is the area's tallest remnant of the volcanic era. Today, magma still simmers below the hills, producing the area's powerful geysers and Calistoga's soothing mineral water. Another vivid reminder occurs on occasion: earthquakes. The San Andreas fault runs up the center of Bodega Head on the coast, and the more timid Rodger's Creek fault sits beneath Santa Rosa and Healdsburg.

When the ancient sea receded, it left bays and lagoons that became fertile valleys. The Napa and Russian Rivers formed and for eons roamed back and forth over the face of the Napa and Santa Rosa plains, mixing the soil and volcanic ash. Napa Valley, 5 miles wide and 40 miles long, lies east of the Mayacamas. The land to the west was more vast, with dozens of smaller valleys: Sonoma the largest and most temperate, the parched Alexander and Dry Creek Valleys to the north, and near the ocean the lush Russian River Valley, where redwoods the width of two-car garages began to grow. All the while the Pacific continued to pound western Sonoma, even today eroding its jagged coastline.

It's hard to imagine a land more made-to-order for wine. The soil is rich with minerals from ancient oceans and volcanic ash, and the rocky nature of the land creates excellent drainage. Cool air masses from the Pacific meet the dry desert air from the east, creating a unique climate. Fog chills the mornings, then burns off as the days turn ideally warm; and as the sun sets, the crisp air returns. And perhaps most important: rain. Typically, Napa and Sonoma Counties are drenched from December through April; then things dry up until November. In all, a perfect spot for wine.

Beer hops were a big business in Sonoma County in the early 1900s, and hop kilns were abundant.

Courtesy Sonoma County Museum

As humans were entering stage right, Napa and Sonoma Counties already pulsed with life. Cougars, lynx, rattlesnakes, wolves, elk, and deer roamed along with the mightiest of all, grizzly bears. Hawks, buzzards, and eagles glided above the hillsides. Sturgeon and salmon swarmed in the rivers, and along the coast, whales, otters, and sea lions prospered, and the great white shark lurked. Many have survived the arrival of man, though in reduced numbers. Others were not so lucky.

SOCIAL HISTORY

FIRST INHABITANTS

Brave the occasionally harrowing California freeway system, and you'll inevitably see this bumper sticker: CALIFORNIA NATIVE. How natives do moan about newcomers. It's rather silly, of course, since people are such a recent addition to Northern California — 5,000 years, in the big scheme of things, is hardly enough time to unpack.

Miwok Indians thrived along the coast of Sonoma County for generations.

Courtesy Sonoma County Museum

The earliest "newcomers" crossed the land bridge that once connected Asia and Alaska and wandered south. The first known inhabitants were the Pomo and Miwok tribes in Sonoma, and the Wappo who lived in Napa Valley and eastern Sonoma County. It was a plentiful place and allowed an unhurried way of life, the men hunting and the women gathering berries, mussels, and other food. They assembled near the streams when salmon returned but were careful because the grizzly bear had a taste for human flesh, as well. Communities thrived. Most were small, but some villages had populations of

1,000 or more. Coastal Miwok used shells as money, and Pomo women achieved great expertise as basket makers. Pomo men lived away from their wives in communal lodges, which also served as ceremonial sweat houses as well as impromptu schools for boys. These early inhabitants gave special names to this land of theirs, names that remain today. Not that historians particularly agree on what the words mean. *Mayacamas* is a Spanish adaptation of an Native American word that meant "howl of the mountain lion." *Napa*, depending on which story you believe, is Wappo for "grizzly bear," "fish," or "bountiful place." *Petaluma*, a city in southern Sonoma County, may be Pomo for "flat back" or Miwok for "behind the hill" — both referring to the Sonoma Mountains and the flat Petaluma plain. *Cotati*, another Sonoma County city, sounds poetic, but its possible Pomo meaning is anything but romantic: "punch in the face." One name that didn't stick was *Shabakai*, or "long snake" — that's what natives called the Russian River.

The first Europeans arrivals were heavily outnumbered. As many as 12,000 Wappo lived between Napa and Clear Lake to the north, and 8,000 Pomo prospered in what are now Sonoma, Lake, and Mendocino Counties. That would quickly change.

Sonoma County was the first to be explored by the white man, and as explorers often seem to do, they stumbled onto it by accident. Lt. Francisco de Bodega y Cuadra was piloting his Spanish ship the *Sonora* along the coast in search of San Francisco Bay. Startled Indians paddled out in canoes to greet the *Sonora*, presenting the crew with elaborate feather and shell offerings. Rough seas and a damaged skiff prevented Bodega y Cuadra and crew from actually coming ashore, but Bodega's name stuck somehow: Bodega Bay. The first expedition actually to land in Sonoma County came the following year, when a small party of Spanish set out from their *presidio*, or military outpost, in San Francisco. Crossing the bay, they entered the mouth of the Petaluma River with the crazy notion that it ended up in Tomales Bay and the vast Pacific. (Always looking for shortcuts, those explorers.) It didn't, of course, so Lt. Fernando Quiros and his crew explored the Petaluma plain instead.

Russians and not the Spanish, however, were the first to establish an outpost in the area. By the early 1800s the Russian-American Company, a private entity supported largely by imperial Russia, was expanding south after the Alaskan fur trade began to play out. In 1809 Ivan Kuskov and crew landed in Bodega Bay and scouted the area. They returned in 1812 and established a colony they called Rumiantsev. Exploring the coastline further, Kuskov selected a blustery bluff a few miles to the north and established Fort Ross the following year. The fort became the hub of Russian activity and Rumiantsev their major port. Though a prime location for fur trade, Fort Ross was not the most habitable place. Even today the bluffs overlooking the Pacific are fogged in much of the year, and the wind and dampness can be severe. One early visitor wrote: "It is so easy to catch cold here that even those inhabitants of Ross who were born here are sick almost every year." Later, ranches were established inland where the climate was more moderate, and the Russians grew much-needed grain and produce for their Alaskan settlements. The slaughter of sea otters, meanwhile, was ruthless and devastating. By 1821, the annual catch had dropped from hundreds to 32.

THIS LAND IS WHOSE LAND?

Wine Country's first settlement: Mission San Francisco in Sonoma.

Thomas Hallstein/Outsight

The Spanish weren't keen on the Russians hanging around just to the north. They were determined that their presidio in San Francisco would be the dominant force in the area. Even when Mexico declared independence from Spain in 1822, that didn't lessen the importance of the land north of San Francisco. California had been explored and established largely through the mission system, which began in 1769 as a way to civilize the "heathen" natives and convert them to Catholicism. It was also a way to establish a Spanish presence and, if the mission was successful, add greatly to the wealth and power of the church.

In 1823 Father Jose Altimira, an ambitious young priest at San Francisco's Mission Dolores, became convinced that a new mission was needed in the northern territory. Church authorities, cautiously considering their waning influence with the new Mexican government, balked, so Altimira turned to Don Luis Arguello, Mexican governor of California. Arguello saw an opportunity to thwart the Russians and approved the idea. Altimira set out that year with a party of 14 soldiers to explore the land north of the bay, from Petaluma to Napa to Suisun. According to legend, he marked his path by sowing mustard seed, which today blooms bright yellow every spring. Altimira was most impressed by Sonoma Valley, with its mild climate and tall trees.

On July 7, 1823, with a makeshift redwood cross, Altimira blessed the mission site in what is now the city of Sonoma, and the San Francisco Solano

Mission was established. It was California's last mission and the only one established under Mexican rule. In the early years the mission was a great success, and despite having the reputation of being a harsh taskmaster, Altimira converted more than 700 Indians. In the fall of 1826, Indian laborers had just brought in a bountiful harvest when they staged a violent uprising. The mission was partially burned, and Father Altimira fled for his life. He was replaced, the mission rebuilt, and in 1834 the mission was at the height of its prosperity when the Mexican Congress secularized the mission system and returned the acquired wealth to the people. It was the beginning of a new era.

Lt. Mariano Guadelupe Vallejo was an enterprising 28-year-old officer given the opportunity of a lifetime. The Mexican government sent him to Sonoma to replace the padres and also to establish a presidio and thereby thwart Russian expansion. Vallejo's ambitions were far greater than even that; he soon became one of the most powerful and wealthy men in California. As commandant general, Vallejo ruled the territory north of San Francisco and eventually set aside more than 100,000 acres for himself. He laid out the town of Sonoma around an eight-acre plaza — the largest in California — and for himself built the imposing Petaluma Adobe in 1836. It would be the largest adobe structure in Northern California and the first crop-producing rancho in the area.

It was Vallejo who pushed for the settlement of Napa and Sonoma Counties. He found an ally in frontiersmen like George Yount. Others had been exploring Napa Valley since 1831, but Yount was the first to explore with the notion of settlement. Befriending the already powerful Vallejo, Yount requested a land grant. Vallejo consented, but only after Yount converted to Catholicism and became a naturalized Mexican citizen. (Zoning laws were *really* tough then.) Yount never became an upstanding Catholic, but he did establish the 11,814-acre Rancho Caymus in 1836, now the Yountville area of central Napa County. About that same time, Vallejo was giving Sonoma land grants to family members, who established the rancho predecessors of Santa Rosa, Kenwood, and Healdsburg. Mexican influence continued to expand, particularly after 1839, when the Russians, having wiped out the otter population, gave up and sold Fort Ross.

Otters weren't the only inhabitants facing annihilation. Indian uprisings were not uncommon, and Yount's house in Napa Valley was half home, half fortress. Vallejo occasionally led campaigns against rebellious Indians, but perhaps the most devastating blow came in 1837 when a Mexican corporal inadvertently brought smallpox to Sonoma Valley. This white man's disease all but wiped out Sonoma County's Native population.

BEAR FLAG REVOLT

Throughout the 1830s and early 1840s, American settlers streamed into California, lured by stories of free land. Mexican rule, however, denied Americans land ownership, and this led to confrontations. Tensions peaked in 1846 when rumors spread that Mexico was about to order all Americans out of

A sketch of the original Bear Flag

Chris Alderman

California. At dawn on June 14, some 30 armed horsemen from Sacramento and Napa Valleys rode into Sonoma. So began the Bear Flag Revolt, 25 eventful days when Sonoma was the capital of the independent Republic of California. Though significant, it was a revolution of almost comic proportions. Few soldiers still guarded the Sonoma outpost when the riders arrived, and the insurrectionists captured Sonoma without a single shot. Vallejo was roused from his bed and tied to a chair. One story has it that he tried sly negotiations with the rebels, freely offering the leaders his brandy and getting them drunk. Whether that's truth or folklore, the rebels prevailed. By noon, William Ide was elected leader of the new republic, and a makeshift flag was hoisted to the top of a pole in the plaza. Saddle maker Ben Dewel crafted this flag for the new government, using a grizzly bear as the chief symbol. (Some said it looked more like a prized pig, not a bear.) The Bear Flag Republic had a short reign. In July, an American navy vessel captured the Mexican stronghold of Monterey and claimed California for itself. The Bear Flag boys immediately threw in with the Americans, and four years later, in 1850, California became a state. Eventually, in 1911, the Bear Flag was adopted as the state flag.

The 1840s and 1850s were formative years for Napa and Sonoma Counties. The Gold Rush of 1848 sent Americans by the thousands into the Sierras. Once-powerful Sonoma almost became a ghost town as residents left to pan gold and San Francisco achieved new significance. Other towns were born of miner commerce, such as the river ports of Napa and Petaluma.

A FIRST GLASS OF WINE

During this time, California's wine industry was conceived. Oats and wheat had been the primary crops of Napa and Sonoma Counties, and sheep and cattle were also dominant. Vallejo and Yount grew the crude mission grapes brought north by the priests for sacramental wine, but it wasn't until 1856, when a Hungarian aristocrat named Agoston Haraszthy arrived in Sonoma, that the idea of a wine industry first took root. Haraszthy had attempted vineyards in San Diego and San Mateo and immediately recognized potential in the soil and climate of Sonoma and Napa Valleys. Purchasing land and a winery northeast of the Plaza, Haraszthy established Buena Vista, "Beautiful View."

Workers toiled in a stone quarry to build the Sebastiani winery in Sonoma, circa 1880s.

By 1858 Haraszthy had already surpassed Vallejo's accomplishments as a winemaker and even inspired a German apprentice named Charles Krug, who founded Napa Valley's first winery in 1861. That same year, convinced that the mission grape wasn't the only variety that would thrive in California, Haraszthy toured the wine regions of Europe and returned with cuttings from 300 classic varieties. It was his experimentations with these grapes that brought Haraszthy fame and earned him the title "Father of the California Wine Industry." Wineries began to spring up throughout Napa and Sonoma Counties, the beginnings of wine dynasties such as Beringer and Inglenook that still live today.

The later part of the century was a boom period. Between 1850 and 1860, Napa County's population grew from 400 to almost 5,000. By 1869, Sonoma County's residents numbered 19,000. Petaluma, its largest city, was on its way to becoming the egg capital of the world. The burgeoning city of Santa Rosa had snatched the county seat from Sonoma in 1854, and with the completion of the San Francisco and North Pacific train line in 1870, its destiny as the North Bay's largest city was established. It was the era of the highwaymen, as the legendary Black Bart and others robbed stagecoaches around the North Bay. It was also an era of genius. Calling the area a "chosen spot," horticulturist Luther Burbank created varieties of fruit trees that brought the curious from around the country. And it was a time of pleasure — the resort town of Calistoga, founded by California's first millionaire, Sam Brannan, had become a vacation mecca — as well as a time of creativity — Robert Louis Stevenson was inspired by a stay in Napa Valley and called its wine "bottled poetry."

The wine industry was small but growing in the late 1800s, though it shared the land with other important crops: hops, timber, and apples in Sonoma and wheat in Napa. Wine making and drinking in those days was anything but the chic activity it is today. Wine was sold almost exclusively in bulk and often wasn't even blended until it reached its selling point. It was vended from barrels in saloons and stores, with customers usually bringing their own containers. Gustave Niebaum of Inglenook and the old Fountaingrove Winery in Santa Rosa were among the first to bottle their own wine. Niebaum was also the first to use vintage dates on his wine and to promote "Napa Valley" on his labels.

Arnold Tubbs and family picnicking at Chateau Montelena in 1888.

Courtesy Chateau Monelena

Wine making received two blows late in the century: the depression of the 1870s and phylloxera. The wine industry somehow weathered the economic hard times, though people like Haraszthy were not so lucky. His winery failed, and business setbacks forced him to pursue dealings in Central America, where he met his death. — accounts say he was devoured by an alligator while crossing a Nicaraguan river. As for phylloxera, it attacked the vineyards of Napa and Sonoma Counties with equal fervor.

Phylloxera, a microscopic voracious aphid that infests vine roots, first appeared in Europe in the 1860s, devastating the vineyards of Chateau Margaux, Chateau Lafitte, and others. Only by grafting their vines to American root stock were the Europeans able to save their classic wines. While the European wine industry recovered, California wine began to receive its first world notice. Sonoma County — not Napa — had been the undisputed capital of California wine, but fate and phylloxera would change all that. Phylloxera surfaced first in Sonoma Valley in 1875, and it slowly spread north to the Russian River. By 1889 Sonoma County's vineyards were in ruin when the French invited American wines to compete in the World's Fair. Napa Valley's wines scored well, raising Napa from obscurity to fame. The crown had been snatched by the time phylloxera finally invaded Napa. Growers tried everything to kill the bug, from chemicals to flooding their fields, but nothing worked. Eventually most were forced to pull out their vines. Some planted again, using resistant stock. Others gave up and planted fruit trees.

Three renowned Americans meet in Santa Rosa in 1915: Thomas Edison, Luther Burbank, and Henry Ford.

Courtesy Sonoma County Museum

Not long after that, just after the turn of the 20th century, famed writer Jack London began buying property in Glen Ellen. Saying he was tired of cities and people, he retired to the mountain retreat he called Beauty Ranch, becoming the first of a long line of celebrities drawn to life in Wine Country.

Just another day at a Santa Rosa saloon near the turn of the 20th century.

Courtesy Sonoma County Museum

A COMPLAINT FROM MOTHER NATURE

A new century brought new tragedy. Downtown Calistoga was leveled by a fire in 1901, and on April 18, 1906, what became known as the San Francisco Earthquake equally devastated Sonoma County, particularly in Santa Rosa. Built on the loose foundation between two creek beds, Santa Rosa shimmied like gelatin, laying waste to the downtown and killing 100 people. (It didn't help that the brick buildings were poorly constructed.) Three large downtown hotels, one reporter wrote, "fell as if constructed of playing cards." It would be years before Calistoga and Santa Rosa recovered. San Francisco, of course, took a beating, but a fact not often reported was the impact that event had on the California wine business. Many of the wineries stored their wine in the cooler climate of San Francisco, and the quake destroyed almost two-thirds of the state's wine supply. The castlelike wineries of Napa County — Greystone Cellars, Beringer, Inglenook, and the others that harked back to the grandeur of Bordeaux — were spared the earthquake. But looming even more dangerously on the horizon was something called Prohibition.

Fruit of the Vine — Who's on First

Spanish missionaries are usually credited with bringing the first wine grapes to Sonoma and Napa, but that might not really be the case. Russian colonists at Fort Ross apparently imported vines from Peru as early as 1817, predating the Spanish by a good seven years. But the padres made up for it in volume. Father Jose Altimira, founder of Mission San Francisco Solano in Sonoma, planted 1,000 vines of mission grape, a rather coarse variety brought north from Mexico for sacramental wine.

Napa's first vineyard was planted in 1838 by Napa's first white settler, George Yount. He brought mission vines east from Sonoma and made wine for his own use. It didn't take long before the entrepreneurial spirit set in, and Gen. Mariano Vallejo of Sonoma was the first to succumb. Vallejo became California's first commercial winemaker in 1841, eventually planting 70,000 vines. His wine sold under the name Lachryma Montis, or "Tears of the Mountain," and became the toast of San Francisco. The winery was hardly a chic shop; his cellar, press, and sales outlet were housed in an army barracks. As for a tasting room . . .

Prohibition had been a growing movement in the United States since the turn of the century and, by 1917, a majority of states had outlawed alcohol. The United States Congress cinched it with the Volstead Act and on January 1, 1920, Prohibition began. In Sonoma County alone it left three million useless gallons of wine aging in vats. Sebastiani in Sonoma, Beaulieu in Rutherford, and a handful of other wineries survived by making religious wine and medicinal spirits. But most wineries closed — almost 200 alone in Sonoma County and more than 120 in Napa Valley. By the time Prohibition was repealed in 1933, the Great Depression was on, followed by World War II. Recovery of the wine industry took time.

The 1906 San Francisco earthquake was equally disastrous in Santa Rosa.

Courtesy Sonoma County Library

In 1937 the opening of a single bridge would forever change Sonoma County. It wasn't just any bridge, mind you, but the Golden Gate, spanning the mouth of the San Francisco Bay. Sonoma County became a thoroughfare in California's major north-south corridor, the Redwood Highway. And Sonoma County became its own destination — for example, the Russian River area, already a popular resort spot for San Franciscans, boomed.

After World War II, the vineyards of Europe were once again devastated, and with the flow from Europe cut off, America turned to its own wine. The end of the war began the slow rebirth of the wine industry, and Napa and Sonoma began prospering in the 1950s and 1960s. By the early 1970s, a small tourist industry began forming around the wineries. Tourists were drawn to free wine tastings; restaurants and hotels began to appear. When corporations began eyeing the family-owned wineries, there was no question that Napa and Sonoma were ripe with potential *and* profit. Inglenook was the first to go corporate when United Vintners bought it in 1964; Beaulieu and others followed. In Napa Valley new wineries began opening; some were small operations called "boutiques" in industry lingo; others were more dramatic such as Sterling, a towering white villa perched on a hill south of Calistoga. Brash young winemakers like Robert Mondavi promoted California wine like no one had in the past. By the 1970s even the French, who so often had turned up their noses at California wine, saw California's potential, particularly for sparkling wine. Moet-Hennessy was the first to arrive, building Domaine Chandon in Yountville in 1975. Others were to follow.

Napa and Sonoma Counties also became a favorite location of filmmakers. Alfred Hitchcock immortalized Bodega Bay in *The Birds*; thousands stop each year for a photo of one of Sonoma County's most recognizable landmarks, the Bodega School. Later, wine life at its most ruthless was portrayed in *Falcon Crest*, which used Spring Mountain Vineyards in St. Helena as a backdrop.

Wine Country's greatest achievement and the final turning point for Napa and Sonoma came in the summer of 1976. At the now infamous Paris tasting (see below), French wine experts for the first time picked several California wines over the classic wines of Bordeaux and Burgundy in a blind tasting. History was made, and Napa and Sonoma Counties' prominence in the world of wine was set.

Today, Napa and Sonoma Counties continue to grow, much to the chagrin of long-standing residents. Tourism bureaus report that each year about five million people travel to Napa Valley, and five million visit Sonoma Valley, drawn increasingly by wine, landscape, and climate. Santa Rosa is a small but blossoming metropolis of suburbs. Highway 29, the main road through Napa Valley, pulses with activity. How different it is from the days of grizzly bears and Wappo, yet Napa and Sonoma remain strikingly beautiful places.

Upstaging the French

California and French wine lovers have a long-standing love-hate relationship — California loves French wine and France hates California's. We exaggerate — but only somewhat. California wine makers have always aspired to the quality and reputation of Bordeaux and Burgundy wines, while French enthusiasts ignored California. That is, until May 24, 1976.

It began with British wine merchant Stephen Spurrier, who had a taste for California wine but had a difficult time convincing his English and European customers. Spurrier hit upon the idea of staging a blind tasting of California and French wine, using the nine greatest palates of France. It was unheard of. California had beaten French wines in past tastings, the but the judges were always American, and what did they know.

Judges knew they were sampling both French and American wines, though the bottles were masked. As the tasting progressed, the tasters began to point out the wines they believed were Californian and their comments about them grew increasingly patronizing. When the sacks were removed, the judges were mortified: the wines they thought classic bordeaux or burgundy were in reality Californian. Six of the 11 highest-rated wines were, in fact, from California, almost entirely from Napa. The 1973 Stag's Leap cabernet beat 1970 vintages of Chateau Mouton-Rothschild and Chateau Haut-Brion, and a 1973 Chateau Montelena bested Burgundy's finest whites. France contested the findings, of course, but it was too late. California, particularly Napa, had earned its place on the international wine map.

CHAPTER TWO
Getting There
TRANSPORTATION

Why not tour wineries in style? Rent a 1947 Packard.

Thomas Hallstein/Outsight

Gridlock is not the rarity it used to be in Wine Country, so it pays to know your way around. Highways 101 and 29, the main thoroughfares through Napa and Sonoma Counties, are always hectic, especially on weekends. Not that the terrain doesn't conspire against smooth travel — any approach requires a minor mountain expedition.

Perhaps that's why in the late 1700s the earliest explorers came by way of water. The Sonoma coast was the area's first highway marker. And as sailing ships from around the globe made for the New World, the Napa and Petaluma Rivers, which connect with San Pablo Bay, allowed early settlers a fast way inland.

By the mid-1800s trails from the central valley would take travelers along Clear Lake to Bodega Bay as well as south and east along the bay to Benicia. Carts and stagecoaches brought folks along primitive roads, stirring up dust in the summer and churning up mud in the winter.

By the 1860s steamships were chugging up and down the Napa and Petaluma Rivers, but soon railroads steamed into the scene with names like Southern Pacific and San Francisco North Pacific, and they connected the towns of the two budding counties to the East Bay.

The automobile changed everything, for better and for worse. Sonoma County remained somewhat innocently isolated from San Francisco — it's a long loop around that bay — until the big day in May 1937. That's when the Golden Gate Bridge opened a speedier route north, and Napa and Sonoma

Counties became one of the travel destinations for San Francisco and for the world. Today, in fact, 50 percent of the people who visit Wine Country each year originate their getaway in San Francisco.

There are any number of ways to get to and get around Wine Country. Let us be your guide.

GETTING TO NAPA & SONOMA

Harking back to the days that wine was made by hand, the grape crusher statue greets visitors to Napa.

Thomas Hallstein/Outsight

BY AIR

Air travelers bound for Wine Country can arrive and depart from one of three major airports handling numerous domestic and international airlines.

San Francisco International (SFO), *Oakland International* (OAK), and *Sacramento Metropolitan* (SMF) are all within easy driving distance of Napa and Sonoma Counties. Currently there are no commuter services or connecting flights in or out of the Napa airport.

BY CAR

Although planes and trains will bring you to the threshold of Wine Country, a car is a necessity in Wine Country proper. Public transportation is limited,

NAPA & SONOMA ACCESS

Approximate mileage and times by car between towns and cities:

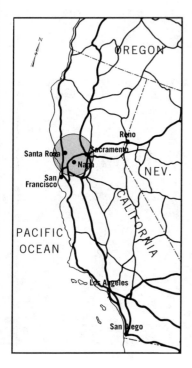

Napa County	Time	Miles
Napa (the city) to:		
Eureka	4 hrs.	255
Los Angeles	8 hrs.	439
Oakland	1 hr.	46
Reno	3 1/2 hrs.	200
Sacramento	1 hr.	61
San Francisco	1 hr.	56
San Diego	11 hrs.	600

Sonoma County	Time	Miles
Santa Rosa to:		
Eureka	4 hrs.	219
Los Angeles	8 hrs.	431
Oakland	1 hr.	60
Reno	4 hrs.	229
Sacramento	2 hrs.	97
San Francisco	1 hr.	56
San Diego	11 hrs.	600

Napa (the city) to:	Time	Miles
Calistoga	1/2 hr.	25
St. Helena	20 min.	18
Rutherford	10 min.	11
Sonoma	15 min.	12
Santa Rosa	1 hr.	36
Yountville	10 min.	8

Santa Rosa to:	Time	Miles
Bodega Bay	3/4 hr.	22
Geyserville	25 min.	21
Healdsburg	15 min.	15
Jenner	3/4 hr.	32
Petaluma	20 min.	16

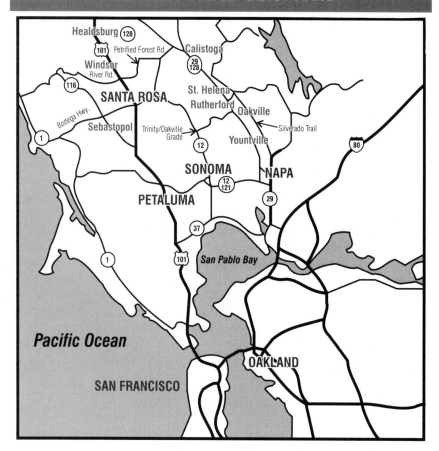

WITHIN WINE COUNTRY

Moving north or south in Napa and Sonoma Counties is easy going. Highway 29, Napa Valley's main street, cuts a long and straight path from the San Pablo Bay north to Lake County. Most of Napa's wineries are along this two-lane road, so traffic can back up. Silverado Trail to the east is a quieter two-lane, though it has its share of wineries, as well. In Sonoma County, Highway 101 will take you north and south at interstate speeds. Moving between Napa and Sonoma generally takes more patience. Highway 12 offers the smoothest path, although it has its own winding hills. The Oakville Grade/Trinity Road is a roller coaster around Mt. Veeder that offers some of the best views of both counties. Petrified Forest and Spring Mountain roads scale the northern Mayacamas Mountains and, at the top, merge with Calistoga Road from Santa Rosa. Low gear on these roads is a good idea. Weather is never a problem. It rarely snows in Wine Country, and when it does it melts quickly, even in the highest elevations.

and the landscape is so vast that you'll need your own wheels. Traffic is common on Saturday and Sunday and during peak summer months, so an ambitious itinerary can be cut short by the weekend tourist crush. If you're close enough to drive to Wine Country, here's how to find Napa and Sonoma Counties.

From the north: Travelers from the north can reach Wine Country via two major roadways. Highway 101 brings visitors into the heart of Sonoma County. If Napa Valley is your destination, take the Highway 128 east exit at Geyserville; it's a beautiful route, a two-lane road that leads you right into Calistoga.

If you're arriving via Interstate 5, connect with I-505 near Sacramento. For a scenic route, or if upper Napa Valley is your destination, exit at Highway 128 in Winters. Follow it west along the beautiful Howell Mountain. If you're in a hurry, or Sonoma County is where you're headed, from I-505 connect with I-80 West; then take the Highway 12 exit, which leads to the cities of Napa and Sonoma.

From the south: Like visitors from the north, drivers arriving from southern California can choose between Highway 101 or I-5.

Traveling Highway 101 brings you through the heart of San Francisco. Stay alert — 101 empties onto the streets of the city and can be a bit confusing. Continue across the Golden Gate Bridge through Marin County and into central Sonoma County. To reach the city of Sonoma or Napa Valley, exit on Highway 37 in Novato, and connect with Highway 121. From I-5 connect with I-580, and continue into downtown Oakland; there connect with eastbound I-80. Exit on Highway 12, which leads to the cities of Napa and Sonoma.

From the east: Wine Country is an easy jaunt from Sacramento or Reno. From I-80, connect with Highway 12. Take it west to Napa and then onto Sonoma Valley.

Renting a Car

Since a car is almost a requirement in Wine Country, visitors arriving by air inevitably rent a vehicle. Most major rental companies, of course, work out of the metro airports, and they're typically helpful in plotting routes and will often supply drivers with basic maps to reach their destinations. Just in case, a few directions:

San Francisco International Airport: To find your way to Wine Country from the Bay Area's largest airport, take Highway 101 north into San Francisco. The highway empties onto the streets, so watch the signs carefully. Continue through the city across the Golden Gate Bridge, and you'll soon find yourself in central Sonoma County. To reach the town of Sonoma or Napa Valley, take Highway 37 in Novato, and connect with Highway 121.

Miles: 72 to central Sonoma County; 82 to Napa Valley
Time: 90 minutes

Oakland International Airport: To reach Napa County and the city of Sonoma, take I-80 north through Oakland and connect with Highway 29 north. For Napa, stay on Highway, and for the city of Sonoma take Highway 12/121. To reach central Sonoma County, take I-80 north through Oakland, exit on I-580, and then connect with Highway 101 north, which takes you into the heart of Sonoma County.

Miles: 82 to central Sonoma County; 46 to Napa Valley
Time: 1 hour to Sonoma; 45 minutes to Napa

Sacramento Metropolitan Airport: Take I-5 South, and connect with the I-80 West bypass; follow the signs to San Francisco. Take Highway 12 to Napa, continuing west to the cities of Sonoma and Santa Rosa.

Miles: 61 miles to Napa; 97 miles to central Sonoma County
Time: 90 minutes to Napa; 2 to 2 1/2 hours to central Sonoma County

You can also rent a car after arriving in Napa and Sonoma Counties. Local information and reservation numbers are listed below. Reservations up to a week in advance are recommended.

Napa County

Budget Rent-A-Car: 707-224-7845
Enterprise Rent-A-Car: 707-253-8000
Hertz: 707-265-7575 or 800-654-3131

Sonoma County

Avis: 800-331-1212
Budget Rent-A-Car: 707-545-8013, 800-527-0700
Encore Rent-A-Car: 707-579-4833
Enterprise Rent-A-Car: 800-325-8007
Hertz: 707-528-0834 or 800-654-3131

Airport Shuttle

Here's an alternative to renting a car at the airport. Reasonably priced express shuttle buses and vans operate to and from the San Francisco and Oakland airports. These comfortable vehicles operate 16 to 20 hours a day, seven days a week. Shuttles depart from airports about every one to two hours, depending on the operator, and deliver passengers to selected drop-off points in Wine Country.

One-way fares (cash only) range from $18 to $35, depending on the operator, the drop-off point, and any excess luggage requirements. Reservations are not usually required, but on weekends and in peak seasons buses fill up, and you may be forced to stand in the aisle. Schedules fluctuate, so it's smart to reserve shuttle services in advance.

Airport Express: SFO to Santa Rosa, 707-837-8700
Evans Airport Service: SFO and OAK (Oakland) to Napa, 707-255-1559, 707-944-2025
Sonoma Airporter: SFO to the town of Sonoma, 707-938-4246

BY BUS

G reyhound bus service to Sonoma and Napa Counties is very limited. It is also possible to ride Greyhound to San Francisco, then make connections on Golden Gate Transit to reach Wine Country. A travel agent will have the most up-to-date information on Greyhound schedules and connections.

   Greyhound in San Francisco: 415-495-1569

   Golden Gate Transit: (for travel between San Francisco and Sonoma County) 415-923-2000, 707-541-2000; one-way fare from San Francisco to Santa Rosa is $5.70.

Once inside Wine Country, public bus service is available through *Sonoma County Transit* and *Napa Valley Transit*. This method of travel could be indispensable for the Wine Country visitor on a tight budget. One drawback: Bus stops, which can be few and far between, are usually not close to wineries and other tourist attractions.

One-way fares average between $1 and $2.50, and weekend service is limited. If buses will be your primary form of transportation, it may be essential to gather together the most current timetables and route maps, which are updated frequently. The cities of Santa Rosa, Napa, Healdsburg, and Petaluma also offer bus service within those city boundaries.

Napa County

The V.I.N.E.: Napa city bus travels mainly along Highway 29 between Calistoga and Vallejo, with bus and ferry connections to and from San Francisco, 800-696-6443, 707-255-7631
Intercity Van-Go: Limited service between most Napa Valley towns, 707-252-2600

Sonoma County

Sonoma County Transit: (for travel within Sonoma County) 707-576-7433
Santa Rosa Transit: (city bus) 707-543-3333
Petaluma Transit: (city bus) 707-778-4460
Healdsburg In-City Transit: (city bus) 707-431-3324

BY TRAIN

Amtrak's westbound *California Zephyr* and north-to-south *Coastal Starlight* trains drop off Napa County-bound passengers in the city of Martinez, about 40 miles south of Napa. Amtrak has continuing ground transportation that delivers passengers directly to Napa but not Sonoma.

For Amtrak information and reservations, call 800-872-7245. It is advisable to consult a travel agent for assistance in booking Amtrak.

Just for the record, the *Napa Valley Wine Train* is actually a gourmet restaurant on rails and not a true form of transportation. (For details, see Chapter Five, *Restaurants & Food Purveyors*.)

BY LIMOUSINE

The ultimate in personal transportation is the limousine, and for many visitors to Wine Country, chauffeured travel goes hand-in-hand with wine tasting. For others, the pricey three-hour ride to the Sonoma Coast can be a romantic and unforgettable luxury.

Both Napa Valley and Sonoma County have an abundance of professional limousine services that will map out wine-tasting itineraries for the novice or deliver connoisseurs to wineries of their choosing. Most also offer day-long, fixed-rate touring packages with extras, such as gourmet picnic lunches or evening dining, included in the price. Per-hour rates range from $45 on weekdays to $165, depending on the limo and the tour. That doesn't include taxes, driver gratuities, parking fees, or bridge tolls. A three- or four-hour minimum is standard, and complimentary champagne is often served. Reservations are required at least two or three days in advance and as much as a week in advance during peak vacationing months. Some recommend booking at least a month ahead of time.

For your added safety, the limousine service you engage should be both licensed and insured. Ask your hotel concierge to recommend a service, or talk to your travel agent. Listed below are some of Wine Country's most popular limousine services. Companies may be based in one county, but they frequently take passengers all over Wine Country and beyond.

Napa County

Antique Tours: 707-226-9227
Evans Inc.: 707-255-1557
Executive Limousine: 707-257-2949

Sonoma County

AAAA Pure Luxury Limousine: 707-795-1615, 800-626-5466
All Occasions Limousine: 707-584-0701
Lon's Limo Scene: 707-539-5466

BY TAXI

When buses are too inconvenient and limousines too expensive, call for an old standby: the taxicab. The companies below are on duty 24 hours a day, seven days a week. Per-mile fares average $2–$3.

Napa County

Napa Valley Cab: 707-257-6444
Taxi Cabernet: 707-963-2620

Sonoma County

Bill's Taxi Service, Guerneville: 707-869-2177
Bear Flag Taxi: 707-996-6733
George's Taxi Yellow Cab, Santa Rosa: 707-544-4444

NEIGHBORS ALL AROUND

The opening of the Golden Gate Bridge in 1937 made Napa and Sonoma Counties easily accessible to San Francisco.

Courtesy Sonoma County Museum

TO THE SOUTH

The striking countryside and tony hamlets of Marin County are directly south. In San Rafael, just east of Highway 101, don't miss the dramatic Marin Civic Center, one of the last buildings designed by Frank Lloyd Wright. If you're not in a hurry, consider trekking north or south on Highway 1, the winding two-lane that hugs the rugged coastline. It will take you by Muir Woods, home to some of the tallest redwoods north of the Bay, and also to the majestic Mount Tamalpais. Drive to its 3,000-foot summit for a spectacular view of San Francisco (clear weather permitting, that is). Point Reyes Lighthouse is also worth a stop along Highway 1, as are the many oyster farms near Marshall.

Farther south is one of the most intriguing, romantic, and ethnically diverse cities in America: San Francisco. It's just a one-hour drive from Wine Country. Ride a cable car, snack on scrumptious dim sum in Chinatown, gorge on culture and shopping, or just admire the view. (See Chapter 4, *Culture*, for more suggestions.) Across the Bay is Oakland and the ever-eclectic Berkeley, both stops worth making.

TO THE EAST

While motoring your way to Sacramento along I-80, your thoughts may turn to . . . onions. The aroma of onions and other commercially grown produce fills the air in fertile Sacramento Valley, where fruits and vegetables are tended in endless flat fields. The city of Sacramento, the state capital and once a major hub for rail and river transportation, is proud of its historic center: Old Town, a faithful recreation of the city's original town center, with a multitude of shops, restaurants, and museums.

TO THE NORTH

Not to be outdone by Napa and Sonoma, Mendocino County is also a major player in the game of fine wine, with several premium wineries along Highway 101 and in beautiful Anderson Valley. The coastal hamlet of Mendocino, one of Hollywood's favorite movie locations, is also a treasure trove for shoppers. Its art galleries, antiques shops, and fine dining, and its New England-like atmosphere make it a popular second destination for Wine Country visitors.

CHAPTER THREE
A Place to Call Your Own
LODGING

A handsome guest room in The Gables Inn, an 1877 Victorian in Santa Rosa.

Thomas Hallstein/Outsight

Just 20 years ago there were only 50 bed-and-breakfast inns in California; today there are more than 800, with new ones hanging out shingles every year. One of the largest concentrations of B&Bs in the state is in Wine Country, where they are scattered through towns and vineyards.

The list of amenities at finer inns includes: private balconies and decks, pools and saunas, evening wine tastings, home-baked chocolate chip cookies, and the like. Private baths are not only standard these days, but many are equipped with whirlpool tubs for two.

The morning meal has evolved from the standard "light continental" fare to a breakfast that is often a gourmet delight, including creative egg entrées, quiche, sausages, waffles or pancakes, oven-fresh breads with homemade jams, fresh fruit, and champagne.

If you're more at ease staying at a familiar motel chain, or if the budget is your first consideration, Wine Country offers several delightful options. Many of these are listed in the motel section included at the end of this chapter.

Don't expect a B&B to be less expensive than a conventional hotel or motel. Unlike its budget-wise British cousin, the Wine Country B&B is an intimate, serene, and often pricey luxury accommodation — and almost always worth it. Keep in mind that over time, policies, amenities, and even furnishings may change at some inns, as will the complimentary goodies.

NAPA AND SONOMA LODGING NOTES

Minimum Stay: A majority of inns and B&Bs require a two-night minimum on weekends; a three-night minimum is the norm on holiday weekends. (Virtually all inns and B&Bs are open year-round in Wine Country.)

Reservations/Cancellations: Make reservations at popular inns and hotels several weeks in advance, as most fill up on weekends even in the off-season. A deposit by credit card for the first night is usually required. Expect a charge for last-minute cancellations.

Restrictions: Smoking is not permitted inside most inns, and pets are prohibited almost unanimously. As a general rule, children under 12 are discouraged, but some inns welcome kids and infants. In-room telephones and televisions are not usually furnished at B&Bs; likewise, room service is limited. Always ask about restrictions before booking.

Rates and credit cards: High season for Wine Country innkeepers is generally from April to October; off-season runs November to March. Many inns, however, make no distinction between the seasons and may charge the same rate year-round. At those that do recognize off-season, expect to pay 20 percent to 30 percent less. Likewise, midweek rates may be significantly less than weekend rates. The following price codes are based on per-room, double-occupancy, high-season weekend rates at B&Bs and the better lodgings.

Inexpensive:	Up to $100
Moderate:	$100 to $150
Expensive:	$150 to $250
Very Expensive:	Over $250

Credit cards are abbreviated as follows:

AE — American Express	DC — Diner's Club
CB — Carte Blanche	MC — Master Card
D — Discover Card	V — Visa

Coastal Rentals: Few places in Northern California are more wild and beautiful than the rugged Sonoma Coast. Fortunately, there are scores of rental properties. Most are privately owned homes with equipped kitchens, etc. Many have full ocean views. Bed linens, towels, and maid service may or may not be provided. There is usually a two-night minimum and fees vary greatly, depending on the number of occupants, the location of the home, the amenities, and the season.

Several property management companies arrange for condo rentals on the Sonoma Coast: *Vacation Rentals USA* (707-875-4000); *Don Berard Associates* (707-884-3211); *Beach Rentals* (707-884-4235).

LODGING IN NAPA COUNTY

Napa

ARBOR GUEST HOUSE
Innkeepers: Chris and
   Andrea Chadwick.
707-252-8144;
   fax 707-252-7385.
www.arborguesthouse.com.
1436 G St., Napa, CA 94559.
Lincoln Ave. exit E. off Hwy.
   29.
Price: Expensive.
Credit Cards: AE, D, MC, V.
Handicap Access: Yes.

Built in 1906, this white Victorian is reminiscent of Grandmother's Midwestern farmhouse, done in antiques, flowered wallpaper and curtains. In the heart of a residential area near downtown, the inn is a quiet haven with a lovely backyard and garden. There are five guest rooms in the main house and carriage house. Two-person whirlpool tubs near fireplaces make the Winter Haven and Autumn Harvest rooms popular, and Rose's Bower, the top floor of the carriage house, is requested often. The Chadwicks are attentive innkeepers, quick with recommendations for dinner and sightseeing. Breakfast is excellent, often featuring thick French toast, chicken sausage, and fresh fruit.

BEAZLEY HOUSE
Innkeepers: Jim and Carol
   Beazley.
707-257-1649, 800-559-1649;
   fax 707-258-1518.
www.beazleyhouse.com.
innkeeper@beazley
   house.com.
1910 1st St., Napa, CA 94559.
1st St. exit E. off Hwy. 29.
Price: Moderate to Very
   Expensive.
Credit Cards: MC, V.

One of Napa's first B&Bs, this wood-shingled circa-1902 mansion has six charming and cozy rooms. Even more desirable is the carriage house, built in 1983, with a fireplace and two-person spa standard in each of its five rooms. The main house is a beauty; the dining and common rooms have coved ceilings and oak floors with mahogany inlays. The Sherry Room is pleasantly done in blue wallpaper and rich cherry wood, but if you're sensitive to street noise, request a room in the carriage house. The garden is a peaceful refuge with an old-fashioned swing. The Beazleys offer a warm welcome at breakfast, and Carol — a former nurse — concocts healthy but tasty fare served buffet style.

BLUE VIOLET MANSION
Innkeepers: Bob and Kathy
   Morris.
707-253-2583, 800-959-2583;
   fax 707-257-8205.

This graceful Queen Anne Victorian, built in 1886, is one of the newest B&B additions to Old Town Napa. The inn is situated on a lush acre that has a garden gazebo, a vine-covered deck, and a

Blue Violet Mansion was built in 1886.

Thomas Hallstein/Outsight

www.bluevioletmansion
.com.
bviolet@napanet.net.
443 Brown St., Napa, CA
94559.
1st St. exit E. off Hwy. 29.
Price: Expensive to Very
Expensive.
Credit Cards: AE, MC, V, D,
DC.

pool. And it's been delightfully restored. Antiques and artwork decorate each of the 17 rooms; at least 11 have gas fireplaces, and 14 have whirlpool tubs. Two rooms also open onto the front balcony. Four rooms on the Camelot Floor are done in Old English decor with stained-glass highlights. A full breakfast is served, and private candlelight dinners can be arranged.

BROOKSIDE VINEYARD

Innkeepers: Tom and Susan
Ridley.
707-944-1661.
3194 Redwood Rd., Napa,
CA 94558.
Off Hwy. 29.
Price: Moderate to
Expensive.
Credit Cards: None.
Special Features: Pool.

Not just a B&B, Brookside is a working vineyard and Christmas tree farm. During grape harvest season, guests are welcome to hike out in the chardonnay vineyard and help Tom test sugar levels. Built in the 1950s, the Mission-style residence is set along a lush creek. The three guest rooms are in a separate wing of the house, offering plenty of privacy, and the atmosphere is casual and unfussy, as though you're staying at a friend's house in the country. The three guest rooms are pleasantly done up in Laura Ashley prints, and the furnishings are a blend of family treasures and antiques. The Britannia room has a fireplace, sauna, and private patio. Breakfast is served buffet style in a gazebo that overlooks the creek.

CANDLELIGHT INN OF THE DUNN LEE MANOR

Innkeepers: Johanna and
Wolfgang Brox.

This 1929 English Tudor-style mansion is in the heart of suburbia, but the one-acre grounds along Napa Creek are beautifully parklike. There are six romantic suites, all with two-person

707-257-3717;
  fax 707-257-3762.
www.candlelightinn.com.
1045 Easum Dr., Napa, CA
  94558.
1st St. exit W. off Hwy. 29.
Price: Expensive to Very
  Expensive.
Credit Cards: AE, D, MC, V.
Handicap Access: Yes.
Special Features: Pool.

whirlpool baths, balconies or decks, and fireplaces. One has a cathedral ceiling and a stained-glass window. The inn has a total of nine rooms. A three-course candlelight breakfast is served overlooking the lovely gardens that surround the house.

A bed-and-breakfast with distinction, Churchill Manor in Napa is a Victorian circa 1889.

Thomas Hallstein/Outsight

CHURCHILL MANOR
Innkeepers: Joanna Guidotti
  and Brian Jensen.
707-253-7733.
www.churchillmanor.com
relax@churchillmanor.com.
485 Brown St., Napa, CA
  94559.
1st St. exit E. off Hwy. 29.
Price: Expensive.
Credit Cards: AE, D, MC, V.
Handicap Access: Limited.

From the moment you spy Churchill Manor, you'll know it's special. The inn, now a National Historic Landmark, was built in 1889 on a lush acre, and has the Greek Revival columns, wraparound verandahs, and grand parlors of days gone by. The 10 guest rooms are on all three floors of this graceful mansion, and all have private baths and queen- or king-size beds. Handpainted Delft tiles, 24-carat gold trim, and an antique beaded opera gown are among the rich details in the rooms. A generous buffet-style breakfast is served in the marble-tiled solarium, where wine and cheese are offered in the evening.

CROSSROADS INN
Innkeepers: Sam and Nancy
  Scott.
707-944-0646;
  fax 707-944-0650.

Stunning valley views are just one of the attractions at CrossRoads Inn. The three-story chalet on 23 mountainous acres is surrounded by oak trees, wildflowers, and hiking trails. The common room has a wall of windows and an unusual circu-

www.napavalleybedand
   breakfast.com.
info@crossroadsnv.com.
6380 Silverado Trail, Napa,
   CA 94558.
Off Silverado Trail, S. of
   Yountville Cross Rd.
Price: Very Expensive.
Credit Cards: MC, V.
Special Features: Pool,
   whirlpool, hiking trails,
   fabulous views.

**ELM HOUSE INN, BEST
   WESTERN**
Manager: Anetha Kouns.
707-255-1831.
800 California Blvd., Napa,
   CA 94559.
1st St. exit E. off Hwy. 29.
Price: Moderate to Very
   Expensive.
Credit Cards: AE, MC, V.
Handicap Access: Yes.
Special Features: Whirlpool.

**EMBASSY SUITES NAPA
   VALLEY**
Manager: Reynaldo
   Zertuche.
707-253-9540;
   fax 707-253-9202.
www.embassynapa.com.
info@embassynapa.com.
1075 California Blvd., Napa,
   CA 94559.
1st St. exit E. off Hwy. 29.
Price: Very Expensive.
Credit Cards: AE, DC, MC,
   V.
Handicap Access: Yes.
Special Features: Indoor and
   outdoor pools, sauna,
   whirlpool, and restaurant.

HENNESSEY HOUSE
Innkeeper: Alex Feit.
707-226-3774;
   fax 707-226-2975.
www.hennesseyhouse.com.
inn@hennesseyhouse.com.

lar fireplace that rises 20 feet. The four guest rooms, all with whirlpools and king-size beds, are named after Beatrix Potter characters, and each is in a separate wing of the house. All have private baths and decks. Scott's stylish breakfasts are served in your room — a nice touch — or on the deck if weather permits.

Sheltered by three huge, historic elm trees, this wood-shingled inn is modern but done in the style of an old European village. There are Italian marble fireplaces in many of its 17 rooms (all with private baths) and each has a TV, phone, and stocked refrigerator. There's also a honeymoon suite with high ceilings, chandelier, and a private whirlpool. The inn's elevator also makes it accessible to wheelchairs. A breakfast buffet is served in the courtyard when weather permits. On a busy intersection.

All 205 rooms in this hotel are two-room suites with French country furnishings and are equipped for light cooking with mini-refrigerators, coffeemakers, and microwave ovens. In addition, all rooms have wet bars, phones, and TVs. Daily complimentary full breakfast is cooked to order, and two hours of complimentary cocktails are served each evening. Outside there's a pond with swans and ducks and a tropical atrium with a skylight for dining. This is an elegant business-class hotel that's also ideal for leisure travelers. A $4.5 million renovation was completed in 1997.

This home on the National Register of Historic Places is a stunning example of a perfectly restored 1889 Eastlake-style Queen Anne. The main house has six rooms, all appointed with antiques and private baths. Larger and more luxurious are the four carriage house rooms, each equipped with

1727 Main St., Napa, CA
  94559.
Lincoln Ave. exit E. off Hwy.
  29.
Price: Expensive to Very
  Expensive.
Credit Cards: AE, D, MC, V.
Special Features: Sauna.

LA BELLE EPOQUE
Innkeeper: Georgia Jump.
707-257-2161, 800-238-8070.
www.labelleepoque.com.
georgia@labelleepoque.com.
1386 Calistoga Ave., Napa,
  CA 94559.
1st St. exit E. off Hwy. 29.
  The annex Buckley House
  is at 1406 Calistoga Ave.
Price: Expensive to Very
  Expensive.
Credit Cards: AE, D, MC, V.

two-person whirlpool tubs. The Bridle Suite is done in masculine tones and has a fireplace and skylight. A full breakfast is served in the dining room, where the restored, hand-painted, and stamped tin ceiling is the focal point. The neighborhood is urban but quiet and a short walk to downtown Napa.

T he stained-glass windows and fine Victorian furniture at this seven-room inn will transport you to another time and place. Built in 1893, this gingerbread beauty is near downtown, and the residential area is still a little funky. Family heirloom antiques and collectibles are scattered throughout the guest rooms and the common parlor. All rooms have private baths, and one has a whirlpool. Three rooms have fireplaces. The inn also has two additional rooms tucked away in an annex called the Buckley House. Breakfast is served in the dining room or sun porch.

A cozy setting at La Résidence Country Inn.

Courtesy La Résidence

**LA RÉSIDENCE
  COUNTRY INN**
Innkeepers: Craig Claussen
  and David Jackson.
707-253-0337, 800-253-9203;
  fax 707-253-0382.
www.laresidence.com.
4066 St. Helena Hwy., Napa,
  CA 94558.
On Hwy. 29.

B uilt in 1870 by a New Orleans riverboat pilot who arrived in San Francisco during the Gold Rush, this Gothic Revival inn still has the flavor of the Old South with its plantation shutters and park-like setting. Eleven of the inn's 23 rooms are in Cabernet Hall, a modern building styled after a French country barn. Between the two buildings is a garden with a pool and white gazebo. Nineteenth-

Price: Expensive to Very
Expensive.
Credit Cards: AE, DC, MC,
V.
Handicap Access: Yes.
Special Features: Pool,
whirlpool.

MILLIKEN CREEK INN
Innkeepers: Lisa Holt and
David Shapiro.
707-255-1197; 888-622-5775;
fax 707-255-3112,
www.millikencreekinn.com.
info@millikencreekinn.com.
1815 Silverado Trail, Napa,
CA 94558.
N. on Hwy. 29, to Trancas
exit.
Price: Moderate to
Expensive.
Credit Cards: AE, D, DC,
MC, V.

THE NAPA INN
Innkeepers: Brooke and Jim
Boyer.
707-257-1444, 800-435-1144;
fax 707-257-0251.
www.napainn.com.
info@napainn.com.
1137 Warren St., Napa, CA
94559.
1st St. exit E. off Hwy. 29.
Price: Expensive.
Credit Cards: AE, D, DC,
MC, V.

NAPA RIVER INN
General Manager: Nancy M.
Lochmann.
707-251-8500, 877-251-8504.
www.napariverinn.com.
500 Main St., Napa, CA
94559.
Price: Expensive to Very
Expensive.
Credit Cards: AE, D, MC,
Visa.

century antiques and chandeliers decorate the rooms, many of which have fireplaces. The pace is slow and easy, with lots of porches and decks and a jogging and bicycling trail. A full breakfast is served in the dining room, where guests dine privately at small tables near a fireplace.

Milliken Creek Inn is located at the base of Wine Country. Nestled between the Silverado Trail and the Napa River, this romantic boutique luxury inn beckons you to relax and unwind with the amenities of a large resort and the intimacy of a bed-and-breakfast. This place is set up to pamper: spa and massage services, yoga, jazz, private wine tasting, breakfast in bed, Italian linens, and Napa River views. Great for a romantic getaway.

Music plays a starring role at this unique Victorian-era inn. The parlor is filled with antique instruments, from a player piano to an accordion, violin, and music box. There are seven guest rooms, one with a whirlpool. Painted a warm blue, this 1899 Queen Anne is in a tree-lined historic neighborhood near downtown. A full breakfast is served in the dining room.

Once a mill, later a warehouse, this lovely old brick building right on the Napa River is now a luxury boutique hotel. The inn was built in the 1800s, and many of the rooms are filled with antiques and furnishings from that period. Some rooms have a California Wine Country look while others have a nautical theme.

The 66-room inn is within walking distance to several hot restaurants in the city of Napa. It is not far from COPIA: The American Center for Wine, Food, and the Arts as well as the Historic Napa Valley Opera House. Right next door to the inn is a bakery where guests can breakfast with healthy delights like a yogurt parfait. Perhaps most unusual is the inn's pet policy: It welcomes them. (A rarity in Wine Country.) The inn even treats dogs to biscuits made from Chardonnay grapes called Char-Dog-Nay Biscuits.

**NAPA VALLEY
    MARRIOTT**
Manager: Michael George
707-253-7433, 800-228-9290;
    fax 707-258-1320.
www.marriotthotels.com
    /sfonp.
3425 Solano Ave., Napa, CA
    94558.
Hwy. 29 at Redwood Rd.
Price: Expensive to Very
    Expensive.
Credit Cards: AE, CB, D,
    DC, MC, V.
Handicap Access: Yes.
Special Features: Pool,
    whirlpool, tennis courts,
    fitness room, two
    restaurants.

With 191 rooms and suites, the Marriott is one of the largest inns in the valley. Nicer than a motel, it's not quite a hotel either, but it is comfortably appointed and has the usual services you would expect from a chain hotel. On the north edge of the city, it is convenient to most of the valley.

There's a sense of drama in Annie's Room at The Old World Inn.

Courtesy Old World Inn

THE OLD WORLD INN
Innkeeper: Sam van Hoeve.
707-257-0112, 800-966-6624;
  fax 707-257-0118.
www.oldworldinn.com.
theoldworldinn@aol.com.
1301 Jefferson St., Napa, CA
  94559.
1st St. exit E. off Hwy. 29.
Price: Moderate to
  Expensive.
Credit Cards: AE, D, MC, V.
Special Features: Whirlpool.

One of the most beautifully appointed B&Bs in the valley, the Old World Inn is a charming 1906 Victorian. The interior is impeccably designed, done in tastefully dramatic pastels, draped fabric, and ruffles. The dining and common rooms on the first floor have gorgeous redwood woodwork and polished wood floors, and each of the 10 guest rooms are individually decorated and have fireplaces; most have claw-foot tubs. The Stockholm Room has a whirlpool bath, and the Garden Room has a skylight for stargazing from bed. Breakfast includes the likes of muffins, fresh fruit and a Greek frittata, and guests dine privately at small tables in the dining room. Though on a busy street, the inn is surprisingly quiet.

Silverado Country Club is a leading Napa Valley resort.

Courtesy SilveradoThomas Hallstein/Outsight

SILVERADO RESORT
Manager: Kirk Candland.
707-257-0200, 800-532-0500;
  fax 707-257-2687.
www.silveradoresort.com.
resv@silveradoresort.com.
1600 Atlas Peak Rd., Napa,
  CA 94558.
1 mile NE. of Napa.
Price: Expensive to Very
  Expensive.
Credit Cards: AE, CB, D,
  DC, MC, V.
Special Features: Two 18-
  hole golf courses, 8 pools,
  tennis, restaurant, room
  service, spa, salon.

Golf is king at Silverado. Its two courses are considered the best in Napa Valley. With more than 750 regular members, the area is constantly bustling with activity. The main house, an imposing mansion built just after the Civil War, was remodeled in 1992.

Today there are 280 rooms scattered over the 1,200-acre estate, ranging in size from studios to three-bedroom suites. The units are individually owned by members but rented out like hotel rooms. (The Oak Creek East area is the most secluded; the Clubhouse side is convenient to the tennis courts and golf courses.) All rooms are comfortably furnished to feel like home, and the kitchenettes have just about everything you need for light cooking. The concierge staff is perhaps the best in the valley.

STAHLECKER HOUSE
Innkeepers: Ron and Ethel
  Stahlecker.
707-257-1588, 800-799-1588;
  fax 707-224-7429.
www.stahleckerhouse.com.
stahlbnb@aol.com.
1042 Easum Dr., Napa, CA
  94558.
1st St. exit W. off Hwy. 29.
Price: Expensive to Very
  Expensive.
Credit Cards: AE, MC, V.

This 1948 ranch-style house seems more like a home than a B&B, but it has four appealing guest rooms with canopy beds, antique furniture, and private baths. Two are newly equipped with a whirlpool spa, fireplace, and private patio. Relax on the immense sun deck surrounded by gardens and oak and laurel trees, or read in the living room. The hosts serve a gourmet candlelight breakfast in the dining room and complimentary beverages around the clock.

Yountville

BORDEAUX HOUSE
Innkeeper: Jean Lunney.
707-944-2855, 800-677-6370;
  fax 707-945-0471.
www.bordeauxhouse.com.
6600 Washington St.,
  Yountville, CA 94599.
Off Hwy. 29 at Washington
  St.
Price: Moderate to
  Expensive.
Credit Cards: MC, V.

The inn — a modern, distinctive red brick building — is a far cry from the usual cozy Victorian inn. Likewise the furnishings, done in a contemporary style that's no longer quite so contemporary. Six of the seven guest rooms in this inn have fireplaces, most have balconies or patios, and all have private baths. A full breakfast is served in the common room. It's close to all of Yountville's shops and restaurants. Innkeeper hospitality leaves room for improvement.

BURGUNDY HOUSE INN
Manager: Deanna Roque.
707-944-0889.
6711 Washington St.,
  Yountville, CA 94599.
Washington St. exit off Hwy.
  29.
Price: Expensive.
Credit Cards: MC, V.

A brandy distillery built in 1891, this grand two-story structure is now a five-room inn. Antique furniture and generic contemporary pieces are set amidst the 22-inch-thick walls of rugged fieldstone and river-rock masonry. A decanter of Napa Valley wine helps visitors settle in, and a full breakfast is served in the garden or inside. All rooms have private baths, and one has a fireplace. It is situated close to a street, but noise is minimal at night. However, innkeeper hospitality leaves room for improvement.

CASTLE IN THE CLOUDS
Innkeepers: Jean and Larry
  Grunewald.
707-944-2785;
  fax 707-945-0882.
www.castleintheclouds.com.
jean@napacastle.com.
7400 St. Helena Hwy., Napa,
  CA 94558.

Put simply, this is a castle with a view. Perched on a sprawling eight acres, the inn has world-famous wineries within view: Mondavi, Far Niente and boutique wonders like Harlan Estate. This is one of the most romantic inns in Wine Country. Naturally the Honeymoon Suite is the most decadent with a fireplace at the foot of its king-size bed, a private bathroom, a 19th-century hand-carved

Price: Expensive to Very Expensive.
Credit Cards: AE, MC, V.
Special Features: Perched on a hillside with a stretch of 8 acres; incredible views; romantic rooms.

MAISON FLEURIE
Manager: Virginia Marzon.
707-944-2056, 800-788-0369; fax 707-944-9342.
www.foursisters.com.
6529 Yount St., Yountville, CA 94599.
1 block E. of Washington St.
Price: Moderate to Very Expensive.
Credit Cards: AE, MC, V.
Special Features: Pool, whirlpool.

NAPA VALLEY LODGE
Manager: Erika Cimpher.
707-944-2468, 800-368-2468; fax 707-944-9362.
www.woodsidehotels.com.
jwolfe@napavalleylodge.com.
2230 Madison St., Yountville, CA 94599.
1 block off Hwy. 29.
Price: Very Expensive.
Credit Cards: AE, D, DC, MC, V.
Handicap Access: Yes.
Special Features: Pool, whirlpool, sauna, fitness room.

NAPA VALLEY RAILWAY INN
Manager: Tawnya Trejo.
707-944-2000.
6503 Washington St., Yountville, CA 94599.
Off Hwy. 29.
Price: Moderate.
Credit Cards: MC, V.
Handicap Access: Yes.

bedroom set, and a lovely view from a bay window. All rooms have down comforters and private baths. Plentiful breakfasts include quiche, eggs benedict, French toast. For those who want a country breakfast, there's always the standby: bacon, eggs, and sausage.

Blessed with a colorful past — it was a bordello and a speakeasy — this 13-room inn was recently known as Magnolia Hotel but became Maison Fleurie in 1994. Encompassing three red-brick, vine-covered buildings built in 1873, it is styled after a French country inn, although it's right in the heart of Yountville. Six rooms have fireplaces, while the pool and whirlpool offer relaxation in a private setting. A full breakfast is served family-style in the fireside dining room.

This delightful lodge has 55 well-appointed and spacious rooms and suites — 33 with fireplaces — decorated with wicker and tropical plants and postcard views of the valley. It is styled as a Spanish hacienda with a red-tile roof and balconies. The pool and whirlpool spa are in a pleasant courtyard. In-room coffeemakers and cooler/ refrigerators are provided, and a champagne breakfast buffet is included. This is a restful location surrounded by ripening grapes in the vineyards, and it's an easy walk to Yountville's shops. Special golf packages are also available.

Take a step back to the time that railroads reigned — stay in one of nine turn-of-the-century railroad cars (three cabooses and six rail cars) thoroughly refurbished into pleasant suites. The suites are long and narrow, and feature period furniture and decor that help guests relive the past glory of rail travel. A brass bed, sitting room with a love seat, and a full bath complete each room. Situated in the heart of Yountville shopping, it's next door to Vintage 1870.

Spacious and comfortable quarters at Oak Knoll Inn.

Thomas Hallstein/Outsight

OAK KNOLL INN
Innkeepers: Barbara Passino
   and John Kuhlmann.
707-255-2200;
   fax 707-255-2296.
www.oakknollinn.com.
2200 E. Oak Knoll Ave.,
   Napa, CA 94558.
3 mi. S. of Yountville.
Price: Very Expensive.
Credit Cards: MC, V.
Special Features: Pool,
   whirlpool.

Oak Knoll Inn is a treasure, perhaps our favorite B&B in Napa Valley. It's intimate, with only four guest suites, but the rooms are spacious and luxurious, with tall French windows, rustic fieldstone walls, and vaulted ceilings. The rooms have king-size beds, Italian marble fireplaces, private baths, and sitting areas with overstuffed chairs and sofas. Surrounded by gardens and 600 acres of chardonnay vineyards, it is well off the bustle of Highway 29; the setting is peaceful and the view magnificent. The innkeepers are also gracious and unstuffy.

The phrase "gourmet breakfast" is used loosely at many B&Bs, but not here. Barbara Passino creates truly magnificent breakfasts, including poached eggs in puff pastry and an indulgence called a chocolate taco stuffed with fresh sorbet. Breakfast is served in the dining room or on the verandah near your room. There's also quite a spread set out at the nightly wine-and-cheese hour.

**OLEANDER HOUSE BED
& BREAKFAST INN**
Innkeeper: Kathleen
   Matthews.
707-944-8315, 800-788-0357.
www.oleander.com.
innkeeper@oleander.com.
7433 St. Helena Hwy.,
   Yountville, CA 94599.
On Hwy. 29.
Price: Expensive.
Credit Cards: AE, MC, V.
Special Features: Whirlpool.

A contemporary two-story house with five guest rooms decorated in Laura Ashley fabrics, this is a comfortable base for a Wine Country stay. The high-ceilinged rooms have private baths, antiques, and queen-size brass or four-poster beds. They also have private balconies, wood-burning fireplaces, and spectacular views of the valley. Breakfast is served at a large table where guests get to know each other, and the menu often includes baked pancakes, a fluffy crêpelike creation. Mustards Grill, one of Napa Valley's premier restaurants, is just a few steps away (see Chapter Five, *Restaurants*). Highway 29 is busy during the day but quiets considerably at night.

PETIT LOGIS INN
Innkeepers: Jay and Judith
  Caldwell.
877- 944-2332;
  fax 707-944-2338.
www.petitlogis.com.
jay@petitlogis.com.
6527 Yount St., Yountville,
  CA 94599.
Price: Moderate to
  Expensive.
Credit Cards: AE, MC, V.
Special Features: Fireplaces;
  6-foot whirlpool tubs;
  patios.

This inn has a culinary edge. It's within walking distance of the French Laundry, by many accounts the best restaurant in America. It's also near some other top-rated restaurants, including Bouchon and Bistro Jeanty. All five guest rooms feature a fireplace and a six-foot double Jacuzzi. The shingled lodge with a trellis of vines has a French-country minimalists feel. Breakfast is not served on the premises but awaits at one of two neighborhood restaurants: Pacific Blues or Gordon's Café. Together they offer a total of 10 items to choose from, calorie conscious to decadent. The inn is simple and lovely, and the price is right.

A pool runs the length of the central walkway at the Villagio Inn & Spa in Yountville.

Thomas Hallstein/Outsight

VILLAGIO INN & SPA
Manager: David Shipman.
707-944-2465, 800-351-1133;
  fax 707-944-8855.
www.villagio.com.
reservations@villagio.com.
6481 Washington St.,
  Yountville, CA 94595.
Price: Very Expensive.
Credit Cards: AE, DC, MC, V.
Special Features: Spa with
  10 treatment rooms, a
  40-ft. lap pool, an exercise
  fitness room.

Villagio Inn & Spa has 112 guest rooms, and each features a wood-burning fireplace, a patio or balcony, a refrigerator, and a bottle of chilled chardonnay. Of course the drawing card here is the 3,500-square-foot spa with 10 treatment rooms, a 40-lap pool, and an exercise fitness room.

Yet another plus is the historic Vintage 1870 complex nearby, featuring upscale specialty shops, galleries, cafés, a complete wine cellar, and a hot-air balloon company — all housed within a 130-year-old restored brick winery.

VINTAGE INN
Manager: David Shipman.
Phone 707-944-1112,
   800-351-1133;
   fax 707-944-1112.
www.vintageinn.com.
reservations@vintage
   inn.com.
6541 Washington St.,
   Yountville, CA 94599.
Washington St. exit off Hwy.
   29.
Price: Very Expensive.
Credit Cards: AE, D, MC, V.
Handicap Access: Yes.
Special Features: Pool,
   children welcome, pet
   friendly.

This is an exceptional inn designed with villa-style units clustered around a common waterway. The 80 spacious and beautifully decorated rooms have oversized beds, whirlpool spa tubs, ceiling fans, in-room coffeemakers and refrigerators, private verandahs, and wood-burning fireplaces. Second-story rooms cost a little more but have vaulted ceilings, and the views are worth it. Smoking or nonsmoking rooms are available, as is room service. California bubbly is served with the continental breakfast. The Vintage 1870 shopping complex is next door.

Rutherford

The luxurious complex of Auberge du Soleil scales the mountainside.

Courtesy Auberge du Soleil

AUBERGE DU SOLEIL
Manager: George Goeggel.
707-963-1211.
www.aubergedusoleil.com.
info@aubergesoleil.com.
180 Rutherford Hill Rd.,
   Rutherford, CA 94573.
Off Hwy. 29.
Price: Very Expensive.
Credit Cards: AE, D, MC, V.
Handicap Access: Yes.

Auberge du Soleil is Napa Valley's most luxurious experience. Fifty-two rooms and suites are nestled in olive trees on a remote 33-acre hillside. The style throughout the inn is distinctly southern France, with deep-set windows and wood shutters and doors. Each room or suite has a terrace and private entrance; most have spectacular views of the valley. All furnishings are leather and terra cotta tiling is used generously throughout on floors and countertops, helping to keep rooms cool dur-

Special Features: Restaurant, pool, whirlpool, tennis court.

ing Napa Valley's toasty summer days. The rooms range from standard bedroom and bath to deluxe suites with fireplaces and whirlpool baths. Two private luxury cottages were added in 1997, each with whirlpool tub and fireplaces. Take in the sculpture garden set along a half-mile path. The restaurant is not to be missed (see Chapter Five, *Restaurants*).

RANCHO CAYMUS INN
Innkeeper: Otto Komes.
707-963-1777, 800-845-1777.
1140 Rutherford Rd., PO Box 78, Rutherford, CA 94573.
From Hwy. 29, E. on Rutherford Rd.
Price: Expensive to Very Expensive.
Credit Cards: AE, CB, DC, MC, V.

This romantic hacienda may recall the film *Like Water For Chocolate* (rose petals are optional). The stucco inn with a red-tile roof is built around a serene courtyard garden, and it's clear an artist's hand was involved in the design. The original owner, sculptor Mary Tilden Morton, created an inn distinguished by stained-glass windows, hand-hewn beams, hand-thrown stoneware, and tooled wooden lamps. Ecuadorian and Guadalajaran craftsmen made the colorful furnishings. All 26 rooms are split level, most have private balconies and adobe beehive fireplaces, and four suites have whirlpool baths. A generous continental breakfast is served in the dining room by the fireplace or in the courtyard. The staff is obliging. Restaurant La Toque, opened in September 1998, serves French cuisine (see Chapter Five, *Restaurants*).

St. Helena

ADAGIO INN
Innkeeper: Betsy Buckwald.
707-963-2238, 888-823-2446; fax 707-963-5598.
www.adagioinn.com.
innkeeper@adagioinn.com.
1417 Kearney St., St. Helena, CA 94574.
2 blocks off Main St.
Price: Expensive to Very Expensive.
Credit Cards: DC, MC, V.

The sun-soaked porch at this 1904 Victorian cottage offers relaxation after a day of shopping and wine tasting. The three guest rooms are spacious, unfussy, and filled with light, and all have private baths and queen beds. The Summer Suite has a brass bed, a bay window and a claw-foot tub/shower. The location is nearly ideal, in a quiet residential neighborhood a few steps from St. Helena's Main Street.

AMBROSE BIERCE HOUSE
Innkeepers: Lisa Wild-Runnells and John Runnells.
707-963-3003; fax 707-963-9367.
www.ambrosehouse.com.
ambrose@napanet.net.

This lovely 1872 Victorian was home to renowned writer and curmudgeon philosopher Ambrose Bierce (*The Devil's Dictionary*), before he vanished in Mexico in 1913 (detailed in the 1989 film *Old Gringo*). The inn was recently remodeled and includes three rooms with private baths, and the mystique of Bierce's life and work surrounds guests. Rooms are air-conditioned and decorated

1515 Main St., St. Helena,
CA 94574.
On Hwy. 29.
Price: Expensive to Very
Expensive.
Credit Cards: MC, V.

with antiques; some have a whirlpool bath. The friendly innkeepers serve a deluxe breakfast and wine and cheese at night.

CINNAMON BEAR INN
Innkeeper: Cathye Ranieri.
707-963-4653.
1407 Kearney St., St. Helena,
CA 94574.
2 blocks off Main St.
Price: Moderate to
Expensive.
Credit Cards: MC, V, AE.

Once the home of St. Helena's mayor, this wood-shingled B&B is where the first innkeeper Jenny Jenkins raised her three children. The inn's warm atmosphere is apparent the moment you walk in the door. The common room is rich with dark wood, and lace curtains and multicolored quilts add to the comfortable feel of the guest suites, which all have queen beds and private baths as well as the stuffed teddy bears that lend the inn its name. (The bear motif is not as saccharine as it might sound; the bears are kept to a subtle but sweet minimum.) The Vanilla Room features an antique Italian marble and wood bedroom set with a king-size feather bed. The wraparound porch with its peeled willow furniture is great for reading. This charming and cozy inn is on a quiet street a few blocks off Main Street.

EL BONITA MOTEL
Managers: Pierrette
Therene.
707-963-3216, 800-541-3284.
www.elbonita.com.
195 Main St., St. Helena, CA
94574.
Price: Inexpensive to
Expensive.
Credit Cards: AE, MC, V.
Handicap Access: Yes.
Special Features: Pool,
whirlpool, sauna, garden.

Don't let the "motel" fool you. The 1950s meet the 1990s at El Bonita, a chic Art Deco, pastel-hued classic. It's also Napa's best bargain. Built in 1953, the motel was renovated and newly land-scaped in 1992. With a new wing of deluxe rooms, El Bonita now has 41 units, all cheerfully appointed; a few have kitchens and whirlpool baths. The garden and lawn spans two and a half acres, all sheltered from busy Highway 29. Trees and hedges also help cushion the steady hum of traffic. Continental breakfast service in the lobby.

FOREST MANOR
Innkeepers: Monica and
Peter Lilly.
707-965-3538, 800-788-0364.
415 Cold Springs Rd.,
Angwin, CA 94508.
Price: Expensive to Very
Expensive.
Credit Cards: AE, D, MC, V.
Special Features: Pool,
whirlpool, tennis, hiking
trails.

At this secluded 20-acre English Tudor estate, now a country inn with a honeymoon suite among its three guest rooms, there are vineyards and forest trails to explore. The three-story manor, air-conditioned and furnished in English antiques and Persian rugs, has vaulted ceilings, fireplaces, and verandahs. The rooms have private baths, refrigerators, coffeemakers, down comforters, and oversized beds. The Canterbury Suite is elegant and roomy, with a fireplace and private entrance.

Somerset Suite has a whirlpool bath. A full breakfast — quiche, fresh fruit, and the like — is served in your room, or in the dining room or verandah if you feel social. About five miles from Highway 29, this friendly inn is a romantic getaway from the bustle of Napa Valley.

GLASS MOUNTAIN INN
Innkeeper: Terry Mahoney.
707-968-9400, 877-968-940;
  fax 707-968-9430.
www.glassmountaininn.net.
glassmt@yahoo.com.
3100 Silverado Trail, St.
  Helena, CA 94574.
Price: Expensive to Very
  Expensive.
Credit Cards: AE, MC, V.

This distinctive wood-shingled Victorian is nestled in a shady hillside. The stone dining room, in fact, opens into a cave. There are three remodeled rooms. The Private Reserve Room is at the bottom of the inn's tower and includes a queen-size mahogany four-poster bed, a hand-carved oak fireplace, whirlpool, and private deck. High in the tower is the Vintage Lady, equipped with a king-size iron bed, fireplace, and nine-foot Roman soaking tub. The smallest room is the Victorian Princess, which offers a queen-size iron bed, clawfoot tub, and a private deck with a hot tub. The inn was newly renovated in the spring of 1999.

HARVEST INN
Manager: Meredith Wood.
707-963-9463, 800-950-8466;
  fax 707-963-4402.
www.harvestinn.com.
reservations@harvestinn
  .com.
1 Main St., St. Helena, CA
  94574.
On Hwy. 29 S. of St. Helena.
Price: Expensive to Very
  Expensive.
Credit Cards: AE, D, DC,
  MC, V.
Special Features: Two pools,
  whirlpools.

There's a bit of Old England in Napa Valley: the Harvest Inn, a stately English Tudor-style lodge built from the bricks and cobblestones of old San Francisco homes. Most of the 54 guest rooms have king-size beds, brick fireplaces, wet bars, and refrigerators, and all are furnished with antiques and reproductions. Several suites have whirlpool tubs. The lush landscaping also helps to create the aura of another time and place. The inn's Harvest Centre has a wine bar and dance floor, and a complimentary continental breakfast is served in the dining hall. The inn, which was given a facelift in the spring of 1999, overlooks a 14-acre working vineyard and is within strolling distance of many wineries.

HOTEL ST. HELENA
Manager: Mary Haney.
707-963-4388, 888-478-4355;
  fax 707-963-5400.
www.hotelsthelena.com.
1309 Main St., St. Helena,
  CA 94574.
Price: Expensive to Very
  Expensive.
Credit Cards: AE, MC, V.

In the thick of St. Helena's shopping and dining, this hotel on the town's Main Street is richly furnished with antiques. There are 17 rooms and 1 suite; 14 have private baths. Its turn-of-the-20th-century charm makes it especially homey. There's a wine bar, and continental breakfast is served every morning. The hotel is air-conditioned.

Thomas Hallstein/Outsight

The Ink House Bed-and-Breakfast is an 1884 Italianate Victorian.

**INK HOUSE BED &
BREAKFAST**
Innkeeper: Diane DeFilipi.
707-963-3890;
    fax 707-968-0739.
www.inkhouse.com.
inkhousebb@aol.com.
1575 St. Helena Hwy., St.
    Helena, CA 94574.
On Hwy. 29 1 mi. N. of
    Rutherford.
Price: Moderate to
    Expensive.
Credit Cards: MC, V.
Special features: Garden,
    observatory.

A glass-enclosed, rooftop observatory with a 360-degree view of vineyards distinguishes this yellow 1884 Italianate Victorian listed on the National Register of Historic Places. Each of the seven second-story guest rooms has a vineyard view and period furnishings. Two rooms share a bath; five have private baths. Just for fun, take a lesson on the antique pump organ in the parlor, or take in a sunset from the wraparound porch. A full gourmet breakfast is served, plus wine and hors d'oeuvres at night. This is an exceptional location and setting. While it's right on Highway 29, the inn is remarkably quiet.

**THE INN AT
    SOUTHBRIDGE**
Innkeeper: Cristine Karp.
707-967-9400, 800-520-6800.
www.slh.com/southbridge.
southbridge@slh.com.
1020 Main St., St. Helena,
    CA 94574.
On Hwy. 29, just S. of
    downtown.
Price: Very Expensive.
Credit Cards: AE, DC, MC,
    V.
Special Features: Restaurant,
    health spa.

A classy new addition to St. Helena, this inn features 20 rooms. The complex —owned by the same people behind Meadowood resort — is a sleekly modern Italianate design. All the rooms are on the second floor and are done in handsome and creamy hues with sophisticated wood accents. The rooms feature a fireplace, an over-sized tub, and French doors that open onto a private balcony. A few of the rooms are rather close to Main Street. Just off the lobby is a family-style Italian restaurant named Tomatina; it's not bad for a quick pizza (see Chapter Five, *Restaurants*). Also part of the complex is the Health Spa of Napa Valley (see Chapter Seven, *Recreation*).

Meadowood is one of Wine Country's most exclusive resorts.

Courtesy Meadowood

MEADOWOOD NAPA VALLEY
Manager: Ken Humes.
707-963-3646, 0-458-8080; fax 707-963-5863.
www.meadowood.com.
900 Meadowood Ln., St. Helena, CA 94574.
E. of St. Helena.
Price: Very Expensive.
Credit Cards: AE, DC, MC, V.
Handicap Access: Limited.
Special Features: Health spa, croquet, restaurants, golf, pool, tennis; children welcome.

Meadowood never falters in its interpretation of luxury. Its lodges, reminiscent of New England's turn-of-the-20th-century cottages, are scattered around a gorgeous wooded 250-acre property. The buildings are tiered with gabled windows and porches, all trimmed in white. The staff pamper with style, and a soothing sense of privacy prevails.

Most of the resort's 85 cottages, suites, and lodges have cathedral ceilings, skylights, ceiling fans, and air conditioning. Rooms range in size from one-room studios with fireplaces to four-bedroom suites with sitting rooms. Each room has a private deck with a view of pine trees or gardens, and a queen- or king-size bed with a goose-down comforter.

Breakfast is not included in the tariff; a continental repast can be delivered to your door, or a full feast is available at the Grill. Better still, try a light breakfast by the pool, surrounded by lush lawns and trees. At night, a walk to the Restaurant, Meadowood's premiere dining room, makes for a cozy evening (see Chapter Five, *Restaurants*). Meadowood also has one of the finest health facilities in the valley, with aerobic and exercise rooms and a full spa (see Chapter Seven, *Recreation*).

OLIVER HOUSE COUNTRY INN
Innkeepers: Bob Bates and Fred Zabata.
707-963-4089.
www.oliverhouse.com.
info@oliverhouse.com.
2970 Silverado Trail N., St. Helena, CA 94574.

If typical Victorian architecture isn't your cup of tea, visit Switzerland instead. Tucked away on four acres outside St. Helena, this small chalet-style inn is a slice of Old Europe on Silverado Trail. Four guest rooms (three with French doors) are appointed with antiques (a 120-year-old Scottish brass bed, for example, and an armoire born in Salzburg the same

3/4 mi. N. of Deer Park Rd.
Price: Moderate to Very
    Expensive.
Credit Cards: AE, MC, V.

ROSE GARDEN INN
Innkeepers: Joanne and
    Tom Contreras.
707-963-4417.
www.rosegardeninn.net.
1277 St. Helena Hwy. S., St.
    Helena, CA 94574.
On Hwy. 29 S. of St. Helena.
Price: Expensive.
Credit Cards: MC, V.

**SHADY OAKS COUNTRY
INN**
Innkeepers: Lisa Wild-
    Runnells and John
    Runnells.
707-963-1190;
    fax 707-963-9367.
www.shadyoaksinn.com.
shdyoaks@napanet.
399 Zinfandel Ln., St.
    Helena, CA 94574.
2 mi. S. of St. Helena.
Price: Expensive to Very
    Expensive.
Credit Cards: MC, V.
Handicap Access: One
    room.

year as Mozart); two rooms have wood-burning fireplaces. The top-floor suite has an open-beam ceiling and a balcony. All rooms have private baths, and three rooms have private entrances. The inn serves a full breakfast.

Once a ranch foreman's home, this comfy inn is located on three acres surrounded by vineyards and now houses four spacious and comfortable guest rooms, all with private baths. (One room features a whirlpool tub, fireplace, and private deck.) The shade of century-old trees invites reading and relaxing.

Oak and walnut trees surround this friendly country inn consisting of five guest rooms with private baths, all furnished with antiques. The main house, built in the 1920s, has three lovely rooms. Built in the 1880s, the old stone winery has two more luxurious rooms, one with a vineyard view from a private deck, the other with a distinct stone interior. The inn was recently renovated. A full gourmet champagne breakfast — eggs Benedict or Belgian waffles are the norm — is served in your room or the dining room and garden patio, which is guarded by Roman columns. Premium wines and cheeses are served in the evening.

*There are vineyard views
from the pool at the Vineyard
Country Inn.*

Chris Alderman

VINEYARD COUNTRY INN
Innkeepers: Michael and Monica Wahlen.
707-963-1000;
fax 707-963-1794.
www.vineyardcountry inn.com
201 Main St., St. Helena, CA 94574.
Price: Expensive.
Credit Cards: AE, MC, V.
Handicap Access: Yes.
Special Features: Pool, whirlpool.

This lovely inn takes its inspiration from a French country village. Surrounding a central court, the buildings are crowned with steeply pitched roofs and intricate brick chimneys. There are 21 elegant suites, with exposed beam ceilings, redbrick fireplaces, king- or queen-size beds, and wet bars with refrigerator. Many have balconies with vineyard views. For the breakfast buffet, small tables are grouped around a large dining room fireplace. The inn is along busy Highway 29, but the rooms are relatively quiet.

WHITE SULPHUR SPRINGS INN AND SPA
Inkeeper: Hoffman Institute.
707-963-8588, 800-593-8873;
fax 707-963-28980.
www.whitesulphur springs.com.
3100 White Sulphur Springs Rd., St. Helena, CA 94574.
W. on Spring St. from Hwy. 29.
Price: Moderate to Expensive.
Credit Cards: MC, V.
Special Features: Health spa, mineral pool, whirlpool.

Established in 1852, White Sulphur Springs was California's first resort. A rustic, Old World retreat in a canyon above St. Helena, it is set in 330 acres of redwood, fir, and madrone and has hiking trails and waterfalls. The resort, now newly renovated, has nine cottages and two small lodges — a total of 28 rooms with half or shared baths. The large cottages have kitchenettes, and the sleeping cottages and private rooms have kitchen privileges. A complimentary continental breakfast is available in the communal kitchen. The sulphur spring that gave the resort its name more than a century ago still flows out of the mountain and into an outdoor soaking pool at a temperature maintained between 85 to 92 degrees. Two other pools are maintained at different temperatures. (For details on spa treatments, see Chapter Seven, *Recreation.*)

WINE COUNTRY INN
Innkeeper: Jim Smith.
707-963-7077, 888-465-4608;
fax 707-963-9018.
www.winecountryinn.com.
romance@winecountry inn.com.
1152 Lodi Ln., St. Helena, CA 94574.
Price: Expensive to Very Expensive
Credit Cards: MC, V.
Special Features: Pool, whirlpool.

This 24-room guesthouse is modern, but a tall stone tower gives it an Old World feel. All rooms have private baths and are furnished with antiques; many have alcove beds and balconies or decks with lush views. Fireplaces are standard in most rooms but are inoperable from mid-April to mid-October. The owners are building five new cottages. A buffet-style breakfast is served daily.

Chris Alderman

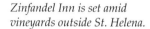

Zinfandel Inn is set amid vineyards outside St. Helena.

ZINFANDEL INN
Innkeepers: Diane and Jerry
  Payton.
707-963-3512.
www.zinfandelinn.com.
800 Zinfandel Ln., St.
  Helena, CA 94574.
1 mi. S. of St. Helena on
  Hwy. 29.
Price: Expensive to Very
  Expensive.
Credit Cards: MC, V.
Sepcial Features: Garden,
  pool, whirlpool.

A striking example of an English Tudor, this luxury getaway is planted in the heart of Wine Country. A fountain and an arched doorway crowned with fieldstone greet you, while the dining room has a beautifully inlaid oak floor. The three guest rooms are all named after grape varieties: The Chardonnay Room may be the most elegant, with its stone fireplace, king-size bed in a bay window, and private entrance. The romantic Zinfandel Room has a private balcony, wood-burning stove and whirlpool tub. The Petite Sirah offers a Victorian-inspired room with a panoramic view of vineyards and mountains.

Calistoga

**BRANNAN COTTAGE
  INN**
Innkeeper: Patrick Brawdy.
707-942-4200.
www.brannancottageinn.com.
innkeeper@brannancottage
  inn.com.
109 Wapoo Ave., P.O. Box 81,
  Calistoga, CA 94515.
Just off Hwy. 29 near
  Brannan St.
Price: Moderate to
  Expensive.
Credit Cards: MC, V.
Handicap Access: Yes.
Special Features: Garden.

B uilt around 1860 by Calistoga founder Sam Brannan, this inn is listed on the National Register of Historic Places and is the only guesthouse constructed for Brannan's Hot Springs Resort that still stands on its original site. Not surprisingly, it's also the oldest building in town. Restoration got under way in the 1980s; reconstruction of the gingerbread gable was based on enlarged vintage photographs.

Today, an eclectic collection of furnishings, including plush and comfortable antiques, furnish the six guest rooms. All have private baths, private entrances, and air conditioning. A generous breakfast may be served in the courtyard under lemon trees. The house is surrounded by gardens, so guests can always find a private, quiet spot to read and relax, and the sunny courtyard beckons after a day of "spa-ing."

CALISTOGA INN
Innkeeper: Michael
  Dunsford.
707-942-4101;
  fax 707-942-4914.
www.calistogainn.com.
info@calistogainn.com.
1250 Lincoln Ave., Calistoga,
  CA 94515.
On Hwy. 29 near Cedar St.
Price: Inexpensive to
  moderate.
Credit Cards: AE, MC, V.
Special Features: On-site
  brewery, beer garden, and
  restaurant.

Wine isn't the only beverage in this neck of the woods. A brewery, Napa Valley Brewing Co. (see Chapter Six, *Wineries*), makes its home in the old water tower next to the Calistoga Inn. This turn-of-the-20th-century hotel is charming, but the 18 guest rooms are basic. Double beds are standard, and baths are shared. A light continental breakfast is served. The inn, about a block from the main highway, is within walking distance to spas and dining.

**CALISTOGA COUNTRY
  LODGE**
Innkeeper: Rae Ellen Fields
  and Laura Apolinar.
707-942-5555;
  fax 707-942-5864.
www.countrylodge.com.
cowgirl@countrylodge.com.
2883 Foothill Blvd.,
  Calistoga, CA.
Price: Moderate.
Credit Cards: AE, MC, V.
Special Features: Great
  views, pool, whirlpool.

This lodge has a refreshingly rustic feel. For those who like to perch and take in the view, this lodge has exquisite views of Mt. Helena and the Mayacamas mountain range. It's located in the foothills of the Mayacamas Mountains, yet it's one mile from downtown Calistoga. All six rooms are decorated in Southwest style and are low tech, with no TV, VCRs, or phones. Four rooms have private baths, two have shared baths. The rooms feature American antiques, Native American artifacts, and a touch of Georgia O'Keeffe.

CARLIN COTTAGES
Innkeeper: Gina Carlin.
707-942-9102, 800-734-4624;
  fax 707-942-2295.
www.carlincottage.com.
1623 Lake St., Calistoga, CA
  94515.
Hwy. 29 N. thru town, W. on
  Lake.
Price: Inexpensive to
  Expensive.
Credit Cards: AE, MC, V.
Special features: Pool,
  whirlpool.

Remember the old auto court motels of the 1950s? Well, Carlin Cottages is a souped-up version of those vanishing classics. There are 15 cottages — ranging from studios to two-bedrooms — and each is agreeably appointed with country Shaker-style furniture. Most of the cottages have kitchenettes, and seven cottages have whirlpool tubs with water fed by a mineral spring. There's a pool in the center of the courtyard, and mature trees shade the entire property. Located on a quiet residential street, Carlin Cottages is a good spot for families.

CHATEAU DE VIE

Innkeepers: Felipe Barragan
and Peter Weatherman.
707-942-6446;
    fax 707-942-6456.
www.chateaudv.com.
chateaudv@aol.com.
3250 Hwy. 128, Calistoga,
    CA 94515.
Price: Expensive to Very
    Expensive.
Credit Cards: AE, MC, V.
Special Features: 8-person
    Jacuzzi outside by the
    garden.

Surrounded by two acres of vineyards, this bed-and-breakfast has an understated elegance appreciated by the discerning. (Ted Kennedy reportedly has been a guest.) The inn has excellent views of Mount St. Helena and great gourmet breakfasts: fresh baked scones, breads and muffins, country sausage, and vegetable quiches. All three rooms have queen-size beds and private baths. An eight-person whirlpool spa sits outside by the garden.

CHRISTOPHER'S INN

Innkeepers: Christopher and
    Adele Layton.
707-942-5755;
    fax 707-942-6895.
www.chrisinn.com.
info@christophersinn.com.
1010 Foothill Blvd.,
    Calistoga, CA 94515.
On Hwy. 29 just S. of
    Lincoln Ave.
Price: Expensive to Very
    Expensive.
Credit Cards: AE, MC, V.
Handicap Access: Limited.

One of Napa Valley's newest B&Bs, this stylish inn has 22 rooms, all with private baths. Its rich antiques and Laura Ashley wallpaper and curtains evoke an English country inn. An architect by trade, Christopher Layton renovated three old summer cottages. The grounds are impeccably tended, bright with color and shaded by tall trees; one room has a private garden patio, and another has a porch shaded by star jasmine. A wing was added in 1997, and many of the new rooms feature fireplaces and whirlpool tubs. A modest continental breakfast is delivered to your room or served in the garden. Location is both an advantage and a disadvantage. Guests can walk to town, but Highway 29 can be noisy during the day. Luckily most rooms are well off the road.

Culver's Country Inn is convenient to Calistoga's popular spas.

Chris Alderman

CULVER'S MANSION
Innkeeper: Jacqueline
  LeVesque.
707-942-4535.
www.culvermansion.com.
1805 Foothill Blvd.,
  Calistoga, CA 94515.
On Hwy. 128 N. of Lincoln
  Ave.
Price: Expensive.
Credit Cards: None.
Special Features: Pool,
  whirlpool, indoor sauna.

A registered historical landmark, circa 1875, this Gothic Revival inn has a unique clipped gable roof. Operated by a British-born host, the inn has six guest rooms, all with private baths, decorated with Victorian furniture. Set on a shady hillside, Culver's is an easy walk to Calistoga's main-street dining and shopping. A full breakfast is served. The inn is also air conditioned, a plus during Calistoga's toasty summers.

COTTAGE GROVE INN
Innkeeper: Valerie Beck.
707-942-8400, 800-799-2284.
www.cottagegrove.com.
innkeeper@cottage
  grove.com.
1711 Lincoln Ave., Calistoga,
  CA 94515.
A few blocks north of
  downtown.
Price: Expensive to Very
  Expensive.
Credit Cards: AE, D, DC,
  MC, V.
Handicap Access: Yes.

This classy inn is actually a group of 16 California Craftsman-style cottages, built on the site of Brannan's original Calistoga resort. The cottages are nestled in a grove of old elms and a short walk to Calistoga's many spas. Each cottage features skylights, hardwood floors, covered front porches with wicker rockers, ceiling fans, wood-burning fireplaces, air conditioning, and two-person whirlpool tubs. Each has a distinct design theme. The Nautical Cottage, for example, takes New England as its inspiration. The Gardener's Cottage sports a picket-fence headboard and floral prints. Some cottages are situated close to the street, but Lincoln Avenue quiets considerably at night.

THE ELMS
Proprietor: Alicia Sylvia.
707-942-9476,
  800-399-ELMS.
www.theelms.com.
info@theelems.com.
1300 Cedar St., Calistoga,
  CA 94515.
Just N. of Lincoln Ave.
Price: Moderate to
  Expensive.
Credit Cards: D, MC, V.

This impressive three-story French Victorian is in a quiet residential neighborhood not far from downtown. Time seemingly stands still inside this grande dame with towering windows and a formal parlor. The seven rooms, all with private baths and some with spa tubs, are beautifully done in European antiques. There is also a cottage for a more intimate getaway, which features a king-size brass bed, kitchenette, double whirlpool, and a private patio. Wine and cheese are served in the main house by the parlor fire every afternoon.

FOOTHILL HOUSE
Innkeepers: Doris and Gus
  Beckert.
707-942-6933, 800-942-6933;
  fax 707-942-5692.
www.foothillhouse.com
gus@calicom.net.

This cozy inn is a find. Shaded by tall trees and set amid lush gardens, the modest turn-of-the-century farmhouse is a soothing getaway. Foothill House offers three elegant suites and a private cottage. All have private baths (three with whirlpool tubs), private patio-door entrances, refrigerators,

A footpath leads you into a garden at the Foothill House.

Thomas Hallstein/Outsight

3037 Foothill Blvd., Calistoga, CA 94515. On Hwy. 128 N. of Petrified Forest Rd.
Price: Expensive to Very Expensive.
Credit Cards: AE, D, MC, V.

and wood-burning stoves or fireplaces. Laura Ashley prints and antiques furnish the rooms, including queen- or king-size four-poster beds.

The cottage, called Quail's Roost, is accented in whitewashed pine and equipped with a kitchenette and a two-person whirlpool that looks out to a waterfall. The Beckerts pamper guests with a generous gourmet breakfast delivered to your room that includes fresh fruit and croissants and such treats as a rich cheese and potato casserole. Afternoon wine and cheese in the sun room is an extravagant spread.

HIDEAWAY COTTAGES
Manager: DeAnn Wiley.
707-942-4108.
www.hideaway
cottages.com.
1412 Fairway, Calistoga, CA 94515.
Just off Lincoln Ave.
Price: Moderate to Very Expensive.
Credit Cards: AE, MC, V.
Handicap Access: Yes.
Special Features: Pool, whirlpool.

These 17 units are comfy but utilitarian, and all are set amid tall mature trees on a quiet residential street close to Lincoln Avenue restaurants and shops. It's a good spot if you're planning an extended stay. Three deluxe cottages are available, and one of the cottages can accommodate groups of four or six. Air conditioning and televisions are standard, and most units have kitchenettes.

HOTEL D'AMICI
Innkeeper: Roger Asbil.
707-942-1007.
www.rutherfordgrove.com.

Above the Cinnabar Restaurant in a historic building on the main business thoroughfare, this inn has four suites, each with private bath,

amici@rutherfordgrove.com.
1436 Lincoln Ave., PO Box
552, Calistoga, CA 94573.
On Hwy. 29 downtown.
Price: Expensive to Very
Expensive.
Credit Cards: AE, MC, V.
Handicap Access: No.

LA CHAUMIERE
Innkeeper: Gary Venturi.
707-942-5139, 800-474-6800;
fax 707-842-5199.
www.lachaumiere.com.
calist9578@aol.com.
1301 Cedar St., Calistoga,
CA 94515.
Just N. of Lincoln Ave.
Price: Expensive.
Credit Cards: MC, V.

**LARKMEAD COUNTRY
INN**
Innkeeper: Tim Garbarino.
707-942-5360.
www.larkmead.com.
1103 Larkmead Ln.,
Calistoga, CA 94515.
S. of Calistoga off Hwy. 29.
Price: Expensive.
Credit Cards: None.
Handicap Access: Yes.

**MEADOWLARK
COUNTRY HOUSE**
Innkeeper: Kurt Stevens.
800-942-5651;
fax 707-942-5023.
www.meadowlarkinn.com.
601 Petrified Forest,
Calistoga, CA 94515.
Price: Expensive to Very
Expensive.
Credit Cards: AE, MC, V.
Special Features: Mineral
pool, whirlpool, and
sauna.

color TV, oak furnishings, and a ceiling fan. Two of the rooms share a balcony.

This is an intimate and homey bungalow in a peaceful residential area not far from downtown. The main house has three guest rooms; one has a private deck, and each has private baths. The inn's jewel is out back: a private cottage under a giant redwood tree. Built in 1932, it has a private deck and a fireplace made from petrified wood. The grounds are lovingly tended. Be prepared for a hearty breakfast. Wine and cheese are served in the afternoon.

Built on land owned in the late 1880s by flamboyant San Francisco heiress Lillie Coit, this inn was originally part of Larkmead Winery, as was Champagne Cellars next door. It is set in the heart of a vineyard and was built by an Italian-Swiss family before Prohibition. The Palladian-style architecture is unique to the area. The main part of the house is upstairs, the better to oversee work in the vineyards and catch afternoon breezes. Four guest rooms, all with private baths, are along a hallway in one wing of the house. Persian rugs, wicker, and colorful fabrics add to the homey feel.

This luxurious inn is just two miles outside Calistoga and it has plenty of land to roam: 20 acres. There are sport horses in the pasture, and a mineral pool, hot tub and sauna. The bedrooms all have private baths and queen-size beds, and some have private decks or terraces to take advantage of the views. Gourmet breakfasts are served, and guests are encouraged to step to the veranda afterward to enjoy the vistas.

MOUNT VIEW HOTEL
Manager: Jeff Niezgoda.
707-942-6877;
    fax 707-942-6904.
www.mountainview
    hotel.com.
info@mountviewhotel.com.
1457 Lincoln Ave., Calistoga,
    CA 94515.
Price: Moderate to Very
    Expensive.
Credit Cards: AE, MC, V.
Special Features: Health spa,
    pool, whirlpool,
    restaurant.

Restored in Art Deco style and on the National Register of Historic Places, this elegant lodge was originally a European-style hotel built in 1917. There are 29 units and three cottages, including nine luxurious suites, one of which is furnished in Art Deco period pieces. It's in the heart of Calistoga shopping and dining. The hotel has its own superb spa (see Chapter Seven, *Recreation*), and others are just a step away. Just off the lobby is one of the valley's best restaurants, Catahoula, where California meets Louisiana (see Chapter Five, *Restaurants*).

THE PINK MANSION
Innkeepers: Toppa and
    Leslie Epps.
707-942-0558, 800-238-7465.
www.pinkmansion.com.
pink@napanet.net.
1415 Foothill Blvd.,
    Calistoga, CA 94515.
On Foothill Blvd. (Hwy. 128)
    near Hwy. 29.
Price: Moderate to Very
    Expensive.
Credit Cards: D, MC, V.
Special Features: Indoor
    pool, whirlpool, garden.

Postcard views of Napa Valley and lush forests await visitors who stay at this 1875 Victorian. The home's pink exterior will catch your attention, while the flowers, rare plants, and exotic palms will hold your interest. The inn features two rooms and four suites with fireplaces; two suites have whirlpools. (The Angel Room also has a treasured family collection of angels; the Forest Room is decorated in green.) Wine and cheese cap off the afternoon. The inn has an indoor pool, and the estate grounds include three acres of landscaped gardens.

SCOTT COURTYARD
Innkeepers: Derek and
    Robin Werrett.
707-942-0948, 800-942-1515;
    fax 707-942-5102.
www.scottcourtyard.com.
1443 2nd St., Calistoga, CA
    94515.
Near downtown.
Price: Expensive.
Credit Cards: AE, D, MC, V.
Special Features: Pool,
    fitness room.

If you've slept in enough Victorian inns to last a lifetime, then this B&B is a refreshing change of pace. In four buildings that cluster around a beautiful and quiet garden courtyard, the inn has three suites with fireplaces, all decorated with tropical-style Art Deco antiques and collectibles. The Rose Suite is cozy with hardwood floors and a private porch. All the suites have queen-size beds and private entrances and baths plus refrigerators. Those who like to make and do rather than simply lounge by the pool will enjoy the artist's workshop, replete with a kiln. A breakfast buffet is served in the common room warmed by a stone fireplace or in the courtyard by the pool. Check out the aviary. This inn is near downtown but quiet, and the hospitality is first-rate.

Thomas Hallstein/Outsight

Guests can gather comfortably at the newly expanded Silver Rose Inn.

SILVER ROSE INN
Proprietors: J-Paul, Sally, and Derrick Dumont.
707-942-9581, 800-995-9381.
www.silverrose.com.
silvrose@napanet.net.
351 Rosedale Rd., Calistoga, CA 94515.
S. of Hwy. 29 just off Silverado Trail.
Price: Expensive to Very Expensive.
Credit Cards: AE, D, MC, V.
Special Features: Winery, restaurant, health spa, 2 pools, whirlpool, fitness room, tennis, conference center, putting green.

Perched on a rocky outcropping and surrounded by ancient oak trees, this striking retreat — or more accurately a complex — has sweeping views of upper Napa Valley and Mount St. Helena. Indeed, this is a unique inn with a small winery and a restaurant on the premises. The main house, Inn on the Knoll, is a spacious contemporary inn with nine rooms, each having a distinct personality. The intimate Turn-of-the-Century Room is decorated with antique dolls. The Oriental Room has Asian rugs, rattan furniture, shoji screens, and a Japanese lacquered headboard; there's also a cathedral ceiling, whirlpool bath, and gorgeous vineyard views. Silver Rose also has an 11-room building called Inn the Vineyard; its most luxurious room is the Vineyard Suite, which has a whirlpool tub for two set against a dramatic fireplace.

Guests gather in the evening for wine and cheese around the large stone fireplaces in each building. Breakfast is served in the dining room, on the deck, or in your room. Breakfast is a hearty continental affair and includes Sally's luscious baked goods such as a delightful Hawaiian Bread. The Dumonts are superb hosts.

WINE WAY INN
Innkeepers: Cecile and Moye Stephens.
707-942-0680, 800-572-0679; fax 707-942-2636.

"Like staying with friends" is the apt motto of this quaint California bungalow. The Stephenses, who bought the inn in 1990, are warm hosts and Cecile's breakfasts are among the best in the valley, with menus that include frittatas with homemade

www.napavalley.com/ wineway.
1019 Foothill Blvd., Calistoga, CA 94515.
Hwy. 29 just S. of Lincoln Ave.
Price: Moderate to Expensive.
Credit Cards: AE, D, MC, V.

salsa and a sticky-sweet "bubble bread." All six guest rooms are modest in size, have private baths, and are nicely done with antiques and quilts. The multilevel deck out back offers a spectacular view of the Palisades. The only negative: The inn is near a busy intersection, so traffic noise may be an issue.

CALISTOGA SPA LODGING

Mineral pools at Calistoga Spa Hot Springs.

Peter Hickey. Courtesy Calistoga Chamber of Commerce

Many spas offer lodging/spa treatment discount packages. For complete spa treatment information, see Chapter Seven, *Recreation*.

Calistoga Spa Hot Springs (Manager: Jan Thomas; 707-942-6269; www.calisto gaspa.com; 1006 Washington St., Calistoga, CA 94515; Moderate; MC, V.) Relaxed and unpretentious, this inn has the amenities of a resort but at more affordable prices. All 57 family-oriented units have kitchenettes, air conditioning, TVs, and telephones. Features include fitness room and four outdoor mineral pools. Children are welcome.

Calistoga Village Inn & Spa (Manager: Gisela Schaefer; 707-942-0991; www. greatspa.com; 1880 Lincoln Ave., Calistoga, CA 94515; Moderate to Expensive; AE, D, MC, V.) This inn has been everything from a motel to a Moonie camp. Rooms are pleasant but modestly appointed. Some suites have whirlpool tubs. Two outdoor mineral pools offer an expansive view of the mountains. There is an inside mineral whirlpool and sauna. A renovation of the spa was completed in fall 1999.

Dr. Wilkinson's Hot Springs (Manager: Mark Wilkinson; 707-942-4102; www. drwilkinson.com; 1507 Lincoln Ave., Calistoga, CA 94515; Expensive; AE, MC, V.) This spa has 42 spacious and functional motel-like rooms, many with kitchenettes. There are two outdoor mineral pools plus an indoor mineral whirlpool. Shopping and dining is within walking distance. Rooms, grounds, and pools have recently been polished up.

Eurospa (Manager: Mitch and Lisa Jaffuel; 707-942-6829; 1202 Pine St., Calistoga, CA 94515; Expensive; MC, V.) Each of the 13 rooms at this inn and spa is decorated in a different theme. Many rooms have private whirlpools, and gas-burning wood stoves. There is an outdoor pool and whirlpool. Close to downtown yet away from the main street bustle.

Golden Haven Hot Springs and Resort (Manager: Deanna Murray; www. goldenhaven.com; 707-942-6793; 1713 Lake St., Calistoga, CA 94515; Moderate to Expensive; AE, MC, V.) Amid towering oak trees and immaculate gardens, this 28-room spa offers five rooms with kitchenettes and all with refrigerators. Rooms with whirlpools, saunas, or waterbeds are also available.

Indian Springs Spa and Resort (Managers: Erik Fair and Mikki Ellis-Marsili; 707-942-4913; 1712 Lincoln Ave., Calistoga, CA 94515; Expensive to Very Expensive; D, MC, V.) Eighteen whitewashed bungalow-style cottages — one is a three-bedroom that sleeps six — overlook 16 acres of palm trees and views of Mount St. Helena. Gorgeous Olympic-size mineral pool. An easy walk to downtown shopping and dining.

Nance's Hot Springs (Managers: Sara Wright and Debbie Fisher; 707-942-6211; 1614 Lincoln Ave., Calistoga, CA 94515; Inexpensive to Moderate; AE, D, MC, V.) A no-frills family-run motel. Rooms include kitchenettes. Indoor mineral pool.

Roman Spa (Manager: Michael Quest; 707-942-4441, 800-250-2457; www.tales .com/roman spa; 1300 Washington St.; Moderate to Expensive; AE, D, MC, V.) Lushly landscaped grounds surround this older but well-tended 60-room motel-like resort. Half of the units have kitchenettes. There is an outdoor mineral pool and whirlpool, plus a large indoor whirlpool and sauna. Newly renovated in spring 1999.

LODGING IN SONOMA COUNTY

Sonoma Valley

BANCROFT HOUSE
Innkeepers: Michael Woods and Diane Wendt Woods.
707-996-4863;
fax 707-996-5618.
www.bancrofthouse.com.

Just when you thought every Wine Country bed-and-breakfast was priced out of reach for the average traveler, here's this delightful inn. This 1906 Queen Anne is stylish yet comfortable, rich with dark wood cabinetry and crown molding.

info@bancrofthouse.com.
786 Broadway, Sonoma, CA
    95476.
3 blocks S. on Broadway
    from Sonoma Plaza.
Price: Moderate to Very
    Expensive.
Credit Cards: D, MC, V.

Breakfast is still served on the big table off the kitchen, full breakfasts on the weekends, continental during the week. There are four rooms and one cottage, and each is named for an Impressionist painting. Here's another B&B rarity these days: Kids are welcome.

There are some great porches for sipping wine at the Beltane Ranch in Glen Ellen.

Thomas Hallstein/Outsight

BELTANE RANCH
Manager: Ann Soulier.
707-996-6501.www.beltane
    ranch.com.
11775 Sonoma Hwy., PO Box
    395, Glen Ellen, CA 95442.
On Hwy. 12 between
    Kenwood and Glen Ellen.
Price: Moderate to
    Expensive.
Credit Cards: None.
Special Features: Tennis,
    hiking trails, working
    vineyard.

This former bunkhouse was built in 1882 and has been everything from a brothel to a turkey farm, but now it's a quiet and unpretentious B&B. It sits on 1,600 acres of land, amid vineyards and olive trees. (The inn even makes it owns Beltane Ranch Olive Oil.) A stylish porch and verandah with an elaborate gingerbread railing were added to the house years ago. There are five guest rooms, each with a private entrance and bath and one with a wood-burning stove. There is also a new cottage with one bedroom and a private garden. A full breakfast is served in the wood-paneled dining room. An added bonus is the remarkable hiking trail on the property, which takes you past vineyards and then follows a stream.

**BRICK HOUSE
    BUNGALOWS**
Innkeepers: Joe Gough and
    B. J. Clarke.

Located just a half a block from the Sonoma Plaza, this inn is near the best restaurants, shops, and historical sites but is hidden in a secluded compound. There's a lovely little garden and a stone

707-996-8091;
fax 707-996-7301.
www.brickhouse
bungalows.com.
info@brickhouse
bungalows.com.
313 First St. E., Sonoma, CA
95476.
1/2 block N. of Sonoma
Plaza.
Price: Very Expensive.
Credit Cards: MC, V.
Special Features: Garden.

**THE COTTAGE INN AND
SPA/THE MISSION
BED-AND-BREAKFAST**
Innkeeper: Robert Behrens
and Marga Friberg.
707-996-0719, 800-944-1490.
www.cottageinnand
spa.com.
cottageinn@aol.com.
302 First St. E., Sonoma, CA
95476.
1 block N, of Sonoma Plaza.
Price: Moderate to Very
Expensive.
Credit Cards: MC, V.
Handicap Access: Yes.
Special Features: Whirlpool,
spa services.

EL DORADO HOTEL
Manager: Bonnie Reynolds.
707-996-3030, 800-289-3031;
fax 707-996-3148.
www.hoteleldorado.com.
info@hotelel dorado.com.
405 First St. W., Sonoma, CA
95476.
On the downtown plaza.
Price: Expensive.
Credit Cards: AE, MC, V.
Handicap Access: Yes.
Special Features: Restaurant,
pool.

GAIGE HOUSE INN
Innkeeper: Ken Burnet.
707-935-0237, 800-935-0237;
fax 707-935-6411.
www.gaige.com

fountain, perfect for relaxing in a chair with good book. There are five bungalows in all, each with a full kitchen and a distinct personality. The Brick House bungalow was built in 1907 and recalls an Italian farmhouse. It has 20-inch thick stone walls, tile floors, fireplace, and claw-foot tub. Hamilton's bungalow and Chelsea's bungalow both have two-story lofts, and each overlooks a private garden.

These two inns are side-by-side on 1st Street East, not far from the downtown plaza but still a quiet oasis. A Mediterranean-style courtyard is enclosed by a high stucco wall and features a fountain and whirlpool. The two inns have seven rooms total between them. Many have private entries or patios, some have fireplaces and whirlpool baths. Fresh-baked goodies are delivered each morning, allowing guests a private continental breakfast.

The El Dorado is a special hotel. Restored to its original elegance, it has 26 rooms, all with private baths. French windows plus terraces offer views of the hotel's Spanish courtyard or the historic plaza. A continental breakfast is included in the tariff, as is a complimentary bottle of wine. The lobby restaurant Piatti serves regional Italian cuisine (see Chapter Five, *Restaurants*).

You could say this inn really rates — literally. Arts and Entertainment Channel included this inn in its top 10 most romantic bed-and-breakfasts in the world. A Queen Anne-Italianate built in the

gaige@sprynet.com.
13540 Arnold Dr., Glen
  Ellen, CA 95442.
Off Hwy. 12.
Price: Very Expensive.
Credit Cards: AE, D, MC, V.
Special Features: Pool, hot
  tub.

1890s, this inn was lovingly restored with 15 pleasant guest rooms. Newly remodeled in 1998, the inn's rooms all have private baths and air conditioning; nine have private entrances, five have whirlpool tubs, and nine have fireplaces. The best is the Gaige Suite, which has a canopied king-size bed, a whirlpool tub, and a private balcony with a grand view. The interior has an eclectic Caribbean feel to it. Full breakfast is served. The pool is a lovely setting, and there's a whirlpool spa in the garden. It's in an ideal location for wine touring and Sonoma dining.

GLENELLY INN
Innkeeper: Kristi Hallamore
  Jeppesen.
707-996-6720;
  fax 707-996-5227.
www.glenelly.com.glenelly
  @glenelly.com.
5131 Warm Springs Rd.,
  Glen Ellen, CA 95442.
Off Hwy. 12 at Arnold Dr.
Price: Expensive.
Credit Cards: MC, V.
Special Features: Whirlpool.

Originally established in 1916 as a railroad inn, this French colonial has grand verandahs on both floors and six rooms, with two additional garden suites nearby. All rooms have stylish country furnishings, queen-size beds with goose-down comforters, and claw-foot tubs with showers. One room holds a personal collection of hats; the Vallejo Suite features mementos of local figure of note, Gen. Mariano Vallejo. All rooms open to the verandah or deck in this quiet, wooded setting with nearby wineries and restaurants. A generous buffet breakfast is served near the stone fireplace in the dining room. A favorite is salsa jack soufflé.

**THE INN AT CEDAR
  MANSION**
Innkeeper: Bob Kowal.
707-938-3206, 800-409-5496.
www.cedarmansion.com.
info@cedarmansion.com.
531 Second St. E., Sonoma,
  CA 95476.
Near Sonoma Plaza.
Price: Very Expensive.
Credit Cards: D, AE, MC, V.
Handicap Access: Yes.
Special Features: Pool,
  whirlpool, tennis court,
  fireplaces, spa services.

The Inn at Cedar Mansion is a classic bed-and-breakfast in every sense. The main house is a remarkable Italianate-style of Victorian, built in 1881. Innkeeper Bob Kowal completed a $1.5 million restoration in 1999, adding a tennis court, swimming pool, and whirlpool, all set amid nearly two acres of lush gardens a short walk from Sonoma Plaza.

There are three suites in the main house and two in carriage house, each luxuriously appointed. The suites in the main house have 13-foot ceilings, tall windows, crown , and marble bathrooms and are furnished with classic furniture. The carriage house suites are more modern in style but have wood-burning fireplaces and whirlpool tubs.

Breakfast is not only gourmet, it's also show time. An exhibition-style professional kitchen allows guests to watch the staff prepare the morning's delicacies.

KENWOOD INN AND SPA
Innkeepers: Terrence and
Roseann Grimm.
707-833-1293 or
800-353-6966;
fax 707-833-1247.
www.kenwoodinn.com.
10400 Sonoma Hwy.,
Kenwood, CA 95452
1 mi. S. of Kenwood. On
Hwy. 12.
Price: Very Expensive.
Credit Cards: AE, MC, V.
Special Features: Heated
pool, health spa.

This intimate resort looks like a small Tuscan village in a grove of oak trees. The inn includes 12 lush and large rooms, each with a fireplace, queen-size feather mattresses on the beds and a pleasant view. At the heart of the compound are the pool and gardens, where a spa facility was added in 1994. Treatments include massage, aromatherapy, and facials, all available on the terrace when weather permits. A full country breakfast is included and there is also a lunch menu offered poolside. Traffic along Highway 12 quiets dramatically at night.

**LODGE AT SONOMA
HOTEL AND SPA**
Manager: Paul Rossi.
707-935-6600, 888-710-8008;
fax 707-935-6829.
www.thelodgeat
sonoma.com.
1325 Broadway, Sonoma,
CA 95476.
1/2 mile S. of Sonoma Plaza.
Price: Expensive to Very
Expensive.
Credit Cards: CB, D, DC,
AE, MC, V.
Handicap Access: Yes.
Special Features: Restaurant,
pool, whirlpool, bar,
fireplaces, health spa.

One of the newest and largest hotels in Sonoma Valley, this 182-room inn is part of the Renaissance/Marriott family of hotels. The nine-acre complex features a main lodge and 18 cottages. Many of the rooms and suites have private entrances and fireplaces. The inn is elegantly designed in a classic California mission style. The courtyard is impressive with its towering Canary Island date palms. The health spa features private cabanas and a mineral water pool. Be sure to check out Carneros (see Chapter Five, *Restaurants*), the inn's restaurant, a handsome space that features fresh pastas, pizzas and steaks, and other treats from the rotisserie.

MACARTHUR PLACE
Manager: Bill Blum.
707-938-2929, 800-722-1866.
www.macarthurplace.com.
info@macarthurplace.com.
29 E. MacArthur St.,
Sonoma, CA 95476.
4 blocks south of Sonoma
Plaza.
Price: Very Expensive.
Credit Cards: AE, MC, V.
Handicap Access: Yes.
Special Features: Restaurant,
pool, whirlpool, health
spa, garden.

MacArthur Place is Wine Country living at its most luxurious. Sixty-four rooms and suites are set in a private seven-acre compound lush with gardens and sculptures. The property was once working vineyard and ranch, and the original house — a grand Victorian built in the 1850s — includes 10 rooms. Twenty-nine deluxe suites were recently added, and each includes a wood-burning fireplace, king-size bed, whirlpool tub, and TV with DVD player with six-speaker sound.

The property's historic barn is now home to a conference center as well as a cocktail bar and the valley's premiere steak house, Saddles. The inn's Garden Spa offers a range of treatments, from a rose petal bath to an olive oil body polish.

A luxurious spa treatment at MacArthur Place.

Courtesy MacArthur Place

RAMEKINS
Innkeeper: Marilyn Piraino.
707-933-0452;
    fax 707-933-0451.
www.ramekins.com.
bandb@ramekins.com.
450 W. Spain St., Sonoma,
    CA 95476.
Price: Moderate to
    Expensive.
Credit Cards: MC, V.
Special Features: Culinary
    school; top-rated
    restaurant next door.

This has to rate as one of the most food savvy bed-and-breakfasts of all. The six guest rooms are on the second floor of Ramekins Sonoma Valley Culinary School, well within reach of delectable aromas. All rooms have antique-pine furniture, custom-made down comforters, and oversized bathrooms. Continental breakfasts feature fresh baked pastries but if you want a bigger spread, a top-rated restaurant called The General's Daughter (see Chapter Five, *Restaurants*) is right next door. Ramekins is also just a few blocks from the historic Sonoma Plaza.

SONOMA HOTEL
Innkeeper: Tim Farfan.
707-996-2996, 800-468-6016;
    fax 707-996-7014.
www.sonomahotel.com.
sonomahotel@aol.com.
110 W. Spain St., Sonoma,
    CA 95476.
On Sonoma Plaza.
Price: Inexpensive to
    Expensive.
Credit Cards: AE, D, DC,
    MC, V.
Handicap Access: No.
Special Features: Restaurant.

Each of the 16 rooms in this hotel is sumptuously appointed with antiques, old oak, and stained glass. All have private baths. The best is the Bear Flag Room, with a glorious antique mahogany bedroom suite. This inn had a major facelift in 1998, with all the rooms remodeled. Complimentary continental breakfast is served. The location is ideal, with downtown Sonoma at your feet. Another plus: On the first floor of the inn, adjacent to the inn's lobby, is a popular dining spot, The Girl & The Fig (see Chapter Five, *Restaurants*).

Courtesy Sonoma Mission Inn

Sonoma Mission Inn is a place to be pampered.

SONOMA MISSION INN AND SPA
Manager: Ulrich Krauer.
707-938-9000, 800-862-4945.
www.sonomamission
inn.com.
18140 Sonoma Hwy., Boyes Hot Springs, CA 95416.
Just N. of Sonoma on Hwy. 12.
Price: Very Expensive.
Credit Cards: AE, DC, MC, V.
Handicap Access: Yes.
Special Features: Health spa, golf course, pool, exercise rooms, two restaurants.

Native Indians considered this spot a sacred healing ground; by the turn of the 20th century it had become a getaway for well-heeled San Franciscans who came to Boyes Hot Springs Hotel to "take the waters." The resort, now the Sonoma Mission Inn and Spa, has been a destination ever since.

The Sonoma Mission Inn is Sonoma County at its most luxurious, from the impressive Mission-style façade to its health spa pamper palace. The rich and famous who have stayed here include Sylvester Stallone, Billy Crystal, and Tom Cruise. The 228 rooms and suites, while not lavish, are done in pastel hues and appointed with plantation shutters and ceiling fans. Many offer views of the inn's shady grounds, and a few have fireplaces. The main building dates to 1927 and has been expanded and renovated over the years. A world-class spa was opened in 1981, and numerous accommodation/spa packages are available. Sixty new luxury suites have been added since 1997, all equipped with fireplaces and baths with whirlpool tubs. In 1993, after years of research, the inn found a new source of mineral water, a 135-degree artesian well 1,100 feet below the surface. Now the inn's whirlpools and two outdoor pools are naturally warmed by this soothing aqua (see "Spas" in Chapter Seven, *Recreation*, for more details).

The 10-acre grounds also include two restaurants: The Restaurant, an uneven, albeit expensive, dining room (see Chapter Five, *Restaurants*), and The Big 3 Dine, an adequate eatery for breakfast and lunch. If there's a drawback to the Sonoma Mission Inn, it is location. While it is convenient to wineries and historic sites of Sonoma Valley, it's located along a hectic and well-developed thoroughfare. The grounds, however, remain peaceful.

**SONOMA VALLEY INN,
BEST WESTERN**
Manager: Tony Woods.
707-938-9200,800-334-5784;
fax 707-938-0935.
www.sonomavalleyinn.com.
550 2nd St. W., Sonoma, CA
95476.
1 block W. from Sonoma
Plaza off Hwy. 12.
Price: Moderate to Very
Expensive.
Credit Cards: AE, CB, D,
DC, MC, V.
Handicap Access: Yes.
Special Features: Pool,
whirlpool, fitness room.

An "intimate motel" may be the best way to describe this exceptional lodge just a block from Sonoma Plaza. Rooms and furnishings are well above average for a motel — most are equipped with kitchenettes, wet bars, whirlpools, or fireplaces. Most of the 71 rooms open onto a lovely courtyard. It's ideal for families visiting the valley. Complimentary continental breakfast is included. Seven new suites were completed in the summer of 1999, and many of the other rooms have been remodeled.

THISTLE DEW INN
Innkeeper: Larry Barnett.
707-938-2909, 800-382-7895.
www.thistledew.com.
tdibandb@aol.com.
171 W. Spain St., Sonoma,
CA 95476.
1/2 block from Sonoma
Plaza.
Price: Moderate to
Expensive.
Credit Cards: AE, MC, V, D.
Handicap Access: Yes.
Special Features: Whirlpool.

This inn is decorated throughout with vintage Mission furniture. Each of the six guest rooms (two in the main house and four in the adjacent cottage) has a private bath, air conditioning, and ceiling fan. Five rooms have private decks and entrances. Three rooms have gas fireplaces, and three are equipped with a large whirlpool tub. A full gourmet breakfast is served in the dining room or on the deck. This is a charming inn, reasonably priced and in an excellent location for strolling to all of Sonoma's finest. A whirlpool tub is in the garden.

TROJAN HORSE INN
Innkeepers: Joe and Sandy
Miccio.
707-996-2430, 800-899-1925;
fax 707-996-9185.
www.trojanhorseinn.com.
trojaninn@aol.com.
19455 Sonoma Hwy.,
Sonoma, CA 95476.
Near Spain St. on Hwy. 12.
Price: Moderate to
Expensive.
Credit Cards: AE, D, DC,
MC, V.
Handicap Access: Yes.
Special Features: Whirlpool.

This early-20th-century B&B inn was originally the home of one of Sonoma's pioneer families. The six guest rooms, all with private baths, are lavishly furnished with antiques and modern conveniences. The Grape Arbor Room and the Country Corner have whirlpool baths. The inn is close to restaurants, wine tasting, and shopping. A special note: The inn is close to a busy intersection along Highway 12, but traffic quiets considerably at night.

Petaluma and Rohnert Park

CAVANAGH INN
Innkeepers: Ray and Jeanne
    Farris.
707-765-4657, 888-765-4658;
    fax 707-769-0466.
www.cavanaghinn.com.
10 Keller St., Petaluma, CA
    94952.
Price: Inexpensive to
    Moderate.
Credit Cards: AE, MC, V.

Snug in a residential district near downtown Petaluma, this inn is within easy walking distance of the town's historic homes, the Petaluma River, and a legion of antique shops. Seven guest rooms — five with private baths — span two houses, a stately 1902 mansion and a 1912 Craftsman cottage. Together they share a lawn shaded by a large magnolia tree. The parlor of the main house has a pleasant fireplace. The guest rooms — comfortable and unfussy — are well priced.

DOUBLETREE HOTEL
Manager: Bill Comstock.
707-584-5466, 800-222-TREE;
    fax 707-586-9726.
www.dtdonoma.com.
1 Doubletree Dr., Rohnert
    Park, CA 94928.
Just off Hwy. 101 at Golf
    Course Dr. exit.
Price: Expensive.
Credit Cards: AE, MC, V.
Handicap Access: Yes.
Special Features: Restaurant,
    lounges, pool, whirlpool,
    fitness room.

A Mission-style hotel surrounded by two 18-hole golf courses, the Doubletree is popular primarily for its conference and banquet facilities. Leisure travelers will also appreciate its full-service hotel amenities. There are 245 rooms, including six suites. The rooms are decorated with standard hotel furnishings, the suites with French country-inspired furniture. There's a martini bar in the lobby and a wine bar called Bacchus in the restaurant. If you're looking for an intimate getaway, steer clear of this sprawling hotel.

Santa Rosa

**FLAMINGO RESORT
    HOTEL**
Manager: Foriann Bynum.
707-545-8530, 800-848-8300.
www.flamingoresort.com.
info@flamingoresort.com.
2777 4th St., Santa Rosa, CA
    95405.
At Farmers Ln.
Price: Inexpensive to Very
    Expensive.
Credit Cards: AE, DC, MC,
    V.
Handicap Access: Yes.
Special Features: Pool,
    whirlpool, tennis, fitness
    center, day spa,
    restaurant, conference
    center.

French country furnishings and lush landscaping make this 270-room resort hotel friendly and comfortable. Sonoma Valley's premium wineries are just minutes east on Highway 12. Guests have access to an adjacent fitness center. Specialty shops and excellent restaurants are just blocks away on Farmers Lane. Popular with both business travelers and tourists. A new wing — The Courtyard — is a hotel within a hotel, with 34 executive rooms catering to business travelers. The lounge offers live music five nights a week.

FOUNTAINGROVE INN HOTEL

Manager: Bill Carson.
707-578-6101, 800-222-6101;
 fax 707-544-3126;
www.fountaingroveinn.com.
101 Fountaingrove Pkwy.,
 Santa Rosa, CA 95403.
Off Hwy. 101 at Old
 Redwood Hwy. exit.
Price: Expensive to Very
 Expensive.
Credit Cards: AE, D, DC,
 MC, V.
Handicap Access: Yes.
Special Features: Heated
 pool, whirlpool, restaurant,
 conference center.

The redwood and stone exterior of this luxury hotel is modern but blends harmoniously with the landscape. And the deliberately low sweep of the architecture affords an unobstructed view of the Round Barn historical landmark just up the hill. The 126 rooms are elegantly simple and decorated with tasteful furnishings. Each room has double queen-size or a king-size beds and a small refrigerator. Continental breakfast is included in the tariff, and standard hotel services are available. The hotel offers wine touring packages as well as golf packages.

THE GABLES

Innkeepers: Michael and
 Judy Ogne.
707-585-7777, 800-GABLESN;
 fax 707-584-5634.
www.thegablesinn.com.
innkeeper@thegables
 inn.com.
4257 Petaluma Hill Rd.,
 Santa Rosa, CA 95404.
Rohnert Park Expwy. E. exit
 off Hwy. 101.
Price: Expensive.
Credit Cards: AE, D, DC,
 MC, V.

The 15 gables over keyhole-shaped windows lend the name to this 1877 High Victorian Gothic Revival inn. Other features include ceilings that reach 25 feet, a mahogany staircase, and three Italian marble fireplaces. There are seven spacious guest rooms (most with private bath with a clawfoot tub), including four suites. The separate William and Mary's Cottage is furnished with a wet bar, a wood stove, two-person whirlpool tub, and a queen-size bed in the loft. The inn is air conditioned throughout. Full gourmet breakfast and afternoon snacks are included.

HILTON

Manager: David Connor.
707-523-7555;
 fax 707-569-5555.
www.hilton.com.
3555 Round Barn Blvd.,
 Santa Rosa, CA 95403.
Off Hwy. 101 at Old
 Redwood Hwy. exit.
Price: Moderate to Very
 Expensive.
Credit Cards: AE, D, MC, V.
Handicap Access: Yes.
Special Features: Pool,
 whirlpool, fitness center,
 restaurant, lounge,
 banquet facilities.

Looking for a nice hotel in Santa Rosa? This is the best bet. Once known as the Doubletree Hotel, it joined the Hilton family in 1997. (To add to the confusion, the Red Lion Inn in Rohnert Park became the DoubleTree.) The accommodations are first-rate, and the inn is on a hillside overlooking the city with easy access to Highway 101. The 246 spacious guest rooms and suites are scattered over several acres. The hotel caters to business travelers; all rooms have telephone-equipped desks. There are full hotel services. Ask for a room with a view when making your reservation. Remodeled in 1998.

HOTEL LA ROSE
Manager: Holly Michalek.
707-579-3200, 800-527-6738;
   fax 707-579-3247;.
www.hotellarose.com.
concierge@hotellarose.com.
308 Wilson St., Santa Rosa,
   CA 95404.
Downtown Santa Rosa exit
   off Hwy. 101.
Price: Expensive to Very
   Expensive.
Credit Cards: AE, CB, D,
   DC, MC, V.
Special Features: Restaurant
   called Josef's, hot tub.

This historic hotel, built in 1907 from stone extracted from the mountain ridges east of Santa Rosa, is in Railroad Square, once the hub of commerce in Sonoma County. Now the square is an eclectic urban area busy with bohemian coffee houses, nightclubs, and a few street folks. Reconstructed in 1985, the hotel and adjacent carriage house have a total of 49 rooms, with English country interiors, private baths renovated in 1998, and televisions. Twenty of the rooms have patios or balconies overlooking a courtyard garden. A European breakfast is included. Josef's Restaurant in the hotel is recommended. Airport shuttle from San Francisco.

MELITTA STATION INN
Innkeepers: Diane Crandon
   and Vic Amstadter.
707-538-7712, 800-504-3099.
www.melittastationinn.com.
5850 Melita Rd., Santa Rosa,
   CA 95409.
5 mi. E. of downtown on
   Hwy. 12.
Price: Moderate to
   Expensive.
Credit Cards: MC, V.

At the north end of the Valley of the Moon (and just minutes from Santa Rosa dining), this home was once a busy railroad station, general store, and post office. Today it's a warm inn with five guest rooms furnished with antiques and collectibles. Five rooms have private baths. One suite has two connecting rooms. The inn is situated close to the road, but it has personality to spare. An ample breakfast is served by the wood-burning stove in the large sitting room or on the balcony.

SAFARI WEST WILDLIFE PRESERVE AND TENT CAMP
Inkeepers: Peter and Nancy
   Lang.
707-579-2551, 800-616-2695;
   fax 707-579-8777.
www.safariwest.com.
safariwest@safariwest.com.
3115 Porter Creek Road,
   Santa Rosa, CA. 95404
Price: Expensive.
Credit Cards: AE, MC, V.
Special Features: African
   wilderness experience
   with exotic animals,
   African cuisine.

This is no Jurassic Park, no danger lurks, but it's based on the same idea: to make the wild accessible. At Safari West you can now stay overnight in authentic canvas African safari tents with hardwood floors, in close proximity but separated from exotic wildlife. Each tent has a king-size bed or two doubles and a bathroom with a shower. A two-hour tour, to be scheduled separately, will take you through the 400 acres of wilderness, revealing some of the 300 exotic mammals and birds. (A tour is not included in the price for an overnight stay.) Authentic African cuisine served.

VINTNERS INN
Manager: Jessica Adams.
707-575-7350, 800-421-2584.
www.vintnersinn.com.
info@vintnersinn.com.

Surrounded by a 93-acre vineyard, Vintners Inn is one of Sonoma County's finest establishments. It's a European-style hotel with an Old-World atmosphere, from its French country decor

Vintners Inn is one of Santa Rosa's finest establishments.

4350 Barnes Rd., Santa Rosa, CA 95403.
Off Hwy. 101.
Price: Expensive to Very Expensive.
Credit Cards: AE, DC, MC, V.
Handicap Access: Yes.
Special Features: Whirlpool, restaurant.

to the central plaza with a fountain. The 44 guest rooms are separated into three buildings that ring the courtyard. Climbing the staircase in each building is akin to going upstairs to bedrooms in an elegant farmhouse. The oversized rooms in this Provençal-influenced inn have beamed ceilings and pine furniture, some dating back to the turn of the century. Many rooms have fireplaces. Ground-floor rooms have patios; second-floor rooms have balconies with vineyard or courtyard views. Continental breakfast is included in the tariff; room service is also available. The inn is convenient to both Sonoma and Napa Valley wineries. Next door is the superb John Ash & Co. restaurant (see Chapter Five, *Restaurants*).

Healdsburg

BELLE DE JOUR INN
Innkeepers: Tom and Brenda Hearn.
707-431-9777;
  fax 707-431-7412.
www.belledejourinn.com.
16276 Healdsburg Ave., Healdsburg, CA 95448.
1 mi. N. of Dry Creek Rd.
Across from Simi Winery.
Price: Expensive to Very Expensive.
Credit Cards: AE, MC, V.

One of the most private and peaceful bed-and-breakfast inns in Healdsburg, Belle de Jour is set on a tranquil six-acre hilltop with lovely views of rolling hills and distant mountains. The Italianate main farmhouse, built around 1873, is where the innkeepers live and prepare scrumptious breakfasts. The five guest suites, all decorated with French-country-inspired furniture and sun-dried linens, are set behind the main house. Two of the rooms have whirlpool tubs for two. The Terrace Room has an intimate whirlpool tub with its views of the unspoiled countryside. There is also a large suite in the new carriage house, and it's equipped with whirlpool tubs for two and showers for two, as well as a gas fireplace. The Caretaker's Suite has a king-size canopy bed and French doors leading to a trellised deck. The Hearns' 1925 antique touring car is available for personally escorted wine-tasting tours. Belle de Jour Inn is elegance and hospitality at its finest.

CAMELLIA INN

Innkeepers: Ray, Del and
   Lucy Lewand.
707-433-8182, 800-727-8182.
www.camelliainn.com.
211 North St., Healdsburg,
   CA 95448.
2 blocks E. of Healdsburg
   Ave.
Price: Inexpensive to
   Expensive.
Credit Cards: AE, MC, V, D.
Special Features: Pool,
   garden, fish pond.

This 1869 Italianate Victorian home entered the turn of the century as Healdsburg's first hospital. It is now a magnificent inn with nine guest rooms, and still has many of its original and unique architectural details, including the twin marble fireplaces in the double parlor. All the rooms in the air-conditioned inn have private baths and are furnished with antiques and accented with chandeliers and Oriental rugs. On a quiet residential street just two blocks from the plaza, the inn is named for the 50-some varieties of camellias that grace its gardens. A full breakfast buffet is served in the dining room, dominated by a mahogany fireplace mantel. Very friendly innkeepers.

DRY CREEK INN, BEST WESTERN

Manager: Aaron Krug.
707-433-0300, 800-222-5784;
   fax 707-433-1129.
www.drycreekinn.com.
198 Dry Creek Rd.,
   Healdsburg, CA 95448.
Off Hwy. 101 at Dry Creek
   Rd. exit.
Price: Inexpensive to
   Moderate.
Credit Cards: AE, D, DC,
   MC, V.
Handicap Access: Yes.
Special Features: Pool,
   whirlpool, exercise room.

This motel is distinguished by its outstanding location for wine touring. There is fairly standard motel decor throughout, but a spectacular view of Dry Creek Valley is the payoff in many rooms. Rooms are equipped with refrigerators and coffeemakers and a continental breakfast is included — great for families. It's well situated for a day of wine tasting followed by dining downtown on the plaza; the down side: The inn fronts busy Highway 101, but the road quiets considerably at night.

GRAPE LEAF INN

Innkeepers: Richard and
   Kae Rosenberg.
707-433-8140;
   fax 707-433-3140.
www.grapeleafinn.com.
grapelf@pacbell.net.
539 Johnson St., Healdsburg,
   CA 95448.
2 blocks E. of Healdsburg
   Ave.

The 12 elegant guest rooms in this 1900 Queen Anne Victorian are furnished with iron beds, armoires, and warm oak accents, and are all named after grape varietals. Seven of the rooms have skylights, and nine have tubs for two; the Chardonnay Suite is the most luxurious, with stained-glass windows and cedar-paneled walls. The quiet porch is perfect for unwinding after a day of wine touring. A full country breakfast is served in the dining

Price: Moderate to
   Expensive.
Credit Cards: MC, V.

room. Wine is served nightly, and on Saturday nights guest vintners occasionally arrive with wine for private tastings. Within walking distance is Healdsburg's historic downtown plaza.

HAYDON STREET INN
Innkeepers: Dick and Pat
   Bertapelle.
707-433-5228, 800-528-3703;
   fax 707-433-6637.
www.haydon.com.
321 Haydon St., Healdsburg,
   CA 95448.
Off Hwy. 101 at Central
   Healdsburg exit.
Price: Moderate to
   Expensive.
Credit Cards: AE, D, MC, V.

In a quiet residential area and surrounded by trees, this Queen Anne Victorian inn has eight charming guest rooms and one suite, all with hardwood floors, antiques, down comforters and private baths. More romantic are the two cottage rooms, both with large whirlpool tubs: The Victorian Room has a queen-size wicker bed, and the Pine Room has a lovely four-poster bed covered in white linens. A generous breakfast buffet is served in the dining room. The inn is a short walk to Healdsburg's plaza.

The Honor Mansion, a bed-and-breakfast in Healdsburg, has a reputation for pampering.

Thomas Hallstein/Outsight

HONOR MANSION
Innkeepers: Steve and Cathi
   Fowler.
707-433-4277, 800-554-4667;
   fax 707-431-7173.
www.honormansion.com.
14891 Grove St.,
   Healdsburg, CA 95448.
Price: Expensive to Very
   Expensive.
Credit Cards: D, MC, V.
Special Features: 100-year-
   old Magnolia trees, lap
   pool, koi pond.

Honor Mansion has won its share of honors. It was named one of the most romantic inns by American Historic Inns. And "The Best Places to Kiss in Northern California" called the inn "[C]lose to flawless. . . ." Built in 1883, this Victorian mansion owes its name to Dr. Herbert Honor, whose family owned the property for more than 100 years. In 1994 Cathi and Steve Fowler bought the inn and remodeled the entire building. And these innkeepers will spoil you outright, from mints on your pillow to full-blown two- to three-course decadent breakfasts. Some dishes include Caramel Apple French Toast and Mansion Eggs Benedict, featured in the Honor Mansion Cookbook. Most of the guest rooms and suites feature queen-size beds, comfy sitting areas, claw-foot tubs, and great views. The inn is near the Healdsburg plaza and just a short drive from many wineries in the area.

HEALDSBURG INN ON THE PLAZA

Innkeeper: Genny Jenkins.
707-433-6991, 800-431-8663;
 fax 707-433-9513.
www.healdsburginn.com.
110 Matheson St.,
 Healdsburg, CA 95448.
Off Healdsburg Ave.
Price: Moderate to Very
 Expensive.
Credit Cards: MC, V.
Special Features: Art gallery.

Right on Healdsburg's delightful downtown plaza, this 11-room inn welcomes guests through the main floor gift shop. Four rooms in the front have bay windows and overlook the plaza with its bevy of shops, restaurants, and tasting rooms. They have king-size beds, fireplaces, and whirlpool tubs for two in their private baths. The back rooms open up to a balcony and each have a queen-size bed, a private bath with an old-fashioned soaking tub, and a fireplace. The solarium and roof garden is the common area where guests take breakfast and afternoon refreshments. In-room TVs and phones are available on request.

HOTEL HEALDSBURG

General Manager: Greg Bye.
707-431-2800.
www.hotelhealdsburg.com.
greg@hotelhealdsburg.com.
25 Matheson Street,
 Healdsburg, CA 95448.
Price: Expensive to Very
 Expensive.
Credit cards: AE, D, DC,
 MC, V.

This contemporary, three story hotel is right on the main square of Healdsburg, a small town that manages to be both quaint and cosmopolitan. The hotel is warm and inviting; the lobby has a stone fireplace inside, and for those who like to people watch, a screened in porch. Right off the lobby is Dry Creek Kitchen, a restaurant owned by star chef Charlie Palmer, best known for his Aurole restaurants in New York and Las Vegas. The restaurant features American cuisine, showcasing food and wine from Sonoma County. It serves lunch and dinner.

Hotel Healdsburg has 55 rooms, and they are designed to pamper: oversized bathrooms done in Italian glass mosaic tile, six-foot soaking tubs, private balconies, down comforters. All this and a continental breakfast delivered to your door.

MADRONA MANOR

Innkeepers: Bill and Trudy
 Konrad.
707-433-4231, 800-258-4003.
www.madronamanor.com.
madronaman@aol.com.
1001 Westside Rd.,
 Healdsburg, CA 95448.

This country inn and restaurant is the grande dame of Sonoma County. With its mansard roof, expansive porch, and surrounding lush gardens, this three-story Victorian built in 1881 is a majestic sight amid a glade of trees. Large and ornate antiques decorate most of the mansion's formal guest rooms. Its 22 rooms have 18 fireplaces, many

From Hwy. 101, Central
Healdsburg exit, W. 1 mi.
Price: Expensive to Very
Expensive.
Credit Cards: MC, V.
Handicap Access: Yes.
Special Features: Pool,
restaurant.

graced with delicate hand-painted borders, and eight of the rooms have balconies or decks. All rooms are air conditioned and include private baths.

Three smaller buildings house five suites and two Jacuzzi tubs. In the Carriage House, ask for Suite 400, which has a fireplace and whirlpool tub. For seclusion, try the Garden Suite, with a fireplace, rattan furniture, and private deck. Well off the main road, a stay at Madrona Manor is guaranteed to be unhurried, a throwback to the slower pace of the home's Victorian heyday. Full breakfast is included in the tariff. The restaurant is also first-rate (see Chapter Five, *Restaurants*).

Geyserville

**HOPE-MERRILL HOUSE
and HOPE-BOSWORTH
HOUSE**
Innkeeper: Ron and Cosette
Scheiber.
707-857-3356, 800-825-4233.
www.hope-inns.com.
moreinfo@hope-inns.com.
21253 Geyserville Ave.,
Geyserville, CA 95441.
1 mi. N. of Geyserville exit
off Hwy. 101.
Price: Moderate to
Expensive.
Credit Cards: AE, D, MC, V.
Handicap Access: Limited.
Special Features: A quarter
acre of zinfandel is on the
premises, pool.

A stagecoach stop in the 1870s and now an enchanting inn, Hope-Merrill House is listed on the Sonoma County Landmarks Register. Aficionados of architectural details will enjoy the historical significance of the structure: a striking example of 19th-century Eastlake-Stick style, the home was built entirely of redwood. Notice the authentic Victorian hand-screened wallpaper. Its eight rooms all have private baths; two have whirlpool tubs. A generous country-style breakfast is served in the dining room. The innkeepers also run the less formal Hope-Bosworth House across the street. Built in 1904, it's a Queen Ann Craftsman style, and it has four guest rooms.

West Sonoma County

APPLEWOOD INN
Innkeepers: Jim Caron and
Darryl Notter.
707-869-9093;
fax 707-869-9170.
www.applewoodinn.com.
stay@applewoodinn.com.
13555 Hwy. 116,
Guerneville, CA 95446.
1/4 mi. S. of Guerneville on
Hwy. 116.
Price: Expensive to Very
Expensive.

This Mission-style inn — hidden in a stand of redwoods — is one of Sonoma County's finest. It's romantic and formal yet familiar, like a wealthy grandmother's house. The site was originally an apple orchard and now harbors a circa-1922 mansion with nine rooms and Piccola Casa, a matching house, added in 1995, with seven rooms. Three new suites and an additional building called the Gatehouse were added in 1999. And no stuffy Victorian-era museum furnishings here — the rooms have been decorated to feel like a private home, blending antiques with con-

A fountain graces the court-yard at Applewood Inn and Restaurant in Guerneville.

Thomas Hallstein/Outsight

Credit Cards: AE, D, MC, V.
Handicap Access: Yes.
Special Features: Restaurant, pool, whirlpool.

temporary pieces and family heirlooms. Rich fabrics drape windows and upholstered furniture, and beds are dressed in fine pastel linens. All rooms have private baths, TVs, and phones. The new rooms have private decks, fireplaces, and whirlpool tubs and showers for two.

The common area is centered around a huge double-sided stone fireplace. Breakfast is served in the inn's freestanding restaurant called Applewood. The restaurant also offers dinner Tuesday to Saturday (see Chapter Five, *Restaurants*).

BODEGA BAY LODGE AND SPA
Manager: Jana Wacholz.
707-875-3525, 800-368-2468.
www.bodegabaylodge.com.
103 Hwy. 1, Bodega Bay, CA 94923.
Price: Expensive to Very Expensive.
Credit Cards: AE, CB, D, DC, MC, V.
Handicap Access: Yes.
Special Features: Restaurant, fitness room, whirlpool, sauna, pool, full-service spa.

This wood-shingled seaside lodge — well-appointed and intimate — is sheltered from coastal winds but close enough for the sound of the surf. All rooms have ocean or bay views and private balconies, and many feature fireplaces, vaulted ceilings, spa baths, refrigerators, wet bars, and coffeemakers. Even the pool and whirlpool offer a breathtaking view. The Duck Club restaurant is, but it's one of the best on the Sonoma Coast (see Chapter Five, *Restaurants*).

BODEGA ESTERO BED & BREAKFAST
Innkeepers: Michael O'Brien and Edgar A. Furlong.
707-876-3300, 800-422-6321.

This bed-and-breakfast is billed as a "modern-day farm." Nestled in a hillside, it has roaming llamas, three types of sheep, and Angora goats. The B&B's geodesic dome architecture features open beam cathedral ceilings that highlight the lush

www.bodegaestero.com.
bodegabb@sonic.net.
17699 Hwy. 1, PO Box 362
Bodega, CA 94922.
Price: Moderate to
Expensive.
Credit Cards: AE, MC & V.
Special Features: Working
farm, hot tub.

**CHANSLOR GUEST
RANCH AND HORSE
STABLES**
Innkeeper: Abby Myers.
707-875-2721.
www.chanslorranch.com.
bedandbreakfast@chanslorr
anch.com.
2660 Hwy. 1, PO Box 1510,
Bodega Bay, CA 94923.
Price: Inexpensive to
Moderate.
Handicapped Access: Yes.
Special Features: Horseback
riding, wetland preserve.

THE FARMHOUSE INN
Innkeeper: Catherine
Bartolomei
707-887-3300, 800-464-6642;
fax 707-887-3311.
www.farmhouseinn.com.
innkeep@farmhouseinn.com.
7871 River Road, Forestville,
CA 95436.
9 mi. W. of Hwy. 101.
Price: Moderate to
Expensive.
Credit Cards: AE, MC, V.
Handicap Access: Yes.
Special Features: Pool.

INN AT OCCIDENTAL
Innkeeper: Jack, Jean, and
Bill Bullard.

coastal hills. Each of the inn's four rooms are spacious and include a private bath with a tub and, best of all, goose-down comforters to take the chill out of the coast. Breakfast is in capable hands: Edgar, the resident chef, was trained at the Culinary Institute of America. In fact, Edgar's scones are such a hit that one guest wanted to trade a 1956 Chevy Truck for his recipe.

This 420-acre working ranch offers an action-packed stay: horseback riding, hiking on nature trails and barbecues. Aside from the small bed-and-breakfast, the coastal ranch operates a horse stable and a 80-acre wetland preserve. As for the B&B, the Ranch House has a great view of the Pacific and the wetlands. All five rooms in the Ranch House have private bathrooms.

Groups or those planning family gatherings or small retreats will likely opt for the whole guesthouse, which sleeps 14 to 18. It has three rooms with private baths and shared living rooms with a fireplace and ocean views.

Colorful is one way to describe this inn's history. Built as a farmhouse in 1878, it later became a horse ranch and a roadhouse lodge before gaining a questionable reputation as a bathhouse. In 1990 the house was remodeled down to its studs, transforming a row of farmhand housing into six lovely guest rooms and two suites. The English country cottage decor is plush, and each room has a private entrance and a ceramic tile whirlpool tub. Most of the rooms have fireplaces and private saunas. The eight guest rooms were all newly remodeled.

The interior of the main house sets a distinct New England tone, with a long Shaker-style dining room where a rich breakfast feast is spread out. The din of traffic on River Road may jangle some nerves, but noise drops considerably at night. Exceptionally friendly innkeeper and staff.

Perched on a hill overlooking the quiet village of Occidental, this comfortable three-story Victorian inn is a jewel, one of Wine Country's best. It is well

707-874-1047, 800-522-6324.
www.innatoccidental.com.
innkeeper@innatoccidental.
com.
3657 Church St., Occidental,
CA 95465.
1 block off Bohemian Hwy.
Price: Expensive to Very
Expensive.
Credit Cards: AE, D, MC, V.
Handicap Access: Limited.

off the beaten path and delightfully so. Guarded by fruit trees and a lush courtyard garden with a fountain, the inn was built in 1877. The 16 rooms and the vacation rental called Sonoma Cottage all have private baths and are sumptuously furnished with antiques that Jack Bullard has collected over the years. The color palette of each room is designed around a specific collectible. The Leaf Umbrella room has a queen-size pine canopy bed; the walls are stenciled to match a watercolor of pink roses, and the room features a cherished collection of umbrella glass. The Tiffany Room features a collection of Tiffany silver as well as a four-poster mahogany bed, fireplace, and private deck. The Sandwich Glass Suite and Marbles Suite feature fireplaces with sitting areas and spa tubs for two.

Bullard is an exceptional host, offering wine, cheese, and homemade cookies by the living room hearth each evening. A superb gourmet breakfast is served in the dining room, which doubles as a wine cellar.

INN AT THE TIDES
Manager: Carlo Galazzo.
707-875-2751, 800-541-7788;
fax 707-875-2669.
www.innatthetides.com.
iatt@monitor.net.
800 Hwy. 1, PO Box 640,
Bodega Bay, CA 94923.
Price: Expensive to Very
Expensive.
Credit Cards: AE, D, MC, V.
Handicap Access: Yes.
Special Features: Indoor/
outdoor pool, whirlpool,
sauna, workout room by
the pool with weights,
restaurant.

Six coastal acres with natural landscaping surround this inn, which is actually 12 separate lodges scattered over a hillside. The 86 guest rooms are agreeably designed, and all have bay or ocean views, with refrigerators, coffeemakers, and a hide-a-bed. The inn is home to Sonoma County's leading winemaker dinner; if interested, inquire when making your reservations. Continental breakfast is served across Highway 1 at the Tides.

RAFORD HOUSE INN
Innkeepers: Jack and Carole
Vore.
707-887-9573, 800-887-9503;
fax 707-887-9597.
www.rafordhouse.com.
10630 Wohler Rd.,
Healdsburg, CA 95448.
Price: Moderate to
Expensive.
Credit Cards: AE, D, MC, V.

In the heart of rural Sonoma County, this inn is ideally located for touring the wineries of Russian River and Dry Creek valleys. An 1880 Victorian, it sits like a jewel on a gentle slope overlooking vineyards and tall redwoods. Stately palm trees stand as sentinels on the front lawn, and at the end of a tall staircase is a wide porch, an ideal place to kick off your shoes and watch the hummingbirds flitter by. Two of the six guest rooms have fireplaces, and all have private baths. Each

The porch of the Raford House offers a soothing view.

Courtesy Raford House

room is decorated in a dominant color; the Blue Room is furnished with a four-poster bed and armoire. The Strawberry Room has a private entrance that opens onto the garden. Friendly innkeepers — and one of Carole's specialties, California-style eggs Benedict — are a real treat.

RIDENHOUR RANCH HOUSE INN

Innkeepers: Chris Bell and Meilani Naranjo.
707-887-1033, 888-877-4466; fax 707-869-2967.
www.ridenhourranchhouse.com.
ridenhourinn@earthlink.net.
River Rd., Guerneville, CA 95446.
12 mi. W. of Hwy. 101.
Price: Moderate to Expensive.
Credit Cards: AE, MC, V.
Special Features: Redwood hot tub.

Within walking distance of Korbel Champagne Cellars and the Russian River, this circa-1906 inn is built of redwood and has eight guest rooms, each with a private bath. The rooms are decorated with English and American antiques, and some have forest or garden views. Hawthorn Cottage has a king-size bed, a fireplace, and a cozy window seat. Madrone has a king-size bed, a sitting area with a sofa and a private brick patio. The inn serves decadent "skip-lunch breakfasts," replete with caloric dishes such as stuffed French toast coupled with a mini soufflé.

RIVER'S END

Manager: Bert Rangel.
707-865-2484.
www.sterba.com/bodega/river.
11048 Hwy. 1, PO Box 1800, Jenner, CA 95446.

The view is spectacular from this modest resort on the edge of a sheer cliff overlooking the Russian River and the Pacific Ocean. The resort includes four cabins, plus three rooms below the restaurant. All are simply appointed and have private baths. Most are wood paneled and have gas

Price: Moderate to
   Expensive.
Credit Cards: MC, V.
Handicap Access: Limited.
Special Features: Restaurant,
   RV camping.

fireplaces and decks for ocean gazing. River's End Restaurant is recommended.

SANTA NELLA HOUSE
Innkeepers: Francis Ranney
   and Kristina Tellfsen.
707-869-9488, 800-440-9031;
   fax 707-869-0355.
www.santanellahouse.com.
santanella@earthlink.com.
12130 Hwy. 116,
   Guerneville, CA 95446.
2 mi. SE. of Guerneville.
Price: Moderate.
Credit Cards: MC, V.
Special Features: Hot tub.

Nestled in a quiet redwood forest, this inn is an 1870 Victorian with a grand wraparound verandah. There are four guest rooms, all with private baths and furnished with functional antiques and queen-size beds. All have wood-burning fireplaces. A full breakfast — Smoked Salmon Benedict is just one of many specialties — is served in the kitchen by the wood-burning stove. The parlor/music room is a favorite gathering place.

SEA RANCH LODGE
Innkeeper: Marianne
   Harder.
707-785-2371, 800-732-7262.
www.searchsearanch.com.
info@searanchlodge.com.
60 Sea Walk Dr., PO Box 44,
   Sea Ranch, CA 95497.
29 mi. N. of Jenner on Hwy.
   1.
Price: Expensive to Very
   Expensive.
Credit Cards: AE, MC, V.
Special Features: Restaurant.

On bluffs above the Pacific Ocean, this lodge has one of the best vistas in Wine Country. All but one of the 20 rooms face the sea, and cozy window seats offer front-row viewing for spectacular sunsets. The location is remote, but if you're in need of a peaceful getaway, this is it. Outside, the weathered wood recalls New England and the interior feels like a rustic cabin, with knotty pine, cathedral ceilings, and quilted bedspreads. Some rooms have fireplaces and hot tubs. Three caveats: Walls are thin, locate your room's flashlight immediately since lighting is poor outside at night, and bring a sweater because fog keeps it cool even in summer. The restaurant is adequate but pricey — but, oh, that view. Hiking trails are well marked along the bluffs, and the inn has a golf course (see Chapter Seven, *Recreation*).

SONOMA COAST VILLA
Innkeeper: Cyrus Griffin.
707-876-9818, 888-404-2255;
   fax 707-876-9856.
www.scvilla.com.
reservations@scvilla.com.
16702 Hwy. 1, Bodega, CA
   94923.
Price: Expensive to Very
   Expensive.
Credit Cards: AE, MC, V.

This Mediterranean-style B&B on 60 acres is great for roaming. The pastoral hillsides are lovely, and there are plenty of meandering gardens. The inn's 18 rooms are all decorated with a touch of Tuscany, and they come with many accessories: mini bars, fireplaces, comforters, and VCRs. Guests have access to an extensive video library with romantic classics like *Casablanca*. Sonoma Coast Villa serves a full country breakfast, and it has a

Handicap Access: Yes.
Special Features: Restaurant, garden.

restaurant that serves a complimentary buffet on Friday and Saturday nights.

MOTELS

Napa Valley

Best Western Inn At The Vines (707-257-1930, 877-846-3729; www.innatthe vines.com; 100 Soscol Ave., Napa, CA 94559; Moderate to Expensive; AE, D, DC, MC, V.) 68 rooms, some wheelchair accessible. Heated pool and spa, restaurant, loft suites available.

Chablis Inn (707-257-1944, 800-443-3490; www.chablisinn.com; 3360 Solano Ave., Napa, CA 94558; Moderate to Expensive; AE, MC, V.) Basic 34-unit motel. All rooms have a coffeemaker, a refrigerator, and either a wet bar or a kitchenette. All rooms have been renovated. Stay includes a continental breakfast.

The Chateau (707-253-9300; www.napavalleychateauhotel.com; 4195 Solano Ave., Napa, CA 94558; Inexpensive to Expensive; AE, D, DC, MC, V.) A well-appointed inn in the heart of the valley. Six suites available. Pool, whirlpool.

Comfort Inn Napa Valley (707-942-9400; 1865 Lincoln Ave., Calistoga, CA 94515; Moderate to Expensive; AE, CB, D, DC, MC, V.) 55 rooms; hot mineral water swimming pool, hot mineral water Jacuzzi, sauna, steam room, continental breakfast.

Discovery Inn (707-253-0892; 500 Silverado Trail, Napa, CA 945598; Moderate; AE, MC, V.) 15 rooms recently remodeled, some with kitchenettes.

John Muir Inn (707-257-7220; www.johnmuirnapa.com; 1998 Trower Ave., Napa, CA 94558; Expensive; AE, D, DC, MC, V.) 60-room, better-than-average motel built in 1986 and redecorated in 2000. Many rooms have kitchenettes and overlook the garden courtyard. Pool, whirlpool, continental breakfast.

Sonoma County

Best Western Garden Inn (707-546-4031, 800-938-4774; www.hotelswest.com /sro/index.html; 1500 Santa Rosa Ave., Santa Rosa, CA 95401; Inexpensive to Moderate; AE, D, DC, MC, V.) Two pools, coffee shop; 78 rooms. Three wheelchair-accessible and nonsmoking rooms. Guest laundry. Nicely landscaped.

Bodega Coast Inn (707-875-2217; 521 Hwy. 1, Bodega Bay, CA 94923; Inexpensive to Very Expensive; AE, D, DC,MC, V.) Once a Holiday Inn, it has 45 attractively appointed rooms and suites with balconies offering lovely views of Bodega Bay harbor. A few rooms have fireplaces, whirlpool tubs, and vaulted ceilings. Some rooms have two-person whirlpools.

Bodega Harbor Inn (707-875-3594; Bodega Ave. at Coast Hwy. 1, Bodega Bay,

CA 94923; Inexpensive to Moderate; MC, V.) 14 rooms, 2 suites, cottages, and homes, some rooms with bay views, decks, fireplaces, and kitchens.

El Pueblo Inn (707-996-3651, 800-900-8844; www.elpuebloinn.com; 896 W. Napa St., Sonoma, CA 95476; Inexpensive to Expensive; AE, D, MC, V.) 39-room motel with a pool and a hot tub. Restaurants nearby. On a busy intersection.

Fairview Motel (707-433-5548; 74 Healdsburg Ave., Healdsburg, CA 95448; Inexpensive to Moderate; AE, D, MC, V.) Pool, whirlpool, complimentary coffee. Restaurants nearby.

Geyserville Inn (707-857-4343, 877-857-4343; www.geyservilleinn.com; 21714 Geyserville Ave., Geyserville, CA 95441; Inexpensive to Expensive; AE, D, MC, V.) A new 38-room inn, pleasantly designed and comfortable. Many rooms have fireplaces, patios. Pool, whirlpool. Complimentary continental breakfast.

Hillside Inn (546-9353; 2901 4th St., Santa Rosa, CA 95401; Inexpensive; AE, D, DC, MC, V.) Tree-surrounded setting with 35 units, pool, sauna, restaurant, and lounge. Suites and kitchenettes available.

Holiday Inn Express (707-829-6677, 800-465-4329; 1101 Gravenstein Hwy. So., Sebastopol, CA 95472; Inexpensive to Expensive; AE, D, DC, MC, V.) Completed in late 1998, this pleasant 82-room inn is just one of two hotels Sebastopol has to offer. Pool, spa, gym, continental breakfast, refrigerators and coffeemakers in each room.

Los Robles Lodge (707-545-6330, 800-255-6330; 1985 Cleveland Ave, Santa Rosa, CA 95401; Inexpensive to Moderate; AE, CB, D, DC, MC, V.) Olympic-sized, year-round heated pool; hot tub; fitness center; coffee; shop; restaurant; 105 rooms.

Santa Rosa Courtyard by Marriott (707-573-9000; 175 Railroad St., Santa Rosa, CA 95401; Moderate to Expensive; AE, D, DC, MC, V.) 138 Rooms. Swimming pool, spa, nonsmoking rooms, café, lounge, room service. Handicap-accessible. Close to downtown and historic Railroad Square shopping area. Airport shuttle stops here.

Salt Point Lodge (707-847-3234, 800-966-3437; www.saltpoint.com; 23255 Hwy. 1, Jenner, CA 95450; Inexpensive to Moderate. MC, V. Just 16 rooms. Restaurant and lounge, hot tub, sauna, sun deck, some ocean-view rooms. Seaside state park and marine reserve nearby.

Timber Cove Inn (707-847-3231, 800-987-8319; www.timbercoveinn.com/timbercove2.htm; 21780 N. Coast Hwy. 1, Jenner, CA 95450; Moderate to Very Expensive; AE, MC, V.) Charming but funky, with a breathtaking location perched on a rocky cliff overlooking the ocean. Many of the 50 rooms have ocean views, and some have fireplaces and private hot tubs. Restaurant and lounge. Two-night minimum on weekends.

Travelodge (707-433-0101; 178 Dry Creek Rd., Healdsburg, CA 95448; Inexpensive to Expensive; AE, MC, V. A new and stylishly pleasant motel close to wineries. There are 22 rooms plus one suite with refrigerators and whirlpool tubs. Indoor whirlpool and sauna. Continental breakfast included.

CHAPTER FOUR
Life Is Sweet!
CULTURE

The Hess Collection features the work of internationally known artists.

Chris Alderman

Blue jeans mingle with black tie in the Wine Country cultural scene, and that's the way we like it. Nearby San Francisco, of course, is a world-class cultural city, and while Napa and Sonoma Counties can't compete with the City by the Bay's museums, opera, and ballet, Wine Country is more than just wineries, food, and scenic views.

Wine Country's literary heritage dates back to writer Robert Lewis Stevenson, who brought a touch of civilization to St. Helena in the 1880s. Later, Jack London, author of *The Call of the Wild,* retired to Glen Ellen and became a gentleman farmer. Carefully preserved historical sites, such as Sonoma's Mission San Francisco Solano, built in 1825, are reminders that we have long honored our culture.

Music, as it always seems to, helped lead the way. In 1927, the Santa Rosa Symphony was the first to be organized, followed a few years later by the Napa Valley Symphony. As the communities began to grow after World War II, and with the renewal of the wine industry in the 1960s, Napa and Sonoma's cultural landscape began to flourish as well.

Artists weary of the city and drawn to the beauty of Wine Country began moving north, making Napa and Sonoma the popular artistic havens they are today. Art galleries appeared, and wineries began to display art in their tasting rooms. The first theater companies formed in the early 1970s, and theaters have proliferated in Sonoma County to become a dominant force in the local arts. Wineries have played a special role in this cultural expansion, promoting the arts as one of life's necessities as well as the perfect accompaniment to wine.

The following pages will give you some idea of the arts and entertainment possibilities in Napa and Sonoma. The best place to find current happenings are the entertainment pages of the *Napa Register* and Santa Rosa's *Press Democrat*. The arts councils of both counties are also good sources of information. For Napa, phone 707-257-2117 and for Sonoma, phone 707-579-2787.

ARCHITECTURE

While Napa and Sonoma may not have the strong architectural traditions found in the East and Midwest, Wine Country has its own grand style. Plain and practical dried-brick buildings called adobes ruled until the first buildings in a European style were built in the 1860s, and many of those — particularly in Sonoma County — were lost in the earthquake of 1906. Architectural gems remain, however, and newer ones have been added.

The most obvious treasures are the castlelike wineries of Napa Valley. Most notable is *Beringer's* stately, German-style mansion called Rhine House, built in the late 1800s. Nearby is the Gothic fortress of *Greystone Cellars*, built in 1889. It was once the winery for Christian Brothers but is now home to the *Culinary Institute of America at Greystone*. *Inglenook's* grand chateau was built in 1887. In Sonoma, *Hop Kiln Winery* along the Russian River is inside a towering hop kiln built in 1880. The building with three tall spires was used to dry beer hops, back when the area was a center for growing that commodity. *Korbel Champagne Cellars* is an ivy-covered brick beauty with a brandy tower.

There are also newer winery wonders. Most striking is the white hilltop villa south of Calistoga of *Sterling Vineyards*. Nearby is the postmodern temple to wine and art, *Clos Pegase*, designed by Princeton architect Michael Graves. Across Napa Valley is the distinctive shake-roofed *Rutherford Hill Winery*, which recalls an early Wine Country barn. The chateaux of *Domaine Carneros* near Napa and Jordan in Sonoma's Alexander Valley are extravagant reminders of France. Open since 1991, the high-tech *Artesa* is spectacularly understated. Built into the side of a Carneros hillside and nearly impossible to make out from the road, it recalls a buried temple. Not too far away is *Viansa*, built to look like a Tuscan village. *Opus One* winery, a joint venture between Robert Mondavi and France's Chateau Mouton-Rothschild, is another extravagant façade, designed by the firm that created San Francisco's Transamerica Pyramid.

The oldest city in the area, Sonoma, also has many of the oldest buildings, including adobes like the simple but majestic *Mission San Francisco Solano*. Surrounding the Sonoma Plaza are a number of historic buildings, including the fading but still regal *Sebastiani Theatre*, built in 1933.

The cities of Napa and Petaluma offer walking tours of downtown Victorian neighborhoods. (Check at visitor centers for maps.) Napa's tour includes the **Napa Opera House,** 1018 Main St., an Italianate beauty built in 1879, now being refurbished. There's also the **First Presbyterian Church** at the corner of 3rd and Randolph Streets, a Victorian Gothic built in 1874. Walking tour maps are available at the **Napa Valley Conference and Visitors Bureau** (1310 Napa Town Center, Napa; 707-226-7459).

A thriving river port in the 1870s, Petaluma has retained many of its beautiful homes, and the downtown is beautifully preserved — the city amazingly was spared during the 1906 quake. Browse along Petaluma Boulevard and Kentucky Street, taking in the antique shops and admiring the classic architecture. Drive through the Victorian neighborhoods and check out the majestic Queen Anne styling of the old **Gilger House** at 111 6th St., or the intricately ornate Spanish Colonial at 47 6th St. Pick up a copy of *The Streets of Petaluma'* at the **Petaluma Area Chamber of Commerce** (799 Baywood Dr., Petaluma; 707-762-2785).

Many of Santa Rosa's great buildings were lost in the 1906 earthquake, though **McDonald Avenue** on the west edge of downtown has survived. Alfred Hitchcock filmed *Shadow of a Doubt* in Santa Rosa. Downtown has changed considerably since then, but the McDonald Avenue residential area, shown extensively in the film, remains the city's architectural prize. Just west of downtown is a lovely neighborhood of large homes, wide streets, and tall trees. The centerpiece is **Mableton** at 1015 McDonald. Built in 1878, it was inspired by the plantation homes of Mississippi.

CINEMA

The Sebastiani Theatre on Sonoma's historic square.

Thomas Hallstein/Outsight

Although few of Napa's or Sonoma's grand old movie houses still stand — blame it on urban renewal or earthquakes — movie-going remains an ardent passion. The *Wine Country Film Festival,* a month-long celebration of the latest foreign and art films, is small but respected. *The Sonoma Film Institute,* staged in a classroom at Sonoma State University but open to the public, is low on atmosphere but high on quality. Finally, Sonoma and Napa are home to many top-name stars, and the two counties' landscapes are cinema stars in their own right — both are favorite locations for Hollywood feature films and commercials.

Seeing Stars

Hollywood seems enamored with Wine Country, Sonoma County in particular. Look closely, and you'll recognize more than a few famous movie and TV sites. The most famous is perhaps the old Bodega School in Bodega, immortalized by Alfred Hitchcock in *The Birds.* It's just off Bodega Highway, a few miles inland from Bodega Bay. Another familiar spot is downtown Petaluma, used for the cruising scenes in *American Graffiti.* More recently, Sonoma County was seen prominently in films like *Phenomenon, Scream,* and *Bandits,* while Napa Valley life was portrayed in *A Walk in the Clouds.*

More than a few celebrities call Napa and Sonoma home, at least part time. The late Charles Schultz, creator of *Peanuts,* was Santa Rosa's most famous denizen. Robin Williams owns a mountaintop ranch between Napa and Sonoma Counties. The late Raymond "Perry Mason" Burr was a well-known Healdsburg resident. Other high profiles include comedian-vintner Tommy Smothers, musician-actor Tom Waits, and Jon Provost, known to millions as Timmy on the old *Lassie* TV show. Jon Lassiter, the man who created *Toy Story,* calls Sonoma home. Film star Winona Ryder was raised in Petaluma.

Napa County

Cameo Cinema (707-963-9779; 1340 Main St., St. Helena, CA 94574) This charming theater in downtown St. Helena was completely refurbished in 1997. It shows first-run films, but as you might expect for a small town, a few weeks after release. Mostly American fare, though occasional art and foreign films come for a stay.

Century Cine Dome (707-257-7700; 825 Pearl St., Napa, CA 94559) Modern eight-theater complex showing first-runs in downtown.

Sonoma County

Airport Cinemas (707-522-0330; 409 Aviation Blvd., Santa Rosa, CA 95403) Opening in 1995, this eight-screen complex is one of the best in Wine Country. It even has a café.

The Raven Film Center (707-433-5448; 115 North St., Healdsburg, CA 95448)

The main Raven theater is easily the finest movie house in Wine Country. The downtown Healdsburg theater, which seats 600, was meticulously restored a few years back, and four smaller theaters were added behind the original theater. The cinemas show first-run movies and the occasional art film.

Rialto Cinemas (707-525-4840; 551 Summerfield Rd., Santa Rosa, CA 95405) Here's a rarity, a theater devoting itself to foreign and cutting-edge art films.

Roxy (707-522-0330; 85 Santa Rosa Ave., Santa Rosa, CA 95404) This state-of-the art cinema has it all: great sound and projection plus stadium seating with rocking chairs. *The* place to see the latest action blockbuster.

Sebastiani Theatre (707-996-2020; 476 1st St. E., Sonoma, CA 95476) A delightful old theater in dire need of refurbishing. Shows late first-run films.

Sebastopol Cinemas (707-829-3456; McKinley St. & Petaluma Ave., Sebastopol, CA 95472) Open since fall 1994, this five-theater cinema is inside a refurbished brandy distillery. Shows first-run films.

Sonoma Cinemas (707-935-1234; 200 Siesta Way, Boyes Hot Springs, CA 95476; at Hwy. 12) This four-plex theater, open since summer 1994, shows first-run movies.

Cinema 6 (707-528-8770; 620 3rd St., Santa Rosa, CA 95404) Compact little multiplex hidden away in downtown. Don't blink or you'll drive right past. First-run films.

Film Festivities

Sonoma Film Institute (707-664-2606; Sonoma State University, Darwin Theater, Rohnert Park, CA 94928) If you can overlook the classroom atmosphere, the Institute is a great place to catch classics and art films. Whether you prefer the Marx Brothers in *Duck Soup* or the latest French import, the Friday and Saturday night double-features are a great bargain.

Wine Country Film Festival (707-996-2536) This annual July and August event is a fast-paced potpourri of movie screenings, workshops, and parties. The events spread throughout Napa and Sonoma Counties. Some of the movies that made their debut at WCFF include *sex, lies, and videotape* and *When Harry Met Sally*. Stars are usually on hand to schmooze, including Gregory Peck, Nicolas Cage, and Dennis Hopper. Caution: The films are excellent, but the festival has a reputation for organizational problems.

GALLERIES

Whether your thing is abstract expressionism or dolphins jumping through rainbows, there's an art gallery for you somewhere in Napa and Sonoma counties. A new gallery seems to open every weekend. The hills of Northern California shelter some of the finest artists in the country.

A painter tries to capture the rolling ranchland of Wine Country.

Thomas Hallstein/Outsight

Each of the galleries has its own specialty. Some galleries are cooperatives, owned and operated by local artists. Others specialize in ceramics or offer paintings and prints of nationally known artists. Vineyards and seascapes, of course, are the dominant themes.

Napa County

CLOS PEGASE WINERY
707-942-4981;
   fax 707-942-4993.
www.clospegase.com.
info@clospegase.com.
1060 Dunaweal Lane,
   Calistoga, CA 94515.
Open: 10:30–5 daily, tours
   11 & 2 daily.
Fee: None.

This winery is a work of art in itself. Designed by the award-winning architect Michael Graves, it looks like a postmodern Babylonian temple. A commanding edifice of tall pillars and archways, done in bold hues of cream and terra cotta, Clos Pegase is an eye-catcher.

The lawn and courtyard serve as a sculpture garden. That collection includes Richard Serra's provocative "Twins," a minimalist masterpiece. The regular winery tour offers a glimpse of owner Jan Shrem's impressive art collection, including 17th- and 18th-century French statuary artfully displayed in the winery's massive underground cave. Also, a casual browse through the visitors center reveals more treasures.

DI ROSA PRESERVE
707-226-5991;
   fax 707-255-8934
www.dirosapreserve.org
5200 Sonoma Hwy. Napa,
   CA 94559
On Hwy. 128/12.
Open: By Appointment
Admission $12

Di Rosa is both an art gallery and nature preserve. The nationally known collection includes more than 1,700 works of San Francisco Bay Area art — sculptures, paintings, etc. It's on display in a former stone winery and even outdoors, set amid 35 acres of the rolling meadows of the scenic Carneros district of southern Napa Valley.

THE HESS COLLECTION
707-255-1144;
   fax 707-253-1682.
www.hesscollection.com.
4411 Redwood Rd., Napa,
   CA 94558
10 mi. W. of Hwy. 29.
Open: 10–4 daily.
Fee: None.

If there's a gallery in Wine Country that deserves the title museum, it's the Hess Collection. Swiss entrepreneur Donald Hess transformed the old Mont La Salle Winery into an ultramodern showcase for his two great passions: art and wine. Built on the rugged slopes of Mt. Veeder, the Hess Collection opened to the public in 1989.

The entrance opens onto a dramatic three-story staircase. The 130-piece collection spans the upper two floors and features the works of internationally know artists such as Francis Bacon, Robert Motherwell, and Frank Stella. A mix of paintings and sculptures, the works are provocative and often haunting, though humor plays a role, too.

I. WOLK GALLERY
707-963-8800.
www.iwolkgallery.com.
1354 Main St., St. Helena,
   CA 94574.
Open: 10–5:30 Wed.–Mon.
Fee: None.

This is an excellent gallery with serious intentions about art, specializing in contemporary paintings, photography, and crafts by emerging American artists. "Contemporary" does not necessarily read "abstract" since the emphasis is on realist imagery. Exhibitions feature single artists, but a wide range of artists is shown continuously.

JESSEL GALLERY
707-257-2350;
   fax 707-257-2396.
www.jesselgallery.com.
jessel@napanet.net.
1019 Atlas Peak Rd., Napa,
   CA 94558.
Open: 10–5 daily.
Fee: None.

Jessel is the essence of what Northern California galleries are all about. The art is not particularly challenging but lovely nonetheless and the atmosphere is laid-back, almost meditative. If you're weary of the bustle of Highway 29, Napa's main drag, make a detour to this delightful gallery. Jessel, an artist who prefers just one name, opened the gallery in 1987, and offerings include gorgeous pastels and watercolors as well as jewelry and ceramics.

Sonoma County

PRESS HOUSE GALLERY
707-938-1266, 800-926-1266;
   fax 707-939-0916.
www.buenavista
   winery.com.
Buena Vista Winery, 18000
   Old Winery Rd., Sonoma.
Mail: PO Box 1842,
   Sonoma, CA 95476
Open: 10–5 daily.
Fee: None.

The artist-in-residence program at Buena Vista is one of Wine Country's best art ideas. The loft of the historic Press House tasting room becomes a gallery and working studio for a different Bay Area artist each month. Visitors taste wine and watch the creative process in action. The artists — most often working in pastels, oils, and watercolors — welcome questions and friendly discussion.

SONOMA MUSEUM OF VISUAL ART

707-527-0297;
fax 707-545-0518.
www.lbc.net.
Luther Burbank Center for the Arts, 50 Mark West Springs Rd., Santa Rosa, CA 95403.
Open: Wed.–Sun.; hours vary.
Fee: $2.

A museum only in name, the gallery-sized Sonoma Museum of Visual Art has nonetheless become one of Sonoma County's most important art spaces. It earns the name "museum" in the way it displays art. The emphasis is not on money but artists — Sonoma artists in particular. The art may be for sale, but this isn't a showroom. Paintings don't fight for space with postcards, T-shirts, and earrings. And rather than displaying whatever art is handy for quick showings, exhibits pride themselves on quality and linger six to eight weeks. Occasionally the work of a single artist is featured, though usually two people or groups share the space.

SPIRITS IN STONE

707-938-2200,
800-4S74-6624;
fax 707-938-2263.
www.spiritsinstone.com.
452 1st St. E., Suite A, Sonoma, CA 95476.
Open: 10–6 daily.
Fee: None.

If you think African art is just masks and primitive carvings, think again. The Shona tribe in Zimbabwe, known as "the people of the mist," carve extraordinary stone sculptures. They believe that each stone hides a unique spirit and the sculptor's task is to remove what has been hiding the spirit. The sculptures — which depict gods, people, and animals — reveal both vivid talent and primitive charm. A second Shona gallery is in Village Outlets, 3111 N. St. Helena Hwy. (Hwy. 29), St. Helena.

OTHER GALLERIES

Napa County

Artesa Vineyards & Winery (707-224-1668; 1345 Henry Rd., Napa, CA 94559) This winery is an architectural work of art; built into a hillside, it looks like a lost tomb. Contemporary art is on display throughout the winery.

Lee Youngman Galleries (707-942-0585; 1316 Lincoln Ave., Calistoga, CA 94515) Southwest art from nationally known artists; oils, watercolors; metal and wood sculptures.

Mumm Napa Valley (707-942-3434; 8445 Silverado Trail, Napa, CA 94558) The long hallways of this winery are devoted to art, and it's a lovely space. Revolving shows are featured and Ansel Adams's "Story of a Winery" is on permanent display.

Raku Ceramics Collection (707-944-9211; 6540 Washington St., Yountville, CA 94599) Raku is a distinctive Japanese style of ceramics that creates a rustlike glaze. Some beautiful pieces here.

RASberry's Art Glass Gallery (707-944-9211; 6540 Washington St., Yountville, CA 94599) A gift shop disguising itself as a gallery. You may consider these garish creations art. We don't.

Robert Mondavi Winery (707-251-4333; 7801 St. Helena Hwy., Oakville, CA 94562; on Hwy. 29) One of the first wineries to show art; rotating shows on display in the Vineyard Room.

SoCo Gallery (707-257-2117; 68 Coombs St., #2D, Napa, CA 94559) Gallery of local artists established by the Arts Council of Napa Valley.

On the Trail of Art

ARTrails (707-579-ARTS) A Sonoma County tradition every October. For two weekends, dozens of artists open their studios to the public. It's rare chance to see artists in their natural habitat, not to mention an opportunity for a bargain since there's no art gallery middleman. Sponsored by the Cultural Arts Council of Sonoma County; handy tour maps are available.

Napa Valley Artists' Open Studio Tour (707-257-2117) Similar to ARTrails: Dozens of artists open their studios to the public during the last two weekends in October. Tour maps available through the Napa County Arts Council for a nominal fee.

Sonoma County

Bodega Landmark Studio (707-876-3477; 17255 Bodega Hwy., Bodega, CA 94923) West county artists a specialty; oils, watercolors, ceramics.

Ren Brown Collection (707-875-2922; 1781 Hwy. 1, Bodega Bay, CA 94923) Modern Japanese prints are the focus of this gallery.

Santa Rosa Junior College Gallery (707-527-4298; 1501 Mendocino Ave., Santa Rosa, CA 94503) Group shows by faculty and students.

Snoopy's Gallery (707-546-3385; 1667 W. Steele Ln., Santa Rosa) More of a museum and gift shop than a gallery, but it's worth checking out if you're a *Peanuts* fan. Creator Charles Schulz was a local, and many of his originals are on display.

Sonoma State University Gallery (707-664-2295; E. Cotati Ave., Rohnert Park, CA 49428) Traveling exhibits of nationally known painters and sculptors as well as student and faculty group shows.

Sonoma Valley Museum of Art (707-939-7862; 551 Broadway, Sonoma, CA 95476) A pleasant gallery devoted to the works of Sonoma Valley artists.

HISTORIC PLACES

Napa County

BALE GRIST MILL
707-938-1519.
3369 St. Helena Hwy, St. Helena, CA 94574.

Just think: If wheat had caught on in Napa Valley, you might be cruising Highway 29 in search of the perfect loaf of bread. When settlers first began arriving in Napa in the 1830s and 1840s, wheat,

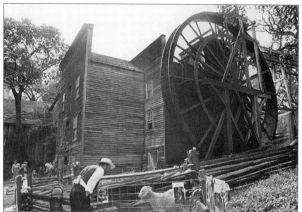

Chris Alderman

Old Mill Days at the historic Bale Grist Mill.

On Hwy. 29, 3 mi. N. of St. Helena.
Contact: Silverado District Headquarters, 20 E. Spain St., Sonoma, CA 95476.
Open: 10–5 daily.
Fee: $1.
Special Features: Gift shop.

corn, and wild oats — not grapes — were the crops of choice. Mills, of course, were a necessity, not only as places to grind grain into meal and flour but also as social centers for the community. Edward Turner Bale's gristmill, built in 1846, was one of three in Napa and the only one that survives.

If traffic or the glitz of wineries gets on your nerves, take an hour for a quiet getaway at the Bale Grist Mill State Historic Park. It seems miles and generations away. The mill is at the end of a short path, a refreshing walk through dense woods and across a lively brook. The first thing you'll notice is the 36-foot-high wooden waterwheel, rolling at a leisurely pace, water trickling down its curved steps. Inside the three-story wood mill house, a woman in a bonnet and period dress greets visitors. She might even offer you a slice of dense bread, made on-site with grain from the mill. The miller may actually crank up the giant millstones and grind flour.

The mill has a colorful past. Its builder, Dr. E. T. Bale, had a reputation as a rogue and scoundrel. He was fond of the bottle and refused to pay his debts. Jailed on a number of occasions, he was publicly whipped and once nearly lynched for shooting a relative of the important Gen. Mariano Vallejo. Finally, Bale settled down and built the mill. It became the gathering spot for the north valley, where friends could exchange gossip and even stage dances. In those days, a miller was a leading citizen in the community, and his counsel in business matters was highly respected.

With the coming of new technology at the turn of the 20th century, the mill fell into neglect. It was restored by the Native Sons of the Golden West in 1925 and then again in 1967. It became a state historic park in 1974.

Sonoma County

FORT ROSS
707-847-3286;
    fax 707-847-3601.
www.parks.sonoma.
    net/fortross.html.
19005 Coast Hwy. 1, Jenner,
    CA 95450.
12 mi. N. of Jenner.
Open: 10–4:30 daily.
Fee: $2 per car.
Special Features: Picnic
    area, gift shop,
    camping.

A quick history quiz: Who were Sonoma's first settlers (besides the Indians, of course)? If you said the Spanish, you're wrong. It was actually the Russians, who established Fort Ross, which predated the Sonoma Mission by 11 years.

The Russian-American Trading Company, a firm controlled largely by the Imperial Russian government, came to California to escape the cruel winters of Alaska and to hunt for valuable sea otters. They landed south in Bodega Bay, which they called Rumiantsev, and explored to the north. On a windy bluff overlooking the Pacific, they built their fort and community, now the centerpiece of Fort Ross State Historic Park.

Under the Russians, the fort thrived for 30 years as a major trading center for trappers and explorers. The Spanish and, later, Mexican settlement of Napa and Sonoma was established largely to thwart the Russian presence at Fort Ross. By 1830 the sea otter population was decimated, and Fort Ross fell into decline. The Russians sold Fort Ross in 1839. It's certainly off the beaten path, miles from the nearest winery, but history buffs won't want to miss it, and the drive along Highway 1 is spectacular.

One structure built by the Russians still stands: the Commandant's House. The two blockhouses, the stockade, and the Russian Orthodox Chapel have been carefully rebuilt. The visitors center and museum offer a look at the fort's past as well as a peek at Russian and Indian artifacts.

Luther Burbank experi-
mented in his garden.

Chris Alderman

LUTHER BURBANK HOME AND GARDEN

707-524-5445.
www.ci.santa-rosa.ca.us/
rp/burbank.
burbankhome@flash
.netdex.com.
Corner of Santa Rosa &
Sonoma Aves., Santa
Rosa.
Mail: PO Box 1678, Santa
Rosa, CA 95402.
Open: Apr.–Oct. 10–4
Wed.–Sun.; garden 8–7
summer, 8–5 winter.
Fee: Docent-led house tour
$3 for adults, free to
children under 12; no fee
for garden.
Special Features: Gift shop.

Plant genius Luther Burbank remains Santa Rosa's favorite son. Seventy-five years after his death, buildings and businesses bear his name. At the turn of the 20th century his fame was international. Burbank arrived from his native Massachusetts in 1877. In a letter home he wrote — and Santa Rosans love to quote this — "I firmly believe . . . this is the chosen spot of all this earth as far as nature is concerned."

From his Santa Rosa garden, Burbank developed more than 800 new strains of fruits, flowers, vegetables, and grasses. Burbank, along with other geniuses like George Washington Carver, transformed plant breeding into a modern science. So great was Burbank's fame that by 1900, 150 people a day came to see the man and his garden. Among his visitors one day in 1915 were Thomas Edison, Henry Ford, and Harvey Firestone.

The house was built in about 1870 and is rather small, a modified Greek Revival cottage. Burbank lived there from 1884 to 1906, when the earthquake damaged the house and Burbank moved. When Burbank died in 1926, his wife Elizabeth returned to the cottage. The property was designated a National Historic Landmark in 1964, and upon Elizabeth's death in 1977, the house and garden became city property.

The half-hour tour of the house is full of facts and artifacts and includes a glimpse inside one of Burbank's original greenhouses. The garden, as you might expect, abounds in Burbank creations, particularly the Paradox Walnut Tree and the Burbank Rose.

MISSION SAN FRANCISCO SOLANO

707-938-1519 (parks dist.
office), 707-938-9560
(mission).
Corner of Spain St. & 1st St.
E., Sonoma Plaza,
Sonoma.
Contact: Parks & Recreation
Dept., 20 E. Spain St.,
Sonoma, CA 95476.
Open: 10–5 daily.
Fee: $1; admission also good
toward entry to Petaluma
Adobe and Vallejo House;
other historic sites are
also along the Plaza.

This is where European settlement really began. Sure, technically, the Russians established the first outpost at Fort Ross, but the true origins of Napa and Sonoma lie at Sonoma's Mission San Francisco Solano. The white adobe mission with a red-tile roof is probably the most popular historic attraction in Wine Country.

To appreciate its significance, it helps to understand the history of California's mission system. The Spanish government and Catholic Church began establishing California missions in 1769, both as a way of converting "heathen" Indians and claiming land for Spain. There were already 20 missions when the young and ambitious Father Jose Altimira received permission from the Mexican governor of California to establish a new one north of the San Francisco Bay. On July 4, 1823, Altimira celebrated Mass with a makeshift redwood cross and blessed the site.

The Sonoma Mission was the last to be established, and the mission system was dissolved in 1833. It became a center of religion and culture under Gen. Mariano Vallejo's rule, but it was sold by the church in 1881. Used over the years as a blacksmith shop and hay barn, the mission was nearly lost until the state intervened in 1906; restoration began three years later.

Today, only the long, low building to the east of the present chapel is original, although the current chapel was only built a few years later, in 1841. Displays explain how adobe buildings are constructed and how the mission was restored. The chapel is decorated with 14 stations of the cross, authentic relics of the mission period. The chapel decor is also patterned after mission interiors of the period, highly stylized primitive renderings by Christianized Indians.

PETALUMA ADOBE
707-762-4871.
3325 Adobe Rd., Petaluma, CA 94954.
3 mi. E. of Petaluma.
Open: 10–5 daily.
Fee: $1; admission also good toward entry to Mission San Francisco Solano and Vallejo House.
Special Features: Picnic tables.

Once the heart of Gen. Mariano Vallejo's sprawling 100-square-mile rancho, the Petaluma Adobe is the area's most meticulously restored adobe. The commanding two-story house was built in 1836 and has three-foot-thick mud walls and a redwood verandah all around.

Authentic is the key word here. The rooms are furnished to the period, and goats and chickens roam the outdoor corridors. Outdoor displays include working replicas of a forge and a large oven for baking bread.

The tour is self-guided; the museum details the history of the adobe and how it was restored.

GENERAL VALLEJO HOME
707-938-1519.
W. Spain St., Sonoma, CA.
1/2 mi. W. of Sonoma Plaza.
Contact: Parks & Recreation Dept., 20 E. Spain St., Sonoma, CA 95476
Open: 10–5 daily.
Fee: $1; admission also good toward entry to Mission San Francisco Solano & Petaluma Adobe.
Special Features: Picnic tables.

Gen. Mariano Vallejo may have been the most powerful man in Northern California in the 1850s, but he had a sense of poetry about him when he named his house *Lachryma Montis*. Latin for "Tears of the Mountain," the name was derived from a mountain spring on the property.

Vallejo was born in Monterey in 1807; his father was a Spanish soldier. Following his father into military service, Vallejo was commander of the presidio, the Spanish fort and settlement in San Francisco, when he was sent north in 1834. He commanded the northern frontier for 14 years and was largely responsible for encouraging the settlement of both Sonoma and Napa Counties.

People who want a glimpse of the Old West will get a kick out of this saddle shop in Vallejo's rancho, circa 1840.

Thomas Hallstein/Outsight

Vallejo's home, finished in 1852, reflects his embrace of the American culture. Instead of an adobe house, he built a two-story Gothic Victorian. The house was prefabricated, designed and built on the East Coast and shipped around the Horn. Vallejo and his family lived in the house for 35 years; the state bought the property in 1933.

The house and grounds are gorgeous, a quiet stop if you need relief from the bustle of Sonoma Plaza. The long driveway is flanked by tall cottonwood trees, and the gardens and vineyards are carefully tended. The self-guided tour begins in a large warehouse, where displays detail Vallejo's life and the history of the house. One detraction: Instead of tasteful ropes in the doorways guarding the rooms as in most historic homes, ugly white metal bars and cages have been installed to protect the considerable collection of artifacts and personal effects on display.

JACK LONDON STATE HISTORIC PARK
707-938-5216.
www.parks.sonoma.net/
JLStory.html.
2400 London Ranch Rd.,
Glen Ellen, CA 95442.
Open: Park open 10–7
summer, 10–5 winter;
house open 10–5 daily.
Fee: $3 per car.
Special Features: Picnic
tables, barbecue pits,
hiking, horseback riding.

"When I first came here, tired of cities and people," Jack London wrote of Glen Ellen, "I settled down on 130 acres of the most beautiful land to be found in California." The writer famed for *The Call of the Wild* and other adventure stories called his home in the Sonoma Mountains "Beauty Ranch."

Today his ranch is in the heart of Wine Country's most beautiful state park, now a vast 880 acres of woodlands, fields, and hiking trails. The remains of the Wolf House is perhaps the park's most prominent feature. The massive castlelike stone building was four stories tall; it was the culmination of Jack and Charmian London's dreams. On the night of August 22, 1913, only days before they were to

This maze of charred stone is Jack London's Wolf House in Jack London State Historic Park.

move in, Wolf House mysteriously burned. The ruins remain today, although it requires a hike to see it. London died in 1916, reminding many of words he once said: "The proper function of man is to live, not exist. I shall not waste my days in trying to prolong them. I shall use my time."

London's grave along the half-mile trail to Wolf House is another popular stop. You can also visit London's ranch house, his stone barn, and pig palace. The House of Happy Walls, built by Charmian after London's death, serves as a museum, displaying an 18,000-volume library, original furnishings, memorabilia, and the Londons' collection of South Pacific artifacts.

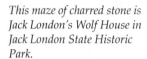

LIBRARIES

Wine Country has two distinguished libraries: the *Napa Valley Wine Library* and the *Sonoma County Wine Library*. Both are exceptional resources.

The Napa Wine Library is inside St. Helena Public Library (707-963-5244; 1492 Library Ln., St. Helena, CA 94574). It has a vast collection, including more than 6,000 books, tapes, etc., detailing everything from the art of winemaking to the history of Napa wine to the current community of wineries throughout the valley.

The Sonoma County Wine Library occupies a small wing inside the Healdsburg branch of the Sonoma County Public Library (707-433-3772; 139 Piper St., Healdsburg, CA 95448). Its collection is similar but somewhat smaller, though no less impressive. The library also subscribes to nearly 75 wine magazines and newsletters.

MUSEUMS

The Sonoma County Museum, a former post office.

Chris Alderman

Napa County

COPIA: THE AMERICAN CENTER FOR FOOD, WINE, AND THE ARTS
707-259-1600.
www.copia.org
mail@copia.org.
500 First St., Napa, CA 94559.
Open: 10–5 Thurs.–Mon. (winter); 10–9 (summer, closed Tues.).
Fee: $12.50.

Copia is the brainchild of vintner Robert Mondavi, who said he wanted to create a place to celebrate and explore the abundance and diversity of America's fine food, wine, and art. The word "copia" means abundance in Italian. The idea is to show how food, wine, and the arts have played a role in people's lives, from the most primitive civilization to the present and into the future.

There are art displays, music, dance and drama performances, wine classes, restaurants, and more. A notable long-term exhibit is called "Forks in the Road: Food, Wine, and the American Table." It explores food and wine in American life and its diversity. It includes historic and geographical influences as well as how sheer individuality helped shape America's food culture. One visual treat is a tower of cookbooks, revealing that Americans are a diverse people who crave a multiplicity of cooking ideas.

NAPA VALLEY MUSEUM
707-944-0500;
 fax 707-945-0500.
www.napavalley museum.org.
55 Presidents Circle, Yountville CA 94599
Open: 10–5 Wed.–Mon.

Since its debut in 1997, this has been an impressive addition to the valley. A stylishly modern take on an old California barn, the $3.5 million museum is devoted to the history, culture and art of Napa, with standing and touring exhibits. One of the standing exhibits is "California Wine: the Science of an Art," a highly interactive education

Fee: $4.50 adults, $3.50 seniors and students, free 6 and younger.

in the making of wine. Another permanent exhibit is "The Land and People of the Napa Valley," an overview of how the valley came to be, from its geological beginnings to the Wappo Indians to its crowning as America's capital of wine.

SHARPSTEEN MUSEUM
707-942-5911;
fax 707-942-6325.
www.napanet.net/vi
/sharpsteen/.
1311 Washington St., PO Box 573, Calistoga, CA 94515.
Open: Noon–4, winter;
10–4, summer.
Fee: None.

If you want a quick lesson in early Napa life, this quaint museum is the place to go. Ben and Bernice Sharpsteen created the museum almost as a hobby after Ben retired as a producer for Walt Disney and the couple moved to Calistoga. Before long it became a community project, and today it is run by volunteers.

The first section of this museum is devoted to the Sharpsteens themselves, and frankly it's rather dull. But the miniature model of early Calistoga that follows is delightful. The town was founded in 1859 as a resort by the flamboyant Sam Brannan. Brannan was a man of many firsts: California's first newspaper publisher, banker, and land developer. He built the first railroad and telegraph. He was also California's first millionaire. His elegant Hot Springs Resort was a gathering place for California's rich and famous, and his vision of Calistoga as a haven of healing waters and relaxation still lives today. Only one tiny Victorian cottage remains from Brannan's resort; it was moved in 1977 and is attached to the museum. Step inside the wonderfully ornate cottage, and you'll step back into the 1860s.

The museum also details a great deal of Northern California history. One display, a Napa Valley timeline, is particularly intriguing, dating back to the first explorers and the Sonoma Mission through the turn of the 20th century. There are also lessons about the early stagecoach days — a restored coach is on display — the first railroad, Robert Louis Stevenson's days in Napa, and more. There are enough old photos, newspapers, and artifacts to keep any history buff happy.

SILVERADO MUSEUM
707-963-3757;
fax 707-963-0917.
1490 Library Ln., PO Box 490, St. Helena, CA 94574.
Open: Noon–4 daily, closed Mon.
Fee: Free.

Writer Robert Louis Stevenson was taken by Napa Valley. In 1880, the author of Dr. Jekyll and Mr. Hyde and Treasure Island honeymooned with his wife in a cabin near the old Silverado Mine. He wrote about the area in *The Silverado Squatters*. He called Napa's wine "bottled poetry," and Mount St. Helena was the inspiration for Spyglass Hill in *Treasure Island*. Although Stevenson spent only a few months in Napa Valley, he has been accepted as an adopted son.

Part of the St. Helena Library Center, the museum has a feeling of a small chapel. Founded in 1969, on the 75th anniversary of Stevenson's death,

Silverado is more a library than a museum. It contains more than 8,000 artifacts, including dozens of paintings and photographs, as well as original Stevenson letters and manuscripts. There are also hundreds of books and first printings.

Sonoma County

An exhibit of baskets at the Sonoma County Museum.

Chris Alderman

SONOMA COUNTY MUSEUM
707-579-1500.
scm@pon.net.
425 7th St., Santa Rosa, CA 95401.
www.pressdemo.com/scmuseum.
Open: 11–4 Wed.–Sun.
Fee: $2 adults, $1 students & seniors.
Special Features: Gift shop.

The Sonoma County Museum building, a classic post office from early in the century, was saved from an insidious fate: progress. When the building was slated for demolition, preservationists prevailed, and it was moved to its present site in 1979. Now on the National Register of Historic places, the structure is beautifully restored. A mix of Spanish and Roman influences, it is considered one of the few remaining examples of classic Federal-style architecture in California. Inside the two-story stucco building are marble floors and rich oak paneling — no better place for a museum. Lobby displays detail the history of the building and its laborious move two blocks north. The main exhibit room offers rotating displays keyed to Sonoma history.

OTHER MUSEUMS

Napa County

Napa Firefighters Museum (707-259-0609; 1201 Main St., Napa, CA 94559) Antique firefighting equipment on display. Hours vary.

Veterans Museum (707-944-4918; California Veteran's Home, Yountville, CA 94599) This fine Spanish Revival complex is home to a collection of military memorabilia.

Sonoma County

Healdsburg Museum (707-431-3325; 221 Matheson St., Healdsburg, CA 95448) Devoted to early Healdsburg history, including Indian artifacts and 5,000 photographs.

Native American Art Museum (707-527-4479; 1501 Mendocino Ave., Santa Rosa Junior College, Santa Rosa, CA 95401) Artifacts and current works by Native American artisans.

Petaluma Historical Museum and Library (707-778-4398; 20 4th St., Petaluma, CA 94952) Devoted to early Petaluma history. Inside a classic 1903 Carnegie Library. A good place to begin a walking tour of Petaluma's classic Victorians.

Sonoma Depot Museum (707-938-1762; 270 First St. W., Sonoma, CA 95476) This rebuilt train depot, home to the Sonoma Valley Historical Society, features a permanent exhibit devoted to the 1846 Bear Flag Revolt plus exhibits detailing the Miwok Indian period and more.

MUSIC

Napa County

NAPA VALLEY SYMPHONY
707-226-8742;
  fax 707-226-3046.
www.napavalley
  symphony.org/
Mail: 2407 California Blvd.,
  Napa, CA 94558.
Lincoln Theater, California
  Veteran's Home,
  Yountville.
Season: Oct.–Apr.; pops
  concerts June & Dec.
Tickets: $10–$37.

The young Asher Raboy is the conductor for this symphony that dates to 1933 when Luigi Catalano first gathered a cadre of amateur and professional musicians. Today there are more than 75 musicians from Napa Valley and the Bay Area in the orchestra.

Each of the season's five concerts feature guest artists performing the great music of the classical repertoire. Past soloists have included pianist Philippe Bianconi and violinist Robert McDuffie. Each summer since 1969, the lovely Robert Mondavi Winery has played host to the symphony's Wine Country Pops, a warm and delightful June evening.

Sonoma County

SANTA ROSA SYMPHONY
707-546-8742;
  fax 707-546-0460.
www.santarosasymphony.
  com.

Jeffrey Kahane has revitalized this small orchestra during the past few years. Musicians — all of respectable talent — come from around the Bay Area. Some are semi-professionals with day jobs; others keep busy roaming from one orchestra to

info@santarosasymphony.
com.
Burbank Center for the
Arts, 50 Mark West
Springs Rd., Santa Rosa,
CA 95403.
Season: Oct.–May.
Tickets: $15–40.

another. Guests of emerging musical reputation are featured in each concert. Recent soloists have included guitarist David Tanenbaum, pianist Andre Watts, and famed cellist Yo-Yo Ma, a close friend of Kahane.

Burbank Center for the Arts, a former church, is a large hall of about 1,500 seats. The acoustics aren't what they might be, but the symphony strives to overcome the limitations. The symphony's Redwood Summer Music Festival is one of the highlights of Sonoma County's musical year.

OTHER MUSIC

Napa County

Chamber Music in Napa Valley (707-253-1411; First United Methodist Church, 625 Randolph St., Napa, CA 94559) This winter series features top chamber performers in intimate settings.

Music in the Vineyards (707-253-8608, various locations) This festival of chamber music happens every August and draws musicians from around the country.

Napa Valley Music & Wine Festival (707-252-4813; Skyline Park, 2201 Imola Ave., Napa, CA 94559) A three-day festival of acoustic music that features Bay Area and national acts.

Robert Mondavi Summer Music Festival (707-963-9611; 7801 Hwy. 29, PO Box 106, Oakville, CA 94562) A tradition since 1969, these June-through-August concerts on the lush lawns of Mondavi's winery bring in top names in popular music: Tony Bennett, David Benoit, and the Preservation Hall Jazz Band.

Sonoma County

Cotati Jazz Festival (707-584-2222; downtown Cotati) Jazz lovers hop between nightclubs listening to the best jazz musicians the Bay Area has to offer. Late June.

Healdsburg Plaza Sunday Concert Series (707-433-6935; downtown Healdsburg) From May through September, an eclectic array of music livens Sunday afternoons on this lovely plaza.

Petaluma Summer Music Festival (707-763-8920; Petaluma, various locales) Cinnabar Theater's annual ode to music and musical theater. Concerts and performances are staged throughout Petaluma during this August series.

Redwood Summer Music Festival (707-546-8742; various locales in Sonoma County) Annual outdoor concert series by the Santa Rosa Symphony. Picnickers spend a carefree day in various outdoor locales listening to Mozart, Gershwin, Copland, and the like.

Courtesy Russian River Jazz Festival

Rodney Strong Music Series (707-433-0919; 11455 Old Redwood Hwy., Healdsburg, CA 95448) A summer-long series of concerts on this winery's lawn.

Russian River Blues Festival (707-869-3940; Johnson Beach, Guerneville) Blues takes its turn at this annual two-day festival in June. The line-up of blues greats has recently included Taj Mahal, Joe Lewis Walker, and Dr. John.

Russian River Jazz Festival (707-869-3940; Johnson Beach, Guerneville) Jazz along the lazy Russian River has made this the most popular music festival in Wine Country. For two days every September, music lovers sun on the beach or listen from floating inner tubes. The line-up of jazz greats has recently included Larry Carlton, Grover Washington, Jr., David Benoit, and Etta James.

Santa Rosa Dixie Jazz Festival (707-539-3494; Doubletree Hotel, Rohnert Park, CA 94928) Sonoma County swarms with Dixie jazz nuts for one weekend every August. A BIG event, bringing in bands from around the world. Don't ask them to play "When the Saints Go Marching In."

NIGHTLIFE

If you're cruising for a good time in Napa Valley at night, you'll discover quickly that things are rather sleepy. It's the nature of the beast. Napa is largely a haven for visitors seeking quiet and relaxation. Tourists, on the other hand, have less of an impact on Sonoma, which has its own large population to entertain. There's plenty to do after 10pm, particularly in Santa Rosa. The Friday edition of Santa Rosa's *Press Democrat* is a good source for what's happening.

Napa County

The happening place right now is *1351 Lounge* (707-963-1969; 1351 Main St., St. Helena, CA 94574), a hip little bar that brings in a steady stream of music, from jazz and rock to the blues. *Downtown Joe's* (707-258-2337; 902 Main St., Napa, CA 94559) and *Silverado Brewing Co.* (707-967-9876; 3020 St. Helena Hwy., N, St. Helena, CA 94574) are two brew ups that have fun atmospheres, live music, and good beer. *Compadres* (707-944-2406; 6539 Washington Ave., Yountville, CA 94599) is a Mexican restaurant with a lively bar atmosphere and outdoor patio. Avoid the food. *Catahoula Saloon* (707-942-2275; 1457 Lincoln Ave., Calistoga, CA 94515) is a stylish watering hole before or after dinner. On a warm evening, try the beer garden at *Calistoga Inn* (707-942-4101; 1250 Lincoln Ave., Calistoga, CA 94515). They brew their own, and it's great stuff; also, a band is often playing in the bar.

Sonoma County

Sonoma County's club scene is thriving. Live music can be found somewhere every night, and DJs seem to be spinning discs in a corner of every bar.

Santa Rosa is the center of Sonoma County's nightlife, although the outlying areas have a number of fine night spots. Sonoma County's premier stage is *Burbank Center for the Arts* (707-546-3600; 50 Mark West Springs Rd., Santa Rosa, CA 95403). Once a sprawling church complex, the center's main stage is the largest hall in the area, seating about 1,500 in cushioned pews. Recent headliners have included k.d. lang, Squirrel Nut Zippers, Collective Soul, Tori Amos, Bonnie Raitt, and B.B. King. Also try The Last Day Saloon (707-545-2343; lastdaysaloon.com/rosa.html; 120 Fifth St., Santa Rosa, CA 95401), which has the best Bay Area rock and blues bands.

Santa Rosa's hotels are another good source for late-night fun. Try *The Flamingo* (707-545-8530; 2777 4th St., Santa Rosa, CA 95405; at Farmers Ln.) and *Equus Lounge* of Fountain Grove Inn (707-578-6101; 101 Fountain Grove Pkwy., Santa Rosa, CA 95403) There are happening pubs in Santa Rosa. Try *Third Street Aleworks* (707-523-3060; 610 Third St., Santa Rosa, CA 95404). Also *The Old Vic* (707-571-7555; 731 4th St., Santa Rosa, CA 95404), which offers live music most nights; it's a dark and casual pub offering a fine selection of British beers. Check out the second floor of *The Cantina* (707-523-3663; 500 4th St., Santa Rosa, CA 95404) if you like to dance to DJs playing 1970s tunes and modern R&B. The crowd is young.

In Sonoma Valley, *Murphy's Irish Pub* (707-935-0660; 464 First St. E., Sonoma, CA 95476) is small but cozy, and it offers a great selection of imported ales. A different crowd entirely hangs out at *Little Switzerland* (707-938-9990; Grove & Riverside, El Verano, CA 95433). This place is a kick! Polka is king at Little Switzerland, a club and restaurant that dates from 1906. The crowd is older, largely serious polka dancers, but they don't care if you show up for a kitsch thrill and make a fool of yourself on the dance floor. The place is delightfully tacky, with plastic flowers and Swiss Alps murals.

Petaluma has one of Sonoma County's most active scenes. *Mystic Theater and Music Hall* (707-765-6665; 21 Petaluma Blvd. N., Petaluma, CA 94952) is another former movie house that discovered live music. Recent acts have included Train and Joan Osborne. Next door is *McNear's* (707-765-2121; 23 Petaluma Blvd. N., Petaluma, CA 94952), a comfortable gathering spot with video games, pool tables, and live music on weekends. It's also one of the few places that serves food late.

West County has another popular stop, *The Powerhouse Brewing Company* (707-829-9171; 268 Petaluma Ave., Sebastopol, CA 95472) is a cozy night spot with a schedule of eclectic music. *Jasper O'Farrell's* (707-823-1389; 6957 Sebastopol Ave., Sebastopol, CA 95472) is another pub that makes you feel at home. There's live music almost every night and it's a potpourri: jazz, bluegrass, folk, rock. Darts are also a serious passion. In Healdsburg, *Bear Republic Brewing Co.* (707-433-BEER; 345 Healdsburg Ave., Healdsburg, CA 95448) may be Healdsburg's hottest night spot, featuring live music and some excellent hand-crafted beers.

THEATER

Theater is just taking root in Napa County; there are just a few community theaters and outdoor Shakespeare festivals. Sonoma, on the other hand, boasts a long tradition of theater. It has one professional company and several highly regarded semi-professional groups, plus a vastly successful summer stock repertory series brings in top college talent from around the country every year. As one local director said of the Sonoma drama scene: "I think there are more people who do theater than see theater."

Sonoma County

CINNABAR THEATER
707-763-8920;
    fax 707-763-8929.
www.cinnabartheater.com.
info@cinnabartheater.com.
3333 Petaluma Blvd. N.,
    Petaluma, CA 94952.
Season: Year-round.
Tickets: Various.

Opera is a scary prospect for a lot of people. Perhaps it's the elitist air that surrounds it, the assumption that it's only for the wealthy and educated. Or perhaps singing in a foreign language turns people off. Whatever the reason, the late Marvin Klebe came to Petaluma in the early 1970s to change that notion. From that began Sonoma County's most eclectic and dynamic theater. "Our main goals are to explore opera as an immediate and human experience to an audience that is not necessarily highbrow," Cinnabar's Elly Lichenstein commented.

Klebe, a powerful baritone, bought the old Cinnabar School on the northern outskirts of Petaluma and set about transforming it into a studio theater. (Luckily, he was also a master carpenter.) Soon, others — musicians, dancers,

Cinnabar Theater performs
La Bohème.

Courtesy Cinnabar Opera Theater

actors, technicians — got involved, and Cinnabar became a small, thriving performing-arts center.

The heart of the place is Cinnabar Opera Theater. There's not a more intriguing theater company north of San Francisco. No, you won't find a tenor from San Francisco Opera on stage, but you will see the finest singers hovering on "the outskirts" of Bay Area opera fame. Productions have run the gamut from *The Magic Flute* to musical chestnuts such as *Fiddler on the Roof.*

PACIFIC ALLIANCE STAGE COMPANY
707-584-3400 (box off.),
707-588-3434 (info.);
fax 707-588-3430.
Spreckels Performing Arts
Center, 5409 Snyder Ln.,
Rohnert Park, CA 94928.
Season: Sept.–May.
Tickets: Call for prices.

Pacific Alliance is the county's first professional Actor's Equity company. The company also has the backing of Spreckels Center, which in turn is backed by the city of Rohnert Park. Artistic Director Michael Grice continues to bring superior talents from around the Bay Area. A few talented local "amateurs" are also earning that all-important union card.

While acting is approaching the level of San Francisco, production values reveal a limited budget. Spreckels is also experimenting with a few offbeat productions in its small studio. It's all very refreshing.

SONOMA COUNTY REPERTORY THEATRE
707-544-7278 (Santa Rosa);
707-823-0177
(Sebastopol).
104 N. Main St., Sebastopol,
CA 95472.

Since its inception in 1995, this company has quickly become the area's leading theater, staging a mix of classics and cutting-edge dramas, comedies, and occasionally a musical. Performances are in a small Sebastopol theater. Artistic director Jim de Priest is a hurricane of energy and a real talent. Top

Season: Year round.
Tickets: $15.

productions have included Shakespeare's *The Tempest* and *Hamlet* as well as *The Glass Menagerie, A Streetcar Named Desire, Lips Together, Teeth Apart,* and *Assassins*.

**SONOMA
   SHAKESPEARE**
707-588-3400;
   fax 505-586-9030.
www.sonomashakes.com.
svsf@pacbell.net.
Mail: 3913 Douglas Drive,
   Santa Rosa, 95405
Venue: On the lawn of
   various wineries.
Season: July–Aug.
Performances: Fri.–Sun.
Tickets: $10–$20.

Looking for a pleasant evening after a busy day of touring? This is it. Pack a picnic, take a blanket, dress casually, and enjoy fine outdoor theater. The hillside above the winery makes for a natural amphitheater, and the festival's all-purpose stage becomes anything from ancient Rome to the Wild West.

Under artistic director Carl Hamilton's guidance, three or more plays are performed in repertory throughout the summer, some pleasantly lower-brow than others. Offerings have included a musical version of *A Comedy of Errors* as well as *Othello* and *Rosencrantz & Guildenstern Are Dead*.

Picasso at the Lapin Agile
*performed by Summer
Repertory Theater.*

Thomas Hallstein/Outsight

**SUMMER REPERTORY
   THEATER**
707-527-4343;
   fax 707-524-1689.
www.santarosa.edu/srt/
1501 Mendocino Ave.,
   Santa Rosa, CA 95401.
Season: June-Aug.
Tickets: $8–$14.

No one has a bigger local following than SRT. Every summer the Santa Rosa Junior College organizes this three-ring circus of theater, bringing in talented student actors and technical people from around the country. Opening several major productions in four weeks and performing them in a repertory format packs a year's experience into two months.

Some summers are better than others, of course. It all depends on the show and the talent pool, but SRT is always worth a try. The play selection is generally rather safe, but SRT has proven its mettle with every genre: comedy, musical, or drama. Recent highlights have included sparkling productions of *Evita* and *Little Shop of Horrors* and an entertaining version of Steve Martin's *Picasso at the Lapin Agile.*

SRT's production values are the highest in the area. Sets are always dynamic, on a par with many professional theaters. It's also significant that SRT is one of the few local companies performing in the summer — thus a perfect choice for tourists looking for a pleasurable evening on the town.

OTHER THEATER

There are more than a dozen other theater companies in Napa and Sonoma. Many are community theaters. We include a selection of the best.

Napa County

The Napa Valley Shakespeare Festival (707-251-WILL; various locations) performs the Bard and other classics in theaters and on lush lawns of local wineries. Recent productions include *Richard III* and *Our Town.* **Dreamweavers** (707-255-LIVE; 101 S. Coombs St., Napa, CA 94559) is a community theater performing favorites such as *Arsenic and Old Lace.* **Magical Moonshine Theater** (707-257-8007; PO Box 2296,Yountville, CA 94599) is an internationally known puppet theater that doesn't have a regular Napa performance space. Look for them locally when they're not away on tour — charming and great for the family.

Sonoma County

Santa Rosa Players (707-546-3600; Burbank Center for the Arts, 50 Mark West Springs Rd., Santa Rosa,CA 95403) is an institution and it has its good runs and bad. But just when you're ready to write them off, they delight you. Not to be outdone by SRJC, **Sonoma State University** (707-664-2353; Rohnert Park) also has a talented theater department and SSU's new performing arts center has the county's best stage for theater. **Sonoma Community Center** (707-938-4626; 276 E. Napa St., Sonoma, CA 95476) is the stage for regular performances.

SEASONAL EVENTS

If there's one thing they know how to do in Wine Country, it's throw a party. If you live in or are visiting Napa or Sonoma Counties and find that you have an open weekend in the summer, then maybe there's something wrong with you. There are enough festivals and fairs to keep you busy all year. We list here some of the most popular seasonal attractions. The agricultural products of the Napa and Sonoma region shine forth at the many county fairs. Wine, of course, is the centerpiece of many festivals; we've included those in a separate section that follows.

At the Bodega Bay Fisherman's Festival, there's an armada of boats for the annual Blessing of the Fleet.

Thomas Hallstein/Outsight

Bodega Bay Fisherman's Festival (707-875-3422; Bodega Bay) A decades-old tradition for this coast town made famous by Alfred Hitchcock's *The Birds*. This mid-April celebration includes bathtub races, harbor tours, kite flying, a golf tournament, and a boat parade. The high point of the weekend is the annual blessing of the fleet.

Calistoga Beer & Sausage Festival (707-942-6333; Napa County Fairgrounds, Calistoga) Napa Valley's way of celebrating Oktoberfest. On tap in September are some of the best beers brewed by area microbreweries, not to mention tasty tidbits from the region's sausage specialists. Fee.

Gravenstein Apple Fair (707-571-8288; Ragle Ranch Park, Sebastopol) Sebastopol was once the apple capital of the world and today specializes in the distinctive Gravenstein variety. There's a potpourri at this mid-August event: arts and crafts, music, hay rides, storytelling, and, of course, apple treats of all kinds. Fee.

Health & Harmony Festival (707-547-9355; Sonoma County Fairgrounds, Santa Rosa) An only-in-California type of event. A celebration of food, music, and "lifestyle," this annual June fair includes everything from puppet theater to psychic palm readers. Fee.

Hometown Harvest Festival (707-963-5706; downtown St. Helena) A rich Napa tradition, celebrating the end of the growing season and the summer's bountiful harvest. One weekend in late October, there's scads of food, arts and crafts, music, and even a parade.

Kenwood Pillow Fights & Fourth of July Celebration (707-833-2440; Kenwood)

The best excuse we know to have a pillow fight astride a greased pole over a mud pit. So silly, it's addicting. A favorite with local celebrities like Tommy Smothers. There's also a parade, live music, and fireworks.

Napa County Fair (707-942-5111; fairgrounds, Calistoga) The usual down-home fun, but with a twist of chic Napa style that includes social gatherings and wine tastings. The usual rides, animals, produce, and music, plus wine, wine, wine. Every July. Fee.

Napa Town and Country Fair (707-253-4900; Napa Exposition Center, Napa) It has the usual: livestock, food and wine tasting, arts-and-crafts displays, a carnival, and entertainment. Every August. Fee.

Napa Valley Mustard Festival (707-259-9020; various locations) Mustard, the beautiful yellow wildflower that blooms throughout Wine Country every winter, is the focus of this series of food and wine events. Late winter. Fee.

Old Adobe Fiesta (707-762-4871; 3325 Adobe Rd., Petaluma) History comes alive every August with period costumes and craft demonstrations at this historic adobe, one of Sonoma County's oldest homesteads.

Petaluma Butter & Eggs Day (707-778-3491; downtown Petaluma) A celebration of this south- county town's early reputation as "The Egg Basket of the World." Poultry, milk, and eggs remain a strong presence in Sonoma. One Sunday every April the town celebrates with a parade, music, and food.

Sebastopol Apple Blossom Festival (707-823-3032; downtown Sebastopol) When the apple trees are in striking form in April, you won't find a more beautiful place than Sebastopol. Apples rule, of course. Eat apple fritters, cobbler, pies. Plus music, games, and arts and crafts.

The midway at the Sonoma County Fair.

Chris Alderman

Sonoma County Fair (707-545-4200; fairgrounds, Santa Rosa) Sonoma County practically shuts down for two weeks every July, as thousands pour in from the countryside for food, music, rides, blue-ribbon animals, and produce. You can even bet on horse races. Fee.

Yountville Days Festival (707-944-0904; downtown Yountville) Celebrate the history of Napa Valley's first settlement. This September event includes a parade, music, food.

WINE EVENTS

We're still waiting to see this sign along a Napa or Sonoma road: GARAGE SALE & WINE TASTING. Wine events are everywhere and all the time in Napa and Sonoma. There's also considerable appeal to sampling and comparing all sorts of wine in one sitting. Most of the following events are staged outside.

The winning bid at the Napa Valley Wine Auction.

Courtesy Napa Valley Vintners Association

Napa Valley Wine Auction (707-963-3388; Meadowood Resort, St. Helena) The chic wine outing. This three-day June event is busy with extravagant parties, dances, and dinners. Auction tickets cost a fortune but are in high demand. All the big names of the Napa wine industry and elsewhere attend, and the auction raises millions for local charities.

Napa Valley Wine Festival (707-253-3563; Napa Exposition Center, Napa) The November wine tasting, dinner, and auction raises money for a local charity and marks the end of the wine season. Fee.

Napa Wine Festival and Crafts Fair (707-257-0322; downtown Napa) A busy event that draws wine as well as arts and crafts buffs from around the county. Every September. Tasting fee.

Russian River Barrel Tasting (707-522-8726; countryside surrounding Healdsburg) Always the first event of the wine season, and helps lift wine lovers out of the winter doldrums. Besides, everyone loves a sneak preview of wine that hasn't been bottled yet. Best of all: It's free.

Russian River Wine Festival (707-433-6935; Healdsburg Plaza, Healdsburg) The wines of 30 wineries in one place. One Sunday every May, the fest also includes delights from local restaurants, arts and crafts, and live music. Fee.

Salute to the Arts (707-938-1133; Sonoma Plaza, Sonoma) A showcase for local artists, writers, restaurants, and wineries. Roam the beautiful historic square, and browse the many booths. Fee for wine and food. July.

Judging wine at the Sonoma County Harvest Fair.

Tim Fish

Sonoma County Harvest Fair (707-545-4200; fairgrounds, Santa Rosa) This event could easily be listed with the regular seasonal offerings, but the wine tasting is the most important in Sonoma County. The fair brings in top wine experts from around the country. Then local wine buffs gather to compare their taste buds to the judges'. Great fun. There's also plenty of food, and the annual grape stomping contest is a crazy attraction. Fee. October.

Things get pretty messy at the annual grape stomping at the Sonoma County Harvest Fair.

Courtesy Sonoma County Harvest Fair

Sonoma County Showcase of Wine & Food (707-586-3795; various locations) A bit less chichi than its Napa counterpart but remains quite the elegant affair. The gala weekend includes tastings, parties, and the auction itself. The event is usually sold out weeks in advance, despite steep ticket prices. July.

Sonoma County Wine & Food Series (707-576-0162; various locations) A long-time favorite with locals. Gatherings at different wineries throughout the summer feature a particular varietal, chardonnay, for example. Wine is paired with food from local restaurants and live music is also included. Fee.

Sonoma Valley Harvest Wine Auction (707-935-0803; various locations) A casual and fun weekend affair that includes winery parties, a main auction, and even a golf tournament. Every September.

NEIGHBORS

Richard Barnes/Courtesy SFMOMA

The San Francisco Museum of Modern Art.

With San Francisco so close, it's impossible to talk of culture without mentioning what that world-class city has to offer.

Museums are one of the most popular excuses for the pleasant hour's drive south. Best known is *The Exploratorium* (415-EXPLORE; exploratorium.edu;

3601 Lyon St., San Francisco, CA 94123), a magnetic place for families because of its hands-on science displays. Likewise, *The California Academy of Sciences* (415-750-7145; calacademy.org; 1 Maritime Plaza, San Francisco, CA 94111; in Golden Gate Park) is a popular spot for kids and families. Art museums include the cutting edge *San Francisco Museum of Modern Art* (415-357-4000; sfmoma.org; 151 3rd St., San Francisco, CA 94103) and the graceful *Palace of the Legion of Honor* (415-863-3330; legionofhonor.org; 100 34th Ave., San Francisco, CA 94122, at Clermont St., in Lincoln Park), which specializes in Rodin sculpture.

The performing arts are still another of San Francisco's many lures. The *San Francisco Ballet* (415-865-2000; sfballet.org; War Memorial Opera House) is one of the best in the country. The *San Francisco Symphony* (415-864-6000; sfsymphony.org; Davies Symphony Hall) is gaining a national reputation as well, and the *San Francisco Opera* (415-864-3330; sfopera.com; War Memorial Opera House) is one of the Bay Area's great artistic traditions. And while San Francisco is hardly Broadway, the theater district around Union Square is a happening place. The *American Conservatory Theater* (415-834-3200; 30 Grant Ave., San Francisco, CA 94133) is the city's most respected, and small off-Broadway style theaters abound. For something uniquely San Francisco, don't miss the wacky musical revue *Beach Blanket Babylon* (415-421-4222; Club Fugazi, 678 Green St., San Francisco, CA 94133)

As for nightlife, San Francisco offers some top clubs. *The Fillmore* (415-346-6000; thefillmore.com; 1805 Geary St., San Francisco, CA 94115) brings in musicals acts like Crosby, Stills & Nash, Counting Crows, and Megadeath. At *The Warfield* (Ticketmaster: 415-421-TIXS; 982 Market St., San Francisco, CA 94102) recent acts have included P. J. Harvey and David Byrne of Talking Heads fame. San Francisco's *South of Market District* is the place to be seen, a former industrial area with nightclubs on almost every corner.

CHAPTER FIVE
Bon Appetit!
RESTAURANTS & FOOD PURVEYORS

Café Lolo in Santa Rosa has great fare, thanks to inventive chef Michael Quigley.

Thomas Hallstein/Outsight

If wine is "bottled poetry," as novelist Robert Louis Stevenson wrote, then fine dining in Wine Country is its culinary equivalent. As wineries have encroached on the farmland of Napa and Sonoma counties, gourmet restaurants have overtaken the burger joints. The urban sprawl of fine dining hasn't upset the natives and certainly not the tourists. Today, Wine Country is widely known as a delicious place.

There are more restaurants than ever that are worth a visit, running the gamut from palatial chateaux to storefront bistros, along with ethnic eateries offering Mexican, Chinese, and Thai fare. There is more to dining out than just the food, of course. We consider atmosphere, for one. Did the restaurant set the tone for the meal to come? Was it warm, interesting, or unique? Most of all, did it work? Service was also key; after all, you are on vacation and deserve to be pampered. We were most interested in knowing how well the servers knew the menu and could make intelligent comments about particular dishes.

Each restaurant is given a price code, signifying the cost of a single meal including appetizer, entrée, and dessert, but not cocktails, wine, tax, or tip. Reviews are organized first by county, then by city or region, then alphabetically. Food purveyors are grouped alphabetically by type, then name of establishment. Every restaurant appears in the general index, too.

Dining Price Code:

Inexpensive:	Up to $20	Expensive:	$30 to $40
Moderate:	$20 to $30	Very Expensive:	$40 or more

Credit Cards:

AE — American Express   DC — Diner's Club
CB — Carte Blanche   MC — Master Card
D — Discover   V — Visa

NAPA COUNTY RESTAURANTS

Napa

Lunch on the patio at Bistro Don Giovanni.

Chris Alderman

BISTRO DON GIOVANNI
707-224-3300.
4110 St. Helena Hwy., Napa, CA 94558.
On Hwy. 29.
Price: Moderate to Expensive.
Credit Cards: AE, D, DC, MC, V.
Cuisine: Italian.
Serving: L, D.

The seduction begins the moment you approach Bistro Don Giovanni. In the evening, when the porch and the lawn are filled with voices and the air is rich with aromas and music, you feel as though you've been invited to an extravagant party. Take a moment to check out the fabulous Comedia dell'Arte fountain. Inside, the setting is romantic, a high-ceilinged room done in warm tones, white linen, and modern art, with vineyard views through tall windows. The perfume from the open kitchen makes you anxious to get down to business: eating. And what fine business it is. Bistro Don Giovanni has usurped Tra Vigne and Piatti as the best Italian dining in the valley.

Reservations:
  Recommended.
Special Features: Outdoor
  dining.
Handicap Access: Yes.

Donna and Giovanni Scala were the founding chefs of Piatti before opening this restaurant in 1993.

With roots in the country cooking of Italy and France, the food is delightfully straightforward. The menu includes the requisite salads, pasta, and risotto as well as pizza from a white-tiled oven. Salads are first-rate, particularly a beet and spinach salad with golden beets, crumbled English Stilton, and sherry vinaigrette. And the Caesar salad is a classic.

Entrées to recommend include a delirious trenne pasta with tender chunks of lamb and baby artichoke hearts. Try the risotto of the day, particularly grilled chicken with roasted sweet peppers and saffron, a potpourri of textures and flavors. Bravissimo the filet of salmon, seared in a pan for a thin crust to protect its moist and flaky heart. It's served with buttermilk mashed potatoes that may cause plate warfare.

Desserts include sensuously intense sorbets and soul-warming pear and sun-dried cherry crisp. The wine list is mostly Napa and Italian and rather pricey. Service is attentive. This place is a find. Don't miss it!

CELADON
707-254-9690;
  fax 707-254-9692.
1040 Main St, Suite 104,
  Napa, CA 94559.
Closed: Sunday.
Price: Expensive.
Credit Cards: AE, DC, MC,
  V.
Cuisine: California.
Serving: L, D.
Reservations:
  Recommended.
Special Features: Creekside
  dining room.
Handicap Access: Yes.

Celadon masters the art of balance better than most restaurants. Its food is top-rate, its service is intelligent and well paced, and its décor is refreshing. It's unfortunate but true that most restaurants don't manage to pull it all together and struggle with at least one of the three.

Most impressive at Celadon is the food. Be sure to start with Dungeness Crab Cake with whole-grain mustard sauce. We almost ordered a second helping. The Braised Algerian Style Lamb Shank is moist and exotic with a whisper of fennel and cardamon. The Pan Roasted Chicken Breast with White Truffle Mashed Potatoes may technically be chicken but this is no low-cal dish. Wow!

To top it off, the Mango and Nectarine Fruit Crisp is choice, loaded with moist, bright fruit with a rich crust. The wine list has a good selection by the glass, and prices across the board are reasonable.

The restaurant's name, Celadon, refers to a type of pottery with a pale green glaze, and there are touches of pale green throughout the smart restaurant, pleasing and subtle. The dinning room is small enough that you feel secreted away. In a way you are. The restaurant is tucked behind a downtown storefront, hidden along Napa Creek.

COLE'S CHOP HOUSE
707-224-6328;
  fax 707-254-9692.

Cole's Chop House is slick. A quiet storefront from the outside, inside it's a bustling, cosmo-

1122 Main Street, Napa, CA 94559.
Price: Very Expensive.
Credit Cards: AE, DC, MC, V.
Cuisine: Steakhouse.
Serving: D.
Reservations: Recommended.
Special features: Creekside patio dining.
Handicap access: Yes.

politan nightclub with a jazz trio playing in the balcony. This place has a pulse. Located inside a circa-1886 building with loftlike 35-foot ceilings, it's a big restaurant with lots of tables and lots of people, but the service is seamless. Besides, Napa is Cabernet country, and that's a wine that demands a slab o' meat.

The beef is all top-of-the line dry-aged Chicago. Real grill masters, of course, are convinced the best steaks are made at home but it's hard to deny the appeal of Cole's. The menu isn't cheap. A prime rib will run you $36, and that's just the steak. Even a potato is extra. But the à la carte side dishes are family-style huge, so two people can share.

Appetizers are typical steak-house fare — Oysters Rockefeller and the like. The Grilled Mexican Prawn Cocktail has plenty of gusto, although the prawns were overcooked. The Center Cut Pork Chop is nicely done, savory, but it lacks a little something. On the other hand, Cole's "Famous" Porterhouse steak is a huge piece of meat, and it was tender, juicy powerfully flavored. For dessert, the Scotch Whisky Bread Pudding sounds tempting, but it was overdone and pasty.

The wine list has a good selection of half bottles and more than a dozen offerings by the glass. There's a good showing of French wines and some older California library wines.

NAPA VALLEY WINE TRAIN
707-253-2111, 800-427-4124.
1275 McKinstry St., Napa, CA 94559.
Price: Very Expensive.
Credit Cards: AE, D, DC, MC, V.
Cuisine: California.
Serving: SB, L, D.
Reservations: Required.
Special Features: Train ride through heart of Napa Valley.

This is one of the biggest disappointments in Wine Country. The train itself is a gloriously restored vintage beauty, and the trip through Napa Valley is a charming and scenic adventure. But oh the price! A dinner excursion tops $150, and the food is adequate at best. A safer bet is riding the deli lunch.

The train, traveling 15 to 25 miles per hour, traverses 21 miles of track from Napa to St. Helena and back again in three hours. As you dine, you glide past world-famous vineyards and wineries. Some locals feel the Wine Train is too "Disneyland," and there is an element of that in the canned commentary that continually crackles "Ahead to your left . . ." through the train's speakers. The train may begin making stops along the way if plans proceed, but staying on board is not a bad proposition, considering the polished mahogany and brass, the velvet swag curtains, etched glass, and white table linens set with bone china. A car with a glass dome was added to the line in 1997.

Meals are prix fixe, and the menu is sorely limited. Dinner typically begins in the lounge car with a pleasant plate of herbed goat cheese, chicken liver and truffle mousse, and olives. Once in the dining car, guests typically select from one of four entrées. The mixed grill — lamb chop, pork tenderloin, and chicken — recalled a July 4th barbecue: tasty but not memorable. If you like poached Pacific salmon, avoid the menu's waterlogged offering. A lobster sauce fails to resuscitate it. Dessert is equally uninspired. The wine list is solid, with a variety available by the glass. Service is genuine but lacks the polish of restaurants in this price range.

SILVERADO RESORT
Two restaurants: Royal Oak
   and Vintner's Court.
707-257-0200;
   fax 707-257-2867.
www.silveradoresort.com.
1600 Atlas Peak Rd., Napa,
   CA 94558.
Closed: Vintner's Court,
   Mon. & Tues.
Price: Very Expensive.
Credit Cards: AE, DC, MC,
   V.
Cuisine: American in Royal
   Oak; California-Asian in
   Vintner's Court.
Serving: D; SB Vintner's
   Court.
Reservations:
   Recommended.

If you don't mind the country-club atmosphere — golf is king at Silverado — the Royal Oak is a good place for thick steaks and chops. The valley's oldest resort (see Chapter Three, *Lodging*), the heart of Silverado is a venerable 1870s mansion built by Gen. John Miller. The Royal Oak had a much-needed face-lift a few years back, and the room is now done in welcoming warmer hues.

At Royal Oak, the Caesar salad is tasty, and the seafood sampler, which includes fresh oysters and clams, is a refreshing overture. Grilled options include an impeccable New York sirloin and a winning duck breast, accented with a black peppercorn butter sauce. At Vintner's Court, the menu is heavy on seafood, and presentation clearly outshines flavor. Starters include tiger eye, ahi sushi with a tempura crust that's yummy enough but not memorable. Entrées include a casserole of baked lobster, scallops, and shrimp in a garlic glaze and served with two crab cakes. The casserole is surprisingly dull and the crab cakes mealy and lifeless. Ditto the grilled prawns in a sake marinade.

The Pan-Asian menu at Vintner's Court is more adventuresome than Royal Oak's but less successful. Vintner's Court is dimly lit, a masculine room with lots of handsome dark wood, and the restaurant's big draw is the Friday night seafood buffet. It's an impressively large spread although the quality will only dazzle landlovers. A half Maine lobster is included, and it usually tastes as though it has been cooking since Tuesday. Still, there's plenty of tasty shrimp and seafood pasta dishes.

Desserts in both restaurants are afterthoughts. Each restaurant has an extensive wine list, high priced and exclusively Napa Valley. Mysteriously, vintage dates are often absent. Service is competent but not at the level you expect for the price.

TUSCANY
707-258-1000.
1005 First St., Napa, CA
   94559.
Price: Moderate to
   Expensive.

Tuscany is a bustling bright-lights kind of stop in the city of Napa. With a full bar along one side of the restaurant, it has a nightclub feel: lots of people with a drink in hand making noisy conversation.

Credit Cards: AE, D, MC, V.
Cuisine: Italian.
Serving: L. Mon.–Fri, D daily.
Reservations: Accepted only for parties of 6 or more.
Handicap Access: Yes.

The food is good, not great. For Italian food, it's a good second choice after nearby Bistro Don Giovanni. The menu is big — and so are the portions — and all the Italian classics are offered. Start with roasted fresh vegetables served with various sauces, and you won't regret it. (Vegetarians could even make a meal of it.) The Fettuccine Al Pescatore is a pleasing stew of fresh mussels, jumbo shrimp and fish. The saffron tomato broth had a nice kick of spice. The Pollo Arrosto is too often overcooked and lacks that fresh juiciness you expect in a fine roasted bird.

The wine list has a good selection of wines by the glass for both reds and whites, nearly 20 of each. Great selection of Italian wines pinot grigio, sangiovese, chianti, etc. Prices are standard.

As for décor, the restaurant emulates a Tuscan village, compete with fake windows, a fake tile roof and murals. The big dinning room is done up in clay and tan colors, and an open kitchen runs along one side of it.

Yountville

The entry at Bistro Jeanty is quaint, charming, and utterly French.

Thomas Hallstein/Outsight

BISTRO JEANTY
707-944-0103.
www.bistrojeanty.com.
6510 Washington St.,
    Yountville, CA 94599
Price: Expensive.
Credit Cards: MC, V.
Cuisine: French.
Serving: L, D.
Reservations: Yes.

After preparing the meticulously elaborate creations at Domaine Chandon for years, chef Philippe Jeanty returned to his roots in 1998 and opened this delightful bistro. The idea, he said, was to create the French country comfort food he grew up with in Champagne. It's hard not to be won over by Jeanty's menu, which is ripe with classics like cassoulet, daube de boeuf, and escargots.

A favorite is Coq au Vin, a hearty red wine stew

Special features: Outdoor dining.
Handicapped Access: Yes.

of moist chicken and mushrooms: delicious. The Ragout de Lapin — rich with rabbit, sweetbread, white beans, and truffle oil — is such an understated concoction that we wished it had a bit more joie de vivre. Pâtés are a specialty of the house, and be sure to try the Rillettes de Canard, a blend of duck and goat cheese. For dessert, go with a sure thing: Crêpe Suzette. There's a reason it's a classic.

The restaurant is a clay-colored storefront in the heart of Yountville. The interior sets a soothing tone with antiques, French restaurant signs, and plenty of elbowroom. The wine list won't impress stuffy collectors; it's a small and impeccable list selected strictly with the menu in mind.

Bouchon is a bistro right off the streets of Paris.

Thomas Hallstein/Outsight

BOUCHON
707-944-8037.
6534 Washington St.,
    Yountville, CA 94599.
Price: Expensive.
Credit Cards: AE, MC, V.
Cuisine: French.
Serving: L, D.
Reservations: Yes.
Special features: Outdoor dining.
Handicapped Access: Yes.

If Bistro Jeanty down the road is trying to corner the market on French country bistros, then Bouchon has Paris in mind. The mood is distinctly urban. Noted New York designer Adam Tihany — famous for Cirque 2000, among others — created a chic den with burgundy, velvet, bold mosaics, and a zinc raw bar handcrafted in France. If this sounds elaborate even by Napa Valley standards, there's good reason: The man behind it is Thomas Keller of The French Laundry. Still, the restaurant had a shaky start in late 1998 but has bloomed into one of the best dining experiences in Wine Country.

If Bouchon has the authentic feel of an upscale brasserie, then it has a menu to match. Specialties include an incredible steak frites (French for steak with fries) and an equally addictive Poulet à la Niçoise, roasted chicken with a ragout of artichokes, onions, and olives. The terrine of duck foie gras is an indulgence worthy to begin any meal, but for something lighter, sample from the raw bar. The oysters are impeccable. The wine list is sharply focused on wines that bring out the menu's best, and prices are average. Service is first-rate, and Bouchon stays open late; the bar is one of the busiest and classiest in the valley.

BRIX
707-944-2749.
www.brix.com.
7377 St. Helena Hwy.,
    Yountville, CA 94599.
On Hwy. 29.
Price: Expensive.
Credit Cards: AE, MC, V.
Cuisine: California-Asian.
Serving: L, D.
Reservations:
    Recommended.
Handicap Access: Yes.

When a menu blends Asia and California with as much bravado as Brix, our interest is piqued. The kitchen isn't always up to its own challenge, but Brix has joined the ranks of Napa Valley's best. Opening in the summer of 1996, Brix quickly established itself as one of Wine Country's most elegant restaurants. With its peaked wood ceiling and warm earthy tones, it recalls a private club in the country. Through a wall of windows, the view is gorgeous — an organic garden, vineyard and the rugged Mayacamas mountain range — and lovely sunsets are staged nightly. The service — professional, experienced, and attentive — is so skilled that it's almost inconspicuous, while the wine list is fairly priced, with a fine selection of modestly priced bottles as well as wine by the glass. It's very extensive with an emphasis on local wineries but it includes international selections.

The menu ranges from the simple to the sublime. Baby greens with sesame citrus dressing is tasty as well as the Ahi Sashimi with a sauce that has a great balance of soy and wasabi. Entrées include the Veal Chop and the New York Strip, both perfectly cooked, tender and flavorful. Desserts include an extravagantly constructed apple and cranberry crisp with a bourbon and caramel sauce.

DOMAINE CHANDON
707-944-2892, 800-736-2892.
www.dchandon.com.
1 Calfornia Blvd.,
    Yountville, CA 94599.
At Hwy. 29.
Closed: Mon. & Tues. L in
    winter.
Price: Very Expensive.
Credit Cards: AE, D, DC,
    MC, V.
Cuisine: French, California.
Serving: L, D.
Reservations: Required.
Special Features: Coat
    requested at dinner;
    outdoor dining.
Handicap Access: Yes.

While Domaine Chandon is not the consummate experience it once was — The French Laundry has stolen some of its thunder — it remains one of Wine Country's best. Few restaurants can say as much after 20 years. Granted, it is not for every taste or pocketbook. Housed in a modern curved-concrete building with terrace views of the landscaped grounds, the restaurant is elegant but not pretentious. Servers dote over the table; we don't mind being pampered.

As part of the Domaine Chandon winery, the emphasis is naturally on sparkling wine. The superb wine list covers America and France with a surprisingly low mark-up, particularly for Chandon bubbly, which sells at retail prices.

Philippe Jeanty, chef de cuisine since 1978, left in 1997 and was replaced by Robert Curry. Like Jeanty, Curry envisions food that complements sparkling wine while combining California innovation with the great traditions of French cooking. The menu changes with the seasons. Appetizers include an exquisite, delicate house-smoked trout. The sautéed foie gras with roasted quince, caramelized pearl onions, and port-cinnamon sauce is a towering presentation, but the cherished foie gras seems lost in the shuffle. For entrées, a standard on the menu — and for good reason — is the caramelized sea scallops, brawny medallions seared with a hint of onion and wild mushrooms. Superb. Exotic but thoroughly comforting is the tornedos of venison with a huckleberry merlot sauce and a luxurious sweet potato napoleon.

Dessert is an ungodly affair. Hot gooey chocolate cake is straightforward but dazzling nonetheless. Rich vanilla ice cream tops a fluffy puck of cake with a heart of rich and lavalike filling

The French Laundry, housed in a romantic stone building, is nationally known.

Faith Echtermeyer

THE FRENCH LAUNDRY
707-944-2380.
6640 Washington St.,
    Yountville, CA 94599.
Closed: Mon., and
    Sun.–Tues. L.
Prix fixe: $105–$120.
Credit Cards: AE, M, V.
Cuisine: California-French.
Serving: L, D.
Reservations: Required.
Special Features: Outdoor
    dining, garden; jackets
    required for men.

Not only is the French Laundry the best restaurant in Wine Country, it's one of the best in the country — period. Owner-chef Thomas Keller was named outstanding chef in the U.S. by the prestigious James Beard Foundation. There's a two-month waiting list for reservations. (If you can get them to answer the phone!) The rich and the famous flock here; Robert Redford is a regular, and Mariah Carey was spotted in the dining room recently. This place is hot. Is it worth all the fuss? Yes, if you can afford it. It's easily the most expensive restaurant in Wine Country.

The grand stone house, which was built in 1900,

was a bar and brothel before becoming a French-style laundry. It was a restaurant of considerable distinction even before Keller took over in 1994. He expanded the gardens and the kitchen. The atmosphere is formal — OK, frankly, it's a little stuffy — and jackets are required for men. You're there to quietly worship the food, and we can live with that. You might call Keller's cuisine "California labor-intensive." Every dish is an artistic feat as well as a culinary joy, and when it comes to butter, the kitchen's motto is: No Fear. At night there are two menus: a five-course prix fixe and a nine-course chef's tasting menu. If money is no object, opt for the chef's tasting menu; you won't regret it. Portions are sized appropriately, but be prepared to indulge yourself. The kitchen's pace is unhurried, although service is attentive. Allow at least two or three hours.

There isn't a false step on the menu, and it's impossible to recommend a particular dish because we've seldom had the same thing twice. That's just how creative this kitchen is. And while the food is serious, Keller reveals his sense of humor in naming certain dishes. You might find Macaroni & Cheese on the menu, but it won't be like anything your mom or Kraft ever made. Then there's the signature dessert, Coffee & Doughnuts; you've never had cinnamon-sugared doughnuts so good, and they're served with a cup of coffee-flavored mousse complete with foam.

The wine list is impressive and expensive, with a superb offering of California and French wines. Wines by the glass are lacking.

Save up your allowance, and make reservations at The French Laundry.

MUSTARDS GRILL
707-944-2424.
7399 St. Helena Hwy.,
    Yountville, CA 94599.
On Hwy. 29.
Price: Moderate.
Credit Cards: D, DC, MC, V.
Cuisine: California.
Serving: L, D.
Reservations:
    Recommended.

After all these years, Mustards Grill still lives up to its reputation. Opened since the early 1980s, and brought to you by the same folks who run Tra Vigne, it was one of the earliest players in Napa's burgeoning restaurant boom. Mustards's secret isn't a secret at all: hearty bistro food prepared with style, at a moderate price and in a lively atmosphere. "Truck-stop deluxe" they call it. The open kitchen takes center stage, dominating an intimate dining room that's rich with dark wood, black-and-white tile and broad, open windows. The tables are close, but the din becomes so loud, it lends an air of privacy. While servers seem harried, they are efficient and friendly.

The menu is comfort food with flair. Chicken, duck, rabbit, ribs, and fish are grilled over wood. A must are the onion rings, a heaping pile that comes thinly sliced and highly seasoned. In the summer, don't miss the first-class heirloom-tomato salad with goat cheese toast.

The list of entrées is ever evolving, but a few favorites are constant. The baby-back ribs will disappoint Southern barbecue fanatics, but our mouths water sufficiently. We prefer the simple pleasures of the grilled boneless

They have a sense of humor at Mustards Grill.

chicken breast with black beans and mango salsa. The kitchen has a way with duck, emphasizing its savory gaminess rather than disguising it. Hamburgers, of course, are big and delicious. A disappointment is the grilled portobello mushroom sandwich with roasted peppers, eggplants, and goat-cheese aïoli. The mushroom is soggy and the toppings blasé.

The wine list is well focused and priced fairly. The wine by-the-glass selection is also first-rate. For dessert, try the Jack Daniels Cake. Though rich and deadly, thankfully it carries nowhere near the kick of its namesake.

NAPA VALLEY GRILLE
707-944-8686.
Washington Square, 6795
   Washington St.,
   Yountville, CA 94599.
On Hwy. 29 at Madison
   (Washington Sq.).
Price: Expensive.
Credit Cards: AE, D, DC,
   MC, V.
Cuisine: California.
Serving: SB, L, D.
Reservations:
   Recommended.
Special Features: Outdoor
   dining.
Handicap Access: Yes.

This restaurant may be part of a small chain, but we appreciate its unpretentious tone and varied menu. In the touristy Washington Square shopping complex, Napa Valley Grille is a fine choice for a quick lunch while browsing or for a more luxurious dinner. The café is done in warm colors, and the kitchen is open and its energy flows through the dining room. The Grille's wine list is not voluminous, but it is nicely done, with a fine offering of wines by the glass.

The menu is large and offers a bit of everything, a stretch many kitchens can't handle. Chef Bob Hurley, whose résumé includes Domaine Chandon and Masa's in San Francisco, pulls it off on most days. Starters include an overly tangy Caesar salad and a delicate smoked salmon burdened by an intense sun-dried tomato tapenade. Main courses include a large selection of pastas. Fish, fowl, and meat are roasted over a wood fire. The filet mignon is moist and tender, and served with marvelous bacon-scallion mashed potatoes. Less successful is the grilled boneless chicken breast, overly dry despite a nice tarragon cream sauce. Desserts include an extravagant chocolate sorbet.

RISTORANTE PIATTI
707-944-2070.
6480 Washington St.,
   Yountville, CA 94599.
Price: Moderate to
   Expensive.
Credit Cards: AE, MC, V.
Cuisine: Italian.
Serving: L, D.
Reservations:
   Recommended.
Special Features: Outdoor
   dining.
Handicap Access: Yes.

Piatti is not the brilliant experience it once was, but considering everything — food, atmosphere, wine list, price — it's hard to beat. Like its sister restaurant in Sonoma, Piatti is styled as an Italian trattoria, with tile floors and braids of garlic. The atmosphere is electric — the hum of diners and the open kitchen pulses throughout the airy dining room. Piatti is rustic and elegant at the same time.

The menu offers the best of Tuscany: pasta, pizzas, and grilled meat and fish. The wood-burning pizza oven produces pies with crusts lighter than air. Starters included a superlative Salmon Carpaccio with Citrus Mascarpone. Equally good is the Torta Capra Formaggio, a delicate and flaky onion tart with fresh farmers cheese.

Entrées include a delightfully fiery Tagliolini con Funghi Arrabiato, thin pasta strands with roasted portabello mushrooms and chili peppers. More understated but no less satisfying is the Ravioli al Limone o Pomodoro, pasta in a tangy lemon sauce. The kitchen has a way with traditional Italian roasted meats, particularly a crisp yet juicy spit-roasted game hen served with creamy arborio rice.

Napa and Italian wines are available, with a hearty Chianti and a few others served by the glass. There's nothing out of the ordinary on the dessert menu, which ranges from gelato to an adequate strawberry crisp. Service is competent but harried.

Oakville/Rutherford

AUBERGE DU SOLEIL
707-967-3111.
www.aubergedusoleil.com.
180 Rutherford Hill Rd.,
   Rutherford, CA 94573.
Credit Cards: AE, D, MC, V.
Price: Very Expensive.
Serving: B, L, D.
Reservations: Required.
Special Features: View,
   outside dining.
Handicap Access: Yes.

If you want a postcard view of Napa Valley, a tapestry woven of vineyards, make a reservation at Auberge du Soleil. Make sure you slip in early enough to grab a table on the outside deck. The check may cause a double take, but the experience is well worth it. Auberge du Soleil, or "Inn of the Sun," is Wine Country's most luxurious resort (see Chapter Three, *Lodging*). The restaurant, a page from *Metropolitan Home* magazine, suggests a villa in southern France, done in soft pastels and accented with rough-hewn wood, a large hearth, and bold arrangements of fresh flowers.

The food is every bit as spectacular as the views and as comforting as the surroundings.

Menus change with the season. Breakfast might begin with griddled corn-bread or hickory-smoked trout scrambled eggs. Lunch might offer chilled salmon, a tasting plate of Middle Eastern specialties, or jerk-spiced shrimp. Dinner entrées could include the Wolf Ranch Quail and the Rabbit Tenderloin, both top-rate. The quail is tender with a crisp skin, a good balance of textures and flavors. The Rabbit Tenderloin is also choice. It's tender and flavorful, with braised celery and stuffed morels.

Desserts are typically dramatic creations. Consider the extravagant Warm Chocolate Gateau and Fresh Cherry Ice Cream, Cherry Thyme Gastrique or the Local Blueberry Tart with Honey Lavender Mascarpone, Cassis Reduction.

Although pricey, the wine list is one of the best in Northern California, with an extensive selection of wine by the glass, including champagne. Service, too, is impeccable but never overly attentive.

LA TOQUE
707-963-9770.
1140 Rutherford Rd.,
    Rutherford, CA 94573.
At Rancho Caymus.
Prix fixe: $79.
Credit Cards: AE, D, MC, V.
Cuisine: Contemporary
    French.
Closed: Monday, Tuesday.
Serving: L Sun., D.
Reservations: Yes.
Special Features: Outdoor
    dining.
Handicapped Access: Yes.

Following the lead of other star chefs, Ken Frank said good-bye to Los Angeles and transplanted to Napa Valley in 1998. The result is La Toque, a romantically chic restaurant that makes you feel like you're in the French countryside. It specializes in contemporary French cuisine, and if presentation is less fanciful than The French Laundry down the road, the food is not far behind. The five-course prix fixe menu is a series of indulgences, from Sucking Pig with fresh Corn Polenta to Antelope with Spaetzle. Don't pass on the additional cheese course, an exceptional offering of fromage. The wine list is practically a book, put together by a team of very wine-savvy people. The service is also top-rate, intelligent, and nimble. The restaurant is a great addition to Napa Valley, clearly one of Wine Country's finest.

RUTHERFORD GRILL
707-963-1792.
1180 Rutherford Rd.,
    Rutherford, CA 94523.
On Hwy. 29 at Rutherford
    Crossroad.
Price: Moderate to
    Expensive.
Credit Cards: AE, MC, V.
Cuisine: American.
Serving: L, D.
Reservations: Not accepted.
Handicap Access: Yes.

So you discovered a big burly cabernet sauvignon while wine tasting? What do you eat with it? California cuisine is not always cabernet friendly, so the arrival of Rutherford Grill in 1994 filled a Napa Valley niche: steak.

The prime rib and filet mignon may not be the best you've ever had, but the beef is tasty and generally tender, and the portions are generous. Steaks and baby-back ribs are grilled over hardwood, and you can watch as your chicken roasts slowly on a spit. The rotisserie chicken can be on the dry side, but it's usually tasty. Appetizers include Maytag Blue Cheese Potato Chips, a less than impressive mound of plain chips topped and quickly saturated by warm cheese. Better is the smoked salmon appetizer served with a dill mayonnaise and tiny toasts. Desserts include a home-made Oreo ice cream sandwich with chocolate sauce, a surprisingly addictive confection.

A modern façade along Highway 29, Rutherford Grill says "chain," and it is one of 30 similar eateries. The atmosphere is classy in a casual sort of way, with a decor that's steak-house-meets-nightclub: dark wood and leather. The open kitchen and table chatter generates a constant hum, yet the booths with overhead lights create a sense of intimacy. The patio is busy at lunch when hamburgers are popular. The wine list is narrow but well focused on Napa, and the service is deft.

St. Helena

PINOT BLANC
707-963-6191.
641 Main St., St. Helena, CA 94574.
On Hwy. 29.
Price: Expensive.
Credit Cards: AE, MC, V.
Cuisine: California, French.
Serving: L, D.
Reservations: Recommended.
Handicap Access: Yes.
Special Features: Outdoor dining.

Joachim Splichal, celebrity chef and owner of Los Angeles' famed Patina Restaurant, opened this bistro with considerable fanfare in the summer of 1996. Splichal is hardly the first star chef to came to Napa. Jeremiah Tower and Thomas Keller arrived first. Pinot Blanc got off to a wobbly start but has finally joined the ranks of Terra and The French Laundry as one of the valley's top restaurants.

Pinot Blanc's blandly conservative interior was given a much-needed freshening up in 1999. The atmosphere is now light and lively. In the summer, the patio is the place to be, where an open hearth shoos away the cool Wine Country evening breeze. The wine list is excellent; the prices are a notch higher than the going rate, but the wine-by-the-glass selection has improved significantly. Service is professional yet often too harried.

The menu offers an expansive list of warm and cold starters but only a modest slate of entrées. The food is innovative yet hearty, and the presentations unfussy. Starters include Seared Scallops with Truffle Vinaigrette, smoky-crispy outside and meltingly tender within; simply brilliant. For entrées, fish seems to be a forte, particularly the Planked Atlantic Salmon with Shallot-Apple Smoked-Bacon Crust. Equally good is the Herb-Crusted Sea Bass; a toasty coating hides a fluffy interior.

Comfort food doesn't get any better than the Grilled Marinated Pork Chop, a monstrous cut that melts off the fork. It's served with hearty horseradish mashed potatoes.

Pinot Blanc's dessert menu has also improved of late, offering both decadence and the simple fruitful pleasures of the season. The Chocolate Croissant Pudding, a variation on bread pudding, is a pleasing way to end a meal.

MIRAMONTE
707-963-1200.

Miramonte is something of an island in Wine Country, a festive place where people have

1327 Railroad Ave., St.
Helena, CA 94574.
Price: Expensive.
Credit Cards: Discover, V,
MC, DC.
Cuisine: Fusion of North,
South, and Central
American cuisines.
Serving: L, D.
Reservations:
Recommended.
Special Features: Full bar,
patio seating.
Handicap Access: Yes

more on their mind than cabernet. We are particularly fond of this place, and we're not the only ones. It's packed most weekend nights — and that says a lot because the place is huge, with seating for 100-plus. Miramonte is unique for two reasons. Its cuisine is a fusion of North, South and Central American flavors, and it has a full bar with wild drinks like the Kentucky Corn-Fed Martini and the Bloody Mira. This place is witty and, for the most part, tasty.

The Sugar and Spice Pork Chop with apple mashed potatoes and hard cider sauce is a creative endeavor. Plenty of sweet flavors to savor, perhaps a tad too cloying in the end. More masterful is the Southern Fried Rabbit, done fried-chicken style, with a tart and crispy crust and a tender interior. The Coconut Tres Leches is a bit unfocused, but it has pleasant flavors.

The wine list showcases wines of the Americas, including some great values from Chile and Argentina. A refreshing twist. And the drinks menu play up both the classic and the exotic.

Miramonte is light and breezy with exposed rafters, custard walls, and pine floors. While the food could be better across the board — the restaurant opened in 2001 and is still working out a few bugs — Miramonte is a welcome retreat from traditional the Wine Country cuisine.

THE RESTAURANT AT MEADOWOOD

707-963-3646, 800-458-8080.
www.meadowood.com.
900 Meadowood Ln., St.
Helena, CA 94574.
Price: Very Expensive.
Credit Cards: AE, DC, MC,
V.
Cuisine: California, Country
French.
Serving: SB, D.
Reservations:
Recommended.
Special Features: Resort
setting, outdoor dining.

The restaurant at Meadowood, at the foot of Howell Mountain in St. Helena, is nestled in a bucolic, wooded setting. The restaurant draws almost exclusively guests of Meadowood Resort (see Chapter Three, *Lodging*), but it's worth seeking out if you can afford the tab. The dining room is modest in size, but the scope is broadened by a cathedral ceiling with exposed beams and views of the plush grounds of Meadowood. The atmosphere is distinctly New England. Although the wine list is weighted to Napa, it also has some Sonoma and European selections. And it's an impeccable list, selected by John Thoreen, Meadowood's learned yet refreshingly down-to-earth wine pro. In addition to the regular menu, prix-fixe dinners are offered.

Appetizers include Sauteed Sea Scallops and Forni Brown Baby Greens. The scallops, in a champagne butter sauce, have delicate flavors and textures. Just a tad overcooked. The greens are a tasty balance of sweet, savory, and acidic. As for the entrées, the Pan Roasted Halibut is choice. It's cooked perfectly, moist and exceptionally flavorful.

Desserts are outstanding. The Summer Berry Pudding is delicious as well as beautiful. Teaming with strawberries, blueberries, and blackberries, it's not oversweetened. It just basks in natural flavors. The Flourless Chocolate Cake is sinful, decadent and delicious. Wowie wow wow.

Courtesy Terra

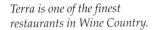

Terra is one of the finest restaurants in Wine Country.

TERRA
707-963-8931.
1345 Railroad Ave., St.
  Helena, CA 94574.
Closed: Tues.
Price: Very Expensive.
Credit Cards: MC, V.
Cuisine: California-Asian.
Serving: D.
Reservations: Required.
Special Features: In the
  historic Hatchery
  Building.

At Terra, East meets West, and the restaurant's Asian influence leaves an indelible mark on California cuisine. Terra's chef, Hiroyoshi Sone, succeeds with daring entrées such as sea bass marinated in sake. The setting is the historic Hatchery Building, and the decor is crisp and elegant: high ceilings, tall arched windows, and fieldstone walls. The duo behind Terra has an impressive resume. Sone led the kitchen at Wolfgang Puck's Spago in Los Angeles, and his wife, Lissa Doumani, was a pastry chef.

Appetizers may include a remarkable lobster flan, a rich but not sweet lobster custard with a touch of curry, or a marvelously realized terrine of foie gras with pear and black currant chutney. Specialty entrées include grilled salmon topped with Thai red curry sauce, an ingenious pairing, and the aforementioned sea bass, which is broiled to a fluffy consistency then paired with shrimp dumplings in shiso broth. Brilliant. Also consider the grilled breast of duck with wild mushroom and salsify vol-au-vent.

The desserts are enticing and you can't miss with the apple and quince tart served with caramel ice cream: a knockout. The wine list is superb with many selections in the $15 to $30 range, and the by-the-glass selection has recently improved. The service at Terra is always attentive, gracious, and knowledgeable. Terra is a rare find indeed.

TOMATINA
707-967-9999.
1016 Main St., St. Helena,
    CA 94574.
Price: Moderate.
Credit cards: D, MC, V.
Cuisine: Italian.
Serving: L, D.
Reservations: Not accepted.

This family-friendly house of pizza has a stylishly casual atmosphere and reasonable prices, which makes it a good lunch stop while you're touring the valley. The dining room is big and airy, with a brick wood-fired pizza oven in full view. There are small tables and large communal tables that seat 12 or more. Don't let the laid-back veneer fool you, though; the people behind Tomatina are the same savvy folks behind Tra Vigne and Mustards Grill.

Guests order at the counter when they walk in, and the menu is the same at lunch or dinner. Ironically, the weakest link here is pizza. It's acceptable but blah. Better is something called piadine, a basic pizza topped with salad, which you fold and eat like a taco; the grilled chicken version is wonderful. The minestrone soup is solid, but the Caesar salad is only adequate. The wine list is appealingly no-nonsense: Everything is $18 a bottle or $3.75 a glass.

TRA VIGNE
707-963-4444.
1050 Charter Oak Ave., St.
    Helena, CA 94574.
Price: Expensive.
Credit Cards: CB, D, DC,
    MC, V.
Cuisine: Italian, California.
Serving: L, D.
Reservations: Required.
Special Features: Outdoor
    dining.
Handicap Access: Yes.

One of Napa Valley's most popular restaurants, Tra Vigne is a sensory delight, from the fragrance of roasted garlic wafting through the courtyard to the neo-Gothic atmosphere of the tall stone building to the pool of herb-infused olive oil at your table. The food is generally cooked with a fiery passion. Most dishes linger on the palate (though a few muster only a mediocre rating). The odds are truly in your favor.

Chef Michael Chiarello has described the cuisine as "American food prepared with the heart, hands, and eyes of an Italian." Perhaps part of Chiarello's success is the freshness. Everything is made at the restaurant, including prosciutto, breads, pastas, cheeses, and gelato. Tra Vigne, which means "among the vines," charms its guests with rows of grapevines just outside the courtyard. Inside, the decor is part Italian villa, part Hollywood, with gold stripes on the molding softened by earth tones. The restaurant swarms with beeper-clad waiters, and the service is impeccable.

Appetizers range from a bland selection of house-cured olives to a winning insalata mista: crisp greens with a citrus vinaigrette served with a warm gorgonzola bruschetta. Be sure to try the Oven-Roasted Polenta bathed in balsamic vinegar. For entrées, don't miss the Coniglio alla Griglia, grilled rabbit with a delicate mustard reduction sauce and teleme layers potatoes. Brilliant. Equally good is the Costata di Bue e Polenta, tender and smoky braised short ribs with garlic polenta. The risotto with prosciutto-wrapped shrimp is good, not great. Desserts range from a marvelous blackberry gelato to your average crème brûlée. The wine list offers the finest of Napa and Italy; diners may also bring their own bottle (the corkage fee is modest and often waived entirely).

WINE SPECTATOR GREYSTONE RESTAURANT
707-967-1010.
www.ciachef.edu/gray
home/html.
2555 Main St., St. Helena,
CA 94574.
On Hwy. 29.
Price: Expensive.
Credit Cards: AE, CB, DC,
MC, V.
Cuisine: Mediterranean.
Serving: L, D.
Reservations:
Recommended.
Handicap Access: Yes.

You expect to be impressed by a restaurant affiliated with the Culinary Institute of America (CIA). Perhaps our expectations are too high, but we've always been disappointed in this restaurant. It's a beautiful spot, and it's popular, but the weak link, ironically, is the food. The kitchen has recently shown improvement, but it can't yet compete with Napa Valley's finest.

The atmosphere is promising, if not downright dramatic. The restaurant is in the north wing of the recently restored Greystone Cellars, an historic Wine Country castle once known as Christian Brothers and now home to the West Coast campus of the CIA. With stone walls and a towering ceiling, the room is cavernous and a bit noisy. The decor is accented with bright colors, and three open kitchen stations lend energy. The recent addition of a grand fireplace with a casual seating area has warmed the interior significantly.

Be sure to start with Temptations, a tower of small plates of tasty bites like grilled prawns with pineapple salsa and salmon mousse with pesto and caviar. Delicious. The entrees, sadly, leave us consistently uninspired. Something like the Rotisserie Duck Breast is savory but little more, and the Lobster Minestrone can be curiously tasteless.

For dessert, try a glorious wedge of the Triple Chocolate Cake. After a shaky start, the wine list has come into its own, with an increasingly wide selection and an adequate offering by the glass. Service is professional but slowly paced.

Calistoga

ALL SEASONS CAFÉ
707-942-9111.
1400 Lincoln Ave., Calistoga,
CA 94515.
Closed: Wed. L.
Price: Expensive.
Credit Cards: MC, V.
Cuisine: French, California.
Serving: L, D.
Reservations:
Recommended.
Handicap Access: Yes.

All Seasons Café has an imaginative menu matched with a modest but urbane setting. Ceiling fans spin slowly over stained-glass lights, the floor is done in black, white, and green tile, and through two walls of windows you can watch downtown Calistoga go by. The wine selection is fabulous. All Seasons, in fact, has a wine shop in back of the restaurant, stocked with new and old vintages and all available at your table for a fair price. Service is professional and warm.

The lunch menu focuses on salads, pizzas, pastas, and sandwiches, while dinner emphasizes grilled fish, duck, beef, and chicken. Included is a Mediterranean-style sandwich with grilled eggplant and roasted peppers; it's tasty but a muddle of flavors. Likewise the smoked trout salad. Far better is the penne pasta with smoked chicken and oven-dried tomatoes, and the icy cold gazpacho is just the thing for a hot summer day. Entrées range from the exotic — Pan-Seared Halibut with North African Sweet Spices — to high-brow comfort food like Braised Lamb Shank with Summer Vegetables. Both are fabulous.

After a meal, linger over the dessert menu. Try something indulgent such as an individual deep-dish berry pie or one of the cafe's impeccable house-made sorbets.

BOSKOS TRATTORIA
707-942-9088.
www.boskos.com.
1364 Lincoln Ave., Calistoga, CA 94515.
Price: Moderate.
Credit Cards: MC, V.
Cuisine: Italian.
Serving: L, D.
Reservations: Not accepted.
Handicap Access: Yes.

This Italian eatery moved across the street in 1994. The food is still basic and hearty and the price is right. With sawdust on the floor, the atmosphere is casual and perfect for families; you order at the counter and seat yourself. Lunch and dinner menus are the same, with a half-order pasta special available for lunch during the week. That's good because portions are generous. Pastas range from the basic spaghetti and meatballs to an enjoyable Palermo fettucine with sautéed onions, sausage, and a creamy tomato sauce. There are also sandwiches, Italian sausage, capocollo, and the like, and pizza from a wood-burning stove. The beer and wine list is adequate.

BRANNAN'S GRILL
707-942-2233.
www.brannansgrill.com.
1374 Lincoln Ave., Calistoga, CA 94915.
Price: Expensive.
Credit Cards: AE, MC, V.
Cuisine: California, American.
Serving: L, D.
Reservations: Recommended.
Handicap Access: Yes.

Brannan's Grill is more adventuresome than it seems at first glance. With seating of 200, we expected the menu to be less exciting and the service to be anything but meticulous. Happily we were wrong on both counts.

Consider the specials carefully because they are a class act here. The Thai Snapper is a great example. It comes to your plate whole — fish, fins, and all — after being lathered in olive oil and massaged with garlic and rice flour. The presentation is extraordinary and the dish exceptionally tasty. Another interesting special is the Lobster Pot Pie.

Unfortunately some dishes fall short of the mark. The Grilled Hanger Steak is moist, grilled to perfection, but the Cabernet Jus de Veau seemed like a chemical concoction with no hint of cabernet. And the Soy & Mirin Glazed Sea Bass is flavorless, a major disappointment. As for dessert, the Sky Hill Chevre Cheese Cake with a wild berry compote was plentiful and the sauces delicious, but the actual cake was flavorless.

The wine list showcases Napa Valley wines, but it is careful to include some less traditional varietals. Rhone reds and whites in particular have a nice showing. The list is a bit pricey, mid $30s and up for most, with a good by-the-glass selection.

Service is attentive and efficient.

Named after Calistoga founder George Brannan, the restaurant is a rare blend: It's traditional with an entrepreneurial spirit. And despite some entrées that miss, it's a great addition to the Calistoga dining scene.

CATAHOULA RESTAURANT & SALOON
707-942-2275.
www.catahoularest.com
1457 Lincoln Ave., Calistoga, CA 94515.
Price: Moderate to Expensive.
Credit Cards: D, MC, V.
Cuisine: Southern-inspired American.
Serving: B Sat. & Sun., L Sat. & Sun., D daily.
Reservations: Recommended.

Wine Country was long on oregano and tarragon and short on cayenne until Catahoula came along. Chef-owner Jan Birnbaum blends the refinement of California cuisine with the earthy flavors of his native Louisiana. On a good night, Catahoula is one of the most high-spirited eating adventures north of San Francisco. A protégé of Paul Prudhomme before making his name at New York's Quilted Giraffe, Birnbaum opened Catahoula, named for the state dog of Louisiana, in 1994. Birnbaum is increasingly in demand as a chef-consultant, so the kitchen strays on occasion, sorely needing his attention to detail. The service is disappointing, off tempo.

The main dining room, which has the panache of a big city restaurant and none of the pretension, is done in vivid green and buttermilk, and one wall is dominated by an abstract construction. Birnbaum and his brick oven is center stage.

The food, for the most part, is delicious. The most stunning entrée is the Crispy Fried Catfish with Lemon-Jalapeno Meuniere and Mardi Gras Slaw. Moist beneath the crust. Deliciously spicy. The Spicy Rabbit Gumbo is also a hit. Long on spice. But be sure to save room for the dessert. We've never tasted a better bread pudding. The Sour Cherry and Chocolate Bread Pudding is masterfully done. Rich, with a streak of tart cherry.

The wine list plays up local wines. It could have bigger half bottle offerings, but it has good offerings by the glass.

All in all, this is a place to go when you when your palate tires of California cuisine and craves spice.

WAPPO BAR AND BISTRO
707-942-4712.
www.wappobar.com.
1226 Washington St.,
Calistoga, CA 94515.
Closed: Tues.
Price: Moderate to Expensive.
Credit Cards: AE, MC, V.
Cuisine: Eclectic.
Serving: L, D.
Reservations: Recommended.
Special Features: Outdoor dining.
Handicap Access: Yes.

The world beat is pounding at this warm-blooded bistro. It's suited for adventurous souls, prepared for an eclectic trip around the culinary world, from Latin America to the Mediterranean, to who knows where. Although the kitchen often goes too far, we don't mind going along for the ride. The narrow dining room — with reddish-brown wainscoting and copper-covered tables and lights — blends European bistro with Southwestern warmth. If the weather is warm, the brick courtyard patio, covered with a grapevine arbor, is a must.

Owners Aaron Bauman and Michelle Mutrux opened the restaurant in 1993, and they share kitchen duties. The menu finds an eccentric match in the wine list, which offers more than the usual chardonnay, and at fair prices. Service is efficient and enthusiastic. Lunch includes sandwiches, salads, and the likes of Thai sweet potato fries, a yummy creation made clumsy by thick breading but saved by an addictive coconut and peanut dipping sauce.

Starters for dinner include a hearty Roasted Basilla Chile Relleno with a Walnut-Pomegranate Sauce. The Empanadas of Baccalao (salt cod in pastry) are lovely but they're overpowered by a chipotle mayonnaise. Main courses include Roast Rabbit with Pumpkin Gnocchi in a mushroom cream sauce, which is surprisingly bland and dry. A real treat is the Ugandan Peanut Chicken with roasted yams and banana and coconut rice. Bravo. Desserts explore the globe and include a lovely Steamed Chocolate Cake with Sherry-Chocolate Sauce.

SONOMA COUNTY RESTAURANTS

Sonoma Valley

CAFÉ CITTI
707-833-2690.
9049 Sonoma Hwy.,
Kenwood, CA 95452.
On Hwy. 12
Price: Moderate.
Credit Cards: MC, V.
Cuisine: Italian.
Serving: L, D.
Reservations: Only for 10 or more.
Special Features: Outdoor dining, deli.

A trattoria in the strictest Italian sense — a casual atmosphere with hearty wine and yummy, inexpensive pasta — Café Citti is a pleasure. There's no menu, just a chalkboard on the wall. Customers order from the counter, cafeteria style. Lunch includes sandwiches: sweet Italian sausage and the usual cold deli fare. Pasta is mix and match; choose penne, linguine, etc., and pair it with the sauce (marinara, Bolognese, etc.) of choice. Other offerings include a zesty Caesar salad and homemade focaccia, plus a luxurious risotto with mushrooms and garlic and a traditional Italian herb-roasted chicken that is to die for. For dessert, don't miss the crème brûlée. For those traveling with kids, this is a perfect place to stop.

CAFÉ LA HAYE

707-935-5994.
www.sterba.com/sonoma/
lahaye.
140 E. Napa St., Sonoma, CA
95476.
Closed: Mon.
Price: Expensive.
Credit Cards:
Cuisine: California.
Serving: SB, D.
Reservations:
Recommended.
Special Features: Close to
the Sonoma Square.
Handicap Access: Yes.

Café La Haye is a classy restaurant yet simple in its sophistication. More importantly, the food stands up to the best in Wine Country. If you're looking for a great meal on the Sonoma Square, this is the spot.

Start with the house-smoked salmon with potato pancake, a fresh yet rich prelude to a meal and given a sweet and sour kick by the the apple-horseradish compote. The Seared Black Pepper-Lavender Filet of Beef is perfectly cooked, a rich, juicy concoction, served with a tasty dollop of Gorgonzola-Potato Gratin. The Pan Roasted Chicken Breast, with a goat cheese-herb stuffing, is so good, you'll be tempted to set the fork and knife aside and attack it fried-chicken style.

The wine list complements the menu, and it's well focused with a good selection of wines from Sonoma County and Napa Valley.

As for the décor, the restaurant is tiny but seems spacious, with high wooden rafters and an upper level of seating. And yet the restaurant still manages to feel cozy.

CARNEROS AT THE LODGE AT SONOMA

707-935-6600.
www.carnerosrestaurant.
com.
1325 Broadway, Sonoma,
CA 95476.
Price: Expensive.
Credit Cards: AE, MC, V.
Cuisine: California.
Serving: B, L, D.
Reservations:
Recommended.
Special Features: patio
dining.
Handicap Access: Yes.

Carneros aspires to be a serious dining destination, and it's well on its way. The food is good, on the cusp of superb, and the service shows promise. The restaurant is part of the Lodge at Sonoma, a 182-room complex owned by Renaissance Hotels (see Chapter Three, *Lodging*). Carneros, to explain, is the wine growing region at the southern base of Napa Valley and Sonoma County, and the restaurant emphasizes wines produced from Sonoma County's 11 appellations.

A superb appetizer is the Wood Oven Asparagus with Serrano Ham, Vella's Special Jack, and Truffled Salad. The asparagus, pristinely roasted, is an excellent foil for the rich ham and cheese. For an entrée, the Rotisserie Ribeye Caramelized Shallot Rosti and Cabernet Sauce is as rich as it sounds and is infused with the essence of wine. The Sonoma Lamb Two Ways with Braised Fennel is less successful, hiding the unique flavor of lamb instead of taking advantage of it. For dessert, the Marscapone Trifle with Lemon and

Blackberry is like tiramisù in a big martini glass, and it seems just as intoxicating.

Prices on the wine are the going rate, and service is solid but needs a little polish. The room itself has a large and airy atmosphere, with an open kitchen and cathedral ceiling, but there's something rather generic about the place. Luckily, not so the food.

Have a hearty plate of pasta at Della Santina's.

Chris Alderman

DELLA SANTINA'S
707-935-0576.
133 E. Napa St., Sonoma, CA 95476.
Price: Moderate.
Credit Cards: AE, D, MC, V.
Cuisine: Italian.
Serving: L, D.
Reservations: Recommended.
Handicap Access: Yes.
Special Features: Patio dining.

Ah, the mighty aromas that escape from this café. Don't overlook this Italian trattoria just off bustling Sonoma Plaza. The food is as authentic and unfussy as the best from Mama's kitchen. The Della Santina family opened shop in 1990 but moved a few storefronts east in 1997, taking over the old Eastside Oyster Bar location. In the summer, the intimate dining room gives way to a glorious garden patio, shady and green. The warm din of the kitchen mingles with Puccini and Verdi.

Appetizers include a Caesar salad that's a vibrant cut above the usual, and the antipasto plate is everything it should be, fat with prosciutto and olives. Entrées include a comforting and velvety risotto with shiitake, portobello, and porcini mushrooms. Roasted meats are a specialty, particularly chicken and rabbit, yet quality varies. One meal the chicken is dry and flavorless, the next it's tender and heavenly. We hope the move to a larger space hasn't influenced quality. For dessert, tiramisù is called for, and Della Santina's version is uneven. Sometimes it's a bit dry, while other times it dances on air.

DEUCE
707-933-3823.

The charming 110-year old Victorian farmhouse that's home to Deuce has a sordid past — it

691 Broadway, Sonoma, CA 95476.
Price: Expensive.
Credit Cards: AE, MC, V.
Cuisine: Contemporary American.
Serving: L, D.
Reservations: Recommended.
Special features: Patio and garden area.
Handicap access: Yes.

was a mortuary years ago — but that doesn't scare off customers. It's one of the most popular restaurants in the valley and rightly so.

The menu offers both comfort and adventure. A favorite is the roasted duck prepared with a Chinese five-spice-rub in a hoisin sauce. Incredible. The roasted Chilean sea bass, a great choice for something on the lighter side, is succulent beneath a tasty crust. The rock shrimp and Maine crab cakes are rich and addictive. And the dessert, the fruit cobbler, is a delicious blend of apple and boysenberry.

The wine list is broad, with more than 100 labels and over a dozen offerings by the glass. Good prices, fair prices. We think it's a savvy move to have a non-vintage Kenwood red and white for $3.50 a glass on the list. Service was gracious and well paced. If the weather is warm, ask for a table in the garden patio.

THE GENERAL'S DAUGHTER
707-938-4004.
400 W. Spain St., Sonoma, CA 95476.
Price: Expensive.
Credit Cards: AE, MC, V.
Cuisine: California.
Serving: SB, L, D.
Reservations: Recommended.
Special Features: Outdoor dining.
Handicap Access: Yes.

This 1883 farmhouse is a true showplace. Suzanne Brangham revitalized this once dilapidated pink house, which belonged to Gen. Mariano Vallejo's daughter Natalia, and opened the restaurant in 1994. The place is gorgeous, with lush landscaping, a wide porch, and a classic interior of hardwood floors, antiques, and lively murals. The bar is done in rich Honduran mahogany.

And with chef Joseph Vitale Jr. in the kitchen, the food finally lives up to the lush atmosphere. The lunch menu offers salads and sandwiches, and dinner is traditionally Californian, with selections of fish, beef, and chicken. A standout appetizer is the Crisp Buttermilk Onion Rings, which come as wispy curls piled high and topped with pepper-blue cheese aïoli. Equally good is the vividly flavored Seared Rare Ahi Tostadas with Spiced Avocado and Salsa Fresca. The Grilled Pacific Salmon is flawless, moist, and rich with a ginger and black pepper beurre blanc. While the Oven-Roasted Half Chicken with Lemon-Honey-Rosemary Glaze is less than inspiring, it is altogether comforting. For dessert, try the warm Orange-Bread Pudding with Whiskey-Soaked Currants; it's not cloyingly heavy-handed as are so many bread puddings.

THE GIRL & THE FIG
707-938-3634.
110 W. Spain St., Sonoma, CA 95476.

The Girl & the Fig has its fans even though food and service is maddeningly inconsistent. Certainly, the restaurant's new location — it used to be in Glen Ellen — is both appealing and con-

Price: Expensive.
Credit Cards: AE, MC, V.
Cuisine: French country
   food.
Serving: L, D.
Reservations:
   Recommended.
Handicapped Access: Yes.
Special Features: Right on
   the Sonoma square, patio
   dining.

venient on the Sonoma Plaza, adjacent to the lobby of the Sonoma Hotel. And it's a pretty stop to spend a couple of hours, with tall broad, wood-framed windows and light, mustard-colored walls. The whole place feels breezy.

The menu certainly sounds promising. Take the Lamb Shank with Polenta, Glazed Carrots and Brussel Sprouts. It was dry when it should have been juicy and tender. Much better was the Duck Confit, with Sausage, Lamb, and White Beans, a savory stew. The Fig Salad, a specialty, was also top notch. But the Almost Flourless Chocolate Cake was another disappointment. A flaky puck of chocolate, the cake's texture was all wrong.

On a positive note, the wine list is refreshing, even daring, and fairly priced. It focuses on California-produced Rhone-style wines, with an emphasis on California syrahs. Few will complain that it's limited in scope because there's plenty to choose from, and Rhone-style wines are, aptly, food friendly.

Chris Alderman

Chris and Karen Bertrand of Glenn Ellen Inn.

GLEN ELLEN INN
707-996-6409.
13670 Arnold Dr., PO Box
   1593, Glen Ellen, CA
   95442.
Price: Expensive.
Credit Cards: AE, MC, V.
Cuisine: California fusion.

The Glen Ellen Inn is quaint: small-town, front-porch-swing kind of quaint. Yet somehow in this quiet corner of the world, chef Chris Bertrand holds his own with Wine Country's finest. Bertrand and wife, Karen, expanded their charming cottage restaurant in 1997, adding more tables and enlarging the kitchen. Removable glass windows have been added to the garden room, so now it's

Reservations:
  Recommended.
Special Features: Outdoor
  dining.
Handicap Access: Yes.

open in the summer, snug in the winter. There's also a secluded garden patio. That's a lot of people to serve in the summer. We miss the intimacy. It used to feel like you were eating in the kitchen, it was that close, but at least the new kitchen remains open to the dining room, and the food has certainly not suffered from the expansion. As for service, it's still first-rate, and the wine list specializes in the best Sonoma Valley wines with a smart list by the glass.

Bertrand was schooled at the Fifth Avenue Grill in Manhattan; he cooks with a French accent, relying on fresh, local ingredients. Salads are exceptional. Fall brings a refreshing autumn salad, a mix of greens tossed with mint, fresh fruit, and sweet pecans. Delightful. Starters include Warm Prawn Croquettes, wonderful fish cakes served with fiery chipotle aïoli. Entrées include a nonfat Late-Harvest Ravioli, stuffed with a lively mixture of pumpkin, walnuts, and sun-dried cranberries. The California Jambalaya lives up to its name: a lighter but still flavorful version of the Louisiana classic. For dessert, a wild creation is the White Chocolate Martini, white mousse infused with Bailey's Irish Cream and topped with a chocolate olive (truffle). Oooh.

KENWOOD RESTAURANT AND BAR

707-833-6326.
9900 Sonoma Hwy.,
  Kenwood, CA 95452.
On Hwy. 12.
Closed: Mon. & Tues.
Price: Expensive.
Credit Cards: MC, V.
Cuisine: California.
Serving: L, D.
Reservations:
  Recommended.
Special Features: Outdoor
  dining.
Handicap Access: Yes.

This bistro, a California roadhouse turned upscale, is in the heart of the Valley of the Moon, one of the most beautiful spots in Wine Country. The patio offers marvelous views of Sugar Loaf Ridge, where vineyards rib the lower slopes. The charm of sipping wine made nearby should not be underestimated, and Kenwood's wine list is a Who's Who of Sonoma Valley vintners.

The decor and chef Max Schacher's food are well matched — both paint a refined picture with subtle strokes. The dining rooms have steep wood ceilings and are done in muted tones brightened by colorful paintings. Likewise, Schacher believes in artistic presentation paired with a sense of understatement, with dishes that emphasize the quality of local duck or fish rather than exotic creations. Frankly, we would like more adventure. Also, the same menu is served lunch and dinner, which makes for a pricey lunch.

Appetizers range from a lively salad of fresh Sonoma greens topped with Roquefort to baked oysters served with an unusual but winning combo of sauerkraut and lemon cream sauce. Entrées include an agreeable pepper-crusted seared ahi tuna with black beans and mangos. Even better is the mushroom linguini with grilled chicken breast, portabello mushrooms, and a lavish goat-cheese sauce. With dessert, relive your childhood with the likes of a brownie sandwich, two chunky cakes with vanilla ice cream and warm caramel sauce. Oooh. Service is always attentive.

MUCCA
938-3451.
14301 Arnold Dr., Glen
  Ellen, CA 95442.
Closed: Mon., Tues. & Wed.
Price: Expensive.
Credit Cards: AE, D, M, V.
Cuisine: Italian.
Serving: D.
Reservations:
  Recommended.
Special Features: Patio
  dining by Sonoma Creek.
Handicap Access: Yes.

Mucca serves authentic Italian food right down to the fresh pasta made in the kitchen. The food is less than inspired, but it's hard to complain in such a pleasant atmosphere. The location — which has been many restaurants over the years — is a circa-1860 mill. It's rustic chic: wooden floors, mustard-colored walls, and vibrant paintings. If the weather is warm, ask for a spot on the desk and listen to the patter of Sonoma Creek nearby.

Brace yourself for caloric cuisine. The Four Cheese Pizza is a thin-crusted pie topped with a rich blend of cheeses: mozzarella, fontina, provolone, and Parmesan. Pizza Hut this isn't! The Pork T-Bone Mostarda di Sonoma is another first-rate pick, savory and cooked to perfection. The Homemade Fries are as thick as carrots, fresh and never greasy. But you'll want to pass on the Peach and Blackberry Crisp. It's a pool of goo with muddled flavors.

Service is pleasant enough but not always savvy, and the wine list is also disappointing because it doesn't play up Italian wines, not even California-produced sangioveses. That said, Mucca does have a range of interesting cabernet sauvignons and merlots. But be forewarned: Prices are high across the board.

RISTORANTE PIATTI
707-996-2351.
405 1st St. W., Sonoma, CA
  95476.
Price: Moderate to
  Expensive.
Credit Cards: AE, DC, MC,
  V.
Cuisine: Italian.
Serving: L, D.
Reservations:
  Recommended.
Special Features: Outdoor
  dining.
Handicap Access: Yes.

Like its twin in Napa Valley, this Piatti is a fun and festive Italian trattoria, with terra-cotta floors and bright murals of tomatoes, asparagus, and braids of garlic. The patio is tranquil, removed from the busy Sonoma Plaza, while the main room hums with happy diners, and the wonderful fragrance of the open kitchen envelops the room like olive oil. Now only if the food matched the atmosphere.

The menu delivers the best of Tuscany: pasta, pizzas, and grilled meat and fish. Starters included an overly salty house-cured salmon and a dull and soggy insalata verde. Better is the bruschetta, a luscious pairing of ripe marinated tomatoes with grilled bread. The wood-burning pizza oven produces pies with crisp and light crusts, particularly a margherita pizza with tantalizing fennel salami. The traditional Italian herb-roasted chicken is good, not great. Pastas include a disappointing Pappardelle Fantasia, a bland concoction of mushy saffron pasta, arugula, and shrimp. A solid selection of Sonoma and Italian wines are available, with a hearty chianti and a few others served by the glass. Desserts range from gelato to a scrumptious warm chocolate bread pudding.

SADDLES
707-933-3191.
www.macarthurplace.com.
29 E. MacArthur St.,
　Sonoma, CA 95476.
Price: Moderate to
　Expensive.
Credit Cards: AE, MC, V.
Cuisine: Steak and seafood.
Serving: L,D.
Reservations:
　Recommended.
Special features: Patio
　dining; part of MacArthur
　Place resort.
Handicap access: Yes.

If you want order up 10-ounce martini and a steak on the side, this is the place to go. Saddles is located in the MacArthur Place resort. (See Chapter Three, *Lodging*.) In Wine Country, a good steak house is a rare find, and the prime cut meats here are outstanding. But don't expect to be wowed by the service.

The Western theme carries throughout the restaurant: cowboy boots, hats and branding irons. A bit overdone. But the steaks make up for it. The 10-ounce Filet Mignon, the 14-ounce New York Strip, and the 24-ounce Porterhouse for Two are great cuts of meat, cooked impeccably. Our only complaint is that the Porterhouse for two didn't seem to satisfy two carnivores. As for the side dishes, the Red Cornmeal Haystack Onion Rings with Blue Cheese Aïoli and the Potato au Gratin, while slightly greasy, still manage to be tasty. Opt for the homemade raspberry ice cream over the peach crisp if you have the option. The ice cream has an excellent texture, and while the raspberry is a bit tart, it's still delicious.

The wine list has a good, solid selection of newer, mostly California wines. Prices are reasonable. A plus: great martini offerings!

SANTE — SONOMA
MISSION INN
707-939-2415, 800-862-4945.
www.sonomamission
inn.com.
18140 Sonoma Hwy.,
　Sonoma, CA 95416
Hwy. 12 at Boyes Boulevard.
Serves: Dinner 6–9 daily.
Price: Expensive.
Credit Cards: AE, MC, V.
Cuisine: California,
　Oriental.
Reservations:
　Recommended.
Special Features: Poolside
　setting, handsome dining
　room.
Handicap Access: Yes.

The renovated restaurant at the Sonoma Mission Inn has a different look . . . and taste. Sante is dark and handsome, refurbished in the Mission style, a better fit with the hotel (see Chapter Three, *Lodging*). It has ark wood beams, iron chandeliers, and wooden floors. As for the food, it's more international in scope, with sushi and dim sum sharing equal status on the menu with tandoori-baked flat breads.

But it's never a good sign when the best thing you can say about a restaurant is its décor. Some things haven't changed. The food still doesn't live up to the price. Appetizers include Pan-Seared Sonoma Foie Gras and Clay-Oven Roasted Prawns. Sadly, the Chicken Kabobs with Four Flavors seem to be missing three. As for entrées, the Two Presentations of Liberty Duck was nearly a disaster. The Crispy Duck Confit seemed hurried — and you can't hurry confit; the flavors need time to come together — and the Grilled Duck Breast was downright a snore.

The wine list is one of the best in Sonoma County, although it comes at premium. If you're a hotel guest and prefer to dine in rather than out, this is a comfortable spot. But if you have the energy, there are far better places to dine nearby.

Santa Rosa

Café Lolo in Santa Rosa is a popular spot for Wine Country diners.

Thomas Hallstein/Outsight

CAFÉ LOLO
707-576-7822.
www.cafelolo.com.
620 5th St., Santa Rosa, CA 95404.
Closed: Sun.
Price: Moderate to Expensive.
Credit Cards: AE, DC, MC, V.
Cuisine: California.
Serving: L, D.
Reservations: Recommended.
Handicap Access: Yes.

This 5th Street storefront has seen many incarnations over the years, but Café Lolo has endured — and for good reason. Chef Michael Quigley's food is inventive yet comforting, plus entrées are priced reasonably, and portions are generous. If we have any criticism, it's the dining room itself. The tables are close together, a bit intrusive if you're on a romantic night out. The elegant decor has recently taken on warmer tones, a welcome improvement.

The food is the main attraction here. Starters include terrine of grilled eggplant, roasted peppers, and Laura Chenel goat cheese as well as a phenomenal house-cured salmon on a jumbo corn pancake. The spiral of salmon sprouts from the plate like a gladiolus. At lunch, don't miss the Grilled Vegetable Sandwich, served with goat cheese on foccacia. Dinner entrées include an appealing Sautéed Filet of Salmon on a bed of green lentils and a fine Pan-Roasted Liberty Duck doused in a port wine sauce. For dessert, try the house special Chocolate Kiss, a temptingly rich puck of chocolate in a puddle of raspberry sauce. Nonchocoholics won't be disappointed with the lemon and rasp-berry sorbet, adorned with a dollop of fresh fruit. The wine list is brief but well chosen, with an excellent selection by the glass.

JOHN ASH & CO.
707-527-7687, 800-421-2584.
4330 Barnes Rd., Santa Rosa,
   CA 95403.
Price: Very Expensive.
Credit Cards: AE, D, MC, V.
Cuisine: California.
Serving: SB, L, D.
Reservations:
   Recommended.
Special Features: Outdoor
   dining.

Chef John Ash continues to pioneer Wine Country cuisine — his book on the subject won a Julia Child Cookbook Award in 1996 — but today, he has nothing to do with the daily opera-tion of the restaurant. His protégé, Jeff Madura, lacks the brilliance of Ash, but the restaurant remains a destination. Madura strives to make each entrée a masterpiece by tending to taste, texture, color, and design.

The lunch menu offers imaginative salads and sandwiches such as a brilliant grilled portobello mushroom club on focaccia. The dinner menu is ever changing. Starters range from crab cakes suc-culently paired with a mild salsa to a simple yet spectacular organic tomato and fresh mozzarella salad.

Entrées vary from a modestly priced margherita pizza to an oven-roasted cedar plank salmon with warm basil cream. A grilled pork tenderloin with a berry-cherry mostarda, served with roasted garlic mashed potatoes, is win-ning, although the berry-cherry sauce is on the sweet side. Better is the smoked and grilled rack of lamb with basalmic reduction sauce; a generous cut of lamb, it is velvety tender.

Desserts include a dramatic creation called Chocolate Stonehenge, an elabo-rate construction of chocolate pâté crusted with walnuts, pine nuts, and hazel-nuts served with a raspberry reduction sauce. Death by dessert, it was as rich as a Godiva truffle. The wine list is one of the best in Wine Country and the by-the-glass selection is excellent. The service staff is attentive and pampering. The setting is a bucolic site next to Vintners Inn (see Chapter Three, *Lodging*), with vineyard views through French windows. The interior had a subtle yet welcome makeover a few years back; once starkly elegant, it now has warm accents of natural wood and teal.

MIXX
707-573-1344;
   fax 707-573-0631.
www.mixxrestaurant.com.
135 4th St., Santa Rosa, CA
   95401.
Closed: Sun.
Price: Expensive.
Credit Cards: AE, DC, MC,
   V.

Where do locals go for great food? Right here. A cornerstone in historic Railroad Square, MiXX also draws its share of tourists. The menu is eclectic, the wine is reasonably priced, and the atmosphere is intimate and elegant without being stuffy. Expanding into the adjacent storefront a few years back, MiXX added elbowroom without sacrificing its Art Nouveau ambiance. The main room is dominated by a magnifi-cent oak and mahogany bar, which was built in Italy

MiXX has a stylish Art Nouveau interior.

Cuisine: California.
Serving: L Mon.–Fri., D
   Mon.–Sat.
Reservations:
   Recommended.
Handicap Access: Yes.

in the late 1800s, shipped to New York, and finally arrived at its present destination around 1904.

Chef Dan Berman oversees the kitchen, leaving wife, Kathleen, to concentrate on desserts. The menu is divided between small plates and large, but the kitchen can enlarge small plates and vice versa. The Bermans take influences from around the culinary world: Cajun, Indian, Italian, and California. Salads include a delectable hearts of romaine that could be called Caesar-light. Berman does imaginative things with fish, and the ravioli of the day is a house specialty. There is the occasional miss, like a risotto with spring vegetables that never quite comes together. The grilled lamb with a sauce of sherry vinegar and black currants demands devotion, but the menu's true star is the Sonoma duck, marinated in a glaze of honey and chili paste and grilled to perfection.

After dinner temptations often include a heavenly crème brûlée, one of the best we've tasted, as well as fresh sorbet that explodes fruit on your tongue.

MARIPOSA
707-838-0162.
www.mariposarestaurant.
   org.
275 Windsor River Rd.,
   Windsor, CA 95472.
Price: Expensive.
Closed: Sun. & Mon.
Credit Cards: D, MC, V.
Cuisine: Seasonal French
   American.
Serving: D.
Reservations:
   Recommended.

Mariposa is a simple, inviting house draped in white lights, and the atmosphere inside is just as appealing. A small place, it feels like you're at a dinner party, not a restaurant.

The food here is always interesting and as for the presentation: art on a plate. The Niman Ranch Beef Liver was the filet mignon of liver, delicate and rich. The Bacon Wrapped Whole Poussin was also appealing, tangy with a mustard green stuffing. The Apple Cobbler was somewhat traditional but still delicious. It was a good mix of Granny Smith apples, dried cherries, and currants.

at www.mariposa restaurant.org.
Special features: patio dining.
Handicap access: yes.

The wine list is fairly broad for the size of the restaurant, featuring a range of local and imported selections. Service was intelligent and well paced. Mariposa is off the beaten wine path, just off Hwy. 101 south of Healdsburg, but it's worth a side trip.

SYRAH
707-568-4002.
www.syrahbistro.com.
205 5th St., Santa Rosa, CA 95401.
Price: Expensive.
Closed: Sun. & Mon.
Credit Cards: AE, MC, V.
Cuisine: French and American cuisine.
Serving: L, D.
Reservations: Recommended.
Special features: Courtyard dining.
Handicap access: Yes.

Syrah will delight serious syrah drinkers who spend as much time lingering over the wine list as they do the menu. Of course the wine list has a fine selection of syrahs, with key French Rhones wines, even though it's weighted to California. The prices are fair, but there could be a better selection by the glass.

Situated in the historic City 205 Building, the restaurant is rustic-chic, with a peaked ceiling, wooden beams, modern art, and an open kitchen.

The food is, on the whole, impressive. A good beginning is the plate of squab livers on a bed of asparagus in a truffle sauce. Mercilessly rich. The Lake Trout, with crab & artichoke stuffing and Champagne white beurre blanc is pleasant but surprisingly bland. The Mixed Grill, a plentiful spread of quail, hanger steak and Tuscan Pork Sausage, always surpasses our expectations. Dessert are well executed, particularly the orange butter cake, layered with strawberry and Seville Orange Jam in a pool of strawberry sauce. Service couldn't have been better — prompt and intelligent. Syrah is a fine addition to the dining scene in Wine Country.

ZAZU
707-523-4814.
3535 Guerneville Rd., Santa Rosa, CA 95401
Price: Expensive.
Closed: Mon. & Tues.
Credit Cards: AE, D, MC, V.
Cuisine: Northern Italian, California.
Serving: D.
Reservations: Recommended.
Handicap access: Limited.

ZaZu might as well post a sign out front: UPSCALE COMFORT FOOD. New chef-owners John Stewart and Duskie Estes purchased the popular Willowside Café, known as a mecca of fine dining in nothing more than a remodeled roadhouse. Today this stop seems to be even more popular in its new incarnation, which proves one thing: Even sophisticated foodies need comfort.

One of the most popular entrees is J. B.'s Balsamic Pork Shoulder with Caramelized Onions. The balsamic vinegar and carmalized onions gives this dish a tart-sweet yin-yang. Outstanding flavors and textures. The Hanger Steak was a bit tough, although it was still tasty. Sublime are the Seared Day Boat Scallops with a melon vinaigrette.

A choice appetizer is the Zucchini Blossoms Fritti in a delicate tempura batter — light, delicate, and crunchy. Another is the Slow Roasted Beets in a Gorgonzola Dolce with Tart Apples.

As for desserts, the ZaZu Bellini rocks. It's an outstanding dish of homemade peach sorbet with a glass of Bonny Doon Moscato del Solo. Other good picks include the Raspberry Almond Shortcake and the Three Tiny Cupcakes.

Although the wine list is small, it plays up local producers and it has some excellent picks. Prices range from moderate to expensive.

The decor of ZaZu hasn't changed much from the Willowside: country chic with eclectic furnishings. The tempo of the service may be off a beat or two, but the servers make up for it with intelligence and warmth.

Healdsburg

BISTRO RALPH
707-433-1380.
109 Plaza St., Healdsburg, CA 95448.
Price: Expensive.
Credit Cards: MC, V.
Cuisine: California.
Serving: L, D.
Reservations: Recommended.
Special Features: Outdoor dining.
Handicap Access: Yes.

Bistro Ralph recalls a Greenwich Village café: elegant in a spare, smartly industrial sort of way. Some might consider the atmosphere chilly, but it has never bothered us. Situated on Healdsburg Plaza, it's a handy spot for lunch or dinner.

The food by chef-owner Ralph Tingle is typically excellent, although there's an occasional miss. The Mussel Bisque is rich but not overwhelming; a great balance of flavors. The Roast Liberty Duck Breast is another good pick, as well as the Grilled Ahi. Bright, fresh flavors. The restaurant can sometimes pull off the Szechuan Pepper Calamari. Other times it's a bit soggy and salty, a disappointment. On the upside, desserts are top rate. An impressive pick is the Chocolate Marquise, a decadent tile of chocolate swimming in a pool of hazelnut crème anglaise. Bistro Ralph has an efficient and modestly priced wine list that plays up the area's best producers. Service is always relaxed and attentive.

DRY CREEK KITCHEN
707-431-0330
317 Healdsburg Ave., Healdsburg, CA 95448
In Hotel Healdsburg.
Price: Expensive.
Credit cards: AE, DC, MC & V.
Cuisine: California.
Serving: L, D.
Reservations: recommended.
Handicap Access: yes.

Given chef/owner Charlie Palmer's track record with his ever-expanding restaurant empire, it won't be long before Dry Creek Kitchen raises the culinary bar in Sonoma County. At its opening in Fall 2001, it remained uneven. The entrées are typical rather than inventive, although many show promise. And the service, while generous and well paced, could be more sophisticated.

The Marinated Early Bird Beets with Redwood Hill Goat Cheese has so many great flavors, but like that line in *Amadeus*, "too many notes": the beets are simply overshadowed. The Pacific Halibut is classically understated, with a rich, yet delicate texture. Less successful is the Pan-seared CK Lamb with a blackberry and pinot noir sauce. The aroma is incredible, but the lamb is so undercooked, it's tough. (And we like rare meat!) The Warm Gala Apple Financier has a dramatic presentation, replete with sliced apples that resemble sails. But the dessert simply fails to deliver. It tastes like an apple cobbler sandwiched in a muffin.

The wine list is true to Palmer's quest to show wines produced from Sonoma County-grown grapes. Palmer said he intends to make the wine list the most extensive list of Sonoma County wines, a wine library of sorts.

The décor is contemporary with big, dramatic beams, and subtle colors, cream with pear-green trim. Comfortable, clean and simple.

Palmer is determined to use Sonoma County-grown product, tracing the county to its roots: farmer's markets. We expect him to succeed over time. For now, everyone in Wine Country is keeping an eye on Dry Creek Kitchen.

MADRONA MANOR
707-433-4231, 800-258-4003.
www.madronamanor.com.
1001 Westside Rd.,
  Healdsburg, CA 95448.
Price: Very Expensive.
Credit Cards: MC, V.
Cuisine: French, California.
Serving: D.
Reservations:
  Recommended.
Special Features: Outdoor
  dining.
Handicap Access: Yes.

It's a shame to approach this 1881 Victorian in the dark. Rising three stories to a steep mansard roof, this inn is a majestic sight set in a quiet glade, amid lush gardens (see Chapter Three, *Lodging*). The dining rooms, which used to be as stark and formal as a starched white shirt, were recently enhanced with warmer yet elegant tones. Service is very attentive, and Madrona Manor has one of the best wine cellars around, particularly if you like newer "blue chip" wines. To top it off, the food can be brilliant.

At night, the menu is prix fixe: $43 for three courses, $52 for four. Starters include Honey Roasted Beets and Spring Lamb Ravioli. The beet dish is earthy, clean and rich, but the ravioli is a bit too heavy.

A great entrée pick is the Grilled Pork Tenderloin because it all comes together, pork, the foie gras dried plums and the green peppercorn sauce. Equally good is the Grilled Filet of Beef, a classic dish grilled to perfection in a Bordelaise Sauce.

The dessert menu is impressive, but chocoholics won't be able to resist the Chocolate Soufflé Cake, blood orange and crème anglaise.

MANZANITA
707-433-8111.
336 Healdsburg Ave.,
  Healdsburg, CA 956448.
Near North St.
Closed: Mon. & Tues.
Price: Expensive.
Credit Cards: MC, V.

Once Manzanita settles in, we expect it to be a steady stop in Healdsburg for the Wine Country traveler. Its food- and wine-savvy owners, Mike and Carol Hale, have been around the block. The Hales were the original owners of one of our favorite Sonoma County restaurants, Willowside, before opening Manzanita in 2001. While the chef

Cuisine: Mediterranean
inspired.
Serving: D
Reservations:
Recommended.
Handicap Access: Yes.

is different here, Carol Hale remains the pastry chef, and that's a welcome treat.

The décor is appealing, modern with the accent on rustic. Overhead are wood rafters, and the restaurant is bordered at the front with stacks of Manzanita logs.

The food isn't outstanding across the board, but it shows promise. One tasty dish is the Wood Oven Bolinas Rockfish in a pool of saffron broth with shellfish and summer vegetables. Great flavors, and our only complaint is that the wood oven left the rockfish a bit dry. However, the Roasted Duck Breast was so understated that it was almost boring. On the upside, the Apricot Cobbler with Vanilla Ice Cream is one of the most delicious cobblers we've come across. The apricots are fresh and tasty, and the cobbler is crusted but moist, the perfect texture.

Another plus: The wine list is well priced with good values from around the world. Though broad, it still manages to have a good showing of Sonoma County wines. However, while Mike Hale is ever the gracious host, the service, always so crisp at Willowside, was rather lax overall. Still, with a more focused eye on food and service, Manzanita could surpass Willowside's rave reviews.

RAVENOUS
707-431-1302.
420 Center St., Healdsburg,
CA 95448.
Closed: Mon. & Tues.
Price: Expensive.
Credit Cards: Not accepted.
Cuisine: California.
Serving: D.
Reservations:
Recommended.
Special Features: Patio
seating out back.
Handicap Access: Yes.

It was close quarters in the original Ravenous, so close you could hear the kitchen sizzle. With it's more spacious new location — just around the block — it may be a little easier to get reservations . On the other hand, with such great reviews, it still may be a struggle. Ravenous has impressed us since it first open although the kitchen has become naggingly uneven recently.

A recent dish, Grilled Pork Tenderloin Medallions and Dry Spice Marinade, is a prime example: great, intense flavors, but the meat was shamefully overcooked. On the other hand, the Capellini is a wonderful stew of mussels, prawns, and day-boat scallops. The tomato-based broth is vibrant and flavorful, but it doesn't overwhelm the delicate flavors of the fish. For dessert, the Mississippi Mud Cake is deep, rich intense chocolate — pure decadence. We joked that it was fuel-injected chocolate.

The wine list is focused with an emphasis on local wineries. The prices are fair, but there could be more offerings by the glass. The new Ravenous has a classy, contemporary look, done up in subdued orange and yellow colors. But most people are less interested in the environment. They've heard Ravenous has incredible food, and they come to devour it.

The day's specials are on the chalkboard at Restaurant Charcuterie.

Chris Alderman

**RESTAURANT
  CHARCUTERIE**
707-431-7213.
www.charcuterierestaurant.
  com.
335 Healdsburg Ave.,
  Healdsburg, CA 95448.
Price: Expensive.
Credit Cards: AE, MC, V.
Cuisine: French, California.
Serving: L, D.
Reservations:
  Recommended.
Handicap Access: Yes.

Don't let the Charcuterie fool you. It may not look like much through the window, but chef-owner Patrick Martin winningly marries the best of France and California. The dining room is small and the decorations are understated, with walls painted light salmon and humorous pig decorations. Wine and menu specials are written on a chalkboard. The wine list is short but well chosen with fair prices. Service, on the whole, is efficient and pleasant, but can be a bit too attentive.

On a positive note, the food is good for the most part, and the portions are generous. If there's a salmon special on the dinner menu, opt for this stunning entrée: seared, moist and flavorful. The Pork Tenderloin with Brown Sugar and Brandy Sauce was perfectly cooked but a bit one note. However, dessert will leave you a fan. The Valrhona Chocolate Gelato managed to be both rich and refreshing.

**ZIN RESTAURANT &
  WINE BAR**
707-473-0946.
www.zinrestaurant.com.
344 Center St., Healdsburg,
  CA 95448.
Closed: Tues.
Price: Expensive.
Credit Cards: AE, MC, V.
Cuisine: California
  Contemporary.
Serving: L, D.

Zin zealots converge at this restaurant, a expansive eatery that feels like an artist's loft: slabs of concrete walls beneath a high ceiling of wooden rafters. Contemporary and yet cozy — the walls are filled with colorful art. A long wine bar sweeps across one side of the restaurant, and whether you're just in for a drink or in for a full meal, you'll love this custom-made menu focused on zinfandel. Even if zinfandel isn't your thing, you'll find plenty of other wines sharing second billing.

Reservations:
   Recommended.
Special Features: Wine bar.
Handicap Access: Yes.

The menu is weighted to California Cuisine, hearty American comfort food, great to pair with zin. The Coq au 'Zin, chicken braised in red wine with applewood bacon, roasted mushrooms and pearl onions was sensuously hearty, albeit a touch salty. The slow-braised Australian Lamb Shank was a bit disappointing. A great starter is the Mexican Beer Battered Green Beans with Mango Salsa. Desserts, like the Gingerbread Pear Upside Down Cake, won't wow you. Despite the casual atmosphere, the service is first-rate.

Geyserville

The Café at the Chateau Souverain is an elegant room with a view.

Chris Alderman

CHATEAU SOUVERAIN WINERY AND CAFÉ
707-433-3141.
www.souverain.com.
400 Souverain Ln.,
   Geyserville, CA 95441.
Independence Ln. exit off
   Hwy. 101.
Closed: Mon.–Thurs.
Price: Expensive.
Credit Cards: AE, MC, V.
Cuisine: California.
Serving: SB, L, D.
Reservations: Recommended.
Special Features: Outdoor
   dining.
Handicap Access: Yes.

From the tall French windows of Chateau Souverain, you can spy the graceful hills of Alexander Valley, a view homeowners dream about. The restaurant's interior is nearly as stunning, a romantic setting with towering cathedral ceilings and a massive fireplace. The food, however, is a disappointment, particularly for those who remember the kitchen's brilliance under chef Gary Danko. It shows in the detail: An otherwise perfectly tangy and tasty Caesar salad has Romaine leaves that are brown around the edges.

The wine list is limited to Chateau Souverain's own, a sound offering of reds and whites with pricing that's fair by restaurant standards. Service is sound but too slowly paced at times. Lunch is perhaps your best bet, since the menu is similar to dinner, and the view is better.

We like the inventive concept behind the open Ravioli of grilled Salmon Filet with Pesto. A juicy filet is casually draped top and bottom with savory sheets of pasta. The pesto, sadly, is a real yawner. The Rib-Eye of Lamb, rubbed with thyme and tarragon, is surpassingly flavorless; even garlic mashed potatoes can't save the day. Desserts include a Fall Fruit Crumble, a creamy crock of apples and nuts, topped with vanilla ice cream; it tastes like what they might serve at Baker's Square.

SANTI
707-857-1790.
21047 Geyserville Ave.,
   Geyserville, CA 95441.
Price: Expensive.
Closed: L on Sun.
Credit Cards: AE, MC, V.
Cusine: European-Italian.
Serving: L, D.
Reservations:
   Recommended.
Handicap Access: Yes.

Tucked in the sleepy town of Geyserville, just north of Healdsburg, is a city-slick restaurant called Santi, a surprising find. Italian for "saint," Santi serves European-Italian cuisine. Chef-owners Thomas Oden and Franco Dunn inspire an authentic European experience with dishes like Spaghettini al Sugo Calabrese, spaghetti with rich sauce of beef and pork ribs, tomatoes, and herbs.

It's rare when a restaurant can impress us with every dish we order, but Santi managed to do that. It might not stand on equal footing with the best you'll find in Italy but it is among the best Italian restaurants in Wine Country.

In winter the menu focuses on hearty northern Italian roasts and braised meats. In warmer weather the menu travels to Southern Italy for lighter fare.

A typical winter dish is Crespelle di Zucca, crepes filled with roasted winter squash and pine nuts topped with smoked ricotta cheese. Decadent, a rather rich beginning for dinner, but how can you go wrong when you're dining with the saints? The Osso Buco di Vitellino, veal shank braised with vegetables, sage, white wine and tomatoes over polenta, is incredible comfort food. Equally good is the Galletto al Mattone, chicken cooked under a brick with sautéed herbs and vegetables. Cap off dinner with the Panna Cotta, an Italian custard in a pool of rhubarb sauce. It's stunningly light and refreshing.

The wine list is broad, the prices are fair, and Santi does a fine job of playing up great local wines. The service is very attentive, although weekends can be harried.

Sonoma West County

APPLEWOOD INN AND RESTAURANT
707-869-9093; 800-555-8509.
www.applewoodinn.com.
13555 Hwy. 116,
   Guerneville, CA 95446.
Closed: Sun. & Mon.
Price: Expensive.
Credit Cards: AE, MC, V.
Cuisine: California.

If you can't spend the night — Applewood is one of the best inns in Wine Country — then dinner is the next best thing. (For details on the inn, see Chapter Three, *Lodging*). The main house, built in 1922, is an architectural gem done in the California Mission Revival style. The restaurant is styled to be the estate's barn. Long and narrow with cathedral ceilings and a stone fireplace, it's handsome and masculine.

Serving: D.
Reservations: Required.
Handicap Access: Yes.

The food is excellent. The Grilled Pork Rack Chop was cooked perfectly, moist inside, charred outside. The Roasted Alaskan Halibut was equally successful, and the Artichoke and Bean Stew highlighted the delicate nature of the fish.

The wine list is impressive, highlighting the Russian River Valley that are hard to get your hands on, while giving a nod to Napa and Italy. The list is not only broad, it's well priced. The service is sharp and intelligent, well-paced, courteous, and professional.

BAY VIEW RESTAURANT AT THE INN AT THE TIDES
707-875-2751, 800-541-7788.
800 Hwy. 1, Bodega Bay, CA 94923.
Closed: Mon. & Tues.
Price: Expensive.
Credit Cards: AE, MC, V.
Cuisine: Seafood, California.
Serving: D.
Reservations:
   Recommended.
Handicap Access: Yes.

If the hectic hum of The Tides or Lucas Wharf is too much and if you seek something more than basic fish, then the Bay View might be an alternative. While the food is simply on par with those two popular restaurants, the presentation has more flair, and the view is more impressive. If that's important, you might not mind the added cost.

The decor is elegantly simple with a beamed cathedral ceiling and Scandinavian furnishings. Servers, wearing black ties and tuxedo shirts, are efficient. The wine list is superbly selected with a credible list by the glass. The menu is dominated by local seafood. Appetizers include ho-hum crab cakes stuffed with far more filler than crab. Main courses include an uninspired pork tenderloin with wild-mushroom gravy. Better is the grilled halibut with a lively pineapple, mango, jalapeno, and cilantro salsa. Desserts include a winning Torta Prieta, a flourless hazelnut chocolate cake with a raspberry and chocolate sauce.

THE DUCK CLUB
707-875-3525.
103 Hwy. 1, Bodega Bay, CA 93923.
At Bodega Bay Lodge.
Price: Moderate to Very
   Expensive.
Credit Cards: AE, D, DC, MC, V.
Cusine: California.
Serving: B, D.
Reservations:
   Recommended.
Special Features: Harbor
   view.

This out-of the-way restaurant — hidden amid the lush landscaping of Bodega Bay Lodge — is worth a search. It offers the best food on the Sonoma Coast. The atmosphere is a bit pedestrian, the decor is strictly country club, but the views over the harbor and wetlands are gorgeous, and a blazing fire warms the room. Service is solid, but the wine list is a bit of a disappointment. Big names but few selections. The wine list does not match the ambiance or the extensive menu.

The menu may be too broad, with the kitchen seemingly stretched at times. Offerings range from seafood, pork chops, steaks, and chicken to pasta, hamburgers, and pizza. Presentation is pleasing but unfussy.

Good picks include the Spinach Salad, with great port-soaked cherries; the Duck Spring Rolls, with its flavorful cilantro vinaigrette dipping sauce; and the Lamb Sirloin served with garlic mashed potatoes. The port sauce was rich but not overpowering.

FARMHOUSE INN & RESTAURANT
707-887-3300, 800-464-6642.
www.farmhouseinn.com.
7871 River Rd., Forestville, CA 95436.
Closed: M,T, W.
Price: Moderate to Expensive.
Credit Cards: AE, MC, V.
Cuisine: Contemporary Californian.
Serving: D.
Reservations: Recommended.
Special features: Nice grounds for a walk; do weddings.
Handicap Access: Yes.

Before you even taste the food, you savor the landscape. Just one of the perks of a restaurant within a bed-and-breakfast setting. (Look for The Farmhouse in Chapter Three, *Lodging*.) On the downside, don't expect the food service to be quite as knowledgeable as some of the top-rated restaurants in Wine Country. Perhaps in time.

Meanwhile, the food is impressive. The Niman Ranch Pork Chop is a good pick. It's flavorful, with hints of ginger and fig. The Rabbit, Rabbit, Rabbit consists of an applewood-smoked bacon-wrapped loin, roasted rack, and confit of leg. A great idea, nicely realized.

Two good appetizers include the Fresh Maine Lobster Sausage and the Pan-Seared Sea of Cortez. Desserts are good, not great. The Summer Fruit–Berry Crisp and the Chocolate Soufflé may underwhelm dessert enthusiasts, but they won't disappoint foodies at large.

The wine list is nice, with a good selection of Sonoma County wines. It has some interesting offbeat reds and whites. Prices are slightly expensive.

The restaurant, done in warm pastels, is elegant, comfortable, and cozy. And just a few paces from your room if you lodge here, as well as dine. Another of the perks of a restaurant within a bed-and-breakfast.

LUCAS WHARF
707-875-3522.
www.lucaswharf.com.
595 Hwy. 1, Bodega Bay, CA 93923.
Price: Moderate to Expensive.
Credit Cards: D, MC, V.
Cuisine: Seafood.
Serving: L, D.
Reservations: Not accepted.
Special Features: Harbor view.

Ask a group of locals the best place to eat seafood on the Sonoma Coast, and you're liable to start an argument. The coast is not nearly as populated with restaurants as, say, Cape Cod — there are just a handful — and people have clear favorites. We find ourselves at Lucas Wharf more often than not. Built on piers overlooking Bodega Bay harbor, it's cozy and romantic, with a fireplace and cathedral ceiling. From your table you'll see great sunsets and fishing boats unloading the catch of the day.

Choose what's fresh off the boat, and you won't go wrong — particularly salmon when it's in season (May through September) and Dungeness crab (November to June). Try the salmon poached or with a Cajun-style spicy and lightly blackened exterior. The seafood pasta is delectable, as is the mixed grill of ling cod, red snapper, and scallops done in an understated curried cream sauce. The wine list and by-the-glass selection has improved, but the selection remains too limited. Lucas Wharf is popular with locals and tourists alike, so be prepared to wait for a table on weekends. Want something more low key? At Lucas Wharf's carry-out counter next door, munch fish and chips and have a cold beer at the picnic tables.

THE TIDES WHARF AND RESTAURANT
707-875-3652, 800-541-7788.
835 Hwy. 1, Bodega Bay, CA 93923.
Price: Expensive.
Credit Cards: AE, D, MC, V.
Cuisine: Seafood.
Serving: B, L, D.
Reservations: Not accepted.
Special Features: Harbor view.

The Tides was immortalized by Alfred Hitchcock in *The Birds*, but you'll never recognize it. The original restaurant, which was attacked by vengeful gulls in a major scene, is long gone, and a new eatery was built in 1997. The new dining room, with its high-raftered ceiling and stunning views of the harbor, is more elegant than the old place but somehow more touristy.

The "catch of the day" is usually a good bet. It's a voluminous list: red snapper, swordfish, ling cod, Pacific oysters. Local specialties include salmon, which is in season May through September, and Dungeness crab, in season November to June. The lunch menu is identical to dinner but a few dollars cheaper. At breakfast, try a crab omelet.

To start, try the succulent fried oysters or the deep-fried calamari, a generous helping of lightly battered beauties. Poached salmon with hollandaise sauce might seem like the thing to order, but the filet is often waterlogged and the sauce comes preprepared in a plastic cup. On the other hand, the crab cioppino, a local classic, is simply brilliant: Dungeness crab, prawns, scallops, mussels, clams swimming in a shallow pool of zesty Italian sauce. The wine list is sound; ditto the service.

FOOD PURVEYORS

A chic restaurant isn't the only place to feast. From Mexican eateries that burn your tongue to old family delicatessens with lingering irresistible smells of smoked meats and cheese, Napa and Sonoma have specialty food shops aplenty.

BAKERIES

Napa County

Alexis Baking Company (707-258-1827; 1517 Third St., Napa, CA 94559) You name it, and ABC has it: bread, pastries, desserts, sandwiches, coffee, or muffins.

The Model Bakery (707-963-8192; 1357 Main St., St. Helena, CA 94574) Everything here is baked in a big brick oven. Sweet or sour baguettes are stacked like kindling in tall wicker baskets, and scones, muffins, and croissants compete for shelf space. Behind the counter are burly loaves of rye, powdered white on top. Also serves coffee and pastries. A handful of tables.

Napa Valley Ovens (707-942-0777; 1353 Lincoln Ave., Calistoga, CA 94515) This is a cozy yet chic bakery, specializing in tasty breakfast goodies as well as foccacia, mini-pizzas, and restaurant-class desserts. Plenty of tables for reading the morning paper.

Sonoma County

Artisan Bakers (707-939-1765; 750 W. Napa St., Sonoma, CA 95476) Some of the finest bread in Wine Country is made right here. Look for loaves in markets around Sonoma County, or stop in the bakery yourself. In 1996, during the baking equivalent of the Olympics, Craig Ponsford achieved the impossible: He baked a better baguette then the French.

Basque Boulangerie Café (707-935-7687; 460 1st St. E., Sonoma, CA 95476) You'll find some lovely loaves here as well croissants, pastries, coffee, and espresso. A few seats inside and out.

The Downtown Bakery & Creamery in Healdsburg is the most popular morning stop for growers during harvest.

Thomas Hallstein/Outsight

Downtown Bakery and Creamery (707-431-2719; 308A Center St., Healdsburg, CA 95448) Fabulous desserts, but it doesn't look like much as you walk in. What's the secret? The Chez Panisse connection. Owners Kathleen Stewart and Lindsey and Therese Shere are veterans of that famed Berkeley kitchen. Tortes and cakes are ungodly delicious, likewise the sticky buns, the monster fig newtons, and blueberry scones. They also have great coffee and ice cream. No seating, but the downtown plaza is across the street.

Mom's Apple Pie (707-823-8330; 4550 Gravenstein Hwy. N., Sebastopol, CA 95472) This roadhouse makes fat pies better than most moms, served in tin pans or by the slice. The coconut cream is to die for. The fried chicken is good, too.

Village Bakery (829-8101; 7225 Healdsburg Ave., Sebastopol, CA 95472) Rustic European-style breads. Pastries, pies, and elegant desserts.

BURGERS, ETC.

Fred's (707-942-9563; 1506 Lincoln Ave., Calistoga, CA 95415) Not much more than a drive-in, but the hamburgers are killer. Eat one outside under the red awning, and watch people stroll by.

Rob's Rib Shack (707-938-8520; 18709 Arnold Dr., Sonoma, CA 95476) This funky roadhouse (note the little pig lights) has been discovered. The succulent baby-back ribs have a sweet-and-spicy sauce.

Taylor's Refresher (707-963-3486; 933 Main St., St. Helena, CA 94574) This is a classic old drive-in restaurant — you have to walk to the window these days — but average Joe's and gourmands alike flock to Taylor's for fast food 1950's style.

The Spot (707-963-2844; 587 St. Helena Hwy., St. Helena, CA 95474) The atmosphere is pure neon, and it's a favorite with both locals and tourists. Great for kids, with a menu of pizza, French fries, and fried chicken. Burgers are the best bet, and sample the soda- fountain goodies.

COFFEE HOUSES

Napa County

Calistoga Roastery (707-942-5757; 1631 Lincoln Ave., Calistoga, CA 94515) A cozy and casual spot for the morning brew. Plenty of seating inside and out.

Napa Valley Coffee Roasting Co. (948 Main St., Napa, CA 94559; 1400 Oak Ave., St. Helena, CA 94574) The premier coffeehouse in the county now has two outlets. The classic old façade in downtown Napa is a popular hangout. Bags of raw greenish beans are open in the back. The St. Helena shop is larger and sunnier with outdoor seating. To go with the brew, there are treats galore.

San Marco Espresso and Bake Shop (707-942-0714; 1336 Lincoln Ave., Calistoga, CA 94515) This recently expanded café still makes an uncompromising cup of coffee, plus fruit and milkshakes are now offered.

29 Joes (707-967-0820; 677 St. Helena Hwy., St. Helena, CA 94574) Good coffee and pastries, plus a pleasant outdoor court for sunny mornings. It also has a drive-up window; perfect for those bleary-eyed days.

Sonoma County

A'Roma Roasters (707-576-7765; 95 5th St., Santa Rosa, CA 95401) Facing historic Railroad Square, A'Roma is a touch bohemian, with exposed rafters, a copper countertop, and a coffee-bean roaster as a centerpiece. Lots of tables, and you'll roll your eyes over goodies like blackberry pie.

Catz (707-829-6600; 6761 Sebastopol Ave., Sebastopol, CA 95472) This funky café is like the tea room of a Victorian train station. There's also an outdoor patio.

The Coffee Garden (707-996-6645; 415 1st St. W., Sonoma, CA 95476) This café looks plain enough, but it's in an adobe built in the 1830s. The main draw is the lovely garden patio.

Flying Goat Coffee Roastery (707-433-9081; 324 Center St., Healdsburg, CA 95448) A stylish spot for a cup of java. Have a muffin while you smell the roaster at work.

Healdsburg Coffee Co. (707-431-7941; 312 Center St., Healdsburg, CA 95448) Inside a historic storefront on the downtown plaza, this is a pleasant spot to savor a cup and scone or cookie.

Wolf Coffee Co. (614 4th St. or 1810 Mendocino Ave., Santa Rosa, CA 95401) Maybe the best cup of coffee in Sonoma County. The 4th Street shop is a classy downtown affair with marble counters. The Mendocino shop is a popular take-out in the Santa Rosa Junior College area.

DELI & GOURMET SHOPS

Napa County

Just like a still-life painting, fresh fruits and vegetables in the courtyard of Tra Vigne.

Thomas Hallstein/Outsight

Cantinetta Tra Vigne (707-963-8888; 1050 Charter Oak Ave., St. Helena, CA 94574) This classic stone building may be the best lunch spot in Napa Valley. The menu is limited but superbly done. Breakfast offers sinful brioche sticky buns and egg dishes. Lunch brings stuffed focaccia and sandwiches such as smoked salmon. Don't miss the eggplant stack, a lasagnalike side dish. Beer and wine are available by the glass for a peaceful lunch in the quiet court-yard.

Dean & Deluca (707-967-9980; 607 South St. Helena Hwy., St. Helena, CA 94574) Manhattan's upscale gourmet food shop opened an outlet in Napa Valley in 1997. It's quite a place, with all sorts of carry-out goodies such as sandwiches, cheese, fresh produce, smoked salmon, duck pâté, olives, baked goods, coffee and cookies, jams, olive oils, vinegars, cakes, and rotisserie chicken.

Genova Delicatessen (707-253-8686; 1550 Trancas Ave., Napa, CA 94558) You can almost smell Genova from two blocks off, so rich is the bouquet of dried salami, roasting chicken, and simmering pastas. With a history that dates from 1926, Genova is home to marbled cold cuts and glass-case treasures like potato salad, antipasto, and olives. There are a handful of tables.

Gordon's Café & Wine Bar (707-944-8246; 6770 Washington St., Yountville, CA 94599) This old grocery is now a hip café. There's a modest menu of salads and sandwiches, plus coffee, wine by the glass, goodies, and breakfast. Eat lunch at the communal tables, or take it to the park nearby.

Napa Valley Olive Oil Manufacturing Co. (707-963-4173; 835 Charter Oak Ave., St. Helena, CA 94574) This faded white barn is a glorious time warp. The shop dates from the 1920s, when Napa Valley was largely populated by Italian farmers. You're as likely to hear Italian inside as English, and the deli counter looks like your (Neapolitan) grandmother's kitchen. Picnic tables outside.

Oakville Grocery Co. (707-944-8802; 7856 St. Helena Hwy., Oakville, CA 94562) What looks like an old country store, with its giant red Coca-Cola sign on the side and wooden screen doors, is actually a gourmet grocery. Goodies include duck pâté, cold cuts, and even caviar. Sandwiches include turkey with pesto and a glorious lavosh. There's also coffee by the cup, bakery treats, and local wines. A café opened next door in 1997, and it features pizza from the wood-burning oven as well as sandwiches, pasta, and salads.

Picnicking on the lawn at V. Sattui Winery in St. Helena.

Chris Alderman

Palisades Market (707-942-9549; 1506 Lincoln Ave., Calistoga, CA 94515) A real find, this modest grocery has an excellent deli — try the roast beef and brie on onion focaccia — plus fresh bread, produce, baked goods, cheese, and wine.

V. Sattui Winery (707-963-7774; 1111 White Ln., St. Helena, CA 94574; at St. Helena Hwy.) Most wineries have a picnic table tucked somewhere, but V. Sattui is lawn-lunch central, shaded by tall oaks. The tasting room doubles as a deli shop.

Sonoma County

Basque Boulangerie Café (707-935-7687; 460 1st St. E., Sonoma, CA 95476) More than a bakery, this stylish storefront has sandwiches and a wine bar. However, for some reason it has yet to master a classic croissant.

Dry Creek General Store (707-433-4171; 3495 Dry Creek Rd., Healdsburg, CA 95448) A rural gathering spot for more than a century, this is a landmark of Sonoma's rustic heritage. The floors are wooden and warped, and under the carport is a tattered upright cola machine. Fancier trappings have been added over the years — a wine rack and a few gourmet goodies. Super deli sandwiches.

Jimtown Store (707-433-1212; 6706 Hwy. 128, Healdsburg, CA 95448) An Alexander Valley landmark for a century, this former general store and gas depot was abandoned for years. John Werner and Carrie Brown resuscitated the place in 1991, retaining quaintness while adding a touch of gourmet chic, drawing national attention along the way. Sandwiches are first-rate, and the aisles include old-fashioned candy, toys, and memorabilia.

Korbel Delicatessen (707-869-6313; 13250 River Rd., Guerneville, CA 95446) Under a cathedral ceiling, on an acid-wash floor, five or six tables offer shady views through tall windows. Outside there are plenty of tables. You can get muffins, salads, sandwiches, beer on tap, wine by the glass, and ales of all kinds (amber, pale, port, golden wheat). Breads, jams and jellies, and vinegars, too.

Cucina Viansa (707-935-5656; 400 First St., E., Sonoma, CA 95476) Viansa Winery and Italian Marketplace opened this outlet on Sonoma Plaza a few years back. The salads and sandwiches are first-rate. Plenty of tables inside and out. Wines are available for a taste or by the glass.

Oakville Grocery, Healdsburg (707-433-3200; 124 Matheson St., Healdsburg, CA 95448) Napa Valley invaded Sonoma with this satellite of the successful upscale grocery. Goodies include duck pâté, cold cuts, cheese, olives, fresh produce, artisan breads. Order a sandwich, pizza, or a rotisserie chicken. There's even wine available by the glass. Take the food with you, or eat on the patio.

The Olive Press (707-939-8900; Jack London Village, 14301 Arnold Dr., Glen Ellen, CA 95442) If you're tired of watching people make wine, switch to olive oil. This smart den makes and sells olive oil that rivals Italy's best. Try a complimentary taste.

Ethnic Food in Wine Country

CHINESE

The best Chinese in Wine Country is found at *Gary Chu's* (707-526-5840; 611 5th St., Santa Rosa, CA 95404). The room is an elegant blend of Chinese and Art Deco and the food is stylishly gourmet. Impeccable ingredients are cooked with light sautés instead of oppressive sauces. Try the spicy plum sauce pork. In Napa, *Golden Harvest* (707-967-9888; 61 Main St., St. Helena, CA 94574) offers solid Chinese fare. Likewise *Soo Yuan* (707-942-9404; 1354 Lincoln Ave., Calistoga, CA 94515). A standard like Kung Pao chicken is competently done, hearty and mildly spicy.

JAPANESE

This close to San Francisco and the Pacific Ocean, we take our sushi seriously. A local favorite is *Sushi Mambo* (707-257-6604; 1015 Coombs St., Napa, CA 95449) and another good bet is *Yoshi-Shige* (707-257-3583; 3381 California Blvd., Napa, CA 94558), just off Trancas St. near Hwy. 29. Sonoma County has several fine Japanese restaurants. Our favorites are *Hana* (707-586-0270; 101 Golf Course Dr., Rohnert Park, CA 94928; at Doubletree Plaza) and Osake (707- 542-8282; 2446 Patio Ct., Santa Rosa, CA 94505), which is just off busy Farmer's Lane.

MEXICAN

In Napa Valley, there's a certain funky appeal to *Ana's Cantina* (707-963-4921; 1205 Main St., St. Helena, CA 94574), a bar with a pool table and lots of character. The food won't win awards but it goes good with a long-neck. Avoid *Armadillo's* (707-963-8082; 1304 Main St. St. Helena, CA 94574), where the atmosphere recalls a colorful village south of the border, but the food is lackluster. A popular spot is *Compadres* (707-944-2406; 6539 Washington St., Yountville, CA 94599) and it looks promising with a lovely outdoor patio and brick walls. But Compadres is an empty piñata. Every dish is a letdown. The atmosphere is lively at *Pacifico* (707-942-4400; 1237 Lincoln Ave., Calistoga, CA 84515), and the margaritas are knockout. The food is hearty; try the fish tacos. If you can overlook its shopping plaza locale, *Zapata* (707-254-8888; Bel Aire Plaza off Trancas St., Napa, CA 94558) has reliable fare and winning margaritas.

In Sonoma County, chains dominate, and the results are less than impressive. *The Cantina* (707-523-3663; 500 4th St., Santa Rosa, CA) is a slick brick palace with an active bar and a heated patio, but the food is boring. A better chain experience is at *Chevys* (707-571-1082; 24 4th St., Santa Rosa, CA 95401). The food isn't authentic but it is fresh and nicely done, especially the fajitas. The food at *La Casa* (707-996-3406; 121 E. Spain St., Sonoma, CA 95476) is adequate at best. A better choice on Sonoma plaza is the festive *Maya* (707-935-3500; 101 E. Napa St., Sonoma, CA 95476) which serves upscale authentic Mexican and incredible margarhitas. Two inexpensive and low-key shops have the best Mexican in the county. Ignore the atmosphere at *Taqueria El Sombrero* (707-433-3818; 245 Center St., Healdsburg, CA 95448) and *Taqueria Santa Rosa* (707-528-7956; 1950 Mendocino Ave., Santa Rosa, CA 95401 and 707-433-9205; 1063 Vine St., Healdsburg, CA 95448) and relish the food. Both use whole beans, not canned refrieds, and grilled meat.

ETC.

Our favorites include *Thai House* (707-526-3939; 525 4th St., Santa Rosa, CA 95401) and *Rin's Thai* (707-938-1462; 139 E. Napa St., Sonoma, CA 95476). You might also try *Thai Pot* (707-829-8889; 6961 Sebastopol Ave., Sebastopol, CA 95472). *Siam Thai House* (707-226-7749; 1139 Lincoln Ave., Napa, CA 94558) and *Thai Kitchen* (707-254-9271; 1222 Trancas, Napa, CA 94558).

If you need an Indian fix, Wine Country offers two that will do in a pinch. *Sizzling Tandoor* (707-579-5999; 409 Mendocino Ave., Santa Rosa, CA 95401) is a sound dining room, with fiery vindaloos and rich curry barani. A new addition to Napa is *Bombay Bistro* (707-253-9375; 1011 First St., Napa, CA 94559).

Russian River Vineyards Restaurant (707-887-1562; 5700 Gravenstein Hwy., Forestville, CA 95436) is the only Greek food for miles, but we can't recommend it.

Sonoma Cheese Factory (707-996-1931; 2 W. Spain St., Sonoma, CA 95476) This supermarket-size deli doubles as factory and tourist attraction. The Viviani family has made cheese in Sonoma since 1931 and they produce a fantastic array, all available as samples. In the rear is a large window, where you can watch cheese in the making. Sandwiches are fairly standard. There's a covered patio, and shady Sonoma Plaza is nearby.

Traverso's Gourmet Foods (707-542-2530; 106 B St., Santa Rosa, CA 95401) Traverso's has evolved into the county's best gourmet deli and wine shop, never losing touch with its Italian roots. Dangling from the ceiling are flags of Italy and prosciutto. The deli case is a painting of salads, meats, and other treats, from delicate pastries such as a chicken apple yoha to hearty ravioli. Sandwiches are marvelous.

Vella Cheese Company (800-848-0505; 315 2nd St. E., Sonoma, CA 95476) The dry jack is to die for. A Sonoma classic that dates to 1931 and worth a visit.

Cheese in the making at the Vella Cheese Company in Sonoma.

Thomas Hallstein/Outsight

FISH MARKETS

One of the joys of living on the Pacific Ocean is fresh seafood. Most prized locally are Dungeness crab and salmon. Crab season runs from mid-November to the end of May and the local salmon season runs from mid-May to September. There are also a number of oyster farms just south on Tomales Bay, and those beefy Pacific oysters are delicious. Below are a few specialty fish markets.

Omega 3 Seafood Market 707-257-3474; 1740 Yajome St., Napa, CA 94559.
Lucas Wharf Deli 707-875-3562; 595 Hwy. 1, Bodega Bay, CA 94923.
Tides Wharf Fish Market 707-875-3554; 835 Hwy. 1, Bodega Bay, CA 94923.

PRODUCE

Roadside apple stands are revered as much as wine in Sebastopol.

Thomas Hallstein/Outsight

The bounty of Wine Country goes well beyond grapes, particularly in Sonoma County. Fine produce stands abound in Wine Country. Look for *The Fruit Basket* (707-996-7433; 18474 Hwy. 12, Sonoma, CA 95476) and *Amstead's* (707-431-0530; 102 Healdsburg Ave., Healdsburg, CA 95448).

Sonoma County Farm Trails is an informal collective of farms. Worth seeking out is *Timber Crest Farm* (707-433-8251; 4791 Dry Creek Rd., Healdsburg, CA 95448), which produces "Sonoma" brand dried tomatoes and vegetables. Another fun spot is *Twin Hill Ranch* (707-823-2815; 1689 Pleasant Hill Rd., Sebastopol, CA 95472), which specializes in apples, nuts, and dried fruit. There's a roaring fire on chilly days. *Kozlowski Farms* (707-887-1587; 5566 Gravenstein Hwy. N., Forestville, CA 95436) is an orchard turned down-home gourmet enterprise. This Sonoma County treasure specializes in jams and jellies, apple butter, raspberry and other vinegars as well as apples and other fresh produce.

Pizza & Pizzerias

Pizza may not be the obsession here that it is in cities like Chicago and New York, but folks here do like their cheese pies. You know what to expect from Pizza Hut and the rest, so we've rounded up a sampling of the little guys — the independents and small chains.

If you like a bit of panache in your pizza, check out *Checkers Pizza & Pasta* (707-942-9300;1414 Lincoln Ave., Calistoga, CA 94515; 523 4th St., Santa Rosa, CA 95401). Both outlets are festive with abstract art and polished pine and black tile. There are traditional pies of sausage and pepperoni, of course, but there's also Thai pizza, topped with marinated chicken, cilantro, and peanuts.

In St. Helena, try family-friendly *Tomatina* (707-967-9999; 1020 Main St., St. Helena, CA 94574). There's a full review earlier in this chapter. Another good place for families is *Frankie, Johnnie & Luigi Too* (707-944-0177; 6772 Washington St., Yountville, CA 94599)

For those who demand New York-style pizza, there's *La Vera* (707-575-1113; 629 4th St., Santa Rosa, CA 95404) The cheese stretches for a city block and the meats are little explosions of pepperoni and sausage. The crust is that perfect unison of crunchy and chewy. The atmosphere is more formal than most pizza shacks, with polished brass and wood.

La Prima Pizza (707-963-7909; 1010 Adams St., St. Helena, CA 94574) makes a pleasant pie, with a puffy crust that's crisp on the bottom. The toppings are generous and of good quality. *Mary's Pizza Shack* (five locations in Sonoma and one in Napa) is fairly safe American pizza. The crust is a tad salty and the meat toppings rather bland, but the cheeses and veggies are top-rate.

WINE SHOPS

The specialty wine shops in Napa and Sonoma counties, as you might imagine, are among the finest in the nation, offering a huge variety as well as hard-to-find treasures. You'll be surprised to learn that wine is seldom cheaper at the wineries than local retail shops, unless you catch a sale or buy by the case. You also run the risk, of course, of not being able to find a wine you loved at the winery. It's your gamble.

Napa County

All Seasons Café (707-942-6828; 1400 Lincoln Ave., Calistoga, CA94515) In the rear of this chic café is a cool cellar of wine, with current vintages and a few old treasures. Prices are the going rates.

Brix (707-944-2749; 7377 St. Helena Hwy., Yountville, CA 94599) Don't be fooled from the outside; this restaurant has an excellent wine shop just inside the front door.

Calistoga Wine Stop (707-942-5556; 1458 Lincoln Ave., Calistoga, CA 94515) Housed in an 1866-vintage Central Pacific railroad car, this shop has a solid line-up of current Napa and Sonoma wines. Prices are average.

Dean & Deluca (707-967-9980; 607 South St. Helena Hwy., St. Helena, CA 94574) This gourmet food store has a large and superb selection of Napa and Sonoma. Prices are the going rate.

JV Warehouse (707-253-2624; 426 1st St., Napa, CA 94559) There's a big selection and good prices at this large outlet.

St. Helena Wine Center (707-963-1313; 1321 Main St., St. Helena, CA 94574) One of Napa's oldest, dating to 1953, this shop believes in the notion of "only the best," offering few bargains. It has a small but extremely select library of Napa and Sonoma current wines. There's also a tasting bar.

St. Helena Wine Merchants (707-963-7888; 699 St. Helena Hwy., St. Helena, CA 94574) A giant selection of new and older vintages but no bargains here. There's also a notable assortment of large bottles. Tasting bar.

Vintage 1870 Wine Cellar (707-944-9070; 6525 Washington St., Yountville, CA 94599) This historic building, with polished wood floors and exposed rafters, has a vast stash of wine and microbrewery beers. No bargains. Tasting bar.

Sweets & Treets

Napa County

Anette's Chocolate & Ice Cream Factory (707-252-4228; 1321 1st St., Napa, CA 94559) This is a dangerous place for weight watchers, offering everything from fresh chocolate turtles and truffles to jelly beans, milkshakes, and sundaes.

The Candy Cellar (707-942-6990; 1367 Lincoln Ave., Calistoga, CA 94515) Relive your childhood as you browse this general store with its wooden barrels stuffed with goodies such as taffy, butterscotch, fireballs, candy necklaces, gum, A&W root-beer barrels, and the like.

Gillespie's Ice Cream & Chocolate (707-944-2113; Vintage 1870, Yountville, CA 94599) Stop for a treat while you browse the shops of Vintage 1870. Offers homemade candy and Double Rainbow ice cream.

San Marco Espresso Co. (707-942-0714; 1408 Lincoln Ave., Calistoga, CA 94515) A small shop with a potpourri of goodies, from muffins and scones to lemon squares, fresh chocolates, decadent cakes, ice cream, and espresso.

Sonoma County

Chocolate Cow (707-935-3564; 452 1st St. E., Sonoma, CA 95476) These folks are udderly cow crazy; black-and-white heifers are everywhere, from T-shirts to stuffed animals. The place also stocks candy, chocolates, fudge, and ice cream.

Screamin' Mimi (707-823-5902; 6902 Sebastopol Ave., Sebastopol, CA 95472) They make their own ice cream and sorbets here, and it's all wonderful.

Sonoma County

Bottle Barn (707-528-1161; 3331 Industrial Dr., Santa Rosa, CA 95403) This warehouse has a huge selection, with a few hard-to-find wines and generally bargain prices.

Root's Cellar (707-433-4937; 113 Mill St., Healdsburg, CA 95448) This small wine shop is packed with some of the top wines in Sonoma and Napa.

Traverso's Gourmet Foods (707-542-2530; 3rd & B Sts., Santa Rosa, CA 95401) This Italian deli doesn't carry a huge selection of wine but offers only the best quality in all price ranges. Bill Traverso knows wine but is so unpretentious about it that you don't have to pretend you do. Traverso's has the best stock of Italian wines in the region.

Twisted Vines (707-766-8162; 16 Kentucky St., Petaluma, CA 94952) This is an exceptional wine bar. Prices are reasonable, and the atmosphere is stylish. The food is pretty good, too.

Wine Exchange of Sonoma (707-938-1794; 452 1st St. E., Sonoma, CA 94576) There's an air of restrained refinement to this shop. Few discounts, but look for the best current releases and a few vintage wines. There's also an enormous selection of specialty beers. Another plus is the wine and beer tasting bar in the back.

The Wine Shop (707-433-0433; 331 Healdsburg Ave., Healdsburg, CA 95448) An excellent wine shop right on the Healdsburg plaza.

CHAPTER SIX
Poetry Uncorked
WINERIES & SPECIALITY BREWERS

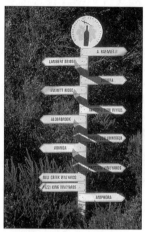

Finding wineries is easy. Just follow the arrows.

Thomas Hallstein/Outsight

Wineries, like the wines they make, come in different styles and qualities. You can even use the same words to describe them. Is it a sweet or sour experience? Subtle or bold? Is it friendly from the first, or does it grow on you? In compiling our list of wineries, we asked ourselves: "What makes a winery worth visiting?" Is it the wine? A pilgrimage to the source of your favorite cabernet sauvignon has great appeal. Is it the fame? "Wow! There's Beringer — we have to stop there." There's also the tour to consider. And is there a fee? Can you picnic? And so on.

Old-timers, of course, remember a different Wine Country. As recently as the 1960s, visitors arrived at local wineries with empty jugs and bottles in hand, ready for a fill-up right from the barrel. But as Napa and Sonoma have gained prominence in the wine world, so has their appeal as vacation meccas. More than eight million tourists come to Napa and Sonoma counties each year. Winery hopping has become an avid pastime, and tasting rooms have evolved into bustling centerpieces, sometimes rustic, sometimes chic, but always inviting and fun. Drinking wine has always been a rich man's hobby, at least in the United States. These days, winery touring is equally expensive, with many wineries charging for tours, and a $10 fee to taste wine is not unusual anymore.

These days wineries have competition from a new generation of specialty beer brewers. These microbreweries or brewpubs are springing up all over Napa and Sonoma counties. With this edition, we devote a special section to these specialty brewers at the end of this chapter.

Fall is the favorite touring season for many — the vineyards resplendent in rich golds and reds, the wineries and fields hectic with the harvest, or "crush" as it's called. Our favorite time is spring, when the mountains and fields are lush and green, the vines budding, the trees flowering, and the fields covered with the yellows of wild mustard.

We've included not only the wineries that regularly offer tours and tastings but also those that are open by appointment only. The wineries are organized first by region, then alphabetically. Here are a few guidelines to keep in mind when winery touring and wine tasting.

1) Have a designated driver. Those small samples can creep up on you, especially if you're new to wine tasting. Also, you don't have to try every wine, and wineries are not offended if you pour out a leftover sample.

2) Don't be intimidated by wine's snobbish image. Be yourself. Ask questions. Have fun. A glossary is provided later in this chapter if you need handy details.

3) Bring the right equipment. Take notes. They don't have to be voluminous, just a brief note like "1999 Simi Chardonnay — great" to jog your memory later. While touring, take along crackers and bottled water. It helps to cleanse your palate between wineries.

4) One tour is not much different from the next. One or two is enough. Also, try different kinds. Korbel and Beringer are rich in history, while Mumm and Mondavi are technical marvels.

5) Most wineries in both counties now charge a fee to taste wine, usually $3 to $10. Some even charge for tours. Usually a souvenir glass is thrown in, and the fee may be waived if you buy wine.

6) Don't let "open by appointment only" scare you off. These are often smaller wineries that want to discourage heavy traffic, and many are restricted by recent zoning laws. If you're a casual tourist, stick to the big wineries with the big welcome, but if you're serious about wine, these smaller wineries are serious about you.

7) Most wineries have a picnic area. It's good courtesy to buy a bottle before picnicking.

Sonoma County Wine and Visitor Center

This is a great idea, although we wish it were in the heart of Wine Country, not in Rohnert Park. Yet, if you're driving up Highway 101 and looking for tourist information, this is a convenient stop. Part of the Doubletree shopping complex, the visitor center is open 9 to 5 daily and is just off the Golf Course Drive exit of Highway 101. The center is home to the Sonoma County Wineries Association and a selection of wines is offered for sale and tasting. There is also a demonstration vineyard and winery, and various displays and maps on the wines, wineries, and history of the county. A similar wine center is in the works for the city of Napa. **Sonoma County Wine and Visitor Center**: 707-586-3795; 5000 Roberts Lake Rd., Rohnert Park, CA 49428.

NAPA COUNTY WINERIES

Napa & Carneros

ACACIA WINERY
Winemaker: Michael
　Terrien.
707-226-9991;
　fax 707-226-1685.
2750 Las Amigas Rd., Napa,
　CA 94559.
Tasting & Tours: 10–4:30
　Mon.–Sat., noon–4:30 Sun.
　by appt.
Tasting Fee: $5 for reserve
　wines only.

Named after a tree that grows throughout the area, Acacia specializes in chardonnay and pinot noir. Acacia was established in 1979 and sold in 1986 to Chalone Inc., which owns Carmenet and Edna Valley. The winery is a modern California barn that sits on the slopes of the Carneros district, which shoulders the top of the San Pablo Bay. Acacia uses grapes from surrounding vineyards, a region suited to Burgundian grapes.

A statue of mother and child in the courtyard of Artesa Winery in the Carneros.

Thomas Hallstein/Outsight

ARTESA VINEYARDS & WINERY

Winemakers: Stephen Tebb and Don Van Staaveren.
707-224-1668;
  fax 707-224-1672.
www.artesawinery.com.
info@artesawinery.com.
Old Sonoma Rd. N. from Hwy. 12/121, L. on Dealy Rd.
Mail: 1345 Henry Rd., Napa, CA 94559.
Tasting: 10–5 daily.
Tours: 11 & 2 daily.
Fee: $4–$6.
Special Features: Art gallery.

Artesa began life in 1991 as sparkling wine specialist Codorniu Napa. Spain's Codorniu, has been making bubbly since 1872 but couldn't make a go of it in California. A few years ago, the winery changed its name and switched to still wine — pinot noir, chardonnay, merlot, sauvignon blanc, syrah. So far, the wines are quite promising.

This $23-million winery is a spectacular understatement. Covered with earth and native grasses, the winery is an enigma from the road, recalling a buried temple. The mystery begins to unravel as you approach the entrance, a long staircase with a waterfall cascading down the center. Inside it seems anything but a bunker, with elegant decor, a sun-baked atrium, and spectacular views through grand windows. It's a must for any student of architecture.

BOUCHAINE VINEYARDS

Winemaker: David Stevens.
707-252-9065,
  800-654-WINE;
  fax 707-252-0401.
www.bouchaine.com.
info@bouchaine.com.
1075 Buchli Station Rd., Napa, CA 94559.
Tasting: 10:30–4 daily.
Tasting Fee: No.
Tours: By appt.

Well off the tourist path, on the wind-swept hills of Southern Carneros, sits this modern redwood winery. Built on the vestiges of a winery that dates from the turn of the century, Bouchaine's new winery is a grand redwood barn that sits alone on rolling hills that lead to the San Pablo Bay. A fire warms the tasting room on cool Carneros days. and a deck offers lovely views when the sun allows. Chardonnay and pinot noir are a specialty, but try the crisp and spicy gewürztraminer.

CARNEROS CREEK WINERY

Winemaker: Scott Rich.
707-253-9463;
  fax 707-253-9465.
www.carneros-creek.com.
wineinfo@carneros creek.com.
1285 Dealy Ln., Napa, CA 94559.
Tasting: 10–5 daily.
Tasting Fee: $5.
Tours: By appt.

Situated along the stream that lends its name, Carneros Creek was a key player in the revival of Carneros as a wine-growing region. It produces a lovely but lean chardonnay and several pinot noirs, including Fleur de Carneros, an easy quaff perfect for picnics. A new winery was added in 1998, and a new visitors center — a lovely white villa — opened in April 2001.

DOMAINE CARNEROS

Winemaker: Eileen Crane.
707-257-0101;
  fax 707-257-3020.

The Domaine Carneros winery is an exclamation point along Highway 12, towering on a hilltop surrounded by vineyards. Built in the style of an 18th-century French chateau, Domaine Carneros is

Domaine Carneros is modeled after an 18th-century French Chateau.

Chris Alderman

www.domainecarneros.com
admin@domainecarneros
.com.
1240 Duhig Rd., PO Box
5420, Napa, CA 94581.
Off Hwy. 12/121, 5 1/2 mi.
W. of Napa.
Hours: 10:30–6 daily.
Tasting: Sold by the glass or
bottle.
Tours: On the hour 11–4
weekends & daily
Apr.–Oct.; on the hour
11–4 weekends & daily 11,
1, & 3 Nov.–Mar.

no everyday winery — but then sparkling wine isn't your everyday libation. Owned in part by champagne giant Taittinger, Domaine Carneros makes a $14 million statement about its French heritage.

The terrace of this cream-and-terra cotta chateau overlooks the lovely rolling hills of the Carneros district, which has a climate similar to Champagne. Inside are marble floors and a maple interior crowned with ornate chandeliers. Behind the stylish front is a state-of-the-art winery that released its first wine in the fall of 1990. Domaine Carneros's nonvintage brut is a light, elegant sparkler, a melding of French and American tastes. A top-notch pinot noir was recently added.

**HAKUSAN SAKE
GARDENS**
707-258-6160 or
800-KOHNAN1;
fax 707-258-9371.
www.hakusan.com.
sake@hakusan.com.
One Executive Way, Napa
CA 94558.
Hwy. 12/29 at Jameson
Canyon Rd., 4 mi. S. of
Napa.
Hours: 10–5 daily.
Tasting Fee: $2.
Tours: Self-guided.
Special Features: Japanese
garden.

You're driving along a Napa back road, admiring the scenery: wide skies, stately mountains, eminent wineries, and field upon field of — rice? Rice isn't really grown in Napa Valley, but grapes aren't the only source of wine. Sake, a rice wine, is the traditional wine of Japan, and Hakusan has been making sake in Napa since 1989.

Kohnan Inc., the firm behind Hakusan, came to Napa because its high-tech plans clashed with certain Japanese traditions. You'll watch a short video on sake while sipping cold and warm sake. (Heat brings out sake's nutty flavor.) After tasting, you can follow a self-guided tour along the outside of the brewery, viewing the process through large windows.

THE HESS COLLECTION
Winemaker: Dave Guffy.
707-255-1144;
  fax 707-253-1682.
www.hesscollection.com.
info@hesscollection.com.
4411 Redwood Rd., PO Box
  4140, Napa, CA 94558
10 mi. W. of Hwy.
Tasting: 10–4 daily except
  major holidays.
Tasting Fee: $3.
Tours: Self-guided.
Special Feature: Art gallery.

On the rugged slopes of Mt. Veeder, Donald Hess, a Swiss mineral magnate, transformed the old Mont La Salle Winery into a showcase for his two passions: wine and art. The Hess Collection is both a winery and a museum of modern art, boasting the most impressive art collection north of San Francisco.

Up a winding road through the thick glades of Mt. Veeder, the ivy-covered winery dates to 1903. It was the first Napa Valley home of Christian Brothers before Hess renovated it and opened it to the public in 1989. Inside, a towering three-story atrium with an elevator and staircase leads to two floors of painting and sculpture, a 130-piece collection that includes the works of Francis Bacon and Robert Motherwell. A self-guided tour allows you to view both art and winery. A porthole next to one painting, for example, provides views of the bottling line. Don't miss the Barrel Chai, a dark, cool cellar where wine ages in barrels for up to 22 months. For a more in-depth look at the winery, watch a brief video.

Before leaving, stop in the tasting room. Hess concentrates on two wines: cabernet sauvignon and chardonnay. The chardonnays are stylish and oaky; the cabernets are well made. There's something about mountain vineyards that makes a rich, intense cabernet.

The wine trails of Napa and Sonoma are well marked.

Chris Alderman

MAYACAMAS VINEYARDS
Winemaker: Bob Travers.
707-224-4030;
  fax 707-224-3979.

High on the brushy slopes of Mt. Veeder, and literally in the dome of an extinct volcano, this winery traces its origins to 1889, when a San Francisco pickle tycoon built the still-sturdy stone winery. Bob and Elinor Travers have run Maya-

www.mayacamas.com.
mayacama@napanet.net.
1155 Lokoya Rd., Napa, CA
 94558.
Off Mt. Veeder Rd.
Tasting & Tours: Mon.–Fri.
 by appt.
Tasting Fee: No.

**MONTICELLO
  VINEYARDS**
Winemakers: Geoff Murray.
707-253-2802, 800-743-6668;
 fax 707-253-1019.
wine@monticellovineyards.
 com.
4242 Big Ranch Rd., Napa,
 CA 94558.
Off Oak Knoll Ave.
Tasting: 10–4:30 daily.
Tasting Fee: $5.
Tours: 10:30, 12:30, & 2:30
 daily by appt.
Special Feature: Picnic area.

**RMS BRANDY
  DISTILLERY**
Brandy Master: Rick Estes.
707-253-9055;
 fax 707-253-0116
www.rmsbrandy.com.
1250 Cuttings Wharf Rd.,
 Napa CA 94559.
1 mi. S. of Hwy. 12/121.
Hours: 10–4:30 daily.
Tasting: No.
Tours: 10:30–4 daily by appt.

SAINTSBURY
707-252-0592;
 fax 707-252-0595.
www.saintsbury.com.
1500 Los Carneros Ave.,
 Napa CA 94559.

camas since 1968. The vineyards are 2,000 feet above sea level, and the trek from Highway 29 is not for the squeamish. The winery — which was used as backdrop for a scene in *A Walk in the Clouds* — still produces the strapping monster cabernet sauvignons on which it built its reputation in the 1970s.

If the visitor center of this winery looks familiar, check the nickel in your pocket. It's modeled after Thomas Jefferson's home, Monticello. A Jefferson scholar, owner Jay Corley paid tribute to one of America's first wine buffs. Corley began as a grape grower in the early 1970s and started making wine in 1980. Cabernet sauvignon has of late superseded chardonnay as the winery's specialty. The cabernet is generally well structured and elegant.

If drinking a cognac in front of a glowing fire is your idea of ecstasy, then Carneros Alambic will reveal the secret behind your fantasy. Carneros Alambic's brandy isn't technically cognac — that comes only from Cognac in France. However, Remy Martin of France does own Carneros Alambic.

The distillery has eight red and copper stills — imported from France — that look like oversized Arabian teapots. The aging cellar, a large building half-buried in the ground, has an extraordinary perfume — they call it "Angel's Share" — which comes from the alcohol evaporating from the aging brandy. It's like standing in a huge brandy snifter. Inside, you'll see thousands of Limousin oak barrels in which the brandy ages for at least five years. California law prohibits tasting, but this brandy house does offer comparative sniffs. Don't scoff. It's rather fun.

David Graves and Richard Ward came to Carneros in search of Burgundy. Enthused by the district's potential for Burgundian grapes chardonnay and pinot noir, the duo formed Saintsbury — named for the author of the classic *Notes on a Cellar-Book* — in 1981. We have a soft spot for Saintsbury's moderately

Tasting & Tours: By appt.
Tasting Fee: No.

priced Garnet pinot noir, and its Carneros pinot and chardonnay are typically lush and complex. With its unassuming design, weathered redwood siding, and steeply sloped roof, the winery fits snugly amid the grapevines in this rural area.

SIGNORELLO VINEYARDS
Winemaker: Pierre Birebent
707-255-5990;
    fax 707-255-5999.
www.signorellovineyards
    .com.
info@silveradovineyards
    .com.
4500 Silverado Tr., Napa,
    CA 94558.
Tasting: 10–5 daily.
Tasting Fee: $10.
Tours: No.

This small winery has garnered attention for its vibrant chardonnay and semillon, a cousin of sauvignon blanc. Its stable of red wines includes a powerful cabernet sauvignon, as well as merlot, and pinot noir. Ray Signorello's first vintage was 1985 and he prefers a low-tech, natural approach to winemaking. The winery, built in 1990, is a stylish but low-key affair.

TREFETHEN VINEYARDS
Winemaker: Peter Luthi.
707-255-7700;
    fax 707-255-0793.
www.trefethen.com.
winery@trefethen.com.
1160 Oak Knoll Ave., PO Box
    2460, Napa, CA 94558.
Tasting: 10–4:30 daily.
Tasting Fee: $5 reserve
    wines only
Tours: By appt.

Shaded by a hundred-year-old oak, this winery was built in 1886 by Hamden W. McIntyre, the architect behind Inglenook and Greystone Cellars. The Trefethen family bought the winery in 1968 and restored it, painting the redwood beauty a pumpkin orange. Tours highlight the three-level gravity-flow system designed by McIntyre, in which grapes are crushed on the third floor, juice is fermented on the second, and wine is aged in barrels on the ground level. Since its first vintage in 1973, Trefethen has made its name with chardonnay.

WILLIAM HILL WINERY
Winemaker: Jill Davis.
707-224-4477;
    fax 707-224-4484.
www.williamhill.com.
whw_club@adsw.com.
1761 Atlas Peak Rd., Napa,
    CA 94558.
Tasting: 10–4:30 daily by
    appt.
Tasting Fee: $5.
Tours: 3 Sat., by appt.

William Hill developed high-profile vineyards now harvested by Atlas Peak, the Hess Collection, and Sterling. Hill's first wine was the 1976 vintage, but this sleekly modern winery wasn't built until 1990. Hill sold the winery in 1991, but it continues without its namesake, producing consistently good cabernet sauvignons and chardonnays. The tour follows a walkway above the cellar, allowing premium views of the winemaking process.

Yountville & Stag's Leap

S. ANDERSON WINERY
Winemaker: Tim Milos.

A family-owned winery that offers a personal touch, S. Anderson specializes in sparkling

707-944-8642, 800-428-2259; fax 707-944-8020.
www.4bubbly.com.sav
wines@4bubbly.com.
1473 Yountville Crossroad, Yountville, CA 94599.
Tasting: 10–5 daily.
Tasting Fee: $5.
Tours: 10:30 & 2:30 daily.
Special features: Cave tour.

CHIMNEY ROCK WINERY
Winemaker: Doug Fletcher.
707-257-2641, 800-257-2641; 707-257-2036.
www.chimneyrock.com.
retail@ chimneyrock.com.
5350 Silverado Tr., Napa, CA 94558.
Tasting: 10–5 daily.
Tasting Fee: $7.
Tours: No.

wine and chardonnay, although its limited-release cabernet sauvignon is snatched up quickly. The tasting room is a quaint stone building at the end of a garden path. The aging caves, carved out of a nearby hillside, are the highlight of the tour.

Cabernet sauvignon has replaced putting greens at Chimney Rock. Owner Sheldon "Hack" Wilson bought the Chimney Rock golf course in the early 1980s and converted nine of the holes to vineyards. The winery is inspired by the architecture of South Africa, where Wilson was an executive in the soft-drink business. Emphasis has recently shifted from white wines to cabernet, which prosper in the Stag's Leap District.

Courtesy Clos du Val

Clos de Val winemaker Bernard Portet.

CLOS DU VAL
Winemaker: Bernard Portet.
707-259-2200, 800-993-9463; fax 707-252-6125.
www.closduval.com.
cdv@closduval.com.
5330 Silverado Tr., Napa, CA 94558.
Tasting: 10–5 daily.

Bernard Portet was raised among the casks and vines of Chateau Lafite-Rothschild, where his father was cellar master. The Bordeaux influence is strong here, both in the wines and the winery. An elegant and understated building surrounded by vineyards, Clos du Val evokes a small country winery, with red roses marking the end of each vine row, in typical French fashion. The tasting room

Tasting Fee: $5, complimentary with tour.

has a vaulted ceiling and windows that open into the cellar.

Established in 1972, Clos du Val helped pioneer the notion that cabernet sauvignons need not be muscular monsters to age well. To anyone who has tasted a Lafite-Rothschild this is no secret, but it wasn't the established thinking in Napa Valley at the time. Clos du Val's cabernets are typically elegant and complex. The winery's roster includes a wonderfully fleshy zinfandel, but the merlot and pinot noir can be inconsistent.

COSENTINO WINERY
Winemaker: Mitch Cosentino.
707-944-1220, 800-764-1220; fax 707-994-1254.
www.cosentinowinery.com.
finewines@ cosentino winery.com.
7415 St. Helena Hwy, PO Box 2818, Yountville, CA 94599.
Hwy. 29.
Tasting: 10–5:30 daily.
Tasting Fee: $5.
Tours: No.

Cosentino specializes in blends with romantic names. Cosentino's bordeaux-style blend of cabernet sauvignon, merlot, and cabernet franc is called The Poet, and it's typically big and tannic. The reserve chardonnay is dubbed The Sculptor. The merlot and pinot noir lack nom de plumes, but they are nicely done. The winery is a modest manor with a friendly tasting room.

DOMAINE CHANDON
Winemaker: Wayne Donaldson.
707- 944-8844; fax 707-944-1123.
www.chandon-usa.com.
customerservice@chandon .com.
One California Dr., Yountville, CA 94599.
Hours: 10–6 daily Apr. 1–Dec.1, 10–6 Wed.–Sun. late Jan.–Mar.31.
Tasting Fee: $8–$12; by the glass $4-7.
Tours: On the hour, 11–5 daily.
Special Features: Restaurant.

The turning point for California sparkling wine came in 1973 when Moet-Hennessy built this ultramodern winery in the hills west of Yountville. If that famed French champagne house believed in Napa's potential, then California winemaking had come of age. Thus began the rush of European sparkling wine firms to Northern California.

Driving along Highway 29, you'd hardly notice the glass and native-stone bunker built into an oak-covered knoll. Inside is a museum with artifacts and explanations of *méthode champenoise*, the classic French process of making bubbly. The tour is thorough, and takes visitors past the mechanized riddling racks, the bottling line, etc.

Domaine Chandon makes a variety of sparkling wines, from a round and refreshing brut to the expensive and intense Etoile. Most are available by the glass in the stylish tasting salon, where on warm days you can sit on the sun-drenched terrace. The restaurant is considered one of Napa Valley's best (see Chapter Five, *Restaurants & Food Purveyors*).

PINE RIDGE WINERY

Winemaker: Stacy Clark.
707-253-7500, 800-575-9777;
    fax 707-253-1493.
www.pineridgewine.com.
info@pineridge wine.com.
5901 Silverado Tr., Napa, CA
    94558.
Tasting: 10:30–4:30daily.
Tasting Fee: $5–$10.
Tours: 10:15, 1, & 3 by appt.
Tour Fee: $10.
Special Features: Picnic area,
    cave tour.

Pine Ridge is an unassuming winery sequestered among the hills along Silverado Trail. The tasting room recently expanded. Take your glass on the patio or explore the shady grounds. There's even a swing. The tour begins in the vineyard and treks through the aging caves, where samples from oak barrels are offered. The winery's cabernet sauvignon has recently recovered from a slump, and its chenin blanc is one of the best in Wine Country.

ROBERT SINSKEY
VINEYARDS

Winemaker: Jeff Virnig.
707-944-9090, 800-869-2030;
    fax 707-944-9092.
www.robertsinskey.com.
rsv@robertsinskey.com.
6320 Silverado Tr., Napa, CA
    94558.
Tasting: 10:30–4:30 daily.
Tasting Fee: $10 (goes
    toward wine purchase of
    2 or more bottles).
Tours: By appt.
Special Features: Cave tour.

On a rise overlooking Silverado Trail, this winery blends a modern design with the warmth of stone and redwood. The ceiling of the tasting room stretches 35 feet high, wisteria entwines courtyard columns, and through a huge glass window you can get a good view of the winery at work. The tour includes a walk through the winery's extensive cave, which is dug into the hillside behind the winery, as well as a hike through the winery's culinary garden. The pinot noir is one of the best in Napa, and the merlot is first rate.

SHAFER VINEYARDS

Winemaker: Elias
    Fernandez.
707-944-2877;
    fax 707-944-9454.
www.shafervineyards.com.
shafer@shafer vineyards.com.
6154 Silverado Tr., Napa, CA
    94558.
Tasting & Tours: Mon.–Fri.
    by appt.; closed weekends
    & holidays.
Tasting Fee: No.

Dynamite is not often required to plant vineyards, but back in 1972 John Shafer was convinced that hillsides were the best place to grow cabernet sauvignon. Mountain vineyards may be the rage now, but they weren't then. The soil is shallow on the hills below the Stag's Leap palisades, so dynamite was required to terrace the vineyards. The vines struggle against the bedrock to find water and nourishment, and these stressed and scrawny vines produce intense wines.

Shafer's winery is a classic California ranch. The tasting room opens through French doors onto a second-floor verandah with an expansive view of lower Napa Valley. Under the vine-covered hill behind the winery is an 8,000-square-foot cave that the Shafers completed in 1991. Carved out of solid rock, the cave — cool and immaculately clean — is the high point of the tour.

Shafer's top cabernet sauvignon is the Hillside Select and it is typically brawny. The Stag's Leap District cab is usually blended with merlot, which makes it softer. Merlot is also bottled separately, along with chardonnay and a recent addition dubbed Firebreak, a blend of cabernet and sangiovese, the chianti grape.

SILVERADO VINEYARDS
Winemakers: Jonathan Emmerich and Jack Stuart.
707-257-1770, 800-997-1770; fax 707-257-1538.
www.silveradovineyards. com.
info@silverado vineyards. com.
6121 Silverado Tr., Napa, CA 94558.
Tasting: 10:30–5 daily (summer), 11–4:30 daily (winter).
Tasting Fee: $7.
Tours: By appt.

Rare is the winery that shines with cabernet sauvignon and chardonnay. Add the challenge of merlot and sauvignon blanc, and the odds are stacked against it. Somehow, Silverado pulls it off, regularly producing outstanding examples of each. Best of all, its wines remain reasonably priced.

Built by the Walt Disney family in 1981, Silverado offers a dramatic view from its perch atop a Silverado Trail knoll. Silverado doesn't pour all its wines in its denlike tasting room, but there's no going wrong. The cabernet is lush and ripe with raspberry fruit; the reserve cabernet is a knockout, as is the reserve chardonnay.

STAG'S LEAP WINE CELLARS
Winemaker: Warren Winiarski and Michael Silacci.
707-944-2020; fax 707-257-7501.
www.stagsleapwinecellars .com.
info@cask23.com.
5766 Silverado Tr., Napa, CA 94558.
Tasting: 10–4:30 daily.
Tasting Fee: $5; free with tour.
Tours: By appt.

Stag's Leap Wine Cellars falls into the select pilgrimage category. In 1976, it achieved instant fame when its 1973 cabernet won the famous Paris tasting, which changed the way the world looked at California wine. Hidden within an oak grove, Stag's Leap is an ever-growing village of buildings. Founded by the Winiarski family in 1972, the winery has an unassuming charm, despite its fame. The tasting room is merely a table tucked among towering wooden casks in one of the aging cellars.

A handful of wines are offered for tasting every day. Don't expect to sample the winery's premier bottling Cask 23, a cabernet blend with a steep price tag, but the other reserve cabernets are rich with velvety fruit and are often on the list. Be sure to try their lean and crisp chardonnays.

Oakville & Rutherford

BEAULIEU VINEYARD
Winemaker: Joel Aiken.
707-967-5230, 800-264-6918; fax 707-967-1066.
www.bv-wine.com.
bvfeedback@udvna.com.
1960 St. Helena Hwy., PO Box 219, Rutherford, CA 94573.

If you could sum up Napa Valley winemaking with a single bottle of wine, it would be the Georges de Latour Private Reserve Cabernet Sauvignon by Beaulieu. Though no longer the best cabernet in the valley, it has been the yardstick against which all other cabernets have been measured.

Pronounced *bowl-you*, or called BV for short, Beaulieu is one of Napa's most distinguished winer-

Beaulieu Vineyards revolutionized California cabernet.

Thomas Hallstein/Outsight

On Hwy. 29.
Tasting: 10–5 daily.
Tasting Fee: $5; $25 for private reserve wines.
Tours: 11–4 daily, on the hour.
Special Features: Gifts.

ies, dating back to 1900 when Frenchman Georges de Latour began making wine. In 1938 Latour hired a young Russian immigrant, Andre Tchelistcheff, who went on to revolutionize California cabernet. Today, though, Beaulieu struggles to maintain that rich tradition.

Built of brick and covered with ivy, the winery isn't particularly impressive, but a tour can be an eye-opener, particularly passing the forest of towering redwood tanks. A video in the visitor center briefs guests on Beaulieu's past and present. Three or four wines are offered; sip as you browse through the museum of old bottles and memorabilia. The crisp sauvignon blanc is good for the price, and the chardonnays are much improved. Tastings of the Private Reserve are offered in a special tasting room.

CAKEBREAD CELLARS
Winemaker: Bruce Cakebread.
707-963-5221, 800-588-0298; fax 707-967-4012.
www.cakebread.com.
cellars@cakebread.com.
8300 St. Helena Hwy., PO Box 216, Rutherford, CA 94573.
On Hwy. 29.
Tasting: 10–4:30 daily, except major holidays.
Tasting Fee: $5 and $10.
Tours: By appt.

The Cakebread clan runs this winery set in prime cabernet sauvignon territory. Jack and Dolores Cakebread began making wine in 1973 and have won a loyal following. A striking new winery, surrounded by gardens and vineyards, opened in 1996. While you're in the tasting room, try the melony sauvignon blanc — one of the best. Cakebread's cabernet sauvignons and chardonnay, lean and rigid on release, bloom after a few years.

CAYMUS VINEYARDS
Winemakers: Chris Phelps and Jon Bolta.
707-967-3010.
707-963-5958.
www.caymus.com.
8700 Conn Creek Rd., PO Box 268, Rutherford, CA 94573.
Tasting: By appt.
Tasting Fee: No.

No American wine is more highly regarded than the Caymus Special Selection cabernet sauvignon. OK, you could argue in favor of cabernets by Dunn or Harlen Estate or new players like Screaming Eagle, but few wines make the "Best of . . ." lists of critics and wine lovers as often as Caymus SS. At release, people crowd the winery for the honor of paying $100 a bottle.

Caymus remains a low-frills family outfit and tampers little with its wines. The main 40-acre vineyard lies east of the Napa River in the heart of Napa Valley's cabernet country, a blessed location. The tasting room is in a modern winery made of sturdy fieldstone. Don't expect to taste the Special Selection, but the regular cabernet and the white blend Conundrum are exceptional.

CHAPPELLET WINERY
Winemaker: Phillip Corallo-Titus.
707-963-7136, 800-4-WINERY; fax 707-963-7445.
www.chappellet.com.
winery@chappellet.com.
1581 Sage Canyon Rd., St. Helena, CA 94574.
Tasting & Tours: 10:30 & 2 Mon.–Fri. By appt.
Tasting Fee: $7.

Styled like a pyramid, this winery would make a striking statement along Highway 29. Instead, it is hidden among the rustic hills east of the valley. Built in the late 1960s by Donn and Molly Chappellet, the winery was only the second to open in the county after Prohibition. The vineyards are steeply terraced and produce a firm cabernet sauvignon as well as something called Old Vines Cuvee, a classic white blend made mostly from chenin blanc.

CHATEAU POTELLE
Winemaker: Marketta Fourmeaux.
707-255-9440; fax 707-255-9444.
www.chateaupotelle.com.
info@chateau potelle.com.
3875 Mt. Veeder Rd., Napa, CA 94558.
Tasting: 11–5 Thurs.–Mon., varies in winter.
Tasting Fee: No.
Tours: By appt.
Special Features: Picnic area.

High on the crest of Mt. Veeder, Chateau Potelle is a respite from busy Highway 29. Bordeaux-born Jean-Noel and Marketta Fourmeaux du Sartel bought Vose vineyards in the early 1980s and renamed it for the family's 900-year-old castle in France. Specialties include cabernet sauvignon and zinfandel. The picnic area has an imposing view.

FRANCISCAN OAKVILLE ESTATE
Winemaker: Larry Levin.
707-963-7111, 800-529-9463; fax 707-963-7111.

Franciscan is the home base of four labels: Estancia, Mt. Veeder, Pinnacles, and of course Franciscan. Each has its niche, and combined they are a formidable presence. Franciscan focuses on Oakville grapes, including a delightful zinfandel and

The handsome tasting room of Franciscan Vineyards in Rutherford.

Thomas Hallstein/Outsight

www.franciscan.com.
amy@franciscan.com.
1178 Galleron Rd., PO Box 407, Rutherford, CA 94574.
At Hwy. 29.
Tasting: 10–5 daily.
Tasting Fee: No.
Tours: No.
Special Features: gifts.

a complex reserve chardonnay dubbed Cuvée Sauvage. Estancia is the bargain label, but there's nothing second-rate about its cabernet sauvignon from Alexander Valley. Mt. Veeder specializes in burly mountain-born cabernets, and Pinnacles makes fine pinot noir and chardonnay from Monterey grapes. A stylish new visitors center opened in 2001.

FROG'S LEAP WINERY
Winemaker: John Williams.
707-963-4704, 800-959-4704; fax 707-963-0242.
www.frogsleap.com.
ribbit@frogsleap com.
8815 Conn Creek Rd., PO Box 189, Rutherford, CA 94573.
Retail: 10–4 Mon.–Sat.
Tasting & Tours: By appt. only.
Tasting Fee: No.

It's rare to find a winery with a sense of humor as well oiled as Frog's Leap. Ribbit is printed on every cork and the weathervane atop the winery sports a leaping frog. The name, a take-off of Stag's Leap Wine Cellars, was inspired by the winery's original site, an old St. Helena frog farm. Founders Larry Turley and John Williams parted ways in 1994, and Williams moved Frog's Leap south and restored a winery that dates from 1884. All five wines — cabernet sauvignon, zinfandel, merlot, chardonnay, and sauvignon blanc — are reliable and often superb. Tastings take place in the vineyard house behind the winery.

GRGICH HILLS CELLARS
Winemaker: Mike Grgich.
707-963-2784, 800-532-3057; fax 707-963-8725.
www.grgich.com.
info@grgich.com.

French wine lovers worship the land, but in California the winemaker is king. Cult followings have a way of developing, as with Mike Grgich, one of Napa Valley's best-known characters. The scrappy immigrant from the former Yugoslavia became a star in 1976 when as winemaker at

Chris Alderman

Winemaker Mike Grgich enjoys a sip of cabernet sauvignon in the barrel room of his winery.

1829 St. Helena Hwy., PO Box 450, Rutherford, CA 94573.
On Hwy. 29.
Tasting: 9:30–4:30 daily, except major holidays.
Tasting Fee: $5 weekends.
Tours: 11 & 2 Mon.–Fri., 11 & 1:30 weekends, by appt.

Chateau Montelena his 1973 chardonnay beat Burgundy's best whites in the famous Paris tasting. Later, Grgich joined with Austin Hills and opened this winery.

An ivy-covered stucco building with a red-tile roof, Grgich's winery remains a house devoted to chardonnay. Elegant and rich, it's consistently among the finest in California. Grgich also makes a graceful fumé blanc and has considerable luck with zinfandel and cabernet sauvignon. All this can be sampled in Grgich's modest tasting room, where the smell of oak and wine float in from the barrel-aging room nearby. You might see a feisty little fellow with a black beret — that's Grgich.

GROTH VINEYARDS AND WINERY
Winemaker: Michael Weis.
707-944-0290;
 fax 707-944-8932.
www.grothwines.com.
ccilurzo@grothwines.com.
750 Oakville Cross Rd., PO Box 390, Oakville, CA 94562.
Tasting: 10–4 Mon.–Sat., by appt.
Tasting Fee: $5.
Tours: 11 & 2 Mon.–Fri., 11 Sat.

This California Mission-style winery is a grand sight along the Oakville Cross Rd. It's also home to one of California's most sought-after cabernet sauvignons, the Groth Reserve. A former executive with Atari — the hallway near the barrel room is lined with video games — Dennis Groth began making wine in 1982, and his graceful winery was completed in 1990.

The tour is enlightening, beginning on a terrace that overlooks the vineyards, continuing past the bottling line and the cavernous barrel aging room, ending finally at the tasting bar. Groth cabernets typically have a lush elegance married with a firm backbone.

**MINER FAMILY
VINEYARDS**
Winemaker: Gary
Brookman.
707-945-1270, 800-366-9463;
fax 707-945-1280.
www.minerfamilywines
.com.
info@minerwines.com.
7850 Silverado Tr., PO Box
367, Oakville 94562.
Tasting: 11–5 daily.
Tasting Fee: $5.
Tours: By appt.

Arecent addition to Napa Valley, this winery is already making some impressive cabernet sauvignons and zinfandels. David Miner, a former software salesman, purchased a 60-acre vineyard high above the valley in 1989. A new winery recently sprung up along Silverado Trail, and it's a smart-looking edifice, done in a rich golden hue and a modern Mediterranean style. The tasting room, sleek in its polished wood tones, offers a grand view of the valley. Visitors can watch the winery in action through wide windows that overlook the barrel and fermentation rooms.

*A toast on the terrace of
Mumm Napa Valley.*

Chris Alderman

MUMM NAPA VALLEY
Winemaker: Greg Fowler
and Rob McNeil.
707-942-3434,
800-MUM-NAPA;
fax 707-942-3467.
www.mummcuvee
napa.com.
concierge@ sparkling.com.
8445 Silverado Tr., PO Box
500, Rutherford, CA
94573.
Hours: 10–5 daily.
Tasting Fee: Sold by the
glass.
Tours: On the hour, 10–3
daily.
Special Features: Patio, gifts.

Mumm Napa Valley may have a French pedigree, but it's a California child through and through. The winery is a long, low ranch barn with redwood siding and a green slate roof. Mumm blends traditional French *méthode champenoise* with the distinctive fruit of Napa Valley, and the result is some of California's best sparkling wines.

The winery tour offers a detailed look at the French way of making sparkling wine. Guides first lead you inside a football field of a room housing giant tanks where the grape juice is fermented. Then they continue through long hallways, allowing gallery views of the winemaker's lab, bottling plant, aging cellars, etc.

Brut Prestige is the main release, a snappy blend

of pinot noir and chardonnay, and Blanc de Noirs is a zesty rosé. The salon is quaint and country, with sliding glass doors that allow easy views of the Rutherford countryside. There's also an outdoor patio when the day begs a seat in the sun.

NAPA WINE COMPANY
707-944-1710, 800-848-9630; fax 707-944-9749.
www.napawineco.com.
retail@napawineco.com.
7830-40 St. Helena Hwy., PO Box 434, Oakville, CA 94562.
On Hwy. 29.
Tasting: 10–5 daily, By appt.
Tasting Fee: $5.

It may just be a large warehouse, but this facility is home to many of Napa Valley's leading wine labels. Dozens of winemakers and wineries — even star winemaker Helen Turley — use the company's equipment and rents space to store barrels. Entering through the tall wooden arched doors of the tasting room, visitors can taste and purchase wines from labels such as Lamborn, Fife, Pahlmeyer, Oakford, and Mason.

Francis Ford Coppola in the "Captain's Room" at the former Inglenook chateau, now home to the Niebaum–Coppola Estate Winery.

Courtesy D. Kopol Bonick

NIEBAUM-COPPOLA ESTATE WINERY
Winemakers: Scott McLeod.
707-968-1177.
www.niebaum-coppola.com.
1991 St. Helena Hwy., PO Box 208, Rutherford, CA 94573.
On Hwy. 29.
Tasting: 10–5 daily.
Tasting Fee: $7.50.
Tours: 10:30 & 2:30 daily.
Tour Fee: $20, includes wine and cheese.
Special Features: Museum devoted to Coppola films and wine history, gifts, café.

Francis Ford Coppola, famed director of *The Godfather* series and *Apocalypse Now,* rescued the Inglenook chateau from potential oblivion in late 1994. Heublein Inc., a conglomerate with little regard for Napa history, had sold the Inglenook brand name to another firm, and seemed prepared to leave the circa-1888 chateau vacant.

Coppola's affections for Inglenook date to the mid-1970s when he bought the former home of Inglenook's founder, Gustave Niebaum, which is next to the winery. Coppola released his own wine, Rubicon, a stout yet elegant bordeaux-style blend, beginning with the 1978 vintage. He now has added zinfandel, chardonnay, plus an everyday red and white done in a hearty Italian style.

Coppola has lovingly restored the chateau, the romantic ideal of what a Napa Valley winery should look like: a sturdy stone castle, shrouded in ivy and enveloped by vineyards. Visitors approach the winery through a long tree-lined driveway. Scottish for "cozy corner," Inglenook originated in 1880 when Niebaum, a Finnish sea captain, came to Rutherford and spent some of the fortune he made in the fur trade on building this towering Gothic structure. The history of the chateau is on display inside, as well as Coppola movie memorabilia such as his Oscar for *Godfather II*.

OPUS ONE
Winemakers: Tim Mondavi
 and Patrick Leon.
707-944-9442;
 fax 707-948-2496.
www.opusonewines.com.
info@opusonewinery.com.
7900 St. Helena Hwy., PO
 Box 6, Oakville, CA 94562.
On Hwy. 29.
Tasting: 10:30–3:30 daily.
Tours: 10:30 daily, by appt.
Tasting Fee: $25.

A joint venture between Robert Mondavi and France's Chateau Mouton-Rothschild, Opus One is an elegant temple, a cross between a Mayan palace and Battlestar Galactica. Designed by the firm that created San Francisco's Transamerica Pyramid, the winery opened in 1991 but was largely inaccessible to the public until 1994. Built of Texas limestone and untreated redwood, the building is partially buried by an earthen berm. The courtyard entrance is a circular colonnade and above is an open-air pavilion that looks out over a sea of vines. The interior blends classic French antiquity with warm California hues.

It's apropos that the winery makes a vivid architectural statement. Opus One has been one of Napa Valley's highest profile wines since its first vintage in 1979. The wine — a blend of cabernet sauvignon, cabernet franc, and merlot — is a classic: rich, oaky, and elegant.

As the tour reveals, few wineries treat their grapes and juice as delicately as Opus One. Arriving in small bins, grapes are sorted by hand — an arduous task — and the juice flows by gravity, not by pump, to the tank room below. The system is advanced in its simplicity. The tasting room fee is extravagant (what do you expect for a $120 bottle of wine?), but the pour is generous.

PEJU PROVINCE
Winemaker: Anthony Peju.
707-963-3600, 800-446-7358.
www.peju.com.
8466 St. Helena Hwy., PO
 Box 478, Rutherford, CA
 94573.
On Hwy. 29.
Tasting: 10–6 daily.
Tasting Fee: $5.
Tours: Self-guided.
Special Features: Garden,
 sculpture collection.

The grounds of this family-owned estate are lovely. Good reason. Tony Peju ran a nursery in Los Angeles before coming north in the early 1980s. A row of beautiful sycamores leads to the French Provincial winery, which is enveloped in white roses and other flowers. There is also a fine collection of marble sculptures. The tour doesn't take long; it's a small place. Cabernet sauvignon and chardonnay are the specialty.

A trek through the vineyard is a highlight of many winery tours, like this one at Robert Mondavi Winery.

Chris Alderman

ROBERT MONDAVI WINERY
Winemaker: Genevieve Janssens.
888-RMONDAVI.
www.robertmondavi winery.com.
info@robertmondavi winery.com.
7801 St. Helena Hwy. PO Box 106, Oakville, CA 94562.
On Hwy. 29.
Tasting: 9–5 daily.
Tasting Fee: $4 to $8.
Tours: Various tour and tasting packages, most have fees; reservations recommended.
Special Features: Art gallery, gifts.

Robert Mondavi has been such an innovator, such a symbol of the "new" Napa Valley, that it's hard to believe that his winery was founded in 1966. Once too flamboyant for conservative Napa County, his Spanish Mission-style winery now seems as natural as the Mayacamas Mountains. Since first setting out on his own from family-owned Charles Krug, Mondavi has been the most outspoken advocate for California and its wines.

Few Napa wineries are busier on a summer day than Mondavi, even though free tastings are available only with a tour, one of the most thorough in the Valley. Several different tours are offered, from a general trip through the winery to an advanced wine-growing tour. (Some tours require a fee and advanced reservations.) The basic tour leads visitors into the vineyards for a lecture on how grapes are grown and harvested, then to the grape presses and a view of all the latest wine wizardry. The tour ends in the tasting room where a selection of wines is offered, along with a minicourse on tasting wine.

Mondavi bottles one of the most extensive list of wines in the valley. Reds seem to be Mondavi's strong suit. The reserve cabernet sauvignons and pinot noirs become more magnificent every year — and so do the prices. Of course, the regular bottlings are hardly slackers.

RUTHERFORD HILL WINERY
Winemakers: David Dobson and Kent Barthman.

The winery here is a mammoth barn, albeit a stylishly realized barn covered in cedar and perched on the hills overlooking Rutherford. Carved into the hillside behind are the largest man-

707-963-7194, 800-637-5681;
fax 707-963-4231.
www.rutherfordhill.com.
info@rutherfordhill.com.
200 Rutherford Hill Rd., PO
Box 427, Rutherford, CA
94573.
Off Silverado Tr.
Tasting: 10–5 daily.
Tasting Fee: $5; $10 for
reserve wines.
Tours: 11:30, 1:30, & 3:30
daily.
Special Features: Picnic area,
gifts, tour includes barrel
tasting.

made aging caves in California, snaking into the rock a half a mile. The titanic cave doors are framed by geometric latticework that recalls Frank Lloyd Wright. A trek through the cool and humid caves is the tour highlight. Merlot is the star here, and it is typically fleshy with a tannic backbone. It remains well-priced.

The smell station is just one of the interactive exhibits at St. Supery.

Chris Alderman

**ST. SUPERY VINEYARD
AND WINERY**
Winemaker: Michael
Beaulac.
707-963-4507, 800-942-0809;
fax 707-963-4526.
www.stsupery.com.
info@ stsupery.com.
8440 St. Helena Hwy,
Rutherford, CA 94573.
On Hwy. 29.
Hours: 9:30–6 daily
May–Oct., 9:30–5 daily
Nov.–Apr.
Tasting Fee: $5 (lifetime
card), $10 reserve wines.
Tours: Guided and self-
guided; call for info.

Wineries, on the whole, aren't the best place to take kids. St. Supery is the exception. It adds a touch of science museum adventure, with colorful displays, hands-on activities, and modern winery gadgetry.

St. Supery was established in 1982, when French businessman Robert Skalli bought Edward St. Supery's old vineyard and built a state-of-the-art winery next door to St. Supery's original Queen Anne Victorian. A second-floor gallery shows off the day-to-day activities. Windows reveal the bottling line, the barrel aging room, and the like. A highlight is the "smell station," where noses are educated on the nuances of cabernet sauvignon and sauvignon blanc. Ever hear cabernet described as cedar or black

Special Features: Interactive wine museum, gifts.

cherry? Hold your nose to a plastic tube, and smell what they mean. Another display gives you a peek under the soil to see the roots of a grapevine. St. Supery offers a solid cabernet sauvignon and an exceptional sauvignon blanc, among other wines.

SEQUOIA GROVE WINERY

Winemaker: James Allen.
707-944-2945, 800-851-7841; fax 707-963-9411.
www.sequoiagrove.com.
info@sequoiagrove.com.
8338 St. Helena Hwy., Napa, CA 94558.
On Hwy. 29 in Rutherford.
Tasting 10:30–5 daily.
Tasting Fee: $5.
Tours: 11:30 & 2, Fri.–Sun.

Dwarfed by century-old sequoia trees, this winery is easy to overlook along Highway 29, but the cabernet sauvignons are worth the stop. Wine was made in the redwood barn before Prohibition, but the wine and the winery had been long forgotten when the Allen family began making wine there again in 1980. Samples are offered from a small table in a corner of the winery. The chardonnay is solid, but the regular and reserve cabernets can achieve greatness.

SILVER OAK CELLARS

Winemakers: Dan Baron.
707-944-8808, 800-273-8809; fax 707-944-2817.
www.silveroak.com.
info@silveroak.com.
915 Oakville Cross Rd., PO Box 414, Oakville, CA 94562.
Tasting: 9–4 Mon.–Sat.
Tasting Fee: $10.
Tours: 1:30 Mon.–Fri., by appt.

Not many wineries can live off one wine, but then Silver Oak isn't just any winery. Here, cabernet sauvignon has been raised to an art form. Low profile by Napa Valley standards, Silver Oak is known to cabernet lovers around the country, and that's all that matters. The Alexander Valley cabernet is typically more accessible than the Napa Valley bottling. But both are velvety and opulent and done in a distinct California style.

Silver Oak was established in 1972 on the site of an old Oakville dairy. Some of the dairy buildings are still used, though a Gothic-style masonry winery became home in 1982. Inside is a tasting room paneled with redwood from old wine tanks.

TURNBULL WINE CELLARS

Winemaker: Jon Engelskirger
707-963-5839, 800-887-6285; fax 707-963-4407.
www.turnbullwines.com.
lflores@turbullwines.com.
8210 St. Helena Hwy., PO Box 29, Oakville, CA 94562.
On Hwy. 29
Tasting: 10–4:30 daily.
Tasting Fee: $5.
Tours: By appt.

A small winery in the heart of cabernet sauvignon territory. The redwood winery was designed by award-winning architect William Turnbull, a former partner in the winery, which originated in 1979. The cabernet is known for its distinct minty quality.

VILLA MT. EDEN WINERY
Winemaker: Mike McGrath.
707-963-9100;
    fax 707-963-7840.
www.villamteden.com.
info@villamteden.com.
8711 Silverado Tr., St.
    Helena, CA 94574.
In Rutherford.
Tasting: 10–4 daily.
Tasting Fee: No.
Tours: By appt.
Special Features: Gifts.

Ⅰn late 1997 the name out front changed from Conn Creek Winery to Villa Mt. Eden. The wines of both labels are made at this modern mission-style winery, but owner Stimson Lane — the company behind Columbia Crest in Washington — is trying to raise Villa Mr. Eden's profile. For good reason. Few wineries are as apt at making both bargain and high-end wines. The winery's basic chardonnay and pinot noir sell for $9 or less and both are gems. Conn Creek has narrowed its list to two wines: a cabernet sauvignon and a classy Bordeaux-style red blend dubbed Anthology.

ZD WINES
Winemaker: Robert
    deLeuze.
707-963-5188, 800-487-7757;
    fax 707- 963.2640.
www.zdwines.com.
info@zdwines.com.
8383 Silverado Tr., Napa, CA
    94558.
Tasting: 10–4:30 daily.
Tasting Fee: $5.
Tours: By appt.

Ⅽhardonnay, pinot noir, cabernet sauvignon — ZD has a way with all three. The winery began life in 1969 in Sonoma Valley and transplanted to Napa ten years later. Crowned with a roof of red tile, the winery was expanded a few years back by the de Leuze family. The star is chardonnay, an opulent beauty, and cabernets are dense and powerful. The pinots are light but intensely fruity.

St. Helena

ANDERSON'S CONN VALLEY VINEYARDS
Winemakers: Gus and Todd
    Anderson.
707-963-8600;
    fax 707-963-7818.
cab@aol.com.
680 Rossi Rd., St. Helena,
    CA 94574.
3 mi. off Silverado Tr.
Tasting & Tours: By
    appt.Tasting Fee: No.

Ⅰ small winery in the foothills east of the valley, it's well off the beaten path, but its cabernet sauvignon is already one of Napa's rising stars. The 1987 vintage was the first for the Anderson family, and their cabernet is intense yet elegant. The Andersons are down-to-earth folks who welcome serious cab fans, although this isn't an extravagant venture, and refreshingly so.

BERINGER VINEYARDS
Winemaker: Ed Sbragia.
707- 963-7115.
www.beringer.com.
2000 Main St., St. Helena,
    CA 94574.
On Hwy. 29
Tasting: 9:30–5:30 daily in
    summer, 9:30–5 daily in
    winter.

Ⅰhere's something almost regal about the Rhine House, the circa-1874 mansion that forms the centerpiece of Beringer Vineyards. Sitting amid manicured lawns and meticulously restored, the Rhine House suggests that Beringer doesn't take its past or its reputation lightly.

This is one of the few wineries that has it all. A prime tourist attraction with a historical tour, it is

The Rhine House at Beringer Vineyards is a historical gem.

Alan Campbell/Courtesy Beringer

Tasting Fee: $3.
Tours: 9:30–5 daily, every half hour.
Tour Fee: $5.
Special Features: Gifts.

also one of Napa's most popular makers of cabernet sauvignon and chardonnay. The oldest continually operated winery in Napa Valley, Beringer was founded by German immigrants, Jacob and Frederick Beringer. The tour offers a few juicy details about the early days.

For a quick taste of wine, go past the Rhine House and up the walk to the Old Bottling Room, where you can take in vino and history. The room is decorated with artifacts like a photo of Clark Gable visiting or a dusty bottle of sacramental wine produced during Prohibition. To taste Beringer's top wines, climb the staircase of the Rhine House to the reserve tasting room. The reserve cabernet is stunning. Of course, there's an additional fee.

The tour takes visitors through the original aging cellar, a stone and timber building built by Chinese laborers. If you want to see a working winery, though, you'll be disappointed. The real action takes place across Highway 29, and it isn't open to the public.

BUEHLER VINEYARDS
Winemaker: John Buehler Jr.
707-963-2155;
  fax 707-963-3747.
www.buehlervine
  yards.com.
uehlers@pacbell.net.
820 Greenfield Rd., St.
  Helena, CA 94574.
Tasting & Tours: By appt.
Tasting Fee: No.

"We're not at the end of the world," John Buehler Jr. likes to say, "but you can see it from here." The winery, a complex of handsome Mediterranean buildings, is not that remote, although it is secluded above the rocky hills that overlook Lake Hennessey. The bread and butter here is zinfandel, both a ripe and tannic red and a dry white. Buehler, in fact, makes one of Napa's best white zinfandels. The cabernet sauvignon is rather inconsistent.

BURGESS CELLARS
Winemaker: Bill Sorenson.
707-963-4766, 800-752-9463;
  fax 707-963-8774.
www.burgesscellars.com.
1108 Deer Park Rd., PO Box
  282, St. Helena, CA 94574.
Tasting & Tours: 10–4 Sat. &
  Sun., weekdays by appt.
Tasting Fee: No.

Built atop the vestiges of a stone winery that dates from the 1880s, Burgess has a low profile and likes it that way. High on the western slopes of Howell Mountain, the two-story stone and red-wood winery is not one tourists happen upon. Tom Burgess began it in 1972 and built a reputation for chardonnay and a firm, age-worthy zinfandel.

CAIN VINEYARD &
  WINERY
Winemaker: Christopher
  Howell.
707-963-1616;
  fax 707-963-7952.
www.cainfive.com.
winery@cain five.com.
3800 Langtry Rd., St.
  Helena, CA 94574.
Off Spring Mtn. Rd.
Tasting & Tours: By appt.
Tasting Fee: No.

A small but elegant complex of buildings sur-rounding a courtyard, Cain Cellars sits on a ridge along Spring Mountain. The surrounding vine-yards are largely devoted to Bordeaux grapes such as cabernet sauvignon, merlot, and malbec, which are used in red blends. The top wine is the reserve blend "Cain Five," a typically lush and seductive bottling that benefits from age. Cain Cuvée is similar but more modestly scaled and priced.

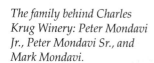

The family behind Charles Krug Winery: Peter Mondavi Jr., Peter Mondavi Sr., and Mark Mondavi.

Vano Photography/Courtesy Krug Winery

CHARLES KRUG WINERY
Winemakers: Jean Moynier
  and Jac Cole.

After working under Agoston Haraszthy in Sonoma, Charles Krug built Napa Valley's first winery in 1861. His massive stone winery was gut-

707-963-5057, 888-747-5784;
    fax 707-967-2291.
www.charleskrug.com.
information@
    pmondavi.com.
2800 Main St., PO Box 191,
    St. Helena, CA 94574.
On Highway 29.
Tasting: 10:30–5 daily.
Tasting Fee: $5.
Tours: 11:30 & 1:30
    Mon.–Fri.
Tour fee: $5.
Special Features: Picnic area.

ted by fire the day after it was finished, but he rebuilt. When the Mondavi family bought Krug in 1943, another Napa dynasty began. Robert Mondavi began his own winery in 1966 after a family feud.

The historic winery building, in disrepair for many years, has recently regained some of its former glory. Wines are still aged inside in its immense 80-year-old redwood tanks. The rest of the winemaking takes place in a facility just behind. The tour is one of the most thorough and educational in the valley, leading visitors into the vineyards and through the winery. Beginning wine tasters are put at ease here. The winery bottles one of the valley's most exhaustive menus of wines, and its cabernet sauvignons have recently regained their former stature.

DUCKHORN
VINEYARDS
Winemaker: Mark Beringer.
707-963-7108;
    fax 707-963-7595.
www.duckhornvineyards
    .com.
welcome@duckhorn
    vineyards.com.
1000 Lodi Lane, St. Helena,
    CA 94574.
Tasting & Tours: 10–4 daily,
    by appt.
Tasting fee: $20.

Duckhorn has finally opened its doors for tasting and tours, pleasing fans to no end. A chic new visitors center opened in fall 2000. Since its first release in 1978, Duckhorn has been the leading producer of merlot. It also makes a robust yet elegant cabernet, and its sauvignon blanc is consistently among the best. The second label, Decoy, offers fine bargains. A recent addition is Paraduxx — a pair of ducks on the label — and it's a unique blend of cabernet sauvignon and zinfandel.

FLORA SPRINGS WINE
CO.
Winemaker: Ken Deis.
707-967-8032;
    fax 707-967-8036.
www.florasprings.com.
tastingroom@florasprings
    .com.
Tasting Room: 677 St.
    Helena Hwy., St. Helena,
    CA 94574.
On Hwy. 29.
Office: 1978 W. Zinfandel
    Ln., St. Helena, CA 94574.
Tasting: 10–6 daily summer,
    10–5 daily winter.
Tasting Fee: $5, $8 for
    reserve wines.
Tours: No.

Flora Springs Winery now has a tasting room on the heavy tourist path of Highway 29. The tasting room is a comfortable space, decorated with humorous murals, and there's a garden in the back where you can sip from a glass on a sunny day. The winery on Zinfandel Lane is a handsome stone edifice that dates from 1888, and current owners Jerome and Flora Komes arrived in 1977. After some shaky years, the wines are coming into their own, with a line-up that includes several solid chardonnays, an exotic sauvignon blanc named Soliloquy, an intriguing red blend dubbed Trilogy, and a first-rate sangiovese.

The tasting room at Folie à Deux is a cozy den.

Chris Alderman

FOLIE À DEUX WINERY
Winemaker: Scott Harvey.
707-963-1160 or
   800-473-4454;
   fax 707-963-9223
www.folieadeux.com.
tasting@folieadeux.com.
3070 St. Helena Hwy. N., St.
   Helena, CA 94574.
On Hwy. 29.
Tasting: 10–5:30 daily.
Tasting Fee: $5.
Tours: 11 & 1 Sat. & Sun.
Special Features: Picnic area.

**FREEMARK ABBEY
   WINERY**
Winemaker: Ted Edwards.
707-963-9694; 800-963-9698;
   fax 707-963-0554.
www.freemarkabbey.com.
wineinfo@freemark
   abbey.com.
3022 St. Helena Hwy., PO
   Box 410, St. Helena, CA
   94574.
On Hwy. 29.
Tasting: 10–4:30 daily.
Tasting Fee: $5.
Tours: Daily at 2.
Special Features: Picnic area;
   gifts.

If two psychiatrists opened a winery, what would they put on the label? An ink blot, of course. No, that's not a joke, that's Folie à Deux. It was conceived by two psychiatrists with a love of wine and a sense of fun. Its name translates as "Folly for Two," a delusion shared by two people. A yellow cottage sitting on a knoll covered with vines, Folie à Deux was a sheep ranch until grapes took over in 1981. In the past, the winery had such a low profile along Highway 29 that it was easy to drive past. Recently a new entrance and winery were added, and the tasting room expanded, without Folie à Deux losing any of its trademark charm. Cabernet sauvignon and zinfandel are the specialties of the house.

Freemark Abbey was a leader in the 1960s and '70s with its Bosche vineyard cabernet sauvignon. But the wine floundered in the '80s and early '90s, only recently regaining some of its stature. An undisputed success is Edelwein Gold, a sweet Johannisberg riesling that's one of California's top dessert wines. Winemaking on the site dates from 1886 when Josephine Tychson built a wood winery, likely the first woman to build a winery in California. The present stone winery was built in 1895, and the tasting room is a lovely space with a wood-beam ceiling.

HEITZ WINE CELLARS
Winemaker: David Heitz.
707-963-3542;
 fax 707-963-7454.
436 St. Helena Hwy. S., St.
 Helena, CA 94574.
On Hwy. 29.
Tasting: 11–4:30 daily.
Tours: Mon.–Fri. at 2, by
 appt.; tours at 500 Taplin
 Rd.
Tasting Fee: No.

Driving along Highway 29, you'd never know that a redwood shack on the outskirts of St. Helena is home to one of America's most coveted wines. But the wine faithful do, and they line up every January to buy Heitz Martha's Vineyard Cabernet Sauvignon.

Curmudgeon and maverick Joe Heitz worked at Beaulieu before going his own way in 1961. Within a few years, he refurbished a stone winery in the hills of the valley's east side, keeping the old winery on Highway 29 as a tasting room. Joe died in 2000, but the winery keeps plugging. The key to Heitz's success seems to lie in the vineyards. Martha's Vineyard is just west of Oakville and produces some of the valley's most distinctive grapes. (Not everyone cares for their minty quality.)

The modest tasting room features a library of old wines for sale, and typically two or three current wines are poured, though seldom the good stuff. Heitz has a chardonnay and pinot noir that garners little notice, but its grignolino, a stout Italian varietal, has considerable charm.

**JOSEPH PHELPS
 VINEYARDS**
Winemaker: Craig Williams.
707-963-2745;
 fax 707-963-4831.
www.jpvwines.com.
jpv@aol.com.
200 Taplin Rd., PO Box 1031,
 St. Helena, CA 94574.
Off Silverado Tr.
Hours: 9–5 Mon.–Sat.,
 10–4 Sun.
Tasting & Tours: By appt.
Tasting Fee: No.

This winery pioneered bordeaux blends in California with its Insignia bottling and, except for a brief slump in the late 1980s, it has been among the best of the breed. Bordeaux blends, to explain, use the traditional grapes of that region: cabernet sauvignon, merlot, petit verdot, etc. Phelps built his large and elegant redwood barn in 1973 and drew immediate attention. The current offerings include a toasty chardonnay and some of the best cabernets in Napa Valley. We're also fans of the winery's syrah and viognier, two lesser-known Rhone-style wines that merit a taste.

MARKHAM WINERY
Winemaker: Kimberlee
 Nicholls.
707-963-5292;
 fax 707-963-4616.
www.markhamvineyards
 .com.
cbeavers@markham
 vineyards.com.
2812 St. Helena Hwy., PO
 Box 636, St. Helena, CA
 94574.

Founded in 1978, Markham quietly went about its business until the Japanese firm Sanraku took over in 1988. The wines were admirable, but the winery was largely overlooked along Highway 29. Following a multimillion dollar face-lift in the early 1990s, the winery and the wines began attracting considerable attention. Beyond large fountains is an expansive and affluent tasting room. The house specialties include merlot, caber-

On Hwy. 29.
Tasting: 10–5 daily.
Tasting Fee: $3–$5.
Tours: No.
Special Features: Art gallery,
gifts.

LOUIS MARTINI WINERY
Winemaker: Michael
Martini.
707-963-2736,
800-321-WINE.
www.louismartini.com.
254 St. Helena Hwy. S., PO
Box 112, St. Helena, CA
94574.
On Hwy. 29.
Tasting: 10–4:30 daily.
Tasting Fee: $3–$10.
Tours: 10–3:30, on the half
hour.
Tour Fee: $6

net sauvignon, chardonnay, and sauvignon blanc, all done with flair.

Run by the third generation of Martinis, this large but unostentatious winery is one of Napa Valley's best known. That's one of the charms of visiting Wine Country. You know the label, why not visit the source? Martini is one of the Valley's great overachievers, producing a voluminous roster that runs from cabernet sauvignon to sherry and other dessert wines. They're all capable and good values. Its top cabernet, Monte Rosso, has recently regained much of its glory.

Originating in Kingsburg, California, in 1922, Martini moved to St. Helena in 1933. Napa's first post-Prohibition success story, Martini flourished under founder Louis M. Martini, one the valley's great characters. Son Louis P. Martini brought the winery into the modern era and today his children, Carolyn and Michael, run it. The winery, like the wine, is a no-frills operation. Industrial outside, the winery's tasting room has a friendly staff and displays that sum up the Martini sense of family.

**MERRYVALE
    VINEYARDS**
Winemaker: Steve Test.
707-963-7777, 800-326-6069
x120; fax 707-963-3018.
www.merryvale.com.
club@merryvale.com.
1000 Main St., St. Helena,
CA 94574.
Tasting: 10–6:30 daily.
Tasting Fee: $3–$12.
Special Features: Gifts,
gourmet foods.

As Sunny St. Helena Winery, this historic stone cellar was the first winery built here after Prohibition, and in 1937 it was the Mondavi family's first venture into Napa Valley. It became home to Merryvale in 1985 when the building was renovated, updating its wine technology while retaining much of its historic charm. Done in rich wood, the tasting room feels like a large cabin and behind the iron gates you'll see the cask room with its massive 100-year-old cask. Steve Test has a gift with many wines, particularly cabernet sauvignon and chardonnay. Profile, a cabernet blend that is the winery's flagship wine, is incredible.

NEWTON VINEYARDS
Winemaker: Su Hua Newton.
707-963-9000;
    fax 707-963-5408.
2555 Madrona Ave., PO Box
540, St. Helena, CA 94574.

It's fitting that spectacular wines are produced from such a spectacular vantage point. Selling his interest in Sterling Vineyards, Peter Newton and wife Su Hua Newton carved out a new vineyard and winery in 1978 on untamed scrub land

Tasting & Tours: 11 Fri., by
appt.
Tasting Fee: No.
Special Features: Garden.

high on Spring Mountain. The vineyards surround the winery on steeply terraced hillsides.

Peter has reproduced the lovely English-style gardens of his homeland, and Su Hua contributed Chinese red lanterns and gates. There is a tank room at the bottom of a three-story pagoda; because of the building's shape, square tanks were required — highly unusual. Beneath all of this is an extensive cave system that stretches several stories down. As part of the tour, tastings are offered in a barrel-aging corridor deep inside one cave. There is no average wine produced at Newton. The merlot is consistently California's best, and the cabernet sauvignon and chardonnays are marvelous.

**PHILIP TOGNI
VINEYARD**
Winemaker: Philip Togni.
707-963-3731;
fax 707-963-9186.
3780 Spring Mtn. Rd., PO
Box 81, St. Helena, CA
94574.
Tasting & Tours: By appt.
Tasting Fee: No.

Creating a name for himself as winemaker for Mayacamas, Chappellet, Chalone, and Cuvaison, Togni began making his own wine in 1983. His cabernet sauvignon is an assertive beauty that has a legion of fans. His sauvignon blanc is rather unusual, lean and too astringent for our tastes. Togni is a meticulous and hands-on winemaker, and the winery is a modest affair.

**PRAGER WINERY AND
PORT WORKS**
Winemaker: James Prager.
707-963-7678, 800-969-7678;
fax 707-963-7679.
www.pragerport.com.
1281 Lewelling Ln., St.
Helena, CA 94574.
Off Hwy. 29.
Tasting: 10:30–4:30 daily.
Tasting Fee: $5.
Tours: By appt.

Bored with plain chocolate (cabernet sauvignon) and vanilla (chardonnay)? Try this small family winery that produces six styles of port, including two whites. Port, of course, is a slightly sweet wine fortified with brandy. Prager also makes small amounts of cabernet and zinfandel, and all the wines are organic. The winery is small, and the atmosphere is low-key.

**RAYMOND VINEYARD
AND CELLARS**
Winemakers: Walter Raymond
and Kenn Vigoda.
707-963-3141, 800-525-2659.
www.raymondwine.com.
director@raymond wine.com.
849 Zinfandel Ln., St. Helena,
CA 94574.
Tasting: 10–4 daily.
Tasting Fee: $2.50 for reserve
wines only.
Tours: By appt.

Though involved in the Napa Valley wine industry since the year Prohibition ended, the Raymond family didn't start their own winery until 1974. The winery is just off busy Highway 29 and has maintained a low profile despite its large production. The Raymonds sold a majority interest in the winery to Japan's Kirin in 1989, but the family remains involved. The cabernet sauvignon and chardonnay are always excellent efforts, and the tasting room is peaceful by Napa standards.

ROBERT KEENAN WINERY
Winemaker: Nils Venge.
707-963-9177.
www.keenanwinery.com.
rkw@keenanwinery.com.
3660 Spring Mtn. Rd., PO Box 142, St. Helena, CA 94574.
Tasting & Tours: By appt.
Tasting Fee: No.

The old Conradi Winery, set in the shady slopes of Spring Mountain, was just a hollow stone shell when Robert Keenan reclaimed it in 1974. The circa 1904 building was reborn as a modern winery. The tasting room is a polished wood loft that runs the length of the building and above the stainless steel tanks and oak barrels. Merlot became Keenan's accidental star when the winery found itself with more merlot than it needed to blend with its cabernet sauvignon. They bottled it separately, and it was a huge success.

V. SATTUI WINERY
Winemaker: Rick Rosenbrand.
707-963-7774, 800-799-2337; fax 707-963-4324.
www.vsattui.com.
info@vsattui.com.
1111 White Ln., St. Helena, CA 94574.
At Hwy. 29 (St. Helena Hwy.)
Tasting: 9–6 daily summer, 9–5 daily winter.
Tasting Fee: No.
Tours: By appt.
Special Features: Deli, picnic area, gifts.

Just about every winery has a picnic table tucked somewhere, but V. Sattui is Lawn Lunch Central. The tasting room doubles as a deli shop. The front lawn is shaded by tall oaks and filled with frolicking kids. Picnickers won't find a heartier welcome in Napa Valley.

While some wineries prefer simply to make wine and not deal with the public, V. Sattui is just the opposite. Its wines are available only at the winery. It's a busy place yet the atmosphere is cordial, not frantic. Though only completed in 1985, the Italian Romanesque winery looks like an old monastery.

V. Sattui is named for Vittorio Sattui, who founded a winery at a different location in 1885. It didn't survive Prohibition, but Vittorio's great-grandson, Daryl, revived the label in 1976. Popular wines here include a light and fruity Johannisberg riesling and a tasty dry rosé named Gamay Rouge.

SPOTTSWOODE WINERY
Winemaker: Rosemary Cakebread.
707-963-0134; fax 707-963-2886.
www.spottswoode.com.
spottswde@aol.com.
1902 Madrona Ave., St. Helena, CA 94574.
Tasting & Tours: 10 Tues. & Fri., by appt.
Tasting Fee: No.

The first Spottswoode wines were made in 1982 in the basement of this estate's 1882 Victorian. Ripe and impeccably balanced, Spottswoode's cabernet sauvignon was quickly regarded as among the best in the '80s, a stature it retains today. The cabernet's success is nearly matched by the sauvignon blanc, a wine that's typically intense in citrus and mineral character. Run by the Novak family, Spottswoode is a small enterprise that welcomes devotees of fine cabernet.

ST. CLEMENT VINEYARDS
Winemaker: Aaron Pott.

Built in 1878, St. Clement's exquisite Gothic Victorian was one of the earliest bonded winer-

St. Clement Vineyards commands an excellent view of the valley.

Chris Alderman

800-331-8266;
   fax 707-963-1412.
www.stclement.com.
info@stclement.com.
2867 St. Helena Hwy., St.
   Helena, CA 94574.
On Hwy. 29.
Tasting: 10–4 daily.
Tasting Fee: $5.
Tours: 10 & 2 Mon.–Fri.; 10
   & 11:30 Sat.–Sun., by appt.
Special Features: picnic area.

ies in the valley. Wine is no longer produced in the stone cellar. In 1979, a modern winery made of fieldstone was built in the hill behind the mansion, which now serves as a stately visitor center. The wide wood porch offers a soothing view of the valley below, and wines are poured in a small parlor. It's so traditional and homespun, it's hard to fathom that St. Clement is owned by Beringer Blass, a division of Australian beer giant Foster's. The winery has an excellent record with chardonnay, cabernet sauvignon, and merlot. The citrusy sauvignon blanc is nicely done.

SUTTER HOME WINERY
Winemaker: Rick
   Oberschulte.
707-963-3104, 800-967-4663;
   fax 707-963-2381.
www.sutterhome.com.
info@sutterhome.com.
277 St. Helena Hwy., PO Box
   248, St. Helena, CA 94574.
On Hwy. 29.
Tasting: 10–5 daily.
Tasting Fee: No.
Tours: Self-guided garden
   only.

Who'd have thought back in the '70s that a simple, sweet rosé would become the Holy Grail — some would say Unholy Grail — of California wine? Since white zinfandel became one of Wine Country's hottest commodities, Sutter Home has grown from one of Napa Valley's smallest wineries to one of its biggest.

Sutter Home's winery dates from 1874; since 1946 it has been owned and operated by Italian immigrant brothers John and Mario Trinchero. Until 1970, Sutter Home specialized in wine in bulk; its motto was: "If you can carry it or roll it through the front door, we'll fill it with wine." In 1972, winemaker Bob Trinchero began tinkering with a rosé-style zinfandel. Sutter Home called it white zinfandel, and it became the best-selling variety in America.

There is no tour — wine is made in a factory up the road — but Sutter

Home's tasting room is an expansive space that doubles as a folksy museum of wine and Americana. Visitors should try the red zinfandel as well as the white; it's sturdy and tasty. There's also a line of nonalcoholic wines dubbed "Fre" (Free).

VIADER VINEYARDS
Winemakers: Charles
 Hendricks.
707-963-3816;
 fax 707-963-3817.
www.viader.com.
1120 Deer Park Rd., PO Box
 280, Deer Park, CA 94576.
Tasting & Tours: By appt.
Tasting Fee: No.

Delia Viader's 18-acre vineyard seems more suited to skiing than grape vines. High above the valley on a rocky 30-degree slope, the vineyard — amazingly — is not terraced. The vines struggle in shallow soil, but these stressed and scrawny vines produce impressive wines. Since her first vintage in 1989, Viader, a native of Argentina, has produced only a single wine, a polished blend of cabernet sauvignon and cabernet franc called Viader.

WHITEHALL LANE
Winemaker: Dean Sylvester.
707-963-9454, 800-963-9454;
 fax 707-963-7035.
www.whitehalllane.com.
greatwine@whitehall
 lane.com.
1563 St. Helena Hwy., St.
 Helena, CA 94574.
On Hwy. 29.
Tasting: 11–5:45 daily.
Tasting Fee: $5.
Tours: By appt.
Special Features: Picnic area.

This handsomely modern winery, seemingly designed with geometric building blocks, is on its third owners since it opened in 1980 and has changed winemakers a number of times, but now the Leonardini family seems to have a firm hand on things. The winery produces first-rate cabernet sauvignon and merlot.

Calistoga

CHATEAU MONTELENA
Winemaker: Bo Barrett.
707-942-5105;
 fax 707-942-4221.
www.montelena.com.
1429 Tubbs Ln., Calistoga,
 CA 94515.
Tasting: 10–4 daily.
Tasting Fee: $10.
Tours: 11 & 2 daily, by appt.

"Not bad for a kid from the sticks," was all Jim Barrett said when Chateau Montelena jolted the wine world by winning the legendary Paris tasting in 1976. A who's who of French wine cognoscenti selected Chateau Montelena's 1973 chardonnay in a blind tasting over the best of Burgundy. Chateau Montelena's star has been shining brightly ever since.

No serious wine lover would think of leaving Chateau Montelena off the tour list. The wines are stunning, and the winery is an elegant and secluded old estate at the foot of Mount St. Helena. Alfred Tubbs founded the original Chateau Montelena in 1882, its French architect using the great chateaux of Bordeaux as inspiration. The approach isn't too impressive, but walk around to the true façade, and you'll discover a dramatic stone castle.

The façade of Chateau Montelana is a classic.

Chris Alderman

During Prohibition the winery fell into neglect, but in 1958, a Chinese immigrant, Yort Franks, created the Chinese-style Jade Lake and the surrounding garden. It is shaded by weeping willows, with swans and geese, walkways, islands, and brightly painted pavilions.

In the handsomely paneled tasting room, three wines are typically poured; the selection varies. Chateau Montelena often pours its older cabernets to give tasters an idea of the wine in its prime. The chardonnays and zinfandels are usually the current vintage, and the chardonnays continue to live up to their reputation as crisp and steely.

CLOS PEGASE
Winemaker: Steve Rogstad.
707-942-4981;
  fax 707-942-4993.
www.clospegase.com.
info@clospegase.com.
1060 Dunaweal Ln.,
  Calistoga, CA 94515.
Tasting: 10:30–5 daily.
Tasting Fee: $2.50, extra for
  reserve wines.
Tours: 11 & 2 daily.
Special Features: Art
  collection.

Clos Pegase is architecturally flamboyant, a postmodern throwback to the Babylonian temple; a shrine to the gods of art, wine, and commerce. This commanding structure of tall pillars and archways, in hues of yellow and tan, is the work of noted Princeton architect Michael Graves. It's an eye-catcher — some locals call Clos Pegase "Hollywood's idea of Egypt."

The name, Clos Pegase, derives from Pegasus, the winged horse that according to the Greeks gave birth to art and wine. Owner Jan Shrem is an avid art collector. The tour offers a glimpse of the collection, including 17th- and 18th-century French statuary artfully displayed in the winery's massive underground cave. Also, a casual browse through the visitor center reveals great treasures, with a sculpture garden featuring the works of Henry Moore, Richard Serra, Mark Di Suvero, and Anthony Caro.

Pegase's wines include a ripe and complex cabernet sauvignon and a

Clos Pegase Winery in Calistoga is a flamboyant Babylonian temple of wine.

chardonnay that is typically refined but with plenty of forward fruit. A perennial star is the merlot, but it's often rather awkward for our tastes.

CUVAISON WINERY
Winemaker: Steve Rogstad.
707-942-6266;
    fax 707-942-5732.
www.cuvaison.com.
info@cuvaison.com.
4550 Silverado Tr., Calistoga,
    CA 94515.
Tasting: 10–5 daily.
Tasting Fee: $5.
Tours: 10:30 daily.
Special Features: Picnic area,
    gifts.

Cuvaison has been around since 1970 but has come into its own recently, particularly since the Schmidneiny family of Switzerland boosted quality by wisely investing in Carneros vineyards. Chardonnay is a specialty here, but the cabernet sauvignon and merlot are not wimps.

A white Mission-style building with a red-tiled roof, Cuvaison is bordered by vineyards and a splendid landscaped picnic area. The tasting room is busy but retains a friendly tone. Tasting begins with the chardonnay, usually a remarkable and elegant wine with rich fruit; the cabernet is equally vibrant, intense, and berrylike. Merlot is the current star.

**SCHRAMSBERG
    VINEYARDS**
Winemaker: Hugh Davies.
www.schramsberg.com.
schramsbrg@aol.com.
707-942-2414, 800-877-3623;
    fax 707-942-5943.

No winery symbolizes the rebirth of Napa Valley better than Schramsberg. Jack and Jamie Davies are the quintessential post-Prohibition wine pioneers. When the Davieses bought the old Schramsberg estate in 1965, it was rich in history but near ruin. In 1862 Jacob Schram had established Napa's

1400 Schramsberg Rd.,
    Calistoga, CA 94515.
Off Hwy. 29.
Tasting & Tours: By appt.
Tasting Fee: $10–$20.

first hillside vineyard and winery and, with the help of Chinese laborers, built a network of underground cellars. After a few years of sweat equity, the Davieses became the country's premiere producer of méthode champenoise sparkling wine, and they remain one of the finest to date.

The grounds of Schramsberg are lovely. The tour offers insight into the winery's history and the art of making bubbly, but it is rather a lecture at times. The highlight is the old cellar caves lined with walls of bottles. In 1994, Schramsberg began offering tastings for the first time with its tour.

The distinctive architecture of Sterling Vineyards.

Thomas Hallstein/Outsight

STERLING VINEYARDS
Winemakers: Greg Fowler
    and Rob Hunter.
707-942-3344, 800-726-6136;
    fax 707-942-3467.
www.sterlingvineyards.
    com.
1111 Dunaweal Ln.,
    Calistoga, CA 94515.
Tasting: 10:30–4:30 daily.
Tasting: Yes.
Tours: Self-guided.
Tasting Fee: No.
Special Features: Aerial
    tramway to winery; $6
    adults, $3 ages 3–20.

Sterling isn't a just winery, it's an experience. A modern white villa perched atop a tall knoll, it just may be Napa Valley's most dramatic visual statement. Sure, there's a touch of Disneyland — you ascend on an aerial tramway — but that's Sterling's appeal. From the top, the view is unsurpassed.

Sterling retains such a contemporary look that it's hard to believe it was built in 1973. A well-marked self-guided tour allows a leisurely glimpse of the winery's workings and finally leads you to one of Napa's most relaxing tasting rooms. After picking up a glass at the counter — usually a sample of sauvignon blanc — visitors sit at tables inside or on the balcony. Once seated, the wines come to you. A varying selection is poured and most are solid efforts. Sterling can occasionally achieve greatness, particularly with its Reserve Cabernet, but inconsistency is a problem. Reserve wines are available to taste for an additional fee.

**STORYBOOK MOUNTAIN
VINEYARDS**
Winemaker: Jerry Seps.
707-942-5310;
　fax 707-942-5334.
www.storybookwines.com.
sigstory@storybookwines
　.com.
3835 Hwy. 128, Calistoga,
　CA 94515.
Tasting & Tours: By appt.
Tasting Fee: No.

With a dramatic gate along Highway 128, and tucked amid rolling hills, Storybook Mountain earns its romantic name. The winery devotes itself to one wine: zinfandel. The regular and the reserve bottlings are typically powerful and long-lived. Jacob and Adam Grimm — the Grimm Brothers, thus the Storybook name- made wine on the property back in the late 19th century. Jerry Seps restored it in 1976, and this small and unpretentious winery remains his baby. The wines reveal a hands-off attitude; the vineyards are organic and Seps tinkers little with the wine in the cellar.

VON STRASSER WINERY
Winemaker: Rudy von
　Strasser.
707-942-0930;
　fax 707-942-0454.
www.vonstrasser.com.
winemaker@vonstrasser
　.com.
1510 Diamond Mtn. Rd.,
　Calistoga, CA 94515.
Off. Hwy.29.
Tasting & Tours: By appt.
Tasting Fee: No.

Its first release arrived in 1993, but von Strasser is already catching the eye of cabernet sauvignon fans. Rudy and Rita von Strasser own prime vineyard space on Diamond Mountain, a stone's throw from the famous Diamond Creek Vineyards. The cab is intensely built and production is small, but the von Strassers are immersed, tending the vineyards and hand-sorting the grapes.

SONOMA COUNTY WINERIES

Sonoma Valley

**ARROWOOD VINEYARDS
AND WINERY**
Winemaker: Richard
　Arrowood.
707-938-5170, 800-938-5170;
　fax 707-935-5947.
www.arrowoodvineyards.
　com.
hospitality@ arrowood
　vineyards.com.
14347 Sonoma Hwy., PO
　Box 1240, Glen Ellen, CA
　95442.
On Hwy. 12.
Tasting: 10–4:30 daily.
Tasting Fee: $3–$10.
Tours: 10:30 & 2:30 daily, by
　appt.

When Chateau St. Jean was at its peak, the winemaker was Richard Arrowood, one of the first to make his name in an increasingly crowded field of celebrity winemakers. In 1986, Arrowood and wife Alis opened this winery, and the wines are among the best in California. A new chapter began with the winery in 2000, when the Robert Mondavi family bought the winery, although the Arrowoods remain on board. A new visitors center opened in early 1998, and it features a dramatic two-story limestone fireplace and views of the vineyard. The winery, a gray-and-white farmhouse with a wide porch, looks deceptively small from the outside. A tour includes the usual crushing facilities, bottling line, and barrel room, ending with a tasting. The king here is chardonnay, rich and complex. Cabernet sauvignon and merlot are also first-rate.

BARTHOLOMEW PARK WINERY

Winemaker: Antoine Favero.
707-935-9511;
    fax 707-935-0549.
www.bartholomew
    parkwinery.com.
info@vineburgwine.com.
1000 Vineyard Ln., Sonoma,
    CA 95476.
Tasting: 10:30–4:30 daily.
Tasting Fee: $5.
Tours: By appt.
Special Feature: Picnic area.

Agoston Haraszthy was the first to plant the classic grapes of France in the state. And this, as tradition holds, is the spot. The winery, a Spanish colonial, was originally a hospital for a women's penitentiary. In 1973 it was restored, and for many years it was Hacienda Winery. More recently it became Bartholomew Park, which specializes in Sonoma Valley vineyards and sells the wine exclusively at the winery. The picnic grove is one of the best in Wine Country. There's also small museum of wine in the tasting room.

Stop for a taste of wine during the tour at Benziger Family Winery.

Chris Alderman

BENZIGER FAMILY WINERY

Winemaker: Joe Benziger.
707-935-3000, 800-989-8890;
    fax 707-935-3016.
www.benziger.com.
greatwine@benziger.com.
1883 London Ranch Rd.,
    Glen Ellen, CA 95442.
Tasting: 10–5 daily.
Tasting Fee: $10 for reserve
    wines only.
Tours: 11:30-3:30 daily.
Special Features: Picnic area,
    art gallery.

If this winery seems familiar, there's a reason. Millions know this spot along the gentle slope of Sonoma Mountain as Glen Ellen Winery, the king of the $5 bottle of vino. From a rundown grape ranch purchased from a naked hippie doctor in 1981, the Benziger clan built a multimillion dollar Goliath. Weary, they sold the Glen Ellen brand in 1994, but kept the ranch, which dates from 1860, and now concentrate on their premium Benziger label.

The Benzigers may have downsized, but the winery grounds are more beautiful than ever. Past an old farmhouse and down the hill is the wooden ranch barn that serves as aging cellar and tasting room.

The tour is largely by motorized tram, leading visitors through the vineyards and grape crush facilities, with a final stop at the tasting room. The Benziger cabernet sauvignons can be a knockout in a good vintage, and the citrusy sauvignon blanc is a winner.

B. R. COHN WINERY
Winemaker: Mike Guylash.
707-938-4064, 800-330-4064.
www.brcohn.com.
linda@brcohn.com.
15140 Sonoma Hwy., Glen Ellen, CA 95442.
On Hwy. 12.
Tasting: 10–5 daily.
Tasting Fee: Reserve wines only.
Tours: No.

Manager for the Doobie Brothers and other rock bands, Bruce Cohn began a second career in wine when he bought Olive Hill Ranch in 1974. Cohn sold his grapes until 1984, when he bottled his first cabernet sauvignon. Ripe and concentrated, it was an immediate hit. Subsequent vintages have faired similarly, but his chardonnay and merlot are more routine. The tasting room, with a wood bar and terra cotta tiles, sits on a knoll covered with olive trees. Olive oil is Cohn's latest passion.

The historic Press House at Buena Vista Winery.

Courtesy Buena Vista Winery

BUENA VISTA WINERY
Winemaker: Judy Matulich-Weitz.
707-938-1266, 800-926-1266; fax 707-939-0916.
www.buenavistawinery.com.
estate@buenavistawinery.com.
18000 Old Winery Rd., PO Box 1842, Sonoma, CA 95476.

This is where it all began — California's oldest premium winery. Buena Vista is where Agoston Haraszthy, known as the father of California wine, began his experiments in 1857. Though others had made wine in Sonoma before this, they had used only the coarse mission variety grapes, brought north by Spanish missionaries for Mass wine. Haraszthy was the first to believe that the noble grapes of Bordeaux and Burgundy could thrive in California.

Tasting: 10–5 daily.
Tasting Fee: $5 for older-
vintage wines.
Tours: Self-guided; guided
historical tour at 11 and 2
in summer.
Special Features: Picnic area,
art gallery.

Visitors to Buena Vista stroll down a gentle quarter-mile path, past thick blackberry bushes and tall eucalyptus trees to the tasting room, set inside the thick stone Press House, built in 1863. Skip the official tour, and read the courtyard displays on your own. The wine is made a few miles away. Buena Vista's reputation has varied widely over the years, and the wines have been particularly disappointing recently.

CARMENET WINERY
707-996-5870, 707-996-8345;
fax 707-996-5302.
www.carmenetwinery.com.
info@carmenetwinery.com.
Winery: 1700 Moon Mtn.
Rd., Sonoma, CA 95476.
Tasting Room: 14301 Arnold
Dr., Glen Ellen
Tasting: 10–5 daily.
Tasting Fee: Older-vintage
wines only.
Tours: By appt.

This estate, high on a rocky and untamed peak of the Mayacamas Mountains, was an "alternative lifestyle community" before the Chalone Wine Group built Carmenet (pronounced *car-men-ay*) in 1982. The easiest place to try the wine is at Carmenet's new tasting room in Glen Ellen. The winery is built of dark wood and recalls a modest chateau. The crush takes place under a large wooden pavilion, and the surrounding hills are a quilt of vineyards. A tour includes a barrel tasting in the underground cellar, blasted from solid granite. Cabernet sauvignon and zinfandel are now the specialties.

Chateau St. Jean Winery draws merlot and cabernet lovers.

Thomas Hallstein/Outsight

CHATEAU ST. JEAN
Winemaker: Steve Reeder.
707-833-4134, 800-543-7572;
fax 707-833-4200.
www.chateaustjean.com.

Surrounded by luxuriant lawns and tall trees, with Sugarloaf Ridge in the distance, Chateau St. Jean is a visual treat. Opening in 1973, Chateau St. Jean drew immediate acclaim for its white wines, particularly the Robert Young Vineyard

8555 Sonoma Hwy.,
Kenwood, CA 95452.
On Hwy.12.
Tasting: 10–5 Sat. & Sun.,
10–4:30 Mon.–Fri.
Tasting Fee: $5–$10.
Tours: No.
Special Features: Picnic area,
deli, gifts.

chardonnay, a luscious and oaky beauty that helped set the standard for chardonnay.

A slump came in the 1980s, and the winery was purchased by Suntory of Japan. Star winemaker Dick Arrowood left in 1990. Chateau St. Jean is now part of the same corporation that owns Beringer, Chateau St. Jean, and other wineries. Ironically, its red wines are now drawing attention. Its cabernet sauvignons and merlot are lush and well structured.

A spacious visitors center was added behind the chateau in 2000. A good thing; the old tasting room was rather cramped on weekends. Be sure to sample the melony Johannisberg riesling, or try a bottle with a picnic; the winery has one of Sonoma's best picnic grounds. The winery is a modern version of a medieval French castle.

The ranchlike tasting room at Cline Cellars in the Carneros has a fish pond out back.

Thomas Hallstein/Outsight

CLINE CELLARS
Winemaker: Matthew Cline.
707-935-4310, 800-546-2070;
fax 707-935-4319.
www.clinecellars.com.
epcline@sonic.net.
24737 Arnold Dr., Sonoma,
CA 95476.
On Hwy. 121.
Tasting: 10–6 daily.
Tasting Fee: No.
Tours: 11, 1 & 3, by appt.
Special Features: Picnic
area.

Cline was Rhone before Rhone was popular. Fred Cline got started in the East Bay in 1982, preferring unsung Rhone-style grapes like carignane and mourvedre. Cline took up shop in Sonoma's Carneros district in, and the tasting room is inside an 1850s farmhouse with a wraparound porch. The pleasant grounds have duck ponds and rose gardens. Nearby, viognier and syrah, Cline's latest Rhone passions, are newly planted. The winery has also had great success recently with zinfandel.

FAMILY WINERIES OF SONOMA VALLEY

www.familywineries.com.
707-833-5504;
   fax 707-833-2883.
jeffmayo@aol.com.
9200 Sonoma Hwy.,
   Kenwood, CA 95452.
On Hwy. 12.
Tasting: 11–6 daily.
Tasting Fee: No.
Tours: No.
Special Features: Gifts.

Seven small wineries banded together in 1997 and opened this tasting room in the heart of Kenwood. You won't find most of these wines back home, which is half the fun, and all are modest, hands-on operations. A bottle or two from each winery is usually open. Wineries include Deerfield Ranch, Mayo Family, Nelson Estate, Sable Ridge, and Tantalus, and no matter what style of wine you prefer, you'll find something worth taking home. That person pouring you a sample just might be a winery owner or a winemaker.

GLORIA FERRER CHAMPAGNE CAVES

Winemaker: Bob Iantosca.
707-996-7256;
   fax 707-996-0378.
www.gloriaferrer.com.
info@gloriaferrer.com.
23555 Carneros Hwy., PO
   Box 1427, Sonoma CA
   95476.
On Hwy. 121
Hours: 10:30–5:30 daily.
Tasting Fee: Sold by the
   glass.
Tours: By appt.
Special Features: Gourmet
   food, gifts.

If you've had the pleasure of paying a mere $10 for Cordon Negro, the simple but tasty little sparkling wine in the ink-black bottles, then you already know the people behind Gloria Ferrer. Freixenet of Spain is the world's largest producer of sparkling wine, and it was drawn to the great promise of California. Gloria Ferrer, named after the wife of Freixenet's president, makes consistently good bubbly at fair prices.

The Carneros location places Gloria Ferrer off the high-traffic areas. Sitting dramatically on a gentle slope of a hill, the winery is a bit of Barcelona, done in warm tones of brown and red. The tasting room fireplace glows in the winter, and during the summer the terrace doors are pushed open to the cool breezes from nearby San Pablo Bay. Gloria Ferrer's tour also has great appeal, particularly the caves carved from the hillside where the sparkling wine ages.

GUNDLACH-BUNDSCHU WINERY

Winemaker: Linda Trotta.
707-938-5277;
   fax 707-938-9460.
www.gunbun.com.
info@gunbun.com.
2000 Denmark St., Sonoma,
   CA 95476.
Tasting: 11–4:30 daily.
Tasting Fee: No.
Tours: Self-guided.
Special Features: Picnic area,
   cave tours on summer
   weekends.

Passionate about wine and Sonoma Valley, Jim Bundschu does not take himself seriously. At a wine auction a few years back, he dressed as Batman, and his winery's humorous posters are classic. He even hijacked the Napa Valley Wine Train and — gasp — gave samples of Sonoma Valley wine. Behind all this frivolity is great wine and rich history. Since 1858, six generations have tended the winery's home vineyard, Rhinefarm. But wine was not bottled from Prohibition until Jim restored the original stone winery in the early 1970s. Located down a winding road, it's worth the trek. Take time to tour the winery's 10,000 square-foot cave. The zinfandels are luscious and assertive.

HANZELL VINEYARDS
Winemaker: Bob Sessions.
707-996-3860, 800-393-4999;
    fax 707-996-3862.
www.hanzell.com.
info@hanzell.com.
18596 Lomita Ave., Sonoma,
    CA 95476.
Off Hwy. 12
Tasting & Tours: By appt.
Tasting Fee: No.

The original boutique winery, Hanzell has greatly influenced California winemaking. The late Ambassador James Zellerbach, who founded the winery in 1956, patterned it after the chateaux of Burgundy. The winery, with its dark wood and pitched roof, was modeled after Clos de Vougeot, and Hanzell was first in California to barrel ferment chardonnay and use French oak barrels for aging. The winery — which makes pinot noir, chardonnay, and cabernet sauvignon — has not always lived up to its old standards.

Kenwood Winery's tasting room makes for great sipping and shopping.

Thomas Hallstein/Outsight

KENWOOD VINEYARDS
Winemaker: Mike Lee.
707-833-5891;
    fax 707-833-1146.
www.kenwoodvineyards
    .com.
info@heckestates.com.
9592 Sonoma Hwy., PO Box
    447, Kenwood, CA 95452.
On Hwy. 12.
Tasting: 10–4:30 daily.
Tasting Fee: No.
Tours: 11:30 & 2:30 daily.
Special Features: Gifts.

Don't let Kenwood Vineyards fool you. The tasting room might be in a rustic little barn, but behind the simple charm is a savvy winery, one of Sonoma County's largest. Here is a homey and relaxed tasting room with wines that will please everyone in your group. Built by the Pagani brothers in 1906, the winery is now owned by Gary Heck, who also runs Korbel Champagne Cellars.

Kenwood doesn't really have a specialty. White or reds, they have luck with both. There's no better wine with fresh oysters than Kenwood's lemony sauvignon blanc. Try Kenwood's cabernet sauvignons, particularly the expensive but outstanding Artist Series, big wines with great aging potential. On occasional weekends Kenwood matches a wine with a particular food, seeking to promote food and wine as partners.

KUNDE ESTATE WINERY
Winemaker: David Noyes.
707-833-5501;
    fax 707-833-2204.
www.kunde.com.
wineinfo@ kunde.com.
10155 Sonoma Hwy. (Hwy.
    12), PO Box 639,
    Kenwood, CA 95452.
Tasting: 10:30–4 daily.
Tasting Fee: No.
Tours: 11–3 Fri–-Mon.
Special Features: Picnic area,
    gifts, cave tours.

Since 1904, five generations of Kundes have grown grapes; and for the first time since World War II, the clan began making wine again in the late 1980s. The Kundes have 2,000 acres of vineyards; they know the personality of each and put that to use. They also brought in a fine winemaker, David Noyes, who worked at Ridge for 10 years. The strengths so far are chardonnay, typically elegant and creamy, and a muscular zinfandel made from 100-year-old vines. The winery is a stylish white barn; in the hillside beyond, the Kundes have carved out a $5 million cave to age wine. Visitors to the tasting room can watch the winery in action through picture windows.

**LANDMARK
    VINEYARDS**
Winemaker: Eric Stern.
707-833-0053;
    fax 707-833-1164.
www.landmarkwine.com.
webmaster@landmarkwine.
    com.
101 Adobe Canyon Rd.,
    Kenwood, CA 95452.
Off Hwy. 12.
Tasting: 10–4:30 daily.
Tasting Fee: No.
Tours: By appt.
Special Features: Gifts, picnic
    area, bocce court, horse-
    drawn wagon tours.

This attractive Mission-style winery, in the shadow of Sugar Loaf Ridge, is a house of chardonnay. Landmark began in Windsor in 1974, but suburban squeeze forced a move south in 1989, when Damaris Deere Ethridge assumed control. The menu includes two impressive chardonnays and a pinot noir. The tasting room is a tasteful space with a cathedral ceiling, fireplace, and granite bar. The cloistered courtyard looks onto the western slopes.

**MATANZAS CREEK
    WINERY**
Winemaker: Even Bakke.
707-528-6464, 800-590-6464;
    fax 707-571-0156.
www.matanzascreek.com.
info@matanzascreek.com.
6097 Bennett Valley Rd.,
    Santa Rosa, CA 95404.
Tasting: 10–4:30 daily.
Tasting Fee: $5.
Tours: By appt.
Special Features: Art gallery.

If you forego the beaten path for this winery, you won't regret it. Matanzas Creek is the only winery in Bennett Valley, a quiet, untouched fold of land west of Kenwood. The first wines were made in 1978 in a converted dairy barn; but these days, if you continue down the long driveway to the foot of the Sonoma Mountains, you'll find a state-of-the-art facility with a modest tasting room.

Jess Jackson, of Kendall-Jackson fame, bought the winery in 2000. Matanzas Creek focuses on three wines. The chardonnay has the delicate finesse of a white burgundy, and the sauvignon blanc is fragrant and flavorful. But the star here is the merlot, a lush, velvety ode to the classic bordeaux of the Pomerol region.

RAVENSWOOD WINERY
Winemaker: Joel Peterson.
707-938-1960, 888-669-4679;
  fax 707-938-9459.
www.ravenswood-wine.
  com.
18701 Gehricke Rd.,
  Sonoma, CA 95476.
Tasting: 10–4:30 daily.
Tasting Fee: $4 Sat. & Sun.
Tours: 10:30 daily by appt.
Special Features: Picnic area,
  gifts.

Cabernet sauvignon may be a passion, but zinfandel is an obsession. Cursed with a shady reputation by its evil twin white zinfandel, red zinfandel was once a second-class citizen. Not anymore. At its best, zinfandel is luscious and jammy, equal to cabernet in most ways and at half the price. Zin lovers have long been wise to Ravenswood.

Ravenswood is now part of the Constellation Brands, a conglomerate that owns Simi and Franciscan wineries as well as Almaden and Paul Masson. Ravenswood is an unassuming stone winery built into the side of a hill; the location fits the label, a classic image of a circle of ravens. In the old tasting room, it was a clash of elbows, so a larger room was added in 1997. None of the old charm was lost. A fire still warms the room in cool months. The welcome, unfortunately, is inconsistent; the staff is jovial one trip, reluctantly civil the next. Also, Ravenswood rarely pours its top zinfandels (Cooke, Old Hill, Dickerson), but its regular zins — and its merlots and cabernet sauvignons — are reason enough to visit.

A sure way to sample the good stuff is to visit in the late winter and spring when the zins are still in the barrel. Ravenswood's tour often includes barrel tasting. Since the winery is small, the tour is brief, but guides are detailed in their discussion of Ravenswood's natural approach to winemaking.

ROCHE WINERY
707-935-7115, 800-825-9475;
  fax 707-935-7846.
www.rochewinery.com.
info@rochewinery.com.
Mail: 28700 Arnold Dr.,
  Sonoma, CA 95476.
One Carneros Hwy. (Hwy
  121), Sonoma, CA.
Tasting: 10–5 daily.
Tasting Fee: Reserve wines
  only.
Tours: No.

On the southernmost edge of Sonoma County, in the cool and foggy Carneros district, Roche occupies a lonely spot near San Pablo Bay. The long porch of the white ranch-style winery has an expansive view. Joe and Genevieve Roche planted wines in the early 1980s, even though popular wisdom said the area was too cold. Chardonnay and pinot noir, they discovered, thrive quite nicely and have become the house specialties.

**ST. FRANCIS WINERY
AND VINEYARD**
Winemaker: Tom Mackey.
707-833-4666;
  fax 707-833-6534.
www.stfranciswine.com.
stfranciswine@ msn.com.
100 Pythian Rd., Kenwood,
  CA 95452.

Merlot is the current popular flavor, and St. Francis makes two of the best, a regular and a reserve. Both are gorgeous and full-bodied, with enough muscle to age a few years. Critics love them. Another success story for St. Francis is its chardonnay, done in a lean and fruity style. Its old-vines zinfandel packs a punch of brilliant fruit. A

Thomas Hallstein/Outsight

St. Francis Winery is an esteemed house of merlot and zinfandel.

Off Hwy. 12.
Tasting: 10–5 daily.
Tasting Fee: $5.
Tours: No.
Special Features: gifts.

SCHUG CARNEROS ESTATE WINERY
Winemaker: Walter Schug.
707-939-9363, 800-966-9365; fax 707-939-9364.
www.schugwinery.com.
schug@schug winery.com.
602 Bonneau Rd., Sonoma, CA 95476.
Off Hwy. 121.
Tasting: 10–5 daily.
Tasting Fee: Reserve wines only.
Tours: By appt.

SEBASTIANI SONOMA CASK CELLARS
Winemaker: Mark Lyon.
707-938-5532, 800-888-5532.
www.sebastiani.com.
389 4th St. E., Sonoma, CA 95476.
Tasting: 10–5 daily.
Tasting Fee: No.
Tours: 10:30–4 daily.
Special Features: Picnic area, gifts.

new winery and visitor's center opened recently, down the road from the winery's original Kenwood location.

Nestled against a windswept hill on the western edge of Carneros is a little bit of Germany. Architecturally, Schug's winery would be more at home along the Rhine, where the winemaker was raised. His wines, too, reflect his European heritage. Schug established his impressive credentials at Joseph Phelps, where he was winemaker from 1973 to 1983. His current wines, poured in a cozy tasting room, are winning, particularly his pinot noirs.

For many people, Sebastiani is another way to spell Sonoma. It's the epitome of the county's wine tradition: an unpretentious family winery, big, old, and Italian. Sonoma County's largest winery — producing six million cases a year — Sebastiani is also one of its most popular tourist attractions.

The winery dates from 1896, when Samuele Sebastiani crushed his first grapes — zinfandel, to be precise — and the press he used is still on display in the tasting room. Samuele's son August, a man with an affinity for bib overalls and stout, simple wines, built the winery's reputation on inexpensive jug wines; since his death in 1980, the family has concentrated on premium wines.

Tours offer a thorough look behind the scenes, from the wine presses to the aging tanks. The highlight is the collection of intricately hand-carved wine casks. The spacious tasting room — renovated and modernized in 2001 — is partly crafted from old wine tanks. Visitors can taste Sebastiani's wide range of wines. Try the Sonoma County cabernet sauvignon and merlot, delightful wines and excellent bargains.

THE WINE ROOM
707-833-6131.
9575 Sonoma Hwy., PO Box
  219, Kenwood, CA 95452.
On Hwy. 12.
Tasting: 11–5 daily.
Tasting Fee: No.
Tours: No.
Special Features: Gifts,
  gourmet foods.

When his career slowed in the 1970s, comedian Tommy Smothers bought a Kenwood ranch and planted grapes. Smothers Brothers wines soon followed, and over the years the fortunes of the wine have risen and fallen, depending on how distracted Tom was by comedy. Dick Arrowood makes the bulk of the wine — now called Remick Ridge — and recent vintages have been impressive. In early 1998, the tasting room became The Wine Room, a co-op with four additional Sonoma Valley Wineries now pouring their latest releases. The line-up includes: Kas, Adler Fels, and Moondance.

VALLEY OF THE MOON WINERY
Winemaker: Pat Henderson.
707-996-6941;
  fax 707-996-5809.
www.valleyofthemoon
  winery.com.
luna@valleyofthemoon
  winery.com.
777 Madrone Road, Glen
  Ellen, CA 95442.
Tasting: 10–4:30 daily.
Tours: By appt.
Special Features: Gifts.

It's not every day that a winery starts over from scratch. Brands like Beaulieu Vineyards and Charles Krug Winery have gotten makeovers in recent years, but those were just tummy tucks and face-lifts compared to Valley of the Moon Winery. When Gary Heck, who owns Korbel and Kenwood Vineyards, bought this winery a few years back it was rundown, and the wines had a nasty reputation. Just about the only thing left from the old days is the winery's original 110-year-old foundation. The new tasting room is sleek and modern, and so is the winery's bottle design, a stark yet dramatic etched bottle. But what about the wines? They're good and getting better, particularly the zinfandel and syrah.

VIANSA WINERY AND ITALIAN MARKET PLACE
Winemaker: Michael
  Sebastiani.
707-935-4700, 800-995-4740;

Sam and Vicki Sebastiani split from the family dynasty a few years back and established this ode to Tuscany high atop a Carneros knoll. Done in warm shades with a terra cotta tile roof and Italian opera music in the background, Viansa is one of

Thomas Hallstein/Outsight

Fermentation tanks are part of the décor at Viansa Winery in the Carneros.

fax 707-996-4632.
www.viansa.com.
tuscan@viansa.com.
25200 Arnold Dr., Sonoma,
CA 95476.
On Hwy. 121.
Tasting: 10–5 daily.
Tasting Fee: No.
Tours: By appt.
Special Features: Gourmet
foods, gifts, picnic area.

WELLINGTON
VINEYARDS
Winemakers: Peter
Wellington and Chris
Loxton.
707-939-0708, 800-816-9463;
fax 707-939-0378.
www.wellingtonvineyards
.com.
wv@wellingtonvineyards
.com.
11600 Dunbar Rd., PO Box
568, Glen Ellen, CA 95442.
Tasting: 11–5 (summer) and
11:30–4:30 (winter) daily.
Tasting fee: No.
Tours: By appt.
Special Features: Picnic area.

Wine Country's most festive spots. Even the stainless steel wine tanks are adorned with colorful faux marble frescoes.

The marketplace offers sumptuous picnic fare, plus a picnic area with a dramatic view. (see Chapter Five, *Restaurants & Food Purveyors*). Viansa is concentrating increasingly — and with considerable success — on Italian-style wines like barbera and nebbiolo and blends that recall a hearty chianti.

Small, family-owned wineries like Wellington are what Sonoma is all about. You'll find it just off Highway 12 north of Glen Ellen. The Wellingtons took over the winery, a white chalet with brown trim, in 1994. The property includes 11 acres of vineyards, the oldest of which dates before the turn of the century. Take a close look at the gnarly carignane vines planted out front, which date to 1933. Those old vines make for some deep, complex wines, including a first-rate zinfandel and a port. Also try the syrah, rich and slightly racy.

Russian River

ARMIDA WINERY
Winemaker: Michael
  Loykasek.
707-433-2222;
  fax 707-433-2202.
www.armida.com.
wino@armida.com.
2201 Westside Rd.,
  Healdsburg, CA 95448.
Tasting: 11–5 daily.
Tasting Fee: No.
Tours: By appt.

Three unique geodesic domes, this winery occupies the border of Dry Creek and Russian River valleys. After tasting, pause on the wooden deck to relish the view. One of Sonoma County's most recent additions, Armida bottled its first wine in 1990 and opened to the public in 1994. Wines include merlot, chardonnay, and pinot noir, all nicely done and fairly priced.

BELVEDERE WINERY
Winemaker: Bob Bertheau.
707-433-8236;
  fax 707-433-2429.
www.belvederewinery.com.
4035 Westside Rd.,
  Healdsburg, CA 95448.
Tasting: 11–5 daily.
Tasting Fee: No.
Tours: No.
Special Feature: Picnic area.
Additional Tasting Room:
  250 Center St. Healdsburg;
  phone 707-433-8236.

The patio of this winery is shaded by greenery; take your glass of chardonnay outside for a soothing sip. Chardonnay is the pillar at Belvedere, which opened in 1979. The winery produces solid wines at reasonable prices, with several first-rate chardonnays and sound zinfandel and cabernet sauvignon, most in the $10 to $20 range. Owner Bill Hambrecht draws from more than 400 acres of his own vineyards. A second tasting room opened just off the Healdsburg Plaza in 1997.

CHALK HILL WINERY
Winemaker: Bill Knuttel
707-838-4306;
  fax 707-838-9687.
www.chalkhill.com
chwtour@aol.com.
10300 Chalk Hill Rd.,
  Healdsburg, CA 95448.
Tasting & Tours: Mon.–Fri.,
  by appt.
Tasting Fee: No.

The white soil gives the Chalk Hill area its name — even though it's really volcanic ash, not chalk. Fred and Peggy Furth established this winery well off the beaten path in 1980 and has hired a series of talented winemakers. White wines thrive in the area and chardonnay is the winery's specialty; it ranges from average to excellent. The sauvignon blanc is consistently a beauty.

DAVIS BYNUM WINERY
Winemaker: David Georges.
707-433-2611, 800-826-1073;
  fax 707-433-4309.
www.davisbynum.com.
info@davisbynum.com.
8075 Westside Rd.,
  Healdsburg, CA 95448.
Tasting: 10–5 daily.
Tasting Fee: No.

Set amid tall cool redwoods and hidden above West Side Road, Davis Bynum relies on the characteristically restrained grapes of the region. These are subtle wines, not overly oaked yet strong in varietal character. Bynum began making wine in Albany in 1965 and moved to his present home in 1973. Best bets are pinot noir and sauvignon blanc. Longtime winemaker Gary Farrell — one of the finest in the business — is now only a consultant at

Tours: No.
Special Features: Picnic area,
　art gallery.

DE LOACH WINERY
Winemaker: Dan
　Cedarquist.
707-526-9111;
　fax 707-526-4151.
www.deloachvineyards.
　com.
1791 Olivet Rd., Santa Rosa,
　CA 95401.
Off River Rd.
Tasting: 10–4:30 daily.
Tasting Fee: No.
Tours: 11 & 2 daily, by appt.
Special Features: Picnic area.

FOPPIANO VINEYARDS
Winemaker: Bill Regan.
707-433-7272.
www.foppiano.com.
12707 Old Redwood Hwy.,
　PO Box 606, Healdsburg,
　CA 95448.
Tasting: 10–4:30 daily.
Tasting Fee: No.
Tours: Self-guided through
　vineyard.

GARY FARRELL WINES
Winemaker: Gary Farrell.
707-473-2900.
www.wines.com/
　gary_farrell.
10701 Westside Rd.,
　Healdsburg, CA 95448.
Tasting & Tours:
　Thurs.–Sun., by appt.
Tasting Fee: No.

HOP KILN WINERY
Winemaker: Steve Strobl.
707-433-6491;
　fax 707-433-8162.
www.hopkilnwinery.com.
6050 Westside Rd.,
　Healdsburg, CA 95448.
Tasting: 10–5 daily, except
　major holidays.

Davis Bynum. Farrell recently opened his own winery nearby.

Name the wine, and De Loach has a knack for it. Its chardonnays, intense and fruity, are among the best. It also produces a masterly collection of zinfandels, made largely from old vines. De Loach's latest success story is sauvignon blanc, typically ripe and grassy. Cecil De Loach began making wine in 1975 while still a San Francisco fireman. Today, the tasting room is in a grand redwood building at the end of a long drive embraced by vineyards.

Five generations of Foppianos have tended vines here. John Foppiano arrived from Genoa in 1896 and planted a vineyard. Wine was sold in bulk and later in jug; the family began moving into premium wine in the 1970s. The winery is unabashedly utilitarian, and the tasting room is in an unassuming wood cottage. The self-guided vineyard tour is worth a few minutes. Foppiano's stars are zinfandel and a beefy petite sirah made from old vines.

Don't let Gary Farrell's quiet demeanor fool you. He's one of the best winemakers in the business. He's been producing wine under his own label for more than a decade but remained the full-time winemaker at Davis Bynum Winery until he recently opened his own winery down the road. He seems to have the touch for just about every varietal, although he's at his best with pinot noir and zinfandel.

Hop Kiln began life as an ode to beer, not wine. Hops were a major crop along Sonoma County's Russian River at the turn of the 20th century. This is one of the few remnants from that era. Built in 1905, the unusual stone barn is topped with three pyramid towers. Dr. Martin Griffin bought and restored the barn and began making wine in 1975.

Hop Kiln Winery in the Russian River Valley of Sonoma County.

Thomas Hallstein/Outsight

Tasting Fee: Limited-release wines only.
Tours: No.
Special Features: Picnic area, lake.

The tasting room inside is rustic but pleasant, warm with wood and history. Tasters can choose from any number of wines. Zinfandel is a specialty and Hop Kiln makes a bold old-style zin that packs in the fruit. Its two generic wines are great bargains: A Thousand Flowers (white) and Marty Griffin's Big Red. Both are delightful, especially for a picnic. Outside, there is a small lake bordered by a sunny patch of picnic tables — be prepared to share with the ducks.

IRON HORSE VINEYARDS
Winemaker: Forrest Tancer.
707-887-1507;
    fax 707-887-1337.
www.ironhorsevine yards.com.
info@ironhorse vineyards.com.
9786 Ross Station Rd., Sebastopol, CA 95472.
Tasting & tours: By appt.
Tasting Fee: No.

This winery amid the undulating hills of Green Valley is Sonoma County's most respected producer of sparkling wine. Barry and Audrey Sterling bought the estate, a former railroad stop, in 1976. Elegant in its sheer simplicity, the winery stretches through a series of wooden barns and is surrounded by vineyards and gardens. The tour reveals the classic *méthode champenoise* process used in making French-style bubbly. In addition to its line of opulent sparkling wine, Iron Horse produces chardonnay and pinot noir, both fine examples.

J WINE CO.
Winemaker: Oded Shakked.
707-431-5400;
    fax 707-431-5410.
www.jwine.com.
winefolk@jwine.com.
11447 Old Redwood Hwy., Healdsburg, CA 95448.

Housed in a sleek concrete and glass structure, this ultramodern winery began life in 1982 as Piper Sonoma. In 1997, Judy Jordan took over the facility to be the new home of its sparkling wine "J." It's a classy bubbly, complex and creamy, and even the sleek-looking green bottle is a knockout. The tasting room is a stylish café. Visitors tour the winery along a concrete

Tasting Fee: Yes.
Tasting: 11–5 daily.
Tours: By appt.

JOSEPH SWAN
VINEYARDS
Winemaker: Rod Berglund.
707-573-3747;
    fax 707-575-1605.
2916 Laguna Rd, Forestville,
    CA 95436.
Off River Rd.
Tasting: 11–4:30 Sat. & Sun.
Tasting Fee: No.
Tours: No.

KENDALL-JACKSON
WINE CENTER
707-571-8100;
    fax 707-546-9221.
www.kj.com.
kjwines@kj.com.
5007 Fulton Rd., Fulton, CA
    95439.
Off. Hwy. 101.
Tasting: 10–5 daily.
Tasting Fee: $2.
Tour: self-guided garden only.
Special Features: Picnic area,
    gifts.

KENDALL-JACKSON
WINE COUNTRY
STORE
Winemaker: Randy Ullom.
707-433-7102.
337 Healdsburg Ave.,
    Healdsburg, CA 95448.
Tasting: 10–4:30 daily.
Tasting Fee: $2.
Tours: No.
Special Features: Gifts.

KORBEL CHAMPAGNE
CELLARS
Winemaker: Paul
    Ahvenainen.
707-824-7000.
www.korbel.com.
info@korbel.com.
13250 River Rd.,
    Guerneville, CA 95446.

balcony that overlooks the entire plant, where the French technique of making sparkling wine called *méthode champenoise* is detailed.

Hardly more than a bungalow, this modest structure belies Joseph Swan's near legendary status in Wine Country. Beginning in 1969, Swan was a pioneer of zinfandel, crafting heroically ripe and long-lived wines. Pinot noir became Swan's star in the 1980s. Swan died in 1989, and son-in-law Rod Berglund is now winemaker. Although the zins are no longer legendary, they remain grand creations.

In 1996, Jess Jackson — the man behind Kendall-Jackson — bought Chateau DeBaun and made it his new visitors center. The chateau itself is rather Disney-like in its notion of grandeur, but the garden is lovely. Inside you can taste a wide range of K-J brands. La Crema's forte is chardonnay and pinot noir, and Robert Pepi makes an excellent sauvigonon blanc and sangiovese. It's hard to find a better value than Calina, a line of hearty Chilean wines.

This storefront tasting room in downtown Healdsburg could be considered an outlet store. Kendall-Jackson is a Wine Country Goliath. What wine lover hasn't tried the eminently sippable Vintner's Reserve chardonnay? Overall, the wine is reliable and occasionally superb, and a varied selection is poured in the tasting room, including several other K-J brands such as La Crema and Calina.

As you drive through the gorgeous redwood forests of the Russian River area, you'll see this century-old ivy-covered stone wine cellar rising nobly from a hillside. Korbel is one of Wine Country's most popular destinations, offering romance, history, and beauty.

In the summer, to avoid the crowds, arrive early

Chris Alderman

Korbel Champagne Cellars has one of the best tours in Wine Country.

Tasting: 9–5 May–Sept., 9–4:30 Oct.–Apr.
Tasting Fee: No.
Tours: 10–3:45 daily, on the hour; garden tours at 11, 1, 3 daily in summer.
Special Features: Picnic area, gifts, garden, deli, microbrewery.

in the morning or late in the afternoon. The half-hour tour is great fun. The Korbel brothers from Czechoslovakia came to Guerneville for the trees, which were perfect for cigar boxes. When the trees were cleared, they planted grapes and made wine using *méthode champenoise*, the traditional French method of making champagne. You'll poke your nose in large wood aging tanks and learn the mystery of the riddling room, where sediment is slowly tapped from each bottle. The tasting room is one of the friendliest, and any or all of its dependable sparklers are offered. In the summer, Korbel's prized antique garden is also available for touring.

MARTINELLI WINERY
Winemaker: Helen Turley.
707-525-0570.
3360 River Rd., Windsor, CA 95492.
Tasting: 10–5 daily.
Tasting Fee: Limited-release wines only.
Tours: No.
Special Features: Picnic area, gifts, art gallery.

This historic hop barn painted a vivid red is home to a prized zinfandel called Jackass Hill. The wine comes from the steepest hillside vineyards in Sonoma County, planted in 1905. Like many old-vine zins, it grabs your taste buds like a two-horse team. Four generations of Martinellis have been farming and the tasting room is a feast of apples, dried fruit, and other goodies.

MILL CREEK VINEYARDS
Winemaker: Hank Skewis.
707-431-2121.
www.mcvonline.com.
tr@mcvonline.com.

It's hard to miss this tasting room, a redwood barn with a waterwheel. The Kreck family has been growing grapes since 1965 and bottled their first wine with the 1974 vintage. Mill Creek helped pioneer merlot but is not among the masters.

Mill Creek Vineyards, a redwood barn with a waterwheel, is a fun stop, especially for the kids.

Thomas Hallstein/Outsight

1401 Westside Rd., PO Box 758, Healdsburg, CA 95448.
Tasting: 10–5 daily.
Tasting Fee: No.
Tours: No.
Special Features: Picnic area.

Sauvignon blanc is the winery's best effort, and it's a delightful companion for a picnic on the winery's deck.

ROCHIOLI VINEYARDS & WINERY

Winemaker: Tom Rochioli.
707-433-2305;
    fax 707-433-2358.
6192 Westside Rd.,
    Healdsburg, CA 95448.
Tasting: 11–4 daily.
Tasting Fee: No.
Tours: No.
Special Features: Picnic area, art gallery.

The pinot noir vineyards of Rochioli are the envy of all winemakers. The top pinots in the business — Gary Farrell, Williams Selyem, and of course Rochioli (pronounced *row-key-OH-lee*) — begin here. Three generations of Rochiolis have been growing grapes along the Russian River. They stay close to the land and because of that, make great wine. In the modest tasting room, which looks out across vineyards toward the river, every wine is a winner. The chardonnay is ripe and buttery and the sauvignon blanc flowery and complex.

RODNEY STRONG VINEYARDS

Winemaker: Richard Sayre.
707-431-1533;
    fax 707-433-0939.
www.rodneystrong.com.
info@rodneystrong.com.
11455 Old Redwood Hwy.,
    Healdsburg, CA 95448.
Tasting: 10–5 daily.
Tasting Fee: No.
Tours: 11 & 3 daily.

A dramatic pyramid of concrete and wood, this winery has weathered many incarnations over the years but is finally coming into its own. The wines are reliable and frequently superb, with cabernet sauvignon, merlot, zinfandel, and pinot noir among the standouts. Balconies outside the tasting room overlook the tanks and oak barrels so a tour may be academic, but the official tour takes you into the vineyards for a close-hand look at grape growing. Windsor Vineyards, a sister winery,

Special Features: Art gallery, picnic area.

also makes wine here. Rodney Strong, a former Broadway dancer and a 30-year veteran of wine, is no longer involved in the day-to-day of the winery

SONOMA-CUTRER VINEYARDS
Winemaker: Terry Adams.
707-528-1181;
　fax 707-528-1561.
www.sonomacutrer.com.
info@sonomacutrer.com.
4401 Slusser Rd., Windsor,
　CA 95492.
Tasting & Tours: By appt.
Tasting Fee: No.

Harvest is called "crush," yet crush is a crude way to describe how Sonoma-Cutrer makes chardonnay. Pampering is more like it. Grapes arrive in small boxes and are then chilled to 40 degrees in a specially designed cooling tunnel. Then they are hand-sorted and, left in whole clusters, put through a gentle membrane press. A tour reveals the entire process as well as an underground aging cellar.

Once the leader in California chardonnay, Sonoma-Cutrer now has keen competition. Brice Cutrer Jones, a jet fighter pilot in the Vietnam War, founded the winery in 1981 and built an ultramodern facility that blends into the hills. Sonoma-Cutrer also has two world-class croquet courts. In 1999. the winery was purchased by conglomerate Brown-Forman, which owns Fetzer Vineyards and other well-known consumer brands such as Jack Daniels, Southern Comfort, and Lenox China.

TOPOLOS AT RUSSIAN RIVER VINEYARDS
Winemaker: Jac Jacobs.
707-887-1575, 800-TOPOLOS;
　fax 707-887-1399.
www.topolos.com.
topolos@topolos.com.
5700 Gravenstein Hwy. N.,
　PO Box 358, Forestville,
　CA 95436.
On Hwy. 116.
Tasting: 11–5:30 daily.
Tasting Fee: No.
Tours: By appt.
Special Features: Restaurant.

Hop kiln meets Greek Orthodox in this eccentric wood winery. The wines are equally offbeat, winning an equal number of fans and foes. Mike Topolos prefers hearty reds made from old vines. Zinfandel is the lead wine, but Topolos also makes petite sirah and alicante bouschet, a full-bodied workhorse rarely bottled anymore. Sharing the winery building is a restaurant that specializes in Greek food.

WILLIAMS SELYEM
Winemaker: Bob Cabral.
707-433-6425.
6575 Westside Rd.,
　Healdsburg, CA 95448.
Tasting & Tours: By appt.
Tasting Fee: No.

Our biggest problem," Burt Williams says, "is allocating the wine and trying to keep the customers happy. That's a good problem to have." Whining about allocations might seem pretentious if Williams Selyem wasn't such an unassuming enterprise. The winery, built in 1989, is a mundane building, basically one long room lit with fluorescents. There is no tasting room and no sign on the road, only a tiny plaque above the door. Yet wine lovers regularly make pilgrimages.

It's the wine, not the winery, that does the talking for Williams and Ed Selyem, who consistently produce some of the best pinot noirs in America. It's a hands-on, seat-of-your-pants affair, originating in a Fulton garage in 1981. New York vintner John Dyson bought the winery in 1998.

WINDSOR VINEYARDS
Winemaker: Toni
  Stockhausen.
707-433-2822, 800-204-9463;
  fax 707-433-7302.
www.windsorvineyards.com.
308-B Center St., Healdsburg,
  CA 95448.
Tasting: 10–5 Mon.–Fri., 10–6
  Sat. & Sun.
Tasting Fee: No.
Tours: No.
Special Features: Gifts.

If you've never heard of Windsor Vineyards, there's good reason. The wine is available only by mail order or at this storefront tasting room situated on the Healdsburg plaza. The quality of the wine, however, belies such relative obscurity. The chardonnays are nicely done in particular.

Alexander Valley

**ALEXANDER VALLEY
  VINEYARDS**
Winemaker: Kevin Hall.
707-433-7209, 800-888-7209;
  fax 707-433-9408.
www.avvwine.com.
avv@avvwine.com.
8644 Hwy. 128, Healdsburg,
  CA 95448.
Tasting: 10–5 daily.
Tasting Fee: No.
Tours: By appt.
Special Features: Picnic area.

Cyrus Alexander, who lent his name to this beautiful valley, built his homestead here. His adobe, constructed in the 1840s, remains. The Wetzel family planted vines in the early 1960s; in 1975 they built a winery with a cool cellar carved into a hill and a gravity flow system that's less stressful to wine. The tasting room is homey, with chairs gathered around a fireplace. The cabernet sauvignons are elegant and easy to drink.

**CANYON ROAD
  CELLARS**
Winemakers: Daryl Groom.
707-857-3417 or
  800-793-9463;
  fax 707-857-9413.
www.canyonroadwinery.com
canyonrd@ sonic.net.
19550 Geyserville Ave.,
  Geyserville, CA 95441.
Tastings: 10–5 daily.
Tours: No.
Tasting Fee: No.
Special Features: Picnic area,
  gifts.

A familiar sight along Hwy. 101, this classic stone building is one of the county's oldest wineries. Frank Nervo went into winemaking back in 1908. Today it's home to Canyon Road Cellars, a value-priced line of wine produced at nearby Geyser Peak Winery. Nearly every bottle is priced below $10, and they're always reliable, particularly the chardonnay and sauvignon blanc. The tasting room, a small building in front of the stone winery, is chock-full of gifts and deli treats.

CHATEAU SOUVERAIN

Winemaker: Ed Killian.
707-433-8281 or
   888-80-WINES.
www.chateausouverain.
   com.
400 Souverain Rd.,
   (Independence Ln. exit off
   Hwy. 101), Geyserville.
Mail: 400 Souverain Rd.,
   Geyserville, CA 95441.
Tasting: 10–5 daily.
Tours: By appt.
Tasting Fee: $2–$4.
Special Features: Restaurant,
   gifts.

The dramatic chalet was inspired by the old hop kilns that once spread across the Russian River Valley. As you climb the stairs and look out over the wide courtyard and huge fountain, the view of Alexander Valley is mesmerizing. Adding to the pleasure, the winery has an excellent café (see Chapter Five, *Restaurants & Food Purveyors*). Souverain's wines have improved dramatically in recent years, particularly the zinfandel and merlot. Prices remain modest.

Built by Pillsbury in 1973, Souverain has gone through a number of owners but is now part of the same company that owns Beringer and Chateau St. Jean. The tasting room in the lower level of the east tower is a stylish spot with a lofty ceiling.

CLOS DU BOIS

Winemaker: Margaret
   Davenport.
707-857-3100, 800-222-3189.
www.closdubois.com.
19410 Geyserville Rd.,
   Geyserville, CA 95441.
Tasting: 10–4:30 daily, except
   major holidays.
Tasting Fee: No.
Tours: No.
Special Features: Gifts,
   gourmet foods, covered
   picnic area.

Clos du Bois, one of Sonoma's largest and most prominent wineries, seems to do everything well and a few things superbly. They may not produce big flashy wines, but their offerings are seldom disappointing — which is surprising, considering the roster.

Vineyards are key to this success; the winery has access to some 1,000 prime acres in Alexander and Dry Creek Valleys. The reserve chardonnays from the Calcaire and Flintwood vineyards are lush and steely, though we often prefer the straightforward character of the regular chardonnay. The cabernet sauvignons are increasingly impressive, particularly the Winemaker's Reserve. The pinot noir and merlots are also contenders.

In late 1994 Clos du Bois moved its tasting room from a prefab warehouse in downtown Healdsburg to its winery just south of Geyserville. The tasting room is a friendly spot, and the staff is knowledgeable, yet they never roll an eye over novice questions.

DE LORIMIER WINERY

Winemaker: Don Frazer.
800-546-7718;
   fax 707-857-3262.
www.delormierwinery.com.
discover@delormierwinery.
   com.
2001 Hwy. 128, PO Box 487,
   Geyserville, CA 95441.
Tasting: 10–4:30 daily.
Tasting Fee: No.
Tours: Self-guided.

Set amid a sea of vines in the north end of Alexander Valley, this winery is well off the beaten path. A modern barn with brown shingles, it dates to 1986 when surgeon Alfred de Lorimier decided to make wine with the grapes he had been growing for years. The biggest success is sauvignon blanc and a crisp and elegant white blend called Spectrum.

FIELD STONE WINERY & VINEYARDS
Winemaker: Tom Milligan.
707-433-7266, 800-54GRAPE;
    fax 707-433-2231.
www.fieldstonewinery.com.
fieldstone1@earthlink.net.
10075 Hwy. 128,
    Healdsburg, CA 95448.
Tasting: 10–5 daily.
Tasting Fee: No.
Tours: By appt.
Special Features: Picnic area.

Cozy inside an Alexander Valley knoll, this winery takes its name from the rugged stone that decorates the façade. Open the wide wooden door and amble past the oak barrels to the tasting room, and you've pretty much taken the tour. The house specialty is petite sirah from circa 1894 vines. It's a ripe bruiser. Cabernet sauvignon and zinfandel are also recommended. Superb picnic grounds.

GEYSER PEAK WINERY
Winemakers: Daryl Groom.
800-255-9463;
    fax 707-857-9402.
www.geyserpeakwinery.com.
tastingroom@geyser
    peakwinery.com.
22281 Chianti Rd., PO Box
    25, Geyserville CA 95441.
Tasting: 10–5 daily.
Tasting Fee: $5, reserve
    wines only.
Tours: No.
Special Features: Picnic area,
    gifts.

The arrival of Australian winemaker Daryl Groom in 1989 put this once-sleepy winery on the map. A former winemaker for Penfolds, he cut his teeth on Grange, one of the world's most respected wines. He has the touch, whether the wine is chardonnay or cabernet sauvignon. Groom's sauvignon blanc is one of the best, and he is crafting his own little Grange with a remarkable new reserve syrah.

Geyser Peak retains much of the rich Sonoma County tradition that Augustus Quitzow originated back in 1880. On the northernmost edge of Wine Country, Geyser Peak is an ivy-covered complex of old and new. Their completely renovated tasting room was completed in the fall of 1998. The staff pours selections from Geyser Peak's large repertoire. Don't miss the soft Johannisberg riesling, which is ripe with lovely peachy fruit, as well as the shiraz and merlot. A conglomerate, Fortune Brands, bought the winery in 1998.

HANNA WINERY
Winemaker: Jeff Hinchliffe.
707-431-4310, 800-854-3987;
    fax 707-431-4314.
www.hannawinery.com.
hannawinery@hanna
    winery.com.
9280 Hwy. 128, Healdsburg,
    CA 95448.
Tasting: 10–4 daily.
Tasting Fee: $2 for reserve
    wines only.
Additional tasting room:
    5355 Occidental Rd.,
    Santa Rosa; open 10–4
    Fri.–Mon.; 707-575-3371.

A noted cardiac surgeon, Elias Hanna went into the wine business in 1985. The winery is well off the tourist path, so Hanna recently opened a tasting room in the heart of its Alexander Valley vineyard. The new building — Frank Lloyd Wright's idea of a pagoda — makes for a striking image among the rolling hills. Hanna owns prime vineyard space around Sonoma County, and the best wines to date are an elegant and sleek pinot noir, plus a solid chardonnay and sauvignon blanc.

**JORDAN VINEYARD &
    WINERY**
Winemaker: Rob Davis.
707-431-5250.
www.jordanwinery.com.
1474 Alexander Valley Rd.,
    Healdsburg, CA 95448.
Hours: 8–5 daily.
Tasting: With tour only.
Tasting Fee: No.
Tours: 11 & 1 Mon.–Sat., by
    appt.

This spectacular French-style chateau rose from a former prune orchard in the mid-1970s to become one of Sonoma County's premiere wineries. Covered in ivy, the chateau seems like a grand classic, but inside is a state-of-the-art winery. The forest of towering wood tanks in its aging room are an impressive sight. Jordan's cabernet sauvignon is elegant and ready to drink on release, one reason it's such a popular wine in restaurants.

**MURPHY-GOODE
    ESTATE WINERY**
Winemaker: David Ready Jr.
707-431-7644;
    fax 707-431-8640.
www.murphygoodewinery.
    com
general@murphygoode
    winery.com.
4001 Hwy. 128, Healdsburg.
Mail: PO Box 158,
    Geyserville, CA 95441.
Tasting: 10:30–4:30 daily.
Tasting Fee: No.
Tours: No.
Special Features: Gifts.

After nearly three decades of growing grapes, the owners of Murphy-Goode own some of the best vineyards in Alexander Valley, and it shows in their wines. The house specialty is a crisp and complex fumé blanc, but Murphy-Goode manages every wine with finesse, from an elegant cabernet sauvignon to one of the best pinot blancs. Step away from the polished wood bar in the tasting room, and peer through the picture window that overlooks the barrel room.

PEDRONCELLI WINERY
Winemaker: John Pedroncelli.
707-857-3531, 800-836-3894.
www.pedroncelli.com.
service@pedroncelli.com.
1220 Canyon Rd.,
    Geyserville, CA 95441.
Tasting: 10–4:30 daily.
Tasting Fee: No.
Tours: No.
Special Features: Art gallery.

One of Sonoma County's oldest wineries — its origins date from 1904 — Pedroncelli is an old reliable. The winery and tasting room are agreeable but not elaborate. The wines are solid, though modestly scaled, and the prices are fair. Two generations of Pedroncellis tend the place. Try the cabernet sauvignon, fumé blanc, and zinfandel — all nicely done.

SAUSAL WINERY
Winemaker: David
    Demostene.
707-433-2285, 800-500-2285.
www.sausalwinery.com.
zinfanz@sonic.net.
7370 Hwy. 128, Healdsburg,
    CA 95448.
Tasting: 10–4 daily.
Tasting Fee: No.
Tours: No.
Special Features: Picnic area.

Zinfandel is the top dog at this small winery. The Demostene family bought the ranch back in 1956 and inherited a plot of zinfandel that was planted before 1877. They began bottling in 1974, and the zin is full-bodied yet smooth. The tasting room sits snugly among the vineyards, and the vine-covered patio is a soothing spot to sip.

SILVER OAK CELLARS
Winemakers: Dan Baron.
707-857-3562, 800-273-8809;
fax 707-857-3134.
www.silveroak.com.
info@silveroak.com.
24625 Chianti Rd., PO Box
558, Geyserville, CA 95441.
Tasting: 9–4 Mon.–Sat.
Tasting Fee: $10.
Tours: 1:30 Mon.–Fri., by
appt.

In 1992 cabernet sauvignon specialist Silver Oak turned the former Lyeth Winery into the new home for its Alexander Valley cab. Consider it Silver Oak West. The winery with its steeply pitched roof and flagstone courtyard remains an elegant spot. While only the Alexander Valley bottling is produced here, all of Silver Oaks wines are poured when available. For the full scoop on Silver Oak, see Oakville/Rutherford earlier in this chapter.

Winemaker Nick Goldschmidt tastes the grapes at Simi Winery.

Courtesy Simi Winery

SIMI WINERY
Winemaker: Nick
Goldschmidt.
707-433-6981;
fax 707-433-6253.
www.simiwinery.com.
16275 Healdsburg Ave.,
PO Box 698, Healdsburg,
CA 95448.
Tasting: 10–5 daily.
Tasting Fee: $5–$7.
Tours: 11, 1, & 3 daily.
Special Features: Gifts.

If we had to choose only one winery to visit — akin to limiting yourself to one glass of champagne on New Year's Eve — that would be a tough call. But we vote for Simi, an alluring combination of history and hi-tech. You never feel as though herded through a factory, even though the winery is hardly small. The staff knows wine but doesn't lord it over you. And best of all: The wines are first-rate.

Hidden in a shady grove of trees on the northern outskirts of Healdsburg, Simi has had a history as shaky as it is long. Italian immigrants Pietro and Giuseppe Simi built the original stone winery in 1890 and called the spot Montepulciano. Over the years, changes in ownership brought good times and bad, until French giant Moet-Hennessy bought Simi in 1981 and restored its former glory.

Simi gives one of the best tours, offering peeks at everything from the oak barrel aging room to the bottling line. The tasting room is a cordial spot. Try the sauvignon blanc, always delightful, and the rich and buttery reserve chardonnay. More impressive still are the cabernet sauvignons. Simi changed hands again in 1998, when New York wine giant Constellation bought it.

TRENTADUE WINERY
Winemaker: Miro Tcholakov.
707-433-3104.
www.trentadue.com
customerservice@trentadue.
com.
19170 Geyserville Rd.,
Geyserville, CA 95441.
Tasting: 10–5 daily.
Tasting Fee: $5, for reserve
wines only.
Tours: By appt.
Special Features: Picnic area,
gifts, gourmet food.
Additional Tasting Room:
320 Center Street,
Healdsburg.

Trentadue makes Arnold Schwarzenegger wines: massive, muscular reds that won't be taken lightly. The Trentadue family has been making wine since 1969, favoring hearty classics like carignane and sangiovese. After a spotty history, wine quality took a leap in the 1990s. The tasting room is packed with gifts and picnic supplies, which you can put to fine use on the trellis-covered picnic patio.

Dry Creek

ALDERBROOK WINERY
Winemaker: T. J. Evans.
707-433-9154;
    fax 707-433-1862.
www.alderbrook.com.
info@alderbrook.com.
2306 Magnolia Dr.,
    Healdsburg, CA 95448.

With its wraparound porch, bleached pine interior, and fireplace, Alderbrook's tasting room is a touch of New England in Wine Country. Not that Alderbrook specializes in stout reds perfect for cool Vermont nights. White wine is the house forte, and the sauvignon blanc and chardonnay are consistently solid. But the zinfandel, merlot, and pinot noir are increasingly impressive.

A. RAFANELLI WINERY
Winemaker: Dave Rafanelli.
707-433-1385.
4685 W. Dry Creek Rd.,
    Healdsburg, CA 95448.
Tasting & Tours: By appt.
Tasting Fee: No.
Special Features: Picnic area.

If you want to try one of the best zinfandels in Wine Country, a trip to this small, folksy redwood barn is a requirement. The wines are nearly impossible to find otherwise. Rafanelli epitomizes old school Sonoma County: good wine, no fuss. Sadly, hospitality at the winery isn't always what it should be. The Rafanellis have been growing grapes for generations and began making wine in 1974, believing their vineyards, not a winery with hi-tech gadgets, did the talking.

DRY CREEK VINEYARDS
Winemaker: Jeff McBride.
707-433-1000, 800-864-9463;
    fax 707-433-5329.

Dry Creek Valley, we've always imagined, is what Napa Valley used to be: small, quiet, and unaffected by it all. It was a land of prunes and pears when Dave Stare, a former railroad engineer,

This sign ushers you into Dry Creek Vineyards, a premium winery in Dry Creek Valley.

Thomas Hallstein/Outsight

www.drycreekvineyards.
com.
dcv@drycreekvineyards.
com.
3770 Lambert Bridge Rd.,
Healdsburg, CA 95448.
Tasting: 10:30–4:30 daily.
Tasting Fee: No.
Tours: No.
Special Features: Picnic area,
gifts.

arrived. The winery will mark its 30th year in 2002. Designed after the small country wineries of France, Dry Creek has always reminded us of a simple country chapel: ivy-covered, with a pitched roof, and set amid a lush lawn and shady trees.

It only adds to the pleasure that Dry Creek's wines are consistently fine, often exceptional, as you'll discover in the tasting room. The atmosphere is laid-back, and the staff is chatty. Visitors can choose four samples from the winery's impressive list — not an easy task. Dry Creek has made its name with fumé blanc, a marvelous, crisp wine that dominates the winery's production. The chenin blanc is so fruity and distinctive that we prefer it over many chardonnays. As for reds, the zinfandel is always one of the best and the cabernet sauvignon has fine character and can be exceptional in a good vintage. The picnic area, largely shaded by tall trees, is one of the best in Wine Country.

**FERRARI-CARANO
VINEYARDS AND
WINERY**
Winemaker: George Bursick.
707-433-6700;
fax 707-431-1742.
www.ferrari-carano.com.
fcwinery@wco.com.
8761 Dry Creek Rd.,
Healdsburg, CA 95448.
Tasting: 10–5 daily.
Tasting Fee: $3–$10.

One of the true stars of California wine, Ferrari-Carano entered the scene in the mid-1980s. Chardonnay, of course, is its flagship, a big, lush, complex wine. The fumé blanc is impressive in its own right, while the cabernet sauvignon and merlot are both solid efforts.

Don and Rhonda Carano own the Eldorado Hotel and Casino in Reno so their arrival in Wine Country has been a dramatic one. Situated in northern Dry Creek Valley, Ferrari-Carano is a bold

Villa Fiore at Ferrari-Carao Vineyards is an opulent mansion.

Chris Alderman

Tours: By appt.
Special Features: Gifts, garden.

statement. Villa Fiore, the winery's visitor center, was completed in late 1994 and it's an extravagant Mediterranean palace surrounded by brushy lawns, flowers, and vineyards. (More than 18,000 tulips bloom every spring.) The tasting room has a faux marble floor and a mahogany and black granite tasting bar. Visitors can descend the limestone staircase to what is possibly the most opulent underground cellar in Wine Country.

J. FRITZ WINERY
Winemaker: James
 Coughlin.
707-894-3389, 800-418-9463.
www.fritzwinery.com
24691 Dutcher Creek Rd.,
 Cloverdale 95425.
Tasting: 11–4:30 Sat. & Sun.,
 by appt. Tues.–Fri.
Tasting Fee: No.
Tours: By appt.
Special Features: Picnic area,
 gifts.

This winery, in the farthest reaches of northern Sonoma Wine Country, is built like a bunker into the side of hill. Well off the road and hidden amid the scrub trees, J. Fritz blends into the countryside. J. Fritz takes zinfandel quite seriously, and it relies on gnarly old vines to make a burly yet graceful zin. Chardonnay and sauvignon blanc are generally fine examples; try the melon, a white that's easy to quaff.

**LAMBERT BRIDGE
 WINERY**
Winemaker: Julia Iantosca.
707-431-9600, 800-975-0555;
 fax 707-433-3215.
www.lambertbridge.com.
wines@lambertbridge.com.
4085 W. Dry Creek Rd.,
 Healdsburg, CA 95448.
Tasting: 10:30–4:30 daily.

Quaint is a woefully abused word, but we can't think of a better way to describe Lambert Bridge. This romantic little winery, with redwood siding and a porch shaded by wisteria, is a comfortable fit among the oaks and vines covering the hillsides that overlook Dry Creek.

Inside, the interior is not nearly as charming as it used to be. We miss the days when the winery was

Tasting Fee: No.
Tours: No.
Special Features: Picnic area.

one cavernous room, lined with cedar and stacked high with oak barrels; wine was sampled at a small table in the corner. A new tasting room was added in 1997. Open since 1969, Lambert Bridge has maintained a low profile. Chardonnay is a specialty, and it's a rich, juicy style with considerable oak. (We've never been impressed with its cabernet sauvignon or merlot.) Also added in 1997 was a new picnic area, making this one of the best wineries around for a casual lunch.

MAZZOCCO VINEYARDS
Winemaker: Phyllis
  Zouzounis.
707-431-8159, 800-501-VINO.
www.mazzocco.com.
vino@mazzocco.com.
1400 Lytton Springs Rd., PO
  Box 486, Healdsburg, CA
  95448.
Tasting: 10–4:30 daily.
Tours: No.
Tasting Fee: No.
Special Features: Picnic area.

This winery is hardly a visual treat, but it occupies prime zinfandel land. Founded by Tom Mazzocco in 1984, the winery has weathered ups and downs but one constant has remained: great zinfandel, big and spicy, yet with considerable finesse. Cabernet sauvignon and chardonnay also have charm. A new tasting room opened in fall 1998.

Picturesque Pezzi King sits amid hillsides ribbed with vineyards in Sonoma County's Dry Creek Valley.

Thomas Hallstein/Outsight

PEZZI KING VINEYARDS
Winemaker: Tim Crowe.
707-431-9388, 800-411-4758.
www.pezziking.com.
pezziking@worldnet.att.net.
3805 Lambert Bridge Rd.,
  Healdsburg, CA 95448.
Tasting: 10–4:30 daily.

A rising star in Sonoma County, PK Vineyards — as it's called — has only been making wine since 1994, but it already has one of the best zinfandels in the business. This zin is powerful, rich, and jammy. The cabernet sauvignon is also a hot item, plush and smooth as satin. The chardonnay and sauvignon blanc are coming along nicely, too. The

Tasting Fee: $2, for limited release wines.
Tours: No.
Special features: Picnic area, gifts.

winery and home vineyard are high in the hills above Dry Creek, but a tasting room — the old Robert Stemmler winery — is in the heart of the valley. The tasting room is shaded by tall trees, and a wide redwood deck offers tranquil views of surrounding vineyards.

A welcoming lawn at Preston Vineyards.

Chris Alderman

PRESTON OF DRY CREEK
Winemaker: Kevin Hamel.
707-433-3372, 800-305-9707;
    fax 707-433-5307
www.prestonvineyards.com.
mail@prestonvineyards.com.
9282 W. Dry Creek Rd.,
    Healdsburg, CA 95448.
Tasting: 11–4:30 daily.
Tasting Fee: No.
Tours: By appt.
Special Features: Picnic area, gifts, bakery.

On the northern edge of Dry Creek Valley, this out-of-the-way winery has been quietly redefining itself in recent years. Lou and Susan Preston began as growers in 1973, specializing in grapes cherished by old Italian farmers: zinfandel, petite sirah, and barbera. A winery followed two years later and Preston made its name with zin and sauvignon blanc. Rhone varietals are the latest emphasis. The viognier is flowery yet dry and complex. The syrah is substantial yet elegant.

The tasting room of this grand California barn was expanded a few years back and it's a comfortable spot, but we miss sipping among the barrels and tanks. There's a plush lawn for picnicking just off the tasting room porch. A bread fanatic, Lou Preston built a bakery on the property in 1997.

QUIVIRA VINEYARDS
Winemaker: Grady Wann.
707-431-8333, 800-292-8339.
www.quivirawine.com.
quivira@quivirawine.com.

Quivira was a wealthy kingdom of legend that explorers believed was hidden in what is now Sonoma County. While the name belongs to antiquity, this Quivira is a modern winery inside and out. Winemaker Doug Nalle, who left in 1989 to

4900 W. Dry Creek Rd.,
  Healdsburg, CA 95448.
Tasting: 11–5 daily.
Tasting Fee: No.
Tours: By appt.
Special Features: Picnic area,
  gifts.

RIDGE VINEYARDS
Winemaker: Paul Draper.
707-433-7721;
  fax 707-433-7751.
www.ridgewine.com.
650 Lytton Springs Rd.,
  Healdsburg, CA.
Mail: PO Box 1810,
  Cupertino, CA 95015
Tasting: 11–4 Fri.–Mon.
Tasting Fee: No.
Tours: No.

concentrate on his own superb zinfandel, set a high standard with zin and sauvignon blanc that Quivira has managed to maintain.

Nervous its cherished supply of Lytton Springs zinfandel grapes would be sold to someone else, Ridge Vineyards purchased this winery in 1991. The corrugated metal winery is not much to see, and the tasting bar is tucked behind the stainless steel tanks; but if you like bold and jammy zins made from old vines, this the place to stop. Selected Ridge wines are sampled. Hours vary in the winter, so call ahead.

SPECIALTY BREWERS

Watch out, wine connoisseurs: Beer lovers are getting serious, too. Microbreweries and brewpubs are cropping up all over Wine Country. It's a return to the old days when any city of size had a brewery or two, bottling suds for the local area. It also harks back to England and Germany, where beers still have character. The San Francisco Bay area is a leader in brewpubs. Also, beer hops were once an important crop in Sonoma County near the turn of the century.

Napa County

**CALISTOGA INN AND
  BREWERY**
707-942-4101;
  fax 707-942-4914.
www.napabeer.com.
info@calistogainn.com.
1250 Lincoln Ave., Calistoga,
  CA 94515.

With its shady beer garden, this is one of our favorite destinations on a warm summer day. If you have lunch while sipping a brew, stick with the basics: a salad or a sandwich. When the weather cools, the action moves inside the historic Calistoga Inn. At night, the dining room is not our first choice in Calistoga for dinner, but stop in the pub for a beer before or after. The beers are all solid, particularly the pilsner and the red ale.

**DOWNTOWN JOE'S
  MICROBREWERY**
707-258-2337;
  fax 707-258-8740.

There's some great beer to be found at this stylish and historic storefront in downtown Napa — plus a comfortable wooden bar and a patio

The Four Ss and a P: The Unpretentious Art of Wine Tasting

"I know how to taste wine," you say. "Put the glass to your lips and swallow, right?" We can't argue with that method. On the other hand, there is an intricate tasting process that experts use — but there's no need for the casual taster to be that correct, either. However, we would like to offer a few tips that will help even novices savor wine more fully. First, understand that palates and preferences are different, but you can distinguish chardonnay from chenin blanc in much the same way you can differentiate pork from beef.

Sight: Hold the glass up and consider the color. Red wines, for example, don't look the same. Pinot noir can be a soft shade of strawberry, while zinfandel is often as dense as blackberry jam.

Swirl: There's a good reason wineries only pour a small amount — aside from the fear of going broke, that is. You can't swirl a full glass without making a puddle. Lightly swirl the glass for a moment, and you'll be surprised how the wine changes. When the wine is infused with air, it releases its aroma.

Sniff: Take a whiff. Your nose is a key player in wine tasting. First, ask yourself, is the aroma pleasant or not? Some wines have very subtle bouquets, while others will rush your nostrils like linebackers. One is not necessarily better than the other. Wines have characteristic smells. Sauvignon blanc, for example, may smell like freshly mown grass.

Sip: Don't take a big gulp. Swish it around your mouth, adding more air to the wine and exposing it to all your taste buds. Is it sweet or dry? Bitter or sour? A cabernet sauvignon, for example, might make you pucker. Those are tannins that help the wine age. Try to sort out the sensations on your tongue. Chardonnay may have an almost buttery taste, and pinot noir may taste lightly of cherry, with a lingering silky sensation.

Pour: We couldn't think of another S-word. Expert tasters always Spit — without it, they'd be passed out on the floor. You don't need to do that, but we would encourage you to take a sip or two and then pour out the rest. Tasting rooms don't mind at all; in fact, they provide buckets especially for it. Also, remember you don't have to try every wine, particularly if you're stopping at a lot of wineries.

www.downtownjoes.com.
902 Main St., Napa, CA
94559.

**SILVERADO BREWING
CO.**
707-967-9876

along the Napa River. The copper brew kettles are in plain sight, so you can watch the brewmaster do his stuff. The food is solid pub fare.

A relatively recent addition to Napa Valley, Silverado leaves room for improvement. The beers are unexciting, and sadly the food is a perfect

3020 St. Helena Hwy., St.
Helena, CA 94574
On Hwy. 29.

match. You have to give it points for atmosphere. The hand-hewn stone building was built in 1895 and was once a winery.

Sonoma County

**BEAR REPUBLIC
BREWING CO.**
707-433-BEER;
fax 707-433-2205.
www.bearrepublic.com.
info@bearrepublic.com.
345 Healdsburg Ave.,
Healdsburg, CA 95448.

This may be Healdsburg's hottest night spot, featuring food, live music, and some excellent hand-crafted beers. The Scottish-style Red Rocket Ale is a specialty, and they also make a yummy hefeweizen, a light German brew perfect for a warm summer day. The atmosphere is lively, and from your table or the bar you can watch brewing at work. As for the food, stick with the basics — burgers, etc. — and you won't go wrong.

DEMPSEY'S ALE HOUSE
707-765-9694;
fax 707-762-1259.
50 E. Washington St.,
Petaluma, CA 94952.

This is Wine Country's best brewpub — period. From the outside, Dempsey's doesn't look like much — it's in a generic shopping center — but there's a handsome interior plus outdoor seating right along the Petaluma River. Peter Burrell brews superior ales, particularly his Red Rooster, and the food is better than you'll find at any pub. Chef Bernadette Burrell worked in the kitchen at Mustards Grill, so expect grilled shark with Indian curry as well as burger and fries.

**THE POWERHOUSE
BREWING CO.**
707-829-9171.
www.powerhousebrewing.
com
268 Petaluma Ave.,
Sebastopol, CA 95472.

A former railroad powerhouse, this brewpub is a hot nightspot. Inside it's cozy and familiar, and when the weather is good, you can sit outside on the wraparound porch. The food and beer are good, but there's plenty of room for improvement. Our favorite brew is a tasty amber called Powerhouse Ale. Most nights there's live music on the menu, whether it's Celtic or zydeco.

**RUSSIAN RIVER
BREWING CO. AT
KORBEL CHAMPAGNE
CELLARS**
707-869-6313.
13250 River Rd.,
Guerneville, CA 95446.

There's beer and bubbly now at Korbel. The beer is brewed and bottled at the winery, and while there isn't a pub, visitors can have a pint or two at Korbel's new delicatessen. The brewery, deep in the heart of the winery facility, is now part of Korbel's extensive tour. The deli is an inviting spot, with tall windows and an open ceiling. The fare is mostly picnic chow, but there's plenty of tables outside to have lunch. The brewery produces a tasty amber ale as well as a golden wheat, a pale, and a porter.

A lineup of tap handles ready to pour some cold ones at the Russian River Brewing Company.

Thomas Hallstein/Outsight

**THIRD STREET
   ALEWORKS**
707-523-3060;
   fax 707-523-3063.
www.thirdstreetaleworks
   .com
610 3rd St., Santa Rosa, CA
   95401.

A popular downtown hangout, this brewpub has a stylish, almost industrial atmosphere, with polished metal highlights and an open balcony. Brewmaster Denise Jones makes some great beer, including the Annadel Pale Ale. The food is better than most pubs, particularly the pizza and the spicy Cajun selections. If the weather is good, there's plenty of room on the patio, and in the balcony there are two pool tables and large communal tables.

Learning the Lingo: A Wine Glossary

No one expects you to be an expert when you're wine tasting, but just in case, here's a cram course in the words of wine, how to say them, and what they mean.

Appellation — A legally defined grape-growing region. Alexander Valley, for example, is an appellation.

Blanc de Blanc (*blonc-deh-blonc*) — A sparkling wine made from white grapes, usually chardonnay. Delicate and dry.

Blanc de Noirs (*blonc-deh-nwahr*) — A sparkling wine made from red grapes, usually pinot noir. Sometimes faintly pink. Fruity but dry.

Blush — A pink or salmon-colored wine made from red grapes. Juice from red grapes is actually white. Red wine derives its color from juice left in contact with the grape skin. The longer the contact, the darker the wine.

Brut (*broot*) — The most popular style of sparkling wine. Typically a blend of chardonnay and pinot noir. Dry.

Cabernet Franc *(cab-er-nay-fronc)* — Red wine of Bordeaux, similar to cabernet sauvignon but lighter in color and body. Often used in blends.

Cabernet Sauvignon *(cab-er-nay-so-vin-yon)* — Red, fragrant, and full-bodied grape of Bordeaux. Dry and usually tannic. Can age in the bottle 5 to 10 years.

Chardonnay *(shar-do-nay)* — California's most popular white grape, famed in France as the essence of white burgundy. Produces wine that is fruity, with hints of citrus or butter.

Chenin Blanc *(shen-nin-blonc)* — A white grape that produces a wine that's more delicate and less complex than chardonnay. Slightly sweet.

Crush — Harvesting and pressing of grapes. The beginning of the winemaking process.

Estate bottled — Wines made from vineyards owned or controlled by the winery.

Fermentation — The conversion of grape juice into wine, using yeast to change sugar into alcohol.

Fumé Blanc *(fu-may-blonc)* — Same as sauvignon blanc. The name has traditionally been used to describe a dry-style sauvignon blanc.

Futures — Wines sold prior to release and delivered later. Usually at a discount.

Gewürztraminer *(geh-vurz-trah-me-ner)* — A white grape that yields a medium-bodied, semi-sweet, and lightly spicy wine.

Johannisberg Riesling *(jo-hahn-is-berg rees-ling)* — A white grape that produces a delicate wine, medium-bodied, semi-sweet, with a melony fruit taste.

Late harvest — Sweet dessert wine made from grapes left on the vine longer than usual. Botrytis cinerea mold forms, dehydrating the grapes and intensifying the sugar content.

Malolactic fermentation — A second fermentation that converts malic acids (which have a tart apple quality) to softer lactic acids (which lend a buttery quality).

Merlot *(mer-low)* — Increasingly popular red grape from Bordeaux. Similar to cabernet sauvignon, but softer and more opulent.

Méthode champenoise *(meh-thowd-sham-pen-nwas)* — Traditional French champagne-making process. Still wine is placed with sugar and yeast into a bottle and then sealed. The yeast devours the sugar, creating bubbles. The wine then "sits on the yeast," or ages in the bottle several years. Finally, the yeast is extracted and the sparkling wine — never once removed from its original bottle — is ready to drink.

Oak — Wine aged in oak barrels picks up some of the smell and taste of the wood. Also contributes to tannins and long aging. Example: "That chardonnay has too much oak for my taste."

Petite Sirah *(peh-teet syr-awh)* — Dark, rich, intense red wine.

Pinot Noir *(pe-no nwahr)* — Silky, fruity, dry red wine that makes the great burgundy of France.

Reserve — A term traditionally used to mean wine held back or reserved for the winery owners, but the meaning has become vague in recent practice. It's now sometimes used to mean better quality grapes or wine aged longer in oak barrels.

Residual sugar — Unfermented sugar that remains in the wine. Wine is considered sweet if it contains more than half a percent by weight.

Riddling — Process used to extract yeast from sparkling wine. A laborious process that slowly shakes deposits to the neck of the bottle, where they can be removed without disturbing the wine.

Sangiovese *(san-jo-vay-ze)* — The sturdy and often spicy red grape used in chianti.

Sauvignon Blanc *(so-vin-yon blonc)* A crisp, light white wine with hints of grass and apples.

Semillon *(sem-me-yawn)* — A cousin to sauvignon blanc, the two are often blended together.

Sparkling wine — Generic term for champagne. Technically, real champagne can come only from the Champagne region of France.

Syrah *(syr-awh)* — Ruby-colored grape of the Rhone region in France. Smooth, yet with rich and massive fruit.

Tannic — The puckery sensation caused by some wines, particularly young reds. Comes from the skin and stalk of the grapes as well as oak barrels. It's thought to further a wine's ability to age.

Varietal — A wine named after the grape variety from which it's made. Example: chardonnay is a varietal, bordeaux is not. (Bordeaux is a region in France; bordeaux wine can contain a number of varietals: cabernet sauvignon, merlot, etc.)

Vintage — The year the grapes for a particular wine are harvested. Non-vintage wines can be blends of different years.

Viognier *(vee-own-yay)* — This highly perfumed white wine is surprisingly dry on the palate. Native to the Rhone area of France, it is increasingly chic in California.

Viticultural area — A wine-growing region. Russian River Valley, for example, is a viticultural area of Sonoma County.

Zinfandel *(zin-fan-dell)* — A spicy and jamlike red wine. A California specialty. Used also to make a blush wine called white zinfandel.

CHAPTER SEVEN
The Great Outdoors
RECREATION

Paddle the day away in a canoe on the Russian River.

Thomas Hallstein/Outsight

In Wine Country, a casual drive down the road is considered recreation. It's that beautiful. Rolling hills laced with vineyards, fertile valleys, a breathtaking coastline, and a mild climate — no wonder so many people are drawn to Napa and Sonoma. But there's more than wine and landscapes. If you crave something more physical, you'll keep busy. From long hikes through a gentle wilderness to rides above it all in hot air balloons, there are recreational adventures to fit every style, taste, and budget.

AUTO RACING

Yes, racing in Wine Country. It's our version of Indianapolis 500, where you can experience the thrill of watching the fastest cars in the world. Sears Point Raceway offers speed aplenty during its season schedule from April through August, which includes races for the hottest factory-backed sports cars, warp-speed dragsters, motorcycles, and even vintage cars. *Sears Point International Raceway* (707-938-8448, 800-733-0345; www.searspoint.com; Hwys. 37 & 121, Sonoma, CA 95476).

BALLOONING

Soaring silently above the vineyards and rolling hills of the Wine Country in a hot air balloon is an experience you won't quickly forget. Rides start early in the day, before surface winds interfere with the launch, and each ride is unique, depending on the whim of the winds.

Some balloon companies provide pickup at your lodging; most provide continental breakfast and a champagne brunch following the ride. Prices vary, but expect to spend about $175 per person. Reservations are necessary.

For a real balloon extravaganza, take in Sonoma County's Hot Air Balloon Classic each June, when 50 balloons fill the sky over the vineyards in Windsor (see "Seasonal Events" in Chapter Four, *Culture*).

Up, Up, and Away!

It's 6 am. A group of early risers fends off the chilly dawn air with hot coffee, waiting for their ballooning adventure to begin. While the balloon isn't in the air yet, anticipation is as the balloon pilot and helpers unroll expanses of magnificent colored fabric onto the open field. Before long, giant fans are steadily blowing air into a flat balloon held open by the pilot. There are signs of life as the balloon grows slowly, like a whale rising above the water's surface. But it is still earthbound. Only when the pilot lights his propane burner and begins to heat the trapped air does the balloon rise.

The heated air, lighter than the cold air around it, gradually lifts the weight of the fireproofed nylon fabric, and within 15 minutes the balloon is inflated, standing on the open field — enormous, beautiful. Six or seven passengers hop into the basket with the pilot, and the lines are released.

Slowly the balloon heads skyward, changing the perspective of the passengers until they can see the other balloons below them on the field, then buildings around the field, then hills in the distance. There is no sensation of movement since they move with the wind; there is no sound except for the barking of a dog below or an occasional *whoosh* from the pilot's burner to keep the air heated.

The balloon follows the wind effortlessly, drifting over the countryside with the pilot's gentle guidance; he can "find" different currents to ride, like a canoeist on a fast-moving stream, but he can't change direction at will. He can turn the balloon in a circle, by opening flaps in the balloon with pulleys, but can't choose his landing place.

After about an hour's flight, the pilot allows the air to cool, and the balloon slowly descends. The pilot maneuvers the balloon to avoid trees while finding an open field for landing. The balloon lands gently; there is usually no more than a gentle bump, though occasionally passengers will get tumbled out of the basket — an undignified though not harmful way to return to earth. The company's vans or trucks have followed the trip from below and are immediately on hand to secure and empty the balloon and load everyone in for the ride back.

The disappointment of returning to earth is diminished by a glass or two of champagne and a gourmet brunch designed to complete a memorable experience.

A hot-air balloon fuels up with a burst of flames.

Thomas Hallstein/Outsight

Napa County

Above the West (707-944-8638, 800-627-2759; www.nvaloft.com; PO Box 2290, Yountville, CA 94599) Pickup from San Francisco and Napa Valley hotels; champagne breakfast; daily flights; family owned & operated.

Adventures Aloft (800-944-4408; PO Box 2290, Yountville, CA 94599) Champagne flights daily; shuttle service; minister available for in-flight weddings; Napa Valley's oldest balloon company. Sunrise launches daily from Vintage 1870.

Balloon Aviation of Napa Valley (800-367-6272; PO Box 2290, Yountville, CA 94599) Flights daily; champagne and brunch flights also available.

Napa Valley Balloons (707-944-0228, 800-253-2224; www.napavalleyballoons.com; PO Box 2680, Yountville, CA 94599) Launches from Domaine Chandon winery; fleet of 14 balloons; picnic brunch and champagne flights.

Sonoma County

Air Flambuoyant (707-83808700, 800-456-4711; 250 Pleasant Ave., Santa Rosa, CA 95403) Operating since 1974; daily flights for small groups.

Above the Wine Country Ballooning (707-829-9850, 888-238-6359; www.balloontours.com; 2508 Burnside Rd., Sebastopol, CA 94572) Romance flights for two; champagne; custom videos.

BICYCLING

Want to slow the pace of your Wine Country tour? Try a bike. With terrain that varies from meandering valleys to steep mountains and a spectacular coastline, there are roads and trails to satisfy everyone from the most leisurely sightseer to ambitious cycling fanatics.

*Exploring Wine Country
back roads on two wheels.*

Courtesy Sonoma County Convension & Visitors Bureau

Mountain bicycling, which started in Marin County just to the south, is extremely popular in Wine Country. **Annadel State Park,** at times, has more mountain bikes than runners on its trails, and **Austin Creek** is also a favorite spot in Sonoma County. Mountain cyclists in Napa County head for **Skyline Park** (Napa) and Mount St. Helena.

Serious enthusiasts race in a number of annual events, including the **Cherry Pie Race** (a Napa tradition) and the **Terrible Two** (a grueling 208-mile course through Sonoma and Napa Counties). Charity races are popular in both counties. Most bike shops have information.

Many local parks have extensive bike trails, including **John F. Kennedy Park** (707-257-9529; Napa), **Skyline Wilderness Park** (707-252-0481; Napa), **Ragle Regional Park** (707-527-2041; Sebastopol), and **Spring Lake County Park** (707-539-8092; Santa Rosa).

Bicyclists of every level are welcome to join the weekend jaunts of the **Santa Rosa Cycling Club** (707-544-4803). The club meets every Saturday and Sunday (weather permitting) for different rides around the county. Call for times and meeting places, or specific ride info can be picked up at local bike shops.

So rent a bicycle, pack a picnic lunch, and explore a park; or point your wheel toward the nearest country road, and enjoy the scenery you would miss from your car. Two excellent guides for specific trails are *Sonoma County Bike Trails* and *Rides In and Around the Napa Valley.*

BIKE RENTALS

Many inns offer bikes for casual day trips and most bike shops rent two-wheelers for the day. Also, **Getaway Adventures** (707-763-3040, 800-499-2453; www.getawayadventures.com; 1117 Lincoln Ave., Calistoga, CA 94515 and 620 E. Washington St., Petaluma, CA 94952) organizes tours through Napa and Sonoma Counties, suggests routes, and includes helmets, etc.

Napa County

Napa Valley Cyclery: 707-255-3377; 4080 Byway E., Napa, CA 94558.
Palisades Mountain Sport: 707-942-9687; 1330B Gerrard, Calistoga, CA 94515; off Washington.
St. Helena Cyclery: 707-963-7736; www.sthelenacyclery.com; 1156 Main, St. Helena, CA 94574.

Sonoma County

Rincon Cyclery: 707-538-0868, 800-965-BIKE; www.rinconcyclery.com; 4927 Sonoma Hwy., Santa Rosa, CA 95409.
Sonoma Valley Cyclery: 707-935-3377; www.sonomavalleycyclery.com; 200799 Broadway, Sonoma, CA 95476.
Spoke Folk Cyclery: 707-433-7171; www.spokefolk.com; 201 Center St., Healdsburg, CA 95448.

BOATING & WATER SPORTS

Sail away on Lake Sonoma.

Thomas Hallstein/Outsight

The dry summer season may be crucial to growing great grapes, but it also means Napa and Sonoma are anything but wetlands. Man, as usual, devised a way around nature, creating reservoirs for community water supplies and for the delight of water-sport fans.

Napa County

LAKE BERRYESSA

The largest man-made lake in the area, Lake Berryessa is about 15 miles east of Rutherford along Highway 128. Some 26 miles long, it's one of northern California's most popular water recreation areas. Berryessa features seven resorts offering complete facilities: full-service marinas, boat rentals for the avid fisherman, sailboats, water ski and jet ski equipment, and overnight accommodations from tent and RV camping to top quality motels. Houseboats are available for rent at Markley Cove for leisurely overnights on the water. Water ski instruction for beginners through competitive-level skiers is available at *Willi's Water Ski Center* (707-966-5502; 1605 Steele Canyon Rd., Napa, CA 94558), run by German champion Willi Ellermeier, at the Steele Park Resort.

Lake Berryessa Marina Resort (707-966-2161; 5800 Knoxville Rd., Napa, CA 94558) Boat launching, cabins, full-service store and snack bar, campsites, RV hookups, boat rentals, jet skis.

Markley Cove Resort (707-966-2134; 7251 Hwy. 128, Napa, CA 94558) Boat launching, fishing boat rentals, water ski rentals, store; no camping.

Putah Creek Park (707-966-2116) Boat launching, campsites, RV hookups, boat rentals, and motel.

Rancho Monticello Resort (707-966-2188; www.ranchomonticelloresort.com; 6590 Knoxville Rd., Napa, CA 94558) Boat launching, campsites, RV hookups.

Spanish Flat Resort (707-966-7700; 4290 Knoxville Rd., Napa, CA 94558) Boat launching, campsites, boat rentals, water and jet ski rentals.

Steele Park Resort (707-966-2123, 800-522-2123; 1605 Steele Canyon Rd., Napa, CA 94558) Boat launching, RV hookups, wave runner and patio boat rental, water ski school, and motel.

Sonoma County

LAKE SONOMA

Sonoma County's Lake Sonoma, 11miles north of Healdsburg on Dry Creek Rd., offers 3,600 surface acres of scenic recreational waters. There are many secluded coves for the quiet boater or angler, while water and jet skiers are allowed in designated areas. Facilities include a public boat ramp, a full-service marina, campsites, both drive-in and boat–accessible only, hiking trails, swimming areas, and a visitor center and fish hatchery near the Warm Springs Dam. For information, try the *Lake Sonoma Recreation Area* (707-433-9483; 3333 Skapps Rd., Geyserville, CA 95441) or *Lake Sonoma Marina* (707-433-2200), which offers boat rentals, including fishing, paddle, sail, ski, canoes, and jet skis.

RUSSIAN RIVER

Since the Pacific Ocean is chilly and the surf a bit rugged (See "The Coast" in this chapter), the Russian River is a good alternative for a leisure day on the water. During the hot summer, the riverside beaches are popular with families who enjoy swimming in the refreshing water while canoes glide past. Canoes and kayaks can be rented near Healdsburg or Guerneville for a leisurely trip, with stops to relax or swim along the way. Don't be surprised if you spot a few nude sunbathers. The county doesn't condone it, but the free-wheeling '60s still live in West County.

Burke's Canoe Trips on the Russian River (707-887-1222; www.burkescanoe trips.com. PO Box 602, Forestville, CA 94536; on River Road at Mirabel, 1 mi. N. of Forestville) Leisurely 10 mi. trip to Guerneville; return shuttle service available, reservations needed, $40 per canoe. Closed mid-Oct. to April.

California Rivers Guided Kayak Tours (707-579-2209; www.calrivers.com; 575 Country Club Dr., Santa Rosa, CA 95401) You can really soak up the beauty of the Wine Country at a leisurely pace on one these guided tours. Local rivers and estuaries are teeming with local wildlife, and since the waters are calm, no experience is necessary.

W. C. Trowbridge Canoe Trips (800-640-1386; www.bikeroute.com/trowbridge .htm; 20 Haldsburg Ave., Healdsburg, CA 95488) Full-day and half-day trips, from 5 to 11 miles; $40–$55 per canoe; shuttle available.

OTHER SITES

Lake Ralphine (707-543-3425; Howarth Park, Santa Rosa) A popular spot for water activities, from boating to feeding ducks. Stocked with fish, this small manmade lake has a city-run boat rental where rowboats, canoes, and paddleboats are available for a minimal fee. Powerboats are not permitted.

Spring Lake (707-539-8092, Off Montgomery Dr., Santa Rosa) A lovely 75-acre lake open only to canoes, rowboats, and sailboats, all of which can be rented during the summer. Windsurfing and rafting are also allowed. There is a separate lagoon for swimming. For boat rentals call 707-537-1834.

CAMPING

Wine Country campgrounds and RV parks are plentiful for the adventurous who like to "rough it." Camping may be a low-key affair, but don't be laid-back about reserving a spot. Campsites fill up quickly in the summer months. Reservations, in fact, are mandatory at most California state parks and beaches and are accepted up to eight weeks in advance or as late as 48 hours

Stoking the morning campfire in Wine Country.

prior to the first day of the reservation if space is available. State campgrounds are noted with an asterisk (*) in the listing.

Camping fees in Wine Country state parks vary with the season and the park. (Fees in mid-2001 ranged from $12 to $29 per night per campsite.) As a rule, campgrounds described as "developed" have flush toilets, hot showers, drinking water, improved roads, and campsites with a table and stove or fire ring. Primitive campsites usually have chemical or pit toilets, tables, and a central water supply. Environmental campsites are primitive sites in undisturbed natural settings. En-route campsites are day-use parking areas where self-contained trailers, campers, and motor homes may park overnight.

To make reservations in state campgrounds, phone 800-444-7275.

Fees at privately operated parks and resorts are generally $15 to $24 per night for tent camping, and from $27 to $30 per night for RV sites with hookups.

Napa Valley

*Bothe-Napa Valley State Park (707-942-4575; 3801 St. Helena Hwy. N., Calistoga, CA 94515; midway bet. St. Helena & Calistoga off Hwy. 29) This 1,920-acre state park has 50 developed campsites. Campers up to 31 feet and trailers to 24 feet can be accommodated; no sanitation station is provided. Horseback riding trails, hiking, swimming pool, picnic area, and exhibits. Handicap accessible in all areas.

Putah Creek Resort (707-966-0794; 7600 Knoxville Rd., Napa, CA 94558; Hwy. 128 to Knoxville Rd. at Lake Berryessa.) A full-service resort with 200 campsites, 55 RV sites, and 26-unit motel. Grocery store, restaurant and lounge, delicatessen, snack bar. Also a marina with fishing supplies, and bait shop.

Rancho Monticello Resort (707-966-2188; www.ranchomonticellorestort.com; 6590 Knoxville Rd., Napa, CA 94558; on Knoxville Rd. about 4 1/2 mi. off Hwy. 128) Travel trailer and camping sites with RV hookups. Restaurant, beer garden, grocery, and snack bar.

Spanish Flat Resort (800-522-2123; www.spanishflatresort.com; 4290 Hwy. 128, Napa, CA 94558; Hwy. 128 to Knoxville Rd., Lake Berryessa) 120 lakeside tent and RV sites, sanitation station, restroom with showers, convenience store, and snack bar.

Sonoma County

*****Austin Creek State Recreation Area** (707-869-2015; Armstrong Woods Rd., Guerneville, CA 95446; 3 mi. N. of Guerneville) A rugged, natural setting of 4,230 acres with just 24 primitive hike-in campsites. Trailers and campers longer than 20 feet are prohibited.

Casini Ranch Family Campground (707-865-2255, 800-451-8400; 22855 Moscow Rd., PO Box 22, Duncans Mills, CA 95430; off Hwy. 116 at Duncan Mills, 1/2 mi. E. on Moscow Rd.) A family campground on the Russian River with 250 pull-through spaces, many riverfront sites. Boat, kayak and canoe rentals, fishing, swimming, playground, general store, laundry.

KOA San Francisco North (707-763-1492; 20 Rainsville Rd., Petaluma, CA 94952; Old Redwood Hwy. exit off Hwy. 101, W. to Stony Point Rd., N. to Rainsville Rd.) A 60-acre rural farm setting with 312 tent and RV sites with full hookups. Swimming pool, hot tub, convenience store, laundromats, playground, camping cabins.

River Bend RV & Campground (707-887-7662; 11820 River Rd., Forestville, CA 95436; about 10 mi. W. of Hwy. 101 on River Road) Full-service with hookups, general store, canoe rentals; 24-hour on-site security.

*****Salt Point State Park** (707-865-2391 or 707-847-3221; 25050 Coast Hwy. 1, Jenner, CA 95450; 20 mi. N. of Jenner on Hwy. 1) 130 developed campsites (no showers); 20 hike-in tent sites, and 30 en-route sites on 6,000 acres. Trailers and campers longer than 31 feet prohibited. No dump station.

*****Sugarloaf Ridge State Park** (707-833-5712; 2605 Adobe Canyon Rd., Kenwood, CA 95452; 7 mi. E. of Santa Rosa on Hwy. 12, N. on Adobe Canyon Rd.) A 2,500-acre park with 50 developed campsites, observatory, 25-miles of nature trail, hiking, horseback riding trails, and exhibits. Trailers and campers to 22 feet long.

The *****Sonoma Coast State Beach** encompasses 5,000 acres, with two developed campgrounds — **Bodega Dunes** and **Wrights Beach** —and two primitive sites: **Willowcreek** and **Pomo.**

Bodega Dunes Campground (707-875-3483, 707-865-2391; Bodega Bay, CA 94923; 1/2 mi. N. of Bodega Bay on Hwy. 1) The larger of the two state beach campgrounds with 99 developed campsites. Trailers and campers up to 31feet; showers; a sanitation station is provided. Picnicking, hiking, fishing, and horseback riding. Most facilities are wheelchair accessible.

Wrights Beach Campground (707-875-3483 or 707-865-2391; Bodega Bay, CA 94923; 6 mi. N. of Bodega Bay on Hwy. 1) 28 developed campsites; trailers and campers to 27 feet allowed. Picnicking, hiking, fishing, and horseback riding. No showers. Some facilities wheelchair accessible.

Willowcreek Campground (707-875-3483 or 707-865-2391; Bodega Bay 94923; Willowcreek Rd., 1 1/2 mi. off Hwy. 1) 11 undeveloped camping sites, a short hike from your car. Picnic tables and fire rings. No showers. Chemical toilets. First come, first served, no reservations.

Pomo Environmental Campground (707-875-3483, 865-2391; Bodega Bay, CA 94923; Willowcreek Rd., 3 mi. off Hwy. 1) 21 undeveloped camping sites, a small hike from your car. Picnic tables and fire rings. No showers. Chemical toilets. First come, first served — no reservations.

THE COAST

Sonoma County's 62-mile coastline has a rustic beauty that is scarcely changed from the days when the Miwok and Pomo Indians were the only inhabitants. Not that the white man hasn't left his mark. Early Russians settlers in the 1800s decimated the sea otter population for the highly prized pelts. Now under government protection, the sea otter is slowly making a comeback — although much to the distress of abalone divers who compete for the otters' favorite food. The Americanization of California, along with the population surge after the Gold Rush, created a need for timber, so the giant redwoods near the coast were heavily harvested. Thankfully, lush forests remain.

Visitors flock to the Sonoma Coast to enjoy some of the most spectacular views in all of California. The rugged cliffs, continually battered by the wild Pacific Ocean, afford a setting of breathtaking beauty. Thanks to the foresight of those who fought to preserve public access to the coast, there are many outlets from which to view the ocean along Highway 1. Particularly popular is the stretch between Bodega Bay and Jenner, where several beaches offer a variety of topography and vistas for hiking, picnicking, wetsuit diving, surfing, or just relaxing.

Whatever your activities, it is always important to remember that the Pacific Ocean can be dangerous. Every year there are deaths caused by unpredictable waves and the strong undertow. Be cautious.

Bodega Bay Harbor offers protection from the rough Pacific surf and is the home port for many commercial fishing boats. Gaining fame as the setting of Alfred Hitchcock's *The Birds,* the town of Bodega Bay has now become a well-known stopover and destination spot for residents and visitors alike. Sportfishing, harbor cruises, and whale-watching trips can be arranged from *Porto Bodega Marina,* off Highway 1 on Bay Flat Road. The gentle beaches on the west side of the harbor afford a perfect spot for windsurfing or sea kayaking.

Kids splash in the surf near Arch Rock on Sonoma County's Goat Rock Beach.

Thomas Hallstein/Outsight

BEACHES

Here are some of the beaches along the coast, listed from north to south. For detailed information, call the *Sonoma County Tourism Program* (800-576-6662). Some of the beaches have a day-use fee.

The Bodega Headlands (707-875-3483; at the end of Bay Flat Rd., off Hwy. 1, Bodega Bay) Originally part of the Sierra Nevadas, the headlands stretch like a curved arm out to sea. For 40 million years they have ridden the Pacific Plate northward, out of step with land on the other side of the San Andreas fault. The cliffs of the Headlands provide a spectacular vista of the Pacific and the coast. They provide the best spots to watch for whales in the winter and early spring. Not a bad idea to bring binoculars and a jacket. Also of interest at the Headlands is the *Bodega Marine Lab* (707-875-2211; www.bml.ucdavis.edu /index/html; 2099 Westside Road, Bodega Bay, CA 94923), open to the public on Fridays from 2 to 4pm. It's educational, and kids will love it.

Doran Regional Park (707-875-3540; Doran Beach Rd., off Hwy. 1, S. of Bodega Bay) A popular family spot because of its level sandy beach and overnight camping facilities. An annual sand castle competition is held every August. Day-use fee.

Salt Point State Park (707-847-3221; 25050 Hwy. 1, N. of Timber Cove) 4,114 acres along 5 miles of shore, offering picnicking, fishing, skin diving, and hiking. More than 14 miles of trails wind through tall forests, windswept headlands, a stunted Pygmy Forest, and grassy valleys along the San Andreas fault. Camping is available. Adjacent to the park is Kruse Rhododendron State Reserve. In May and June, the brilliant pink blossoms of native rhododendrons brighten the forest along the path.

Harbor seals lollygag at the mouth of the Russian River.

Thomas Hallstein/Outsight

Goat Rock Beach (707-875-3483; Off Hwy. 1, So. of Jenner) Named for the huge beach rock that bears a resemblance to the hunched back of a grazing goat. The beach extends from the sandbars along the mouth of the Russian River, where sea lions and their young haul out along the river at certain times of the year. They're fun to watch, but please don't disturb them.

Sonoma Coast State Beach (707-875-3483; Salmon Creek, Bodega Bay) This is actually a chain of many beaches along 18 miles of coastline, from Goat Rock to Bodega Head. Each has its own personality and invites different activities, whether it's tide pooling or a serious game of volleyball. Wildflowers brighten the cliffs in the spring. The coast is always cool in the summer, supplying an escape from inland heat.

SCUBA DIVING & OTHER SURF EQUIPMENT

The Sonoma Coast is Wine Country's busiest recreational spot. Whatever water sport you prefer — scuba diving, abalone diving, surf boarding, kayaking — there's plenty to do on the coast. The water temperatures, ranging from 40 to 55 degrees, make a full wetsuit a minimum requirement, with many divers preferring dry suits for added comfort. Diving is a year-long activity, as long as the sea is calm. Divers must respect the power of the ocean.

Abalone can be harvested from April to December (excluding July). Scuba equipment is not allowed while hunting these succulent creatures, and there is a limit of four per person. You'll also need a license.

Pinnacles Dive Center (707-542-3100; 2112 Armory Dr., Santa Rosa, CA 95401) Diving courses, rentals, equipment sales, diving trips.

Bodega Bay Surf Shack (707-875-3944; www.bodegabaysurf.com; 1400 Hwy. 1, Bodega Bay, CA 94923) Instruction, rentals, sales, tips.

TIDE POOLING

The Sonoma coastline has its own wildlife preserve: the tide pool. Here the rocky coast is as productive as a tropical rain forest. As the tide goes out, twice daily, small oases are left behind among the rocks, shelters for starfish, snails, sea anemone, and a multitude of other visible and almost invisible life forms.

There is little movement at first glance, but with a little patience you'll find there's much to discover. Follow a hermit crab as it creeps out of its turban shell and maneuvers over a rock. Watch the sea anemone's green tentacles entwine a mussel. Track the crayola green fish or sculpins as they dart in and out of the rocks. And search out the starfish playing dead. Tide pools are full of old-timers. Snails may be 20 to 30 years old, and a starfish may be 10 years old.

Please do not remove anything from the pools; even an empty shell might be a hermit crab's mobile home. Tide-poolers are advised to wear waterproof boots for the best exploration. Be cautious. Crabs pinch, octopuses bite, and sea urchin spines are prickly. Also, beware of sleeper waves — those unexpectedly large waves that sneak up and sweep away beachcombers. For additional insight into the world of the tide pool, visit the **Bodega Marine Laboratory** (707-875-2211; www.bml.ucdavis.edu/index/html; 2099 Westside Rd., PO Box 247, Bodega Bay, CA 94923), open to the public on Fridays from 2 to 4pm.

Where are the best places to tide pool? Nearly any rocky place along the **Sonoma Coast State Beach,** which stretches between Bodega Bay and Jenner. The Bodega Marine Lab recommends two. Try the north end of **Salmon Beach,** which is accessible from any Highway 1 pull-off north of the Salmon Creek bridge. **Shell Beach,** a few miles south of Jenner on Highway 1, is more remote, requiring a trip down steep stairs, but it's worth it.

FAMILY FUN

Wine Country isn't just a playground for adults. Kids and kids at heart can find all sorts of fun, from pony rides and water slides to a planetarium show guaranteed to stretch the imagination. Also see "Swimming" and "Boating & Water Sports" in this chapter for other family activity suggestions.

Napa County

Old Faithful Geyser near Calistoga erupts and draws tourists like clockwork.

Chris Alderman

Old Faithful Geyser (707-942-6463; www.oldfaithfulgeyser.com; 1299 Tubbs Ln., Calistoga, CA 94515; 1 mi. N. of Calistoga) One of just three regularly erupting geysers in the world, it shoots steam and vapor 60 feet into the air for 3 minutes; repeats every 40 minutes. Since seismic activity influences the frequency of the eruptions, many believe Old Faithful predicts earthquakes. Open daily; picnic grounds. Admission: $6 adult, $2 children 6–12, children under 6 free.

Petrified Forest (942-6667; 4100 Petrified Forest Rd., Calistoga, CA 94515; 5 mi. W. of Calistoga) Remains of a redwood forest turned to stone by molten lava from the eruption of Mount St. Helena 3 million years ago. The Petrified Forest was discovered in 1870 and immortalized by Robert Louis Stevenson in *The Silverado Squatters*; picnic grounds; museum; open daily. Admission: $5 adults, $4 youth 12–17, $2 children 6–11, children under 6 free.

Sonoma County

The Club House Family Fun Center (707-996-3616; 19171 Sonoma Hwy., Sonoma, CA 95476) Game arcade and miniature golf course that features scale models of historic Sonoma landmarks.

Howarth Park (707-543-3282; Montgomery & Summerfield Rds., Santa Rosa) Popular city-run park offers merry-go-round, pony rides, petting zoo, small railroad; play and picnic areas; paddleboats, canoes, rowboats to rent and ducks to feed on Lake Ralphine. Some activities summer only. Closed Mondays.

J's Amusements (707-869-3102; 16101 Neeley Rd., Guerneville, CA 95446) Go-carts, water slide, picnic areas, roller coaster, arcade.

Pet-A-Llama Ranch (707-823-9395; 5505 Lone Pine Rd., Sebastopol, CA 95472) Feed and pet llamas, miniature horses, petting zoo, group events, horse rides available for $5. Open 10am–4pm Sat. & Sun. Free.

Planetarium (707-527-4465, 800-616-2695; Santa Rosa Junior College, Lark Hall, 1501 Mendocino Ave., Santa Rosa, CA 95401) This excellent planetarium is open to the public on weekends during the school year. Shows at 7 and 8:30pm. Fri. & Sat.; 1:30 and 3pm Sunday; no reservations, so arrive early. No children under 5; $4 general, $2 students.

Safari West (707-579-2551; www.safariwest.com; 3115 Porter Creek Rd., Santa Rosa, CA 95404) A 240-acre park featuring 150 species, including 400 rare and endangered animals. Not a drive-through animal park, but a 2 1/2-hour tour that is comparable to a real African safari. You even get to feed a giraffe. Admission: $48 adults, $24 children.

Scandia Family Fun Center (707-584-1361; 5301 Redwood Drive, Rohnert Park, CA 94926) Little Indy Racers, miniature golf, baseball batting cages, bumper boats, game arcade. A favorite recreation center for kids and families. Packed on summer weekends. There's even a Burger King inside. Separate fees for each activity.

Made for kids and kids at heart: Traintown in Sonoma.

Courtesy Traintown

Traintown Railroad Rides & Petting Zoo (707-938-3912; 20264 Broadway, Sonoma, CA 95476; 1 mi. S. of Sonoma Plaza) Take a 20-minute ride on a scale-model steam train around 10 acres of beautifully landscaped park, through a 140-foot tunnel, across bridges, passing historic replica structures. Open daily June–Sept.; weekends the rest of the year. Admission: $3.75 adults, $3.25 children.

PLAYGROUNDS

If you're touring Wine Country with tikes, they need their share of fun, too. Sometimes 30 minutes on a playground will go a long way. Grab a picnic or a snack, and head to one of these parks. Best of all: It's all free.

Napa County

One of the best playgrounds in Napa Valley is in **Yountville City Park,** which is just off Madison Street on the north edge of town. It's a modern and well-maintained playground, and the park offers plenty of shade for Mom and Dad. In the heart of St. Helena is a modest little playground in **Lyman Park,** which is off Main Street near Adams. In Calistoga, there's a pleasant little playground in **Pioneer Park,** which is on Cedar Street, just off Lincoln Ave. In the city of Napa, head to **Klamath Park,** which is on the north edge of town, just off Highway 29 at Trower Ave.

Sonoma County

In Sonoma Valley, you can't ask for a more convenient playground than **Sonoma Plaza.** It's a beautiful spot with lots of shade, and there's even a duck pond to keep the kids busy. Best of all, Mom and Dad can take turns shopping while the kids blow off steam. In Healdsburg, head for **Giorgi Park** on University Street, and Sebastopol has one of the best playgrounds around in **Libby Park,** on Pleasant Hill Road, just north of Highway 12.

Santa Rosa has two excellent playgrounds. On the east side of town is a new, highly creative playground at **Howarth Park.** It's on Summerfield Road; from Highway 12, take Mission Boulevard south to Montgomery, then make a quick left on Summerfield. On the west side is **Finley Park,** which has a modern playground that will keep the kids busy for hours. To find it, take College Avenue west from Highway 101, then turn south on Stony Point Road.

FISHING

Fishing boats dock in Bodega Bay at Spud Point Marina.

Thomas Hallstein/Outsight

For the expert or the novice, Wine Country offers a fine variety of fishing opportunities. Where else could you hook a giant salmon in the Pacific one morning, then snag a trophy bass in one of California's largest manmade lakes that afternoon?

Remember to pick up a fishing license through a local sporting supply or department store. See "Boating & Water Sports" in this chapter for additional information.

Napa County

Lake Berryessa is a designated trophy lake, boasting trout, bass (both large mouth and black), crappie, bluegill, and catfish. With seven resorts, camping, and full-service marinas, there are unlimited facilities for every type of fishing. For more information, see "Boating & Water Sports" in this chapter.

Lake Hennessey (4 mi. E. of Rutherford on Hwy. 128) A water source for the city of Napa; fishing and boating are allowed, though the only facilities are a car-top launch ramp and picnic grounds.

Napa River can be fished for stripers or sturgeon year-round. *Kennedy Park* (707-257-9529; 2291 Streblow Dr., off Hwy. 121, Napa) provides a boat launch ramp and is a good spot for fishing off the river bank. The *Napa Sea Ranch* (707-252-2799; 3333 Cuttings Wharf Rd., Napa) also offers a boat launch ramp as well as a bait & tackle store and 1,800 feet of river frontage.

Sonoma County

Lake Sonoma (11 mi. N. of Healdsburg on Dry Creek Rd.) offers 53 miles of shoreline and secluded coves for the quiet angler as well as a boat launch ramp and a full-service marina for boat rentals. Fish include bass, Sacramento perch, channel catfish, red ear perch, and blue catfish. Of interest is the fish hatchery, where visitors can watch tankfuls of lively young salmon and steelhead, which are released into Dry Creek when they reach six to seven inches long. *Visitor Center & Hatchery* (707-433-9483) and *Marina* (707-433-2200).

Lake Ralphine and Spring Lake in Santa Rosa are popular destinations with families for low-key fishing expeditions. Both lakes are stocked with catfish, black bass, trout, and bluegill, and practically guarantee beginners a catch. Both lakes offer boat rentals.

The Russian River offers smallish runs of steelhead trout and salmon fishing Nov. through March. The Russian River can be fished from its banks or from canoes and other nonpowered boats.

Bodega Bay is home port for sportfishing boats, offering all-day trips on the Pacific Ocean. Leaving daily (weather permitting), 40- to 65-foot boats search out 200 species of rock and bottom fish and, between April and November, the prized salmon. The cost is about $50–$150 a person. Or you can take the ride just for fun.

Bodega Bay Sport Fishing Center (707-875-3344; 1410 Bay Flat Road, Bodega Bay, CA 94923) Daily charter boats; equipment rentals; sportfishing for many species of rock and bottom fish and salmon; whale-watching tours.

The Boathouse (707-875-3495; The Boathouse, 1445 Hwy. 1, Bodega Bay, CA 94923) Has three boats: the 65-foot *Sea Angler,* 50-foot *Profishn't,* and the 40-foot *Predator;* daily trips for salmon, rockfish, and Dungeness crab.

Fly-fishing enthusiasts will appreciate the fly-casting practice pond constructed in *Galvin Park* (Bennett Valley, Santa Rosa) by the city of Santa Rosa and the *Russian River Flyfishers Club.* Fly fishing clinics are held Thursdays from 4 to 6pm. Call *Lyle's Tackle & Travel* (707-527-9887; 2690 Santa Rosa Ave., Santa Rosa, CA 95407) to reserve a place. For local fishing information, call Lyle's or *Western Sport Shop* (707-542-4432; 2790 Santa Rosa Ave., Santa Rosa, CA 95407).

FLYING

You won't need a pilot's license to zoom low over Wine Country. Take a scenic flying tour above vineyards and mountains, or try aerobatics in a 1940 biplane. For those whose psyches crave an extra thrill, there's hang-gliding and para-gliding by the cliffs near Jenner or Mount St. Helena; rentals can be arranged with *Airtime of San Francisco* (415-759-1177; 3620 Wawona St., San Francisco, CA 94116).

Skydiving is about as close to being airborne on your own as it comes. *Skydive Cloverdale* (707-765-2325; PO Box 750712, Petaluma, CA 94954) offers tandem jumps for beginners. Piggyback with an expert in a specially designed harness for two.

Napa County

Bridgeford Flying Service (707-224-0887; www.bfsnapa.com; 2030 Airport Rd., Napa, CA 94558; at Napa County Airport) Specializes in scenic tours and charter flights. Their Napa Valley tour lasts about an hour and costs $115 for up to three people, $180 for four to five people. Custom coastal and Wine Country tours also available.

Sonoma County

Aero-Schellville (707-938-2444; Schellville Airport, 23982 Arnold Dr., Sonoma, CA 95476) Red Baron, move over. These scenic tours of Sonoma Valley are in vintage biplanes, meticulously restored. Aerobatic flights are also available, offering loops, rolls, and "kamikaze" flights — not for the faint of heart.

GOLF

Gold is popular in Wine Country, although dubs don't come with a corkscrew or wineglass.

Thomas Hallstein/Outsight

Golf courses cover the rich valleys and rolling hills of Wine Country as eagerly as vineyards. One of the region's favorite recreational activities, golf can be played year-round in this mild climate. Where to play? The visitor can stay at a premier resort with its own course, such as Silverado or Meadowood, or at accommodations with courses close at hand, such as Doubletree Inn and Sonoma Mission Inn. Other visitors and residents are free to sample a variety of public and semi-private courses (private clubs that also allow the public to play). Many private clubs allow members of other clubs to enjoy the benefits of their own members.

GOLF COURSES

Greens Fees Price Code   Inexpensive: Under $25
                                        Moderate: $25 to $50
                                        Expensive: Over $50

Napa County

Aetna Springs (707-965-2115; www.aetnasprings.com; 1600 Aetna Springs Rd., Pope Valley, CA 94567) 9 holes; par 35; public course established in the 1890s; driving range; pro; lessons; snack bar. Price: inexpensive.

Chardonnay Club (707-257-1900, 800-788-0136; www.chardonnayclub.com; 2555 Jamieson Canyon Rd., PO Box 3779Napa, CA 94558) Two 18-hole championship courses; par 72; Scottish links-style; semiprivate course; driving range; five pros; shop; clubhouse. Price: expensive.

Napa Municipal Golf Course (707-255-4333; Kennedy Park, 2295 Streblow Dr., Napa, CA 94558) 18 holes; par 72; public course; driving range; instruction; cocktail lounge; reserve tee time seven days in advance. Price: moderate.

Meadowood Resort (707-963-3646, 800-458-8080; www.meadowood.com; 900 Meadowood Ln., St. Helena, CA 94574) Private to members and guests; 9 holes; par 31; tree-lined narrow course. Price: moderate to expensive.

Mount St. Helena Golf Course (707-942-9966; 2025 Grant St., Calistoga, CA 94515) 9 holes; par 34; public course; shop; snack bar. Price: inexpensive.

Napa Valley Country Club (707-252-1114; 3385 Hagen Rd., Napa, CA 94558) Private; 18 holes; par 72; shop; pro; lessons open to public. Price: moderate to expensive.

Silverado Country Club and Resort (707-257-5460, 800-362-4727; www.silver adoresort.com; 1600 Atlas Peak Rd., Napa, CA 94558) Private to members and guests; two 18-hole championship courses; par 72; pro; shop; host to annual Senior PGA tournament in Oct.; considered by many the best course in Northern California. Price: expensive.

Sonoma County

Adobe Creek Golf Course (707-765-3000; www.fairway.com/adobecreek; 1901 Frates Rd., Petaluma, CA 49454) 18 holes; par 72; public course; driving range; putting green; lounge; restaurant. Price: inexpensive to moderate.

Bennett Valley Golf Course (707-528-3673; 3330 Yulupa Ave., Santa Rosa, CA, CA 94505) 18 holes; par 72; municipal course; three pros; shop; driving range; putting green; restaurant; lounge; reserve a week ahead. Price: inexpensive.

Bodega Harbour Golf Links (707-875-3538; 21301 Heron Dr., Bodega Bay, CA 94923) 18 championship holes; par 70; designed by Robert Trent Jones; semi-private course; two pros; shop; lessons; restaurant and lounge; spectacular ocean view from all holes. Price: moderate to expensive.

Fountaingrove Country Club (707-579-4653; 1525 Fountaingrove Pkwy., Santa Rosa, CA 95403) 18 championship holes; par 72; designed by Ted Robinson. Semi-private course; pro; shop; restaurant; tennis courts. Price: expensive.

Mountain Shadows Golf Resort (707-584-7766; 100 Golf Course Dr., Rohnert Park, CA 94928) Two 18-hole championship courses; par 72; public course; pro; shop; driving range; putting green; restaurant; lounge. Price: inexpensive to moderate.

Oakmont Golf Club (707-539-0415; 7025 Oakmont Dr., Santa Rosa, CA 95409) Two 18-hole championship courses; par 72 and 63; designed by Ted Robinson; public course; four pros; two shops; driving range; lessons; reservations suggested. Price: inexpensive to moderate.

Sea Ranch Golf Links (707-785-2468; 49300 Hwy. 1, Sea Ranch, CA 95497) 18 holes; par 72; Scottish links-style designed by Robert Muir Graves; public course; pro; shop; driving range; lessons; snack bar; ocean view from every hole. Price: moderate to expensive.

Sebastopol Golf Course (707-823-9852; 2881 Scott's Right-Of-Way, Sebastopol, CA 95472) 9 holes; par 31; public course; pro; shop; snack bar; picnic facilities. Price: inexpensive.

Sonoma Mission Inn and Country Club (707-996-0300, 800-862-4945; www. sonoma missioninn.com; 17700 Arnold Dr., Sonoma, CA 95476) 18 championship holes; par 72; public course; considered one of the top public courses in the state; $8.5-million renovation in 1990; driving range; putting green; restaurant. Price: moderate to expensive.

HIKING & PARKS

Take in the coastal views while hiking to the ocean.

Thomas Hallstein/Outsight

Whether you choose a trail through sand dunes or redwoods, grassy valleys or mountain forests, there is no better way to appreciate the natural beauty of Wine Country than to pack a snack and leave the roads behind you. Each season has its own personality: brilliant wildflowers in the spring, dry heat and golden grass in summer, colored foliage in the fall, cool breezes and green hills in winter. A number of state and county parks await you, whether you are toting a baby for his first hike or you're ready for serious backpacking. For help with the details of your trip, see Bob Lorentzen's *The Hiker's Hip Pocket Guide to Sonoma County* (includes some hikes in Napa County).

Remember, though you are not likely to find bears, mountain lions are seen occasionally, and rattlesnakes and ticks are common in the back country. Stay away from poison oak, and don't forget to take your own water on summer hikes. *Getaway Adventures* (800-499-2453) offers organized hikes through Robert L. Stevenson, Bothe–Napa Valley and Skyline parks.

Napa County

Bothe–Napa Valley State Park (707-942-4575; 3801 Hwy. 29, 5 mi. N. of St. Helena) Originally home to the Wappo Indians, this land became a country retreat for San Francisco's wealthy Hitchcock family in the 1870s. The History Trail passes a pioneer cemetery to Bale Grist Mill, a partially restored 1846 flour mill; 1,917 acres; day-use fee; 6 miles of hiking trails.

John F. Kennedy Park (707-257-9529; 2291 Streblow Dr. off Hwy. 121, Napa) This 340-acre park features hiking trails along the Napa River and plenty of undeveloped open space as well as softball fields, playgrounds, and boat-launch ramps.

Robert Louis Stevenson State Park (707-942-4575; 7 mi. N. of Calistoga on Hwy. 29) Composed of ancient lava, Mount St. Helena rises 4,343 ft. to provide the highest landmark in Wine Country. In 1841 Russian settlers from Fort Ross scaled the peak, naming it for their commandant's wife, Elena. In 1880 Robert Louis Stevenson spent two months near the mountain, recovering from tuberculosis. It made a lasting impression on him, and he renamed it Spyglass Hill in his most famous work Treasure Island; 3,300 acres; 10- and 6.5-mile round-trips to two summits, past the once-prosperous Silverado Mine; undeveloped except for trails; open daily during daylight hours.

Skyline Wilderness Park (707-252-0481; 2201 W. Imola Ave., Napa) Wilderness close to downtown Napa, with 35 miles of hiking, mountain bike, and horse trails. Its oak-wooded hills are ideal for hiking. On a clear day there are spectacular views of San Francisco from the park's ridges. A small lake offers bass fishing; 850 acres; open daily year-round; day-use fee.

Westwood Hills Wilderness Park (707-257-9529; Browns Valley Road at Laurel Street, Napa) City-owned park with hiking trails, nature museum, native flora and fauna; 111 acres.

White Sulphur Springs (707-963-8588; 3100 White Sulphur Springs Rd., St. Helena) Secluded countryside 3 miles west of St. Helena, with hiking trails throughout; year-round creek and waterfalls. Day-use fee.

Sonoma County

Annadel State Park (707-539-3911; 6201 Channel Dr., off Montgomery Dr., Santa Rosa) Surrounded by an increasingly developed Santa Rosa, Annadel offers 5,000 acres of hills, creeks, woodlands, and meadows, accessible through 40 miles of trails used by hikers, horseback riders, and mountain bikers. Annadel visitors enjoy a small central lake created by the last owner, Joe Coney, and named after himself and his wife, Ilsa, as Lake Ilsanjo; day-use fee.

Armstrong Redwoods State Reserve (707-869-2015; 17000 Armstrong Woods Rd., Guerneville) In the late 1800s Col. James Armstrong sought to preserve this ancient grove of redwoods he had come to love. Because of his efforts and those of his family, Sonoma is fortunate to be able to enjoy this virgin stand of 1,000-year-old trees stretching 300 feet high — one of the largest of which is named after the colonel. Walk among these giants, where even on the hottest day you will feel their cool serenity; 5,000 acres; day-use fee; hiking trails, picnic sites, outdoor theater; open year-round until sunset.

The fog settles in, hovering over the coastal redwoods in Sonoma County.

Thomas Hallstein/Outsight

Austin Creek State Recreation Area (707-869-2015; 17000 Armstrong Woods Rd., Guerneville) Adjacent to Armstrong Grove, this undeveloped park offers miles of trails for hikers and equestrians through canyons, enormous glades, and dark, cool forests; 4,200 acres; day-use fee; camping available.

Hood Mountain Regional Park (707-527-2041; 3000 Los Alamos Road, Santa Rosa) Accessible by car from Alamos Road or by a four-hour hike from Sugarloaf Ridge State Park, Hood Mountain (elevation 2,730 ft.) commands an imposing view of the Mayacamas Range; challenging trails; closed from June to mid-October; day-use fee.

Lake Sonoma (707-433-9483; 3333 Skaggs Spring Rd. near Dry Creek Road, Healdsburg) 40 miles of trails wind through the redwood groves and oak woodlands surrounding Sonoma's newest manmade lake. Visitor Center is at the base of the dam; 3,600 acres; camping, boating, swimming, fish hatchery.

Jack London State Historic Park (707-938-5216; 2400 London Ranch Rd., off Arnold Dr., Glen Ellen) Writer Jack London fell in love with the Valley of the Moon and began buying land there in 1905. By the time he died in 1916, he was immersed in the innovative projects of his "Beauty Ranch." Visitors can see the remains of the London's Wolf House mansion; 7 miles of trails as well as a scenic 3.5-mile climb with breathtaking views of the Valley of the Moon; 800 acres; day-use fee; open daily.

Ragle Ranch Regional Park (707-527-2041; 500 Ragle Rd., off Bodega Hwy., Sebastopol) This former ranch offers trails through a rugged wilderness of oak woodlands and creeks; baseball fields, playgrounds, picnic areas; 156 acres.

Sugarloaf Ridge State Park (800-444-7275; 2605 Adobe Canyon Rd. off Hwy. 12, Santa Rosa) The Wappo Indians lived in this beautiful area before they were decimated by European diseases in the 1830s. Purchased by the state in 1920 as a site for a dam that was never built, Sugarloaf Ridge now offers 25 miles of trails through a varied landscape, including ridges surrounding Bald Mountain and meadows along Sonoma Creek. 2,700 acres; day-use fee; camping.

HORSEBACK RIDING

Horseback riding is a peaceful way to explore Wine Country.

Courtesy Sonoma Cattle Co.

Wine Country adamantly maintains its rural flavor, despite its growing population and worldwide tourist appeal. With an estimated 26,000 horses in Sonoma County alone, there is plenty of interest in horse breeding, competition, and riding. Some 50 horse events take place annually at the Sonoma County Fairgrounds, including top shows such as the California State Horse Show, which attracts visitors from all over the West.

Like Jack London, who was described by one biographer as the "sailor on horseback," many Wine Country residents and visitors take to the hills on horseback to explore the countryside as the early California settlers did before them. Bridle paths and trails can be found at *Annadel, Armstrong Redwoods, Austin Creek, Bothe-Napa Valley, Jack London, Salt Point, Skyline,* and *Sugarloaf Ridge* parks. For those without their own steeds, the following stables rent horses for the day. Trail ride packages start as low as $50 and can go as high as $150 for the more experienced riders.

Napa County

Napa Valley Trail Rides (707-996-8566; www.winecountrytrailrides.com; St. Helena, CA 94574; Bothe–Napa Valley State Park) Guided tours, full-day trips, sunset and full moon rides; barbecue rides.

Sonoma County

Armstrong Woods Pack Station (707-887-2939; Armstrong Redwoods State Park, 17000 Armstrong Woods Rd., PO Box 287, Guerneville, CA 95446) Rentals for trail rides through Armstrong Redwoods and Austin Creek parks; half day or full day with gourmet lunch available.

Chanslor Guest Ranch and Horse Stables (707-875-2721; www.chanslor.com; 2660 Hwy. 1, Bodega Bay, CA 94923) Scenic guided trail rides for riders of all levels; one- or two-hour treks on the ranch and dunes. Open year-round.

Sonoma Cattle Company (707-996-8566; Jack London State Park, 2400 London Ranch Rd., PO Box 877, Glen Ellen, CA 95442) Rentals for Jack London and Sugarloaf Ridge state parks; guided tours for one- or two-hour tours (April through October); sunset and full moon rides; barbecue rides and day trips available.

HORSE RACING

Horse racing fans converge each summer at the *Sonoma County Fair* (707-545-4200; 1350 Bennett Valley Rd., Santa Rosa, CA 95404) to watch California's fastest horses vying for a purse of nearly $2 million. During the rest of the year, the fairgrounds offer *The Jockey Club* (800-454-RACE), with simultaneous broadcasting of races at *Golden Gate Fields, Bay Meadows,* and *Hollywood Park.*

ROCK CLIMBING

For those who like to live on the edge, rock climbing has become a sport with built-in adventure, but it's important to do it right. *Sonoma Outfitters* (528-1920; 145 3rd St., Santa Rosa, CA 95401) offers a complete selection of shoes and equipment.

When you're ready for the real thing, favorite climbing spots in the area are *Sunset Boulder at Goat Rock* on the Sonoma Coast and *Mount St. Helena* in Napa. Check out the book *Bouldering in the Bay Area* for other possible challenges.

RUNNING

Joggers of all ages, sizes, and shapes can be seen on park trails and roadsides in Sonoma and Napa Counties. The fresh air and rural countryside of the Wine Country, along with its mild climate, have made running an extremely popular year-round activity for the health conscious.

For those serious runners looking for competition, several take place each year, including the *Napa Valley Marathon*, which is run from Calistoga to Napa on the second Sunday in March. Another demanding event is the *International Vineman Triathlon*, combining running, bicycling, and swimming competitions. Many races in both counties benefit local causes, such as Sonoma County's *Human Race*. Get specific schedules from the *Sonoma County Tourism Program* (800-5-SONOMA) or the *Napa Valley Conference and Visitors Bureau* (707-226-7459; 1310 Napa Town Ctr., Napa, CA 94559).

SKATING

ICE SKATING

Famed cartoonist and ice-skating buff Charles Schulz built the *Redwood Empire Ice Arena* (707-546-7147; 1667 W. Steel Ln., Santa Rosa, CA 95403) in 1969, and it has become one of Sonoma County's most popular spots. The rink, surrounded by walls painted with Alpine scenes, is the site for recreational and would-be Olympic skaters, birthday parties, and holiday ice shows with professional figure skaters. Next door is *Snoopy's Gallery & Gift Shop* (707-546-3385), filled with every conceivable item relating to Snoopy and the *Peanuts* gang, as well as skating gear including hi-tech in-line skates.

ROLLER SKATING

It's still a fun-time favorite with kids, teens, and adults. After all, they say it's the best aerobic exercise around. *Cal Skate:* 707-585-0500; 6100 Commerce Blvd., Rohnert Park, CA 94928.

SPAS

Long before pioneers came to settle Northern California, Indians knew the locations of hot springs and used the steamy pools, volcanic mud, and mineral waters to heal and soak away pains. Calistoga remains the most popular destination for mud, mineral baths, and professional massage, but health spas are beginning to dot the entire Wine Countryside. Many spas are part of resorts or other places to stay; check Chapter Three, *Lodging*, for more information.

Napa County

AUBERGE DU SOLEIL
707-963-1211.
180 Rutherford Rd.,
 Rutherford, CA 94573.
Open: 8am–8pm daily.
Credit Cards: AE, D, MC, V.

What would Napa Valley's most luxurious resort be without an excellent spa? The facility is top notch, but then so is everything at this inn, hidden in the mountains above Napa Valley. Auberge du Soleil offers a variety of treatments, from aromatherapy and facials to foot massages and Ayurvedic treatments, an ancient East Indian healing system that uses massage and curative oils. If you're staying at the inn, many treatments can be done in your room. One hour massage: $125.

**CALISTOGA SPA HOT
 SPRINGS**
707-942-6269.
www.calistogaspa.com.
1006 Washington St.,
 Calistoga, CA 94515.
Open: 8:30am–5pm
 Mon.–Thu., 8:30am–9pm
 Fri.–Sun.
Credit Cards: MC, V.

Stylishly designed, with hi-tech masonry, polished metal accents, and glass-block walls, this is one of Calistoga's most pleasant spa experiences. Massage rooms are equipped with skylights, a nice touch. Mud baths use a traditional blend of volcanic ash, peat moss, and hot-spring water. Large steam rooms. Staff is extremely attentive. Massage is generally Swedish technique. One of the best pool destinations in Napa, with four naturally heated outside pools, varying from a 83-degree lap pool to a huge 105-degree covered whirlpool. The wading pool signals that kids are welcome here. Pools are open to the public for day use and surrounded by pleasant and private landscaping. Also, large exercise room. Mud bath, mineral whirlpool, and half-hour massage: $78.

**CALISTOGA VILLAGE
 INN AND SPA**
707-942-0991.
www.greatspa.com.
1880 Lincoln Ave.,
 Calistoga, CA 94515.
Credit Cards: AE, D, MC, V.

A small facility removed from the bustle of the downtown strip, this was once known as the French Spa. The name has changed, but the French-style spa equipment remains. Changing rooms are makeshift, but the spa rooms are pleasantly adorned with blue-and-white tiles. Mud treatment is one of best in town, using a pleasant mix of peat moss and white clay, mildly heated by mineral water before you enter. French steam cabinets — contraptions that cover everything except your head — substitute for steam rooms, an enjoyable change. Specialties include herbal wraps and an invigorating salt scrub.

Outside mineral pools have a magnificent view of surrounding mountains. There is a wading pool for kids and the pool house has a whirlpool and sauna. Mud bath, mineral whirlpool, and half-hour massage: $80.

Playing with Mud

Wine Country, along with all its other striking features, is blessed with a little extra something: geothermal activity from down under. The most popular signs of hot steam and bubbling mineral water are the SPA signs along Lincoln Avenue in downtown Calistoga, where salvation is offered to the body and soul in the form of mud and mineral baths.

What exactly is a mud bath treatment? First, you immerse yourself in a thick, warm, black mass of volcanic ash and/or peat moss, mixed with naturally heated mineral water. It's like a warm cocoon enveloping you, but just relax and go with it. The benefits? Relaxed muscles and joints and soft, renewed skin. There are drawbacks, of course. Some may find the mud too warm, and others may feel claustrophobic being engulfed in so much earth. Also, the mud sticks like glue as you wash it off in a lukewarm shower.

Afterward, you soak in warm mineral water, then open your pores in a eucalyptus-scented, geyser-heated steam room. Finish up with a cooling blanket wrap. Ahhhh. If you can handle additional pleasure, expert masseuses will work your body into a silly-putty state.

DR. WILKINSON'S HOT SPRINGS
707-942-4102.
www.drwilkinson.com.
1507 Lincoln Ave.,
Calistoga, CA 95415.
Open: 8:30am–4pm daily.
Credit Cards: AE, MC, V.

John "Doc" Wilkinson was a young chiropractor when he gave his first spa treatment in 1946. One of the most popular spas on Calistoga's main drag, Dr. Wilkinson remains a no-frills outfit. The concrete-block walls of the spa area create a utilitarian atmosphere, the steam room is closet size, and the mineral baths are simple claw-foot tubs. But the staff is first-rate. Mud baths use a traditional blend of volcanic ash, peat moss, and hot-spring water. One of the best massages in Calistoga is found here, with both Swedish and Shiatsu technique. The salon offers five different types of facials as well as a salt glow body scrub. Outdoor pools are not open for day use. Mud bath, mineral whirlpool, and half-hour massage: $99.

EUROSPA AND INN
707-942-6829.
www.eurospa.com.
1202 Pine St., Calistoga, CA 94515.
Open: hours vary, Sun-Thu.
Credit Cards: AE, D, MC, V.

Eurospa takes its lead from the continent, as its name suggests. If the century-old traditions of Calistoga and its thick and hot mud baths lack appeal, Eurospa is a change of pace. In the Pine Street Inn, the spa sets an intimate yet airy mood. Spa rooms have pleasant views of the grounds, and after treatments guests are free to roam outside to use the pool and Jacuzzi. Treatments include various body wraps, aromatherapy facials, body scrubs, and Swedish massage. Mud bath and one hour massage: $135.

GOLDEN HAVEN SPA HOT SPRINGS
707-942-6793.
www.goldenhaven.com.
1713 Lake St., Calistoga, CA 94515.
Open: 8am–8pm daily.
Credit Cards: AE, MC, V.

In a residential neighborhood three blocks from Calistoga's downtown, the Golden Haven is not fancy but has been drawing a following since the 1950s. Service is pleasant and the atmosphere low-key. One of the few spas that offers mud baths and mineral baths for couples — a cozy touch. Mud baths use a mix of peat moss, clay, and mineral water. Specialties include an inch-reducing European body wrap and oatmeal facial scrubs. Massage is Swedish, with Esalen, acupressure, and deep tissue. Spa guests have access to outside Jacuzzi and a large 80-degree pool. Mud bath, mineral whirlpool, and half-hour massage: $78.

HEALTH SPA OF NAPA VALLEY
707-967-8800.
www.napavalleyspa.com.
1030 Main St., St. Helena, CA 94575.
At The Inn at Southbridge.
Open: 6am–8:30pm Mon.–Fri., 7am–8:30pm Sat. & Sun.
Credit Cards: AE, MC, V.

Napa Valley's newest spa, it's located in the heart of St. Helena. It's a first-class facility, with a heated 25-foot outdoor lap pool, outdoor whirlpool, steam rooms, weight room, and spa garden. There's a private room for couples massages. Treatments include Swedish and deep tissue massage, mud and seaweed wraps, facials for men and women, fitness training and assessment. For something out of the ordinary, try a Ayurvedic treatment, an ancient East Indian healing system that uses curative oils. Fifty-minute massage with use of whirlpool, pool, steam room: $95.

Indian Springs in Calistoga is one of the oldest health spas in Napa Valley.

Chris Alderman

**INDIAN HOT SPRINGS
SPA AND RESORT**
707-942-4913.
1712 Lincoln Ave.,
   Calistoga, CA 94515.
Open: 8am–8pm daily.
Credit Cards: D, MC, V.

Wappo Indians built sweat lodges on this site, and later it was home to Calistoga's original resort. Its huge mineral pool — an Olympic-size beauty originally built in 1913 — has bright blue-green water that remains at 80 degrees in the summer. It's even hotter in the winter, when steam rolls off the water and into the sky above Calistoga. The pool is open for day use and draws thousands of summer visitors. Children are welcome. Three active geysers supply water as warm as 212 degrees. The facility is old but well maintained. Mud baths use only volcanic ash, taken from the resort's 16-acre site. Facial treatments are also available. Mud bath and half-hour massage: $125.

LAVENDER HILL SPA
707-942-4495, 800-528-4772.
www.lavenderhillspa.com.
1015 Foothill Blvd.,
   Calistoga, CA 94515.
On Hwy. 29.
Open: 9am–9pm daily.
Credit Cards: AE, MC, V.

This relative newcomer, a charming yellow house that was once a bed & breakfast, caters to couples. It has private, cushioned tubs built for two and double massage tables. One massage room even has a fireplace. Mud baths are a light, warm chocolate-milklike blend of mineral water and powdered volcanic ash. If you're turned off by the thick traditional mud baths, this may be for you. Other treatments include seaweed baths, mineral salt baths, facials, herbal blanket wraps, and massage. There is no pool, but afterward, gather your thoughts in the graceful garden. Mud bath and half-hour massage: $105.

LINCOLN AVENUE SPA
707-942-5296.
www.lincolnavenue
   spa.com.
1339 Lincoln Ave.,
   Calistoga, CA 94515.
Open: 9am–9pm.
Credit Cards: AE, MC, V.

Housed in a sturdy rock building — originally Calistoga's first bank — this spa is in the heart of downtown. Although you won't find any ink pens on chains, the spa has done a good job of preserving the bank's interior, even retaining the vault. Lincoln Avenue offers a few unusual treatments. If being buried in mud is not your cup of tea, try the body mud, in which a balm of warm herbs is applied to your skin, followed by a towel wrap and soothing steam treatment. The mud comes in different "flavors," as well, including seaweed and mint. Other treatments include facials and acupressure face lifts. Treatments for singles or couples. No pools or whirlpools. Body mud and half-hour massage: $79.

MEADOWOOD
707-963-3646, 800-458-8080.
www.meadowood.com.
900 Meadowood Ln., St.
   Helena, CA 94574.

Want to be pampered? The health spa at Meadowood resort is the place. One of Napa Valley's newest and perhaps best spa, it comes at a price, yet a basic massage is priced competitively.

Open: 7am–8pm daily.
Credit Cards: AE, D, DC, MC, V.

Also, if you're addicted to mud, this is not your place. Meadowood specializes in face and body treatments as well as fitness programs. The setting alone soothes the soul. The spa is set in the lush foothills of Howell Mountain and the outside pool and Jacuzzi are surrounded by towering trees. A Meadowood specialty is the chardonnay massage, which uses a pleasant wine-based gel that's invigorating, not oily. Other treatments include something called a "salt glow," as well as facials, waxing, and various therapeutic combinations of all. Massage rooms are darkly lit and light jazz is piped in. Treatments are available to resort guests only. Fifty-minute massage with use of steam room, sauna, and pools: $105.

MOUNT VIEW SPA
707-942-5789, 800-772-8838.
www.mountviewspa.com.
1457 Lincoln Ave.,
  Calistoga, CA 94515.
Open: 9am–9pm daily.
Credit Cards: AE, MC, V.

If you're turned off by the communal locker room atmosphere of many Calistoga spas, this spa has the solitude you crave. Private treatment rooms have lockers, steam rooms, and two-person Jacuzzi tubs, for both singles and couples. Part of the newly restored Mount View Hotel, the spa is elegant yet unpretentiously appointed. Mud treatments come in two forms: fango bath — a light, warm chocolate-milk-like blend of mineral water, herbs, and powdered volcanic ash — as well as mud wraps, in which the body is painted with a glaze of Dead Sea mud, honey, and glycerin, then wrapped in warm blankets. Other treatments include a variety of hydrotherapy baths, facials, and Swedish massage. Choice of hydrotherapy bath with 50-minute massage: $100.

NANCE'S HOT SPRINGS
707-942-6211.
1614 Lincoln Ave.,
  Calistoga, CA 94515.
Open: 9am–5pm Mon.–Fri.,
  10am–7pm Sat. & Sun.
Credit Cards: AE, MC, V.

One of oldest spas, this is a popular spot with folks who relish a simple, old-fashioned Calistoga atmosphere. Co-owner Frank Hughes, in his 70s, is still giving massages after more than 45 years. Spa rooms are low on ambiance, with clawfoot tubs and tiled mud baths. Massage is Swedish. Indoor pool heated with 102-degree mineral water. Mud bath, mineral whirlpool, and half-hour massage: $80.

OASIS SPA
707-942-2122.
1300 Washington St.,
  Calistoga, CA 94515.
Open: 9am–5pm Tues. &
  Wed., 9am–9pm
  Thurs.–Mon.
Credit Cards: MC, V.

A bungalow next to the Roman Spa Motel, Oasis offers a variety of treatments, from traditional mud and massage to herbal facials, foot reflexology, and seaweed baths and wraps. All treatments are for singles or couples. Massage is Swedish and Esalen. Roman Spa's outdoor pool and Finnish sauna are open to Spa guests. Mud bath, mineral whirlpool, and a 25 minute massage: $80.

Chris Alderman

The rock-lined mineral pool at White Sulphur Springs Resort in St. Helena.

WHITE SULPHUR SPRINGS INN AND SPA
707-963-4361, 800-593-8873.
www.whitesulphursprings.com.
3100 White Sulphur Springs Rd., St. Helena, CA 94574.
Open: 9am–6pm daily.
Credit Cards: AE, D, MC, V.

The first resort built in California, White Sulphur Springs dates from 1852. Its first owners were physicians who believed the sulfur springs helped relieve arthritis and rheumatism, and by the turn of the 20th century it was a fashionable watering hole. The grounds cover 330 spectacular acres of redwood, madrone, and fir, explored easily through hiking trails. The lodge and spa were recently updated but retain a sense of history and rustic charm. Spa rooms view the outdoors through high windows. Treatments include massage, facials, and seaweed and mud wraps. Visitors soothe themselves in a free-flowing, rock-lined mineral pool that stays between 85 and 92 degrees. Mud wrap: $75; half-hour massage: $50.

Sonoma County

OSMOSIS
707-823-8231.
www.osmosis.com.
209 Bohemian Hwy., Freestone, CA 95472.
Open: 9am–8pm daily.
Credit Cards: AE, MC, V.

A truly unique experience, Osmosis is the only place in the Western World to experience Japanese-style enzyme baths. The baths are similar to mud baths in only one way: You're covered from neck to toe. In this case it's not mud but a sawdust-like mix of fragrant cedar, rice bran, and more than 600 active enzymes. The concoction ferments and generates gentle and natural heat. Guests don kimonos and begin their treatment in a Japanese sitting room, sipping enzyme tea as they gaze through shoji doors into the Japanese garden. Baths can be taken solo or with a friend. The treatment con-

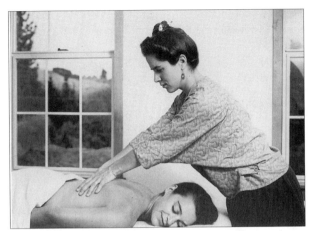

Massages are just one way to pamper yourself in a Wine Country health spa.

Courtesy Osmosis

cludes with a shower and a 30-minute blanket wrap or Swedish massage. Enzyme bath with 75-minute massage: $150.

A SIMPLE TOUCH
707-433-6856.
239 Center St., Healdsburg, CA 95448.
Open: 10am–6pm Sun.–Thurs., 10am–7pm Fri. & Sat.
Credit Cards: MC, V.

An intimate spot just off the Healdsburg Square, this spa is a welcome addition to northern Sonoma County. With a single bath and two treatment rooms, Simple Touch offers individualized care. The lobby welcomes you with soft peach tones and a warm atmosphere. Mud baths are fango style, a light, warm chocolate-milklike blend of mineral water and powdered mud. There are also seaweed and sea-salt baths, as well as rose-petal wraps, herbal facials, and Swedish, Shiatsu, and sports massage. Mud bath and one hour massage: $100.

SONOMA MISSION INN AND SPA
707-938-9000, 800-862-4945.
www.sonomamission inn.com.
18140 Sonoma Hwy., Boyes Hot Springs, CA 95416.
On Hwy. 12.
Open: 6am–9pm daily.
Credit Cards: AE, DC, MC, V.

Who's that lounging in the mineral pool? Billy Crystal? The waters at this Wine Country favorite for the rich and famous have made this site a destination since Native Americans first considered it a healing ground. It's also Wine Country's most expensive spa. The inn has recently tapped into a new source of mineral water, and the soft and lightly green liquid warms the pool and Jacuzzi. The spa house is a stylish combo of Mission and Art Deco, and the pool area is in a peaceful grove of trees. The array of treatments is boggling, from Swedish and sports massage to mud and seaweed body wraps, hair and foot care, waxing, color analysis, and nearly a dozen different facials.

There is also a fitness center. Pools are open to the public for day use during the week. Mineral bath, body wrap and a massage with lavender oil: $200.

SONOMA SPA
707-939-8770.
www.sonomaspaonthe
  plaza.com.
457 1st St. W., Sonoma, CA
  95476.
Open: 9am–9pm daily.
Credit Cards: AE, MC, V.

Opening up shop a few years ago, this spa brought a much-needed dose of indulgence to downtown Sonoma. The Greek Revival storefront looks out onto historic Sonoma Plaza. No traditional mud baths here, but treatments are available for singles and couples. They include Swedish and Esalen massage, as well as rose petal body masques, cooling body mud, herbal wraps, facials, and foot reflexology. Mud and wraps treatments include an herbal sauna. Mud wrap with half-hour massage: $88.

SWIMMING

Summer in the Wine Country brings day after day of blue skies — that is, after the sun breaks through the morning fog. It does get hot in the summer, and a dip in cool water is luscious relief. Remember, the Pacific Ocean — with year-round temperatures around 50 degrees and dangerous undercurrents — is not a good choice. For those whose swimming is more for exercise than for fun, indoor pools with lap lanes are also available year-round. In Calistoga, some spas open their pools to the public for day use for a nominal fee.

Napa County

Windsor Waterworks

You're going to get wet at Windsor Waterworks.

Bothe-Napa Valley State Park (707-942-4575; Hwy. 29, 4 mi. N. of St. Helena) Swimming pool open mid-June through Labor Day; day-use fee.

Lake Berryessa (800-726-1256; W. of Rutherford on Hwy. 128) Miles of clear blue water, with temperatures up to 75 degrees, make this an ideal destination in the summer. Several resorts, including Putah Creek, Spanish Flat, and Steele Park, offer swimming areas. (See "Boating" in this chapter for specific information on resorts.)

St. Helena Community Pool (707-963-7946; 1401 Grayson Ave., St. Helena) Open all summer.

Sonoma County

Lake Sonoma (707-433-9483; 11 mi. N. of Healdsburg on Dry Creek Rd.) Beaches at Lake Sonoma Marina and at Yorty Creek, along with picnic, hiking, and boating facilities.

Morton's Sonoma Springs Rersort (707-833-5511, 800-551-2177; www.sonoma springs.com; 1651 Warm Springs Rd., Kenwood, CA 95452) Two large pools, one wading pool; picnic grounds, volleyball and baseball. Now open year-round. Perfect for group outings.

Russian River residents and visitors alike enjoy swimming in the slow-flowing, deep green Russian River. Swimming areas are at Veterans Memorial Beach in Healdsburg (707-433-1625; Healdsburg Ave.), Monte Rio Beach, and at Johnson's Beach in Guerneville (707-869-2022), both just off River Road, where inner tubes and paddleboats can also be rented.

Spring Lake (707-539-8092; off Summerfield Rd., Santa Rosa) The 72-acre swimming lagoon — separated from the lake's boating and fishing areas — is filled with kids and their families every hot day of summer. A gentle, sandy shoreline, water floats to mark depth, rafts and tubes to rent, and lifeguards help make this a great swimming experience for beginners.

Windsor Waterworks and Slides (707-838-7760; 8225 Conde Ln., Windsor, CA 95492) Outdoor pool, wading pool, picnic sites, and four roller-coaster water slides make this a cool spot to be on a scorching summer day. One ride down the slide and you're hooked.

YMCA (707-545-9622; 1111 College Ave., Santa Rosa, CA 95404) The Y's indoor heated pool is open daily year-round for laps, exercise, instruction, and family fun; day and evening hours.

TENNIS

In an area where the climate is mild, and it rains only six months out of the year, you would expect tennis to be an avid sport. Is it ever. With a variety of both public and private tennis courts offering instruction and competition, Wine Country gives the tennis enthusiast plenty of action.

Napa County

Tennis courts are everywhere in Wine Country.

Janeen Belsardi

Calistoga Public Courts (707-942-2838) are available year-round at Stevenson and Grant Sts., Calistoga; 4 courts; lit; city-run instruction in summer.

Meadowood Resort (707-963-3646; 900 Meadowood Ln., St. Helena, CA 94574) Courts open to members and guests; pro.

Napa Public Courts (707-257-9529) Available during the summer at Napa Valley College (Vallejo Hwy., Napa), Vintage High School (1375 Trower Ave., Napa), Napa High School (2475 Jefferson St.), Silverado Middle School (1133 Coombsville Rd., Napa); city-run instruction.

Napa Valley Country Club (707-252-2299; www.napavalleycc.com; 3385 Hagen Rd., Napa, CA 94558) Private; pro; lessons open to public; active spot.

St. Helena Public Courts (707-963-5706) are available at Robert Louis Stevenson School (1316 Hill View Pl., St. Helena) and St. Helena High School (1401 Grayson Ave., St. Helena); city-operated courts at Crane Park (off Crane Ave.); active women's city league program for A and B players.

Silverado Country Club and Resort (707-257-0200; www.silveradoresort.com; 1600 Atlas Peak Rd., Napa, CA 94558) Open to members and guests; 14 courts, 3 lit; pro.

Sonoma County

Countryside Racquet Club (707-527-9948; 3950 Sebastopol Rd., Santa Rosa, CA 95407) Courts open to members and guests; pro; 8 lit courts; leagues and tournaments; very active.

La Cantera Racquet and Swim Club (707-544-9494; 3737 Montgomery Dr., Santa Rosa, CA 95405) Courts open to members and guests; pro; 12 courts, 4 lit; leagues and tournaments.

Montecito Heights Health and Racquet Club (707-526-0529; 2777 4th St., Santa Rosa, CA 95405) Courts open to members and guests; pro; 5 courts, none lit; leagues and tournaments.

Rancho Arroyo Racquet Club (707-795-5461; 85 Corona Rd., Petaluma, CA 94952) Courts open to members and guests; pro; 7 courts, 2 lit; leagues and tournaments.

Rohnert Park Public Courts (707-588-3456) At seven parks in Rohnert Park: Ladybug (8517 Liman Wy), Dorotea, Eagle, Sunrise, Honeybee (1170 Golf Course Dr.), and Golis. The Recreation Department offers instruction and sponsors the Rohnert Park Tennis Club, a group that draws players from Sonoma, Napa, and Marin counties.

Santa Rosa Public Courts (707-543-3282) are available at Howarth and Galvin parks, Burbank Playground, Santa Rosa Junior College, and Santa Rosa and Montgomery high schools.

WHALE WATCHING

One of the great attractions in California is the opportunity to watch gray whales in their annual round-trip migration between summer feeding grounds in the Bering Sea and their breeding and birthing waters off Baja California. From late May through October, the gray whales feed in the cold waters to build up fat for their 12,000-mile pilgrimage. Then, beginning in late November, they head south, passing close enough to shore to navigate by sight as well as to avoid killer whales in the deeper waters. Their return usually starts in late February and lasts until early June.

The Point Reyes Lighthouse (415-669-1534) At the tip of the Point Reyes National Seashore in Marin County, about a 1 1/2 hour drive from Santa Rosa; offers one of the best vantage points in the state for whale watching. The lighthouse is open from 10 to 4:30 daily except Tuesday and Wednesday, but parking is limited and extremely crowded on weekends. Call ahead to find out if there is any visibility since the lighthouse sits on the windiest and rainiest spot on the entire Pacific Coast.

Sonoma County offers other good whale-watching sites, including *Gualala Point, Stillwater Cove, Fort Ross,* and *Bodega Head.* On a clear day you will have plenty of company to share sightings — all bundled against the sea breezes, toting binoculars and picnic lunches, and ready to spend several hours watching for the telltale white spouts shooting above the blue Pacific waters.

For a close-up view, reserve a place on a whale-watching boat out of *Bodega Bay.* Remember that it's typically 15 degrees colder on the water, so wear plenty of warm clothes. Law prohibits boaters from harassing whales, but the large mammals have little fear of man and often approach boats at sea. All boats leave from Porto Bodega Marina on Bay Flat Rd., off Highway 1. Season is January through April and boats run weather permitting.

Bodega Bay Sport Fishing Center: 707-875-3344; 1410 Bay Flat Road, Bodega Bay, CA 94923.
The Boathouse 707-875-3495; The Boathouse, 1445 Hwy. 1, Bodega Bay, CA 94923.

NEIGHBORS ALL AROUND

Six Flags Marine World is just a short drive south of Napa.

Courtesy Six Flags Marine World

Six Flags Marine World (707-643-6722; www.sixflags.com/mrineworld; 2001 Marine World Pkwy., Vallejo, CA 94589; off I-80) Only a short drive away. This 160-acre facility includes whale and seal shows, elephant rides, and the usual wild creatures. Walk through a glass tunnel surrounded by sharks or see robotic dinosaurs in action. Open daily; closed November–March. Admission: $42.99 adults, seniors and disabled $32.99, $21.50 children 4-12, children 3 and under free.

CHAPTER EIGHT
For the Sport of It
SHOPPING

Peruse the quaint shops in old railroad cars in downtown Calistoga.

Thomas Hallstein/Outsight

Shopping is sporting, an exercise in endurance, an exhausting workout, a test of willpower, and pure capitalistic fun. Just start off your day with a shot of espresso, catalog your credit cards, and set off on a great marathon through Wine Country.

This chapter is organized by city, detailing eight shopping areas. These burgeoning meccas of retail sales are growing at a furious rate, thanks to affluent, latte-drinking tourists and locals with expensive tastes. This chapter will serve as your compass; it will guide you to both traditional and offbeat stores. Some will be within easy reach; others will be off the beaten path.

Some antiques stores listed will make you feel as though you're prowling an attic. Some furniture stores reveal a new breed of artists/designers who create both comfort and style in one sitting. You could lose a day or two wandering through the bookstores listed here. All are user-friendly, equipped with beautiful books, classical music, and — for the most part — helpful clerks. As for clothing, we list shops both conservative and chic. Indeed, if you take our tour of clothing stores, you will come across — perhaps for the first time in your life — a pair of silk boxer shorts priced at $58. We were naturally befuddled. Just when did it begin costing more to undress than to dress?

So, hit an automated teller machine, harvest some cash, and pick a city, any city: Napa, Yountville, St. Helena, Calistoga, Sonoma, Santa Rosa, Sebastopol, or Healdsburg. You'll find as a rule that Sonoma County stores tend to be funkier than their Napa County counterparts.

SHOPPING IN NAPA COUNTY

Shops and restaurants line the main street of St. Helena, Napa County.

Thomas Hallstein/Outsight

Napa

Downtown Napa can look a little bleak on some streets with several vacant storefronts, but don't despair. The shopping has simply shifted to the *Napa Town Center*, a concentrated area in the city's core, and to the *Napa Premium Outlets*, just on the other side of Highway 29. What follows are highlights.

The *Napa Town Center* is bordered by First St., Pearl St., Franklin St., and Main St. It's an upscale, outdoor mall with a brick path that conveniently meanders by the *Napa Valley Visitors Bureau*. Shoppers stroll past outdoor cafés, ice-cream parlors, and storefronts that boast the best in consumer goods. *McCarrlous* (707-255-9375; 1380 Napa Town Center, Napa, CA 94559) A department store with shoes, clothes, cosmetics, housewares, kid ware — one-stop shopping. *The Mustard Seed Clothing Co.* (707-255-4222; 1301 Napa Town Center, Napa, CA 94559) carries upscale weekend and sportswear for women, with lines that include Flax, Carol Anderson, and Gotcha Covered. *Napa Valley Jewelers* (707-224-0997;1317 Napa Town Center, Napa, CA 94559) sells gold and diamond jewelry, and has a designer on site to customize jewelry. *Silver Sensations* (707-252-8953; 1231 Napa Town Center, Napa, CA 94559) is a gift shop with an emphasis on hand-crafted items, including silver jewelry, blue willow china, wine glasses, jewelry, fountains, and hand-blown glass. *Classic Living* (707-251-5650; 1275 Napa Town Center, Napa, CA 94559) has Persian, European and American furniture, reproductions of 17th-century pieces, as well as contemporary items. *Print Your World* (707-226-7484; 1349 Napa Town Center, Napa, CA 94559) is a ceramic studio where you can paint plates, mugs, water pitchers, etc., before firing them in a kiln. Wannabe artists will love this.

Outside the Napa Town Center, you'll find a range of other interesting stores:

At *The Beaded Nomad* (707-258-8004; 1238 First St., Napa, CA 94559), you don't have to be a child of the '60s to relish this jewelry shop that features clothes, books, beads, beads, and more beads. It also has plenty of nifty wall hangings. The *Neighborhood Antique Collective* (707-259-1900; 1400 First St., Napa, CA 94559) is also worth perusing. Check out the water basins, rockers, mirrors and stained glass. The *Irish Pedlar Antiques* (707-253-9091; 1988 Wise Dr., Napa, CA 94558) specializes in upscale country furniture with its oldest piece dating back to the 18th century. Plenty of linens, cookware, and quilts. *Red Hen Antiques* (707-257-0822; 5091 St. Helena Hwy. 29, Napa, CA 94558) is the largest antiques store in Napa Valley, with rare finds ranging from porcelain dishes to old Life and Post magazines.

Bookends Book Store (707-224-1077; 1014 Coombs St., Napa, CA 94559) is a bookstore with a serious, smart feel to it. The store boasts that it has the valley's largest magazine selection as well as an extensive map and travel section and music CDs. *Copperfield's* (707-252-8002; 1303 First St., Napa, CA 94559) is an all-purpose bookstore and a fun stop for folks who like to peruse used books; 50 percent of its stock is used books.

Splash (707-254-0767; 1403 Second St., Napa, CA 94559) caters to beach fanatics with a variety of swimwear and accessories. You can even sport a tan after shopping here because there are 10 tanning rooms. *Napa Valley Traditions* (707-226-2044; 1202 Main St., Napa, CA 94559) is a quaint gift shop and a tasting room for Bayview Cellars. Look for fine dishware, glassware, and a general line of gifts: lotions, hand therapies, etc. It also has an espresso bar with fresh pastries. The *Napa Valley Emporium* (707-253-7177; 1319 First St , Napa, CA 94559) sells customized apparel from T-shirts to aprons to caps as well as grape-related gifts such as wine racks and corkscrews.

Finally, at *Napa Premium Outlets*, (707-226-9876; 999 Freeway Dr., Napa, CA 94558), there's a maze of 40 stores including: Mikasa, J. Crew, Esprit, Liz Claiborne, Tommy Hilfiger, Jones New York Sport, Ann Taylor Loft, Timberland, Nine West, Book Warehouse, and Levi's.

Yountville

The predominant shopping area is *Vintage 1870* (6525 Washington, Yountville, CA 94599) and it plays to tourists. The historic complex was once the Groezinger Winery, and it has stone flooring, brick walls, and wooden rafters. What follows is a glance at some of the shops.

The Silver Tree carries upscale silver jewelry as well as inexpensive items and specializes in contemporary designs. The shop also carries original abstract art. If you have champagne taste on beer money, step into the *Mira Boutique*. The owner knows the magic of Cubic Zirconia, and styles range from traditional to modern. *Hansel & Gretel Clothes Loft* outfits babies, girls up to 16, and boys up to seven. Great clothes, inventive toys, and nice service.

A Little Romance is a sweet, cozy store that carries bed linen, quilts, bath ware, mats, etc. It is — quite literally — like walking through a catalog. *Cravings Gourmet and Cookware* has a little of everything: gourmet foods such as bottled peppers and pastas, cookbooks, and wreaths. It is a fun, albeit cramped, shopping experience.

Two engaging stores are just a stone's throw from Vintage 1870: *Antique Fair* (707-944-8440; 6512 Washington St., Yountville, CA 94599) has large, stately French walnut pieces — huge armoires, tables, bookcases, carved bed frames, and more. *Overland Sheepskin Co.* (707-944-0778; 6505 Washington St., Yountville, CA 94599) was the Yountville Railroad Depot. Today the shop is devoted to fighting Mother Nature's cool winters in Wine Country. Great coats, hats, rain gear, gloves, luggage, etc.

St. Helena

Lost in a book at the cozy Book Cellar in St. Helena.

Chris Alderman

You better schedule a good 12-hour day of shopping in this quaint yet cosmopolitan Main St., U.S.A. St. Helena has some of the best shopping in all of Wine Country.

Bale Mill Designs (707-963-4595; 3431 St. Helena Hwy. N., St. Helena, CA 94574; on Hwy. 29) has a collection of fine antiques and home furnishings in the European tradition. *Erika Hills Antiques, The Painted Illusions* (707-963-0919; 115 Main St., St. Helena, CA 94574) has its own line of furniture as well as furniture from Europe and Mexico. The emphasis here is on painted furniture, old and new. Consider *St. Helena St. Helena Antiques & Collectibles* (707-963-5878; 1231 Main St., St. Helena, CA 94574); the store name with "St. Helena" stated twice hints that this shop is a bit unusual. Step inside and you confirm it as you meander past a large collection of corkscrews and a 6-foot chandelier from a huge hall in Italy, among other 18th- and 19th-century antiques. Some antiques even hail from China, including Chinese hope chests.

R. S. Basso (707-963-0391; 1219 Main St., St. Helena, CA 94574) offers custom-designed upholstery with rows of fabric ranging from vibrant florals to elegant chintz. The shop also sells high-end accessories and country furnishings. *Showplace North* (707-963-5556; 1350 Main St., St. Helena, CA 94574) can custom-build furniture. The store also has upscale antiques from France, as well as mirrors, rugs, and wall hangings.

The Book Cellar (707-963-3901; 1354 Main St., St. Helena, CA 94574) has more than 100 titles of wine-related books. Easily one of the finest bookstores in Wine Country, it feels like a cozy home library. Note its extraordinary collection of classical music and jazz on CD. *Main Street Books* (707-963-1338; 1315 Main St., St. Helena, CA 94574) is a small, quaint bookstore with a few comfortable chairs for the weary. It has a children's corner and a used-book room, but otherwise there is a relatively modest selection of books.

Mario's Great Clothes for Men (707-963-1603; 1223 Main St., St. Helena, CA 94574) carries designer clothes by Nicole Miller, Jhane Barnes, Xanella, and Cole Haan, with clothes from casual to elegant. *D. Champaign Quality Casual Men's Wear* (707-963-1782; 1228 Main St., St. Helena, CA 94574), less formal than Mario's, is a great shop for men who like to look sporting with lines like Tommy Bahama. *Sportago* (707-963-9042; 1224-B Adams St., St. Helena, CA 94574): When the great outdoors beckon, it's best to be prepared. This store is an authorized Patagonia dealer, and it also carries upscale casual wear. At *WilkeSport* (707-963-4323; 1219 Main St., St. Helena, CA 94574), sportswear meets work wear with higher-end European lines such as Zegna for men and Biella for women.

Fashion-minded businesswomen will gravitate to *I.elle* (707-963-8662; 1309 Main St. #A, St. Helena, CA 94574). It carries clothes for special occasions, as well as casual fare, with lines like K.d Spring. Nifty accessories. At *Cricket* (707-963-8400; 1226 Main St., St. Helena, CA 94574) you'll find wool sweaters, hats, dresses, and more; women's clothing with the emphasis on casual. Imelda Marcos would like *Amelia Claire* (707-963-8502; 1230 Main St., St. Helena, CA 94574), which carries upscale shoes from makers such as Cole Haan, Aerosoles, and even Aquatalia — 100 percent waterproof shoes. If you're looking for upscale clothing for women, *Summerset* (707-963-8130; 1367 Main St., St. Helena, CA 94574) is the perfect shop. It features clothing for special occasions, clothing for travel, sportswear, and accessories, including hats. *Reeds* (707-963-0400; 1302 Main St., St. Helena, CA 94574) is a good shop for professional and eveningwear and carries lines such as Mica, Eileen Fisher, and Kevo. *H. B. Country Clothes* (707-963-4336; 1234-A Adams, St. Helena, CA 94574) has casual clothing — traditional and classic — for women, with lines like Ruff-Hewn, Corben, and Ballentine.

Tapioca Tiger (707-967-0608; 1224-A Adams St., St. Helena, CA 94574) celebrates children in all their glory with inventive items such as sunflower and ladybug sleepers, furniture for kids, gifts, and toys. The accent here is on one-of-a-kind handcrafted items for newborns to seven-year-olds. The inventory includes clothing, furniture, toys, books, etc. *Sweet Pea* (707-963-1201; 1309 Main St., St. Helena, CA 94574) bills itself as a quality-clothing, fashion-forward kind of place for infants to six-year-olds. Kids outfitted here definitely look lively.

Vanderbilt & Co. (707-963-1010; 1429 Main St., St. Helena, CA 94574) is brimming with the smart and artsy accessories you might find while flipping through a glossy home-and-garden catalog. From bedding to kitchenware to patio suites, it has everything you need to warm up your home with a little country mirth or cool it off with contemporary savvy. *Murray n'Gibbs* (707-963-3115; 1220 Adams St., St. Helena, CA 94574) is an eclectic home-accessories store that's a "must see" shop. One item says it all: a lamp with a clarinet serving as its base beneath a hand-painted shade covered with musical notes. *Flying Carpets* (707-967-9192; 1152 Main St., St. Helena, CA 94574) is like visiting a traveling exhibit. On occasion you'll find a display of hand-made oriental carpets, wool and silk rugs, masks, and art, aside from rugs from 14 different countries. *Calla Lily* (707-963-8188; 1222 Main St., St. Helena, CA 94574) is the consummate bed and bath shop: furniture, jewelry, unusual items from local artisans, linens, lotions, towels, etc. It's a refreshing stop. Just north of downtown is the *Campus Store and Marketplace* of the *Culinary Institute of America at Greystone* (707-967-2309; 2555 Main St., St. Helena, CA 94574), which has a superb collection of cookbooks and professional kitchenware.

Davids (707-963-0239; 1343 Main St., St. Helena, CA 94574) is essentially a designer's showcase for jewelry, virtually every piece is handcrafted, with styles from traditional to contemporary. *The William Pacific Co.* (707-963-6000; 1269 Main St., St. Helena, CA 94574) sells fine jewelry, gemstones, jade, etc. Aside from fashion jewelry, you'll also find an eclectic collection of gifts from China.

Fideaux (707-967-9935; 1312 Main St., St. Helena, CA 94574) is where Pet Mart meets Fifth Avenue, an appealing place for the discriminating pet owners with nifty stuff for dogs, cats, and people. There's practical stuff like flea collars and litter pans, as well as the avant-garde: wine-barrel doghouses and a

Hurd Beeswax Candles in St. Helena.

Chris Alderman

full line of European coats and sweaters for dogs. *Nature Etc.* (707-963-1706; 1327 Main St., St. Helena, CA 94574) is full of wonder: butterfly catchers, bird-houses, and an assortment of kits like the one that teaches kids how to make a volcano in the privacy of their own home. Yikes. *Valley Exchange* (707-963-7423; 1201 Main St., St. Helena, CA 94574) runs the gamut: whole bean coffee to hammocks, rustic pine furniture to linens and glassware. It's a distracting shop. Odds are you'll walk out with an item you never set out to buy.

Hurd Beeswax Candles & Hurd Gift & Gourmet (707-963-7211; 3020 St. Helena Hwy. N., St. Helena, CA 94574) is not in downtown St. Helena but rather a mile or so north up St. Helena Hwy. It attracts a lot of tourists, but it's fun and worth the trip. All the candles are handcrafted from sheets of pure beeswax, and there are more than 200 designs.

Just north of town is the **St. Helena Premium Outlets** (707-963-7282; 3111 N. St. Helena Hwy., St. Helena, CA 94574), which features 10 upscale stores, including Brooks Brothers, Coach, Donna Karan, Sunglass Outfitters and the Spirits in Stone Gallery,.

Calistoga

Downtown Calistoga is just one shopping area brimming with stores.

Chris Alderman

The hot springs have brought visitors to Calistoga for more than 130 years. You'll be tempted to do nothing but take in a spa, but Calistoga caters to a growing population of relaxed shoppers with soothing shops — fun lotions and potions — as well as offbeat, whimsical gifts. It won't take you too long to cover the strip — a string of four blocks — with the majority of stores on the north side of the street.

It's a good sign when you see a tabby napping in the front window of a bookstore. *Calistoga Bookstore* (707-942-4123; 1343 Lincoln Ave., Calistoga, CA 94515) appeals to the general reader but specializes in Northern California tour guides, local histories, and self-help books that include meditation, mas-sage, and self care. It also carries CDs.

At *Evens Design Group* (1421 Lincoln Ave.; 707-942-0453;) ceramics sell for 40 percent to 90 percent off retail prices. Among the decorative pieces — such as plates, bowls, bases, and candlestick holders — you find Raku ceramics, blown glass, and slumped glass. At *The Artful Eye* (707-942-4743; 1333 A. Lincoln Ave., Calistoga, CA 94515), jewelry is all handcrafted by some 300 local artists, and many of the pieces seem inspired by ancient cultures. The jewelry ranges in price from $8 to $3,000, but the majority of pieces are lower-end sterling silver. *Mr. Moon's* (707-942-0932; 1365 Lincoln St., Calistoga, CA 94515) features nifty products such as candles, cards, scarves, and soaps, but usually with a twist. *Nature Etc.* (707-942-1071; 1371 Lincoln Ave., Calistoga, CA 94515) is fun for spirited people of all ages. There's an entire "Glow In the Dark" section with glow-in-the-dark stars, jump ropes, chalk, etc.

The sweet scent of *Wexford & Woods* (707-942-9729; 1347 Lincoln Ave., Calistoga, CA 94515) beckons with perfumes, massage oils, and all-natural skin care products from around the world. These include the lines Abra and Zia. If you want to pamper yourself, at *Free Time* (707-942-0210; 1348 C. Lincoln Ave., Calistoga, CA 94515) you can pick up plenty of supplies: lotions, massage oils, all-natural body products, aromatherapy paraphernalia, etc.

Calistoga Kids (707-942-0122; 1443 Lincoln Ave., Calistoga, CA 94515) caters to locals, with clothing for newborns to 14-year-olds. *The Bird's Eye* (707-942-6191; 1307 Lincoln Ave., Calistoga, CA 94515) outfits women of all dimensions. The accent here is on colorful, ethnic clothing with main lines Sangam, Caribe, and Be Jay. *Country Vine Clothing* (707-942-4801; 1458 Lincoln Ave., No. 10, Calistoga, CA 94515) features contemporary comfort clothing, lots of cotton, raw silk, rayon, and hemp. If you left your pool get-up at home, stop in *Jeannie Bell's Resort & Swimwear* (707-942-8340; 1227 A. Lincoln Ave., Calistoga, CA 94515) to gear up for some lazy days in this resort town. This shop sells stylish bathing suits and casual clothing, including summer dresses. *Chateau Ste. Shirts* (707-942-5039; 1355 Lincoln Ave., Calistoga, CA 94515) has stylish swimwear and sportswear and even unisex clogs. *Bella Tootsie Shoes & More* (707-942-8821; 1373 Lincoln Ave., Calistoga, CA 94515) is a shoe store and gift shop. It may seem like an odd combination, but it works. Shoes for men, women, and children are coupled with wine-related gifts such as corkscrews and wineglasses.

SHOPPING IN SONOMA COUNTY

Sonoma

The Old World-style Sonoma Plaza is a large park with a duck pond, a rose garden, a swing set, and a slide. This "family friendly" downtown has charm, and buildings such as the Sebastiani Theater, circa 1933, speak of a less complicated time. A closer look reveals that Sonoma is quickly becoming gentrified. A

The town square of Sonoma is a genteel park surrounded by restaurants and shops.

Thomas Hallstein/Outsight

few years ago the downtown square was home to some country shops and some mundane food purveyors. Today it has high-style clothing stores, gourmet food shops, and ethnic stores, and it can get plenty crowded on weekends. Expect to jockey for a parking spot.

Artifax International Gallery & Gifts (707-996-9494; 450-C First St. E., Sonoma, CA 95476) is a true sensory experience. You'll see Asian imports, Chinese baskets, soaps, exotic textiles, beads, jewelry; you'll smell burning incense and hear tapes of evocative African drums and other World Music. Don't miss *Legends* (707-939-8100; 483 First St. W., Sonoma, CA 95476). Inspired by the movie *Dead Poets Society*, the Michlig family migrated west from Melborne, Florida, to create a shop that celebrates American craft artists. Legends debuts fine crafts from across the U.S. The work ranges from paintings, wood sculptures, chimes, lamps, and ties — everything handmade. *Sign of the Bear* (707-996-3722; 435 First St., Sonoma, CA 95476) is for Wine Country gourmands as well as Wine Country gourmand-wannabes. There are vegetable roasters, herb grills, bagel containers, and upscale All-Clad pans.

While *Readers' Books* (707-939-1779; 127 & 130 E. Napa St., Sonoma, CA 95476) may not be the City Lights of Sonoma County, it has the reputation of being urbane and very literary. Expect great classics and fiction, an expansive cookbook section, and a myriad of books for children. *Sonoma Bookends Bookstore* (707-938-5926; 201 W. Napa St., Suite #15, Sonoma, CA 95476) is a general bookstore catering to the tourist with expanded travel and wine sections. It also features local authors. *Plaza Books* (707-996-8474; 40 W. Spain St., Sonoma, CA 95476) is like browsing through your grandfather's library. The stock includes rare and collectible used books. Some are museum-quality tomes more than 100 years old.

Half Pint (707-938-1722; 450 First St. E., Sonoma, CA 95476) outfits newborns to age 14, and it does it with style. Plenty of toys — puppets, puzzles, and tools — and more Madeline dolls than you can count. *Nature Etc.* (707-

938-5662; 450 First St. E., Suite G, Sonoma, CA 95476) This store appeals to the curious — the young, the old, and everyone in between.

At *Milagros* (707-939-0834; 414 First St. E. #D; Sonoma, CA 95476) you'll find colorful folk art: brightly painted vases, flowers, jewelry, blankets, and ponchos. *Uniquely California* (707-939-6768; 28 W. Spain St.; Sonoma, CA 95476) features artwork and gourmet foods. Gift baskets brimming with California products are a hot item here. *Papyrus* (707-935-6707; 452 First. E., Suite B, Sonoma, CA 95476) is practically paneled in cards with every occasion covered and then some — a truly great selection. There's also plenty of stationery, colorful wrapping paper, and a host of small gift items. *Wine Country Gifts* (707-996-3453; 407 First St. W., Sonoma, CA 95476) has a gallery as well as a collection of fine glassware and Italian ceramics. *Kaboodle* (707-996-9500; 453 First St. W., Sonoma, CA 95476) has lots of unique items — candleholders, picture frames, and pillows, among them — with a horde of other items sandwiched in between. You may never find your way out of this clever maze.

Fashion-minded businesswomen will gravitate to *I.elle* (707-938-2282; 23 E. Napa St., Sonoma, CA 95476). It also carries clothes for special occasions as well as casual fare, with lines like K.d. Spring. Nifty accessories.

If you're looking to make a statement or you're just a cowboy at heart, *Rodeo Sonoma* (707-939-7992; 450 First St. E., #H, Sonoma, CA 95476) is for you. Peruse the line up of boots, and then custom order your own.

Eraldi's Men's Wear & Shoes (707-996-2013; 475 First St. W., Sonoma, CA 95476) carries casual men's clothing with lines like Levi's and Wranglers as well as sports coats, dress slacks, and shoes.

Cornerstone Jewelers (707-996-6635; 416 First. St. E., Sonoma, CA 95476) is a direct importer of diamonds and fine jewelry. It also has an assortment of watches, stopwatches, among other products. *Santa Fe Trading Co.* (707-996-7523; 481-A. First. St. W., Sonoma, CA 95476) is a good place to peruse Indian jewelry, pottery, and artifacts. The store features handcrafted goods from American Indians of the Southwest.

Petaluma

While Petaluma has a distinctive downtown, tourists typically find *Petaluma Village Premium Outlets* (707-778-9300; 2200 Petaluma Blvd. N., Petaluma, CA 94952) more appealing. It has more than 50 top name stores including: Off 5th, Saks Fifth Avenue Outlet, Reebok, Mikasa, Ann Taylor Factory Store, Nine West, Brooks Brothers Factory Store, Book Warehouse, OshKosh B'Gosh, Bass, and Corning Revere.

Santa Rosa

Santa Rosa's downtown is on the cusp of a revival, thanks in part to the Barnes & Noble bookstore, which made its home in the old Rosenberg department store. What was once just a cozy blend of bookstores and coffeehouses is

Whistle Stop Antiques in Santa Rosa's historic Railroad Square.

Thomas Hallstein/Outsight

now filling in with interesting gift shops and clothing stores — stores that appear to have staying power.

Barnes & Noble (707-576-7494; 700 Fourth St., Santa Rosa, CA 95404) appeals to the tourist with expanded sections on local authors, local travel, and local wineries. *Copperfield's Books The Annex* (707-545-5326; 650 Fourth St., Santa Rosa, CA 95404) has strong history, literature, and foreign language sections, and about 75 percent of its inventory is used books. *Treehorn Books* (707-525-1782; 625 Fourth St., Santa Rosa, CA 95404) has an extensive collection of children's books, cookbooks, and books on Western Americana. Most of the books are used with some rare books in the mix. If you want to keep current, step into *Sawyers News* (707-542-1311; 733 Fourth St., Santa Rosa, CA 95404), which sells newspapers from all over the world. But the emphasis is on magazines, with more than 2,500 titles offered.

Randolph Johnson Design (707-577-8196; 608 Fifth St., Santa Rosa, CA 95404) offers furniture and accessories with flair. Ask about its custom-design furniture and stone installation. If you're an artist without a medium, try *The Pottery Studio* (707-576-7102; 632 Fourth St., Santa Rosa, CA 95404). Here you select a ceramic piece, paint it, and fire it in the kiln. Ceramic pieces are varied and include vases, birdhouses, and watering cans.

At *Corrick's* (707-546-2423; 637 Fourth St., Santa Rosa, CA 95404), you can peruse upscale gift items and office supplies in one shop. Corrick's carries upscale china with lines such as Lenox and Gorham. *Papyrus* (707-578-7262; 622 Fourth St., Santa Rosa, CA 95404) is practically paneled in cards, with every occasion covered and then some — a truly great selection. There's also plenty of stationery, colorful wrapping paper, and a host of small gift items.

At *Skeeters* (707-523-1651; 626 Fourth St., Santa Rosa, CA 95404), look for a broad range of items: women's clothing, pottery, jewelry, etc. You can even order custom-made maple and cherry cabinets. *Positively Fourth Street* (707-526-3588; 628 Fourth St., Santa Rosa, CA 95404) has an international appeal: Art Deco pens from France, teapots from China, and hand-carved soapstone from Africa.

Practically an heirloom, *E. R. Sawyer* (707-546-0372; 638 Fourth St., Santa Rosa, CA 95404) was established in 1879. It sells fine jewelry and watches — even waterproof watches. It also does custom-design work. *Hampton Court Essential Luxuries* (707-578-9416; 631 Fourth St., Santa Rosa, CA 95404) carries obscure European fragrances, bath and body lotions, and even romantic clothing. *California Luggage Co.* (707-528-8600; 609 Fourth St., Santa Rosa, CA 95404) carries a broad range of luggage, plus convenient travel necessities. It also does repairs for travelers passing through.

The Last Record Store (707-525-1963; 739 Fourth St., Santa Rosa, CA 95404) sells CDs and cassettes, and its eclectic inventory includes rock, jazz, classical, World Music, blues, and Irish. But for true vinyl, you'll have to go to the store's "record" outlet across the street. (707-528-2350; 802 Fourth St., Santa Rosa, CA 95404).

Aside from Santa Rosa's downtown, the best place to shop in Santa Rosa is *Railroad Square*, a quaint shopping area built around a park with a historic train depot. (Check out the depot and the tourist information stocked there.) Most shops in the square sell antiques, but keep your eyes open. There are plenty of other shops that are worth your while.

Whistle Stop Antiques (707-542-9474; 130 Fourth St., Santa Rosa, CA 95401) is a collective with some 35 dealers. Sift through the collectibles and general line of furniture, and note the handy section devoted to supplies for refurbishing furniture. At *Old Town Furniture* (707-575-8287; 110 Fourth St., Santa Rosa, CA 95401), check out the spanking new furniture, replicas of Victorian, Mission, and traditional styles for the home and office. *Furniture Depot* (707-575-3198; 100 Fourth St., Santa Rosa, CA 95401) carries an eclectic mix of cherry and pine furniture for the bedroom, office, and dining room. *The Silver Shop* (707-546-7515; 107 Third St., Santa Rosa, CA 95401) offers a good selection of vintage silverware and also does silver appraisals.

At *Sonoma Outfitter* (707-528-1920; 145 Third St., Santa Rosa, CA 95401), you can answer the call of the wild in high style. There's clothing for men and women with lines such as Patagonia and Sigrid Olsen. Outdoor gear includes kayaks and camping equipment. Step into *Idyllwilde* (707-568-1599; 127 Fourth St., Santa Rosa, CA 95401), and peruse the garden tools, linens, and a host of birdhouses. It's a lovely home and garden shop.

Searching for a new look? *Hot Couture* (707-528-7247; 101 Third St., Santa Rosa, CA 95401) has vintage clothing that dates back to the early 1900s up through the 1960s. It offers rentals year-round. *Disguise The Limit* (707-575-1477; 100 Fourth St., Santa Rosa, CA 95401) carries theatrical goods, gag gifts, and clothing for the avant-garde. It's the most popular shop in town during Halloween season.

Healdsburg

The clock tower in downtown Healdsburg.

Chris Alderman

Taking a stroll at Healdsburg's town plaza is like stepping into a Norman Rockwell print. Healdsburg may just be the town that time forgot. Yet, once you take a closer look, you realize that Healdsburg is an interesting mix: countrified chic, cosmopolitan, yet down to earth — more Land Rover than BMW. What follows is a look at Healdsburg's quaint town square — primo shopping.

Toyon Books (707-433-9270; 104 Matheson St., Healdsburg, CA 95448) has a large "Wines and Vineyards" section at the front of this general-interest bookstore, which offers both new and used books. Specialties include self-help and spiritual awareness as well as a good selection of new fiction. *Levin & Co.* (707-433-1118; 306 Center St., Healdsburg, CA 95448) is a lively shop that caters to the book and music lover. In books, it specializes in the classics and quality fiction. The music collection focuses on jazz and international music, and also carries classical and pop.

Healdsburg is rich with antiques shops. *The Irish Cottage* (707-433-4850; 112 Matheson St., Healdsburg, CA 95448) is a quaint shop on the square with plenty to peruse: pine dressers and tables, 19th-century cabinets, and chests, flow-blue porcelain, majolica, and silver. *Antique Harvest* (707-433-0223; 225 Healdsburg Ave., Healdsburg, CA 95448) has items that range from country pine to Victorian, with lamps, brass, and Art Deco furnishings to boot. Meander through the wares of more than 10 dealers. *Healdsburg Classic Antiques* (707-433-4315; 226 Healdsburg Ave., Healdsburg, CA 95448) is an enormous shop that spans two Quonset huts and includes about 20 dealers. You'll find furniture here from Victorian through Art Deco. At *Pentimento Antiques & Interiors* (707-431-0600; 226 Healdsburg Ave., Healdsburg, CA

95448), look for "one-of-a-kind" items: a Louis XV armoire, an iron French bed, bed linens, custom lamp shades, and mirrors. They have recently started carrying the Mitchell Gold line of upholstered furniture. At ***Healdsburg Classic 214*** (707-433-6122; 214 Healdsburg Ave., Healdsburg, CA 95448), peruse some architectural wonders such as a rod-iron gazebo as well as an old water pump from Ireland. Decorative pieces and garden furniture, as well. At ***City 214*** (707-433-6122; 214 Healdsburg Ave., Healdsburg, CA 95448), you'll find some interesting items: metal Chinese trunks, French armoire with beveled mirrors, and hand-painted china from the 1920s.

The Rose (707-433-6260; 381 Healdsburg Ave., Healdsburg, CA 95448) is a contemporary women's clothing store with everything from casual wear to cocktail dresses. Custom design is the signature style at ***Ann Marie*** (707-433-5053; 122 Matheson St., Healdsburg, CA 95448), and all the work is done on site. Popular pieces include jewelry made with Murano glass, which hails from an island outside of Venice. ***Options*** (707-431-8861; 126 Matheson St., Healdsburg, CA 95448) has a clear sense of style. It's stocked with one-of-a-kind items and sophisticated collectibles. Look for jewelry, furniture, baskets, pottery, and ceramics.

Robinson & Co. (707-433-7116; 108 Matheson St., Healdsburg, CA 95448) could outfit Martha Stewart's kitchen. It has a wide range of kitchenware, tableware, gourmet foods, books, and candles. At ***Friends in the Country*** (707-433-1615; 114 Matheson St., Healdsburg, CA 95448), "embellishment" could be the motto. The shop has a broad range of linens, pottery, table-top accessories, and fine pine and wicker furniture. ***Mr. Moon's*** (707-433-6666; 105 Plaza St., Healdsburg, CA 95448) coaxes window shoppers in with festive displays of cards, candles, clothes, soaps and lotions, and stuffed animals. ***R. S. Basso*** (707-431-1925; 115 Plaza St., Healdsburg, CA 95448) specializes in custom-made upholstered furniture and accessories.

Fabrications (118 Matheson St. 707-433-6243;) will inspire those who love sewing with its exotic collection of natural fabrics from Guatemala, Bali, Africa, and other international locales. Dark batik fabrics and unusual silks are specialties. ***Las Manos*** (707-433-9328; 130 Plaza St., Healdsburg, CA 95448) has ethnic clothing along with mainstream styles. "Clothing for the free-spirited woman" is how this store describes itself. ***S. L. Danner*** (707-431-1297; 120 Matheson St., Healdsburg, CA 95448) focuses on comfortable clothing for women of all ages, emphasizing natural fibers and colors, with lines that include Eileen Fisher, Isda, Worlds Apart, and True Grit. The folks behind ***Out of Hand*** (707-431-8178; 333 Healdsburg Ave., Healdsburg, CA 95448) say the emphasis is on "Wine Country wear" — casual yet fashionable. You'll find plenty of handcrafted leather handbags, plus smart-looking casual clothing as well as fancier items. Main lines include Flax and Karen Alexander.

Toyworks (707-433-4743; 103 B. Plaza St., Healdsburg, CA 95448) is a refreshing toy store of yore. Peruse the goodies: globes, kites, puzzles, and even kits for building your own magic show. ***Cubby House*** (707-433-6861; 107 Plaza St.,

Healdsburg, CA 95448) features great apparel for packaging your kid in smart and whimsical styles. The store outfits infants to children of age seven. *Rainsong Shoes* (707-433-8058; 117 Plaza St., Healdsburg, CA 95448) is a well-heeled shop that emphasizes comfort as well as style, with prices ranging from $30 to $280. Lines include Reikers, and Arche.

Buckingham Cottage (707-431-2995; 320 Healdsburg Ave., Healdsburg, CA 95448) will help you outfit your house with decorative items. The shop has tablecloths, wall hangings, bedding, and paintings. *Midnight Sun* (707-431-7085; 355 Healdsburg Ave., Healdsburg, CA 95448) is a bed and bath place that sells all the fixings for a luxurious bedroom and bath: jammies, sheets, towels, bath oils, and creams — even iron beds and pine armoires. *Papitre* (707-431-8665; 353 Healdsburg Ave., Healdsburg, CA 95448) emphasizes personalized invitations, you'll also see distinctive frames, cards, and stationery.

Sebastopol

Sebastopol is a pretzel of a town. A series of one-way streets downtown make navigating a bit of a chore, but shopping here is interesting nonetheless. This tiny metropolis in west county seems to have a style of its own: New Age Vintage Coastal Funk. You'll have to search out traditional shops, which tend to be overshadowed by the offbeat.

Buddies (707-823-2109; 415 S. Main St., Sebastopol, CA 95472) looks like a gallery with wearable art displayed on clean, white walls. It carries hand-crafted one-of-a-kind clothing — wearable art — and ethnic pieces. Buddies designs and manufacturers all its knits. *Dressers* (707-829-8757; 141 N. Main St., Sebastopol, CA 95472) is an upscale store with stylish clothes and nifty accessories. Main lines include City Lights and Flax. *Global Village* (707-829-4765; 172 N. Main St., Sebastopol, CA 95472) is truly an international affair. Women's clothes come from Bali, Peru, and India — to name a few countries — and there's jewelry, too.

R. S. Basso (707-829-1426; 186 Main St., Sebastopol, CA 95472) specializes in custom-made furniture. *Country Home* (707-829-1793; 150 N. Main St., Sebastopol, CA 95472) is one of the few traditional shops in Sebastopol. Stepping in here is like walking through a *Country Living* magazine, with plenty of seasonal and holiday decorations, crafts, candles, cookie jars, bath lotions, and baskets.

Quicksilver Mine Co. (707-829-2416; 154 N. Main St., Sebastopol, CA 95472) is a devoted fan of Sonoma County artisans. It specializes in products that are made, grown, or created in Sonoma County. It's fun to peruse the handcrafts, clothing, gourmet food, jewelry, and more. *Wild Things* (707-829-3371; 130 S. Main St., Suite 102, Sebastopol, CA 95472) is one of the most hip nature shops you'll ever come across. Inventory includes finger puppets, screen-painted T-shirts, and beautiful cards.

HearthSong Toys (707-829-0944; 156 N. Main St., Sebastopol, CA 95472) is politically correct. It has toys big people feel good about giving: lots of parent/child activity kits such as candle-making and doll-making kits. Its inventory also includes educational toys and wooden toys. *Toyworks* (707-829-2003; 6940 Sebastopol Ave., Sebastopol, CA 95472) is truly a toy store of yore, but instead of penny candy there's 25-cent candy. Blame it on inflation. Peruse the goodies: globes, kites, puzzles, and even kits for building your own volcano.

The clothing in *Shards & Remnants* (707-823-1366; 130 S. Main St., Suite 103, Sebastopol, CA 95472) spans from the '50s to present-day. You'll find some real antiques as well, such as a 1915 black velvet dress with a hobble skirt, plus feather boas and fake furs. Look for fun stuff in *East of Eden* (103 Main St. 707-829-1968;). They carry new fashions, wedding gowns, and accessories with a few vintage items.

Copperfield's Books (707-823-2618; 138 N. Main St., Sebastopol, CA 95472) is a large bookstore that seems to have a "New-Age State of Mind." It bills itself as a general-purpose bookstore, with specialties in fiction, metaphysics, and alternative health. *People's Music* (707-823-7664; 122 N. Main St., Sebastopol, CA 95472) has an admirable assortment of instruments, including banjos, lutes, and harps.

Delvin Jewelry Design (707-823-9152; 139 N. Main St., Sebastopol, CA 95472) offers custom design with a bonus: a goldsmith on the premises. Original designs tend to be contemporary, using gold, gemstones, and diamonds.

Milk & Honey (707-824-1155; 123 N. Main St., Sebastopol, CA 95472) celebrates the Goddess, featuring the feminine in art, music, jewelry, literature, gifts, and body care. *Rosemary's Garden* (707-829-2539; 132 N. Main St., Sebastopol, CA 95472) is an herbal apothecary and gift store that is well stocked with products to soothe the soul, including Chinese herbs, tea blends, and massage oils.

Sebastopol is Antique Central in Wine Country. *Antique Society* (707-829-1733; 2661 Gravenstein Hwy. S., Sebastopol, CA 95472) is Sonoma County's largest antiques collective, with more than 100 dealers. Naturally you'll find a wide assortment of antiques and collectibles from estate jewelry to furniture, including oak, country, and primitive. *Ray's Trading Co.* (707-829-9726; 3570 Gravenstein Hwy. S., Sebastopol, CA 95472) is a salvage company recognized as an important resource for Bay Area people restoring Victorian homes. Ray's stock bins are full of antique doorknobs, drawer pulls, even whole windows and doors. At *Sebastopol Antique Mall* (707-823-1936; 755 Petaluma Ave., Sebastopol, CA 95472) sip a little vino at the wine bar as you peruse upscale antiques. Look for Japanese *tansu* (chests), jewelry, desks, and dining room tables.

CHAPTER NINE
Facts on File
INFORMATION

Adventure in Wine Country is just a phone call away.

Thomas Hallstein/Outsight

A little peace of mind goes a long way when you want to savor Wine Country. The information compiled in this chapter covers emergencies as well as everyday practical matters. It caters to both the tourist and newcomer, with information running the gamut from weather reports and visitors bureaus to real-estate matters and school listings. So acquaint yourself with Napa and Sonoma. You may decide to stretch your two-week stay into a lifetime.

AMBULANCE, FIRE, POLICE, COAST GUARD

S imply dial 911 in both Napa and Sonoma Counties. You will reach an oper-ator who will swiftly put you through to the right agency: Fire and rescue, ambulance, local police, sheriff, California Highway Patrol, or Coast Guard Search and Rescue.

To report rape and sexual assault: Napa Emergency Woman's Services at 707-255-6397 or Sonoma County's Rape Crisis at 707-545-7273.

For the Poison Control Center call 800-523-2222.

AREA CODES, ZIP CODES, CITY HALLS

AREA CODES

Napa and Sonoma counties:	707
San Francisco:	415
Oakland and Berkeley:	510

Area codes for adjacent counties:	
Marin	415
Mendocino	707
Alameda and Contra Costa	510
Lake County	707
Solano	707
Yolo	916, 530

ZIP CODES & CITY HALLS

	Zip Code	City Hall
Napa County		
Calistoga	94515	707-942-2754
St. Helena	94574	707-967-2792
Yountville	94599	707-944-8851
Napa	94558	707-257-9503
	94559	
	94581	

	Zip Code	City Hall
Sonoma County		
Bodega Bay	94923	
Healdsburg	95448	707-431-3317
Sebastopol	95472, 95473	707-823-1153
Santa Rosa	95401–95409	707-543-3010
Sonoma	95476	707-938-3681
Petaluma	94952–94954	707-778-4345
	94999, 94975	

BANKS

If you have a bank card, you're the king of cash in the age of the automated teller. Hungry for a few more traveler's checks? Listed below are a sampling of regional and national banks. Each branch office is equipped with at least one automated-teller machine. Note the systems to which each bank is electronically linked.

Bank of America (707-542-4433, 800-441-6437) Linked to Plus, Star, and Interlink systems.
Locations: 1429 Lincoln Ave., Calistoga
2 Financial Plaza, Napa
1700 1st St., Napa
1312 Trancas St., Napa
2355 California, Napa
1001 Adams St., Helena
35 W. Napa St., Sonoma
19181 Sonoma Hwy., Sonoma
502 Healdsburg Ave., Healdsburg
1155 W. Steele Ln., Santa Rosa
2420 Sonoma Ave., Santa Rosa
10 Santa Rosa Ave., Santa Rosa
7185 Healdsburg Ave., Sebastopol

Wells Fargo Bank (800-869-3557) Linked to Star, Plus, Interlink, Cirrus, and MasterCard systems.
Locations: 1115 Vine St., Healdsburg
2960 Cleveland Ave., Santa Rosa
200 B St., Santa Rosa
150 Bicentennial Way, Santa Rosa
1407 Fulton Rd., Santa Rosa
1980 Santa Rosa Ave., Santa Rosa

1799 Marlowe Rd., Santa Rosa
6585 Oakmont Drive, Santa Rosa
480 W. Napa St., Sonoma

West America Bank (800-848-1088) Linked to Star, Cirrus, Plus, Explore, Maestro, and MasterCard systems.
Locations: 1 Financial Plaza, Napa
1400 Clay St., Napa
1221 Imola Ave., Napa
3421 Broadway, Suite E2, American Canyon
6470 Washington St., Yountville
1000 Adams, St., Helena
1110 Washington St., Calistoga

BIBLIOGRAPHY

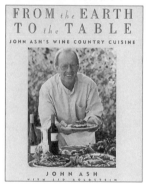

From the Earth to the Table: John Ash's Wine Country Cuisine is the latest book by one of Northern California's leading chefs.

Courtesy John Ash

Browse through our bookshelves. Wine Country can be a curious place, what with the specter of ghost wineries and the mystique of winemaking. Consider, if you will, the two lists compiled: Books You Can Buy and Books You Can Borrow.

"Books You Can Buy" lists titles generally available in Sonoma and Napa bookstores, nationally, or from the publishers.

"Books You Can Borrow" are generally found in Napa and Sonoma local libraries and in most public libraries elsewhere. They are typically no longer for sale.

For wine books, two helpful — and free — sources are the **Napa Valley Wine Library** (707-963-5244; St. Helena Public Library, 1492 Library Ln., St. Helena, CA 94574) and the **Sonoma County Wine Library** (707-433-3772; Healdsburg Public Library, 139 Piper St., Healdsburg, CA 95448) For more information, see "Libraries" in Chapter Four, *Culture.*

BOOKS YOU CAN BUY

WINE AND FOOD

Ash, John, with Sid Goldstein. *From the Earth to the Table: John Ash's Wine Country Cuisine.* New York: Dutton, 1995. 429 pp., photos, $29.95.

———. *American Game Cooking.* New York: Addison-Wesley, 1991. 288 pp., photos, $16.95.

Asher, Gerald. *Vineyard Tales: Reflections on Wine.* San Francisco: Chronicle Books, 1996. 287 pp., $22.95.

Bailey, Lee. *California Wine Country Cooking.* New York: Potter, 1991. 176 pp., photos, $30.

Bernstein, Leonard S. *The Official Guide to Wine Snobbery.* New York: Quill Press, 1982. 160 pp., illus., $4.95.

Cass, Bruce. *The Oxford Companion to the Wines of North America.* Oxford: Oxford University Press, 2000. 301 pages. $45.

Chappellet, Molly. *A Vineyard Garden.* New York: Viking Studio Books, 1991. 291 pp., photos, $40.

DeCarlo, Tessa, and Lynne Tuft. *The Grapes Grow Sweet.* Napa, Calif.: River Press, 1996. 35 pp., color illustrations, $24.

Fisher, MFK. *Here Let Us Feast: A Book of Banquets.* Northpoint Press, 1996. 323 pp., $15.00.

———. *Art of Eating.* Simon & Schuster/Macmillan Co., 1990. 749 pp., $19.95.

Immer, Andrea. *Great Wine Made Simple.* New York: Broadway Books. 2000. 288 pages, $25.

Johnson, Hugh. *World Atlas of Wine.* New York: Simon & Schuster, 1994. 320 pp., color photos, $50.

———. *Vintage: The Story of Wine.* New York: Simon & Schuster, 1989. 464 pp., photos, illus., bibliog., index, $39.95.

Jordan, Michele Anna. *A Cook's Tour of Sonoma.* New York: Addison-Wesley, 1990. 296 pp., illus., $16.95.

Kramer, Matt. *Making Sense of Wine.* New York: William Morrow, 1989. 190 pp., bibliog., index, $16.95.

McCarthy, Ed, and Mary Ewing-Mulligan. *Wine for Dummies.* New York: IDG Books, 1995. 400 pp., black and white illustrations, $16.99.

Thompson, Bob. *The Wine Atlas of California.* New York: Simon & Schuster, 1993. 239 pp., maps, illus., $45.

Robinson, Jancis. *The Oxford Companion to Wine.* 2nd Edition. Oxford: Oxford University Press, 1999. 819 pages. $65.

Roby, Norman S., and Charles E. Olken. *The New Connoisseurs' Handbook of California Wine.* New York: Alfred A. Knopf, 1995. 388 pp., $21.

Steiman, Harvey. *California Kitchen.* San Francisco: Chronicle Books, 1990. 304 pp., photos, $12.95.

Sterling, Joy. *A Cultivated Life.* New York: Villard Books, 1993. 239 pp., illus., $22.

Sullivan, Charles. *A Companion to California Wine: An Encyclopedia of Wine and Winemaking from the Mission Days to the Present.* Berkeley: University of California Press, 1998. 441 pages. $39.95.

Wine Spectator Magazine. *Ultimate Guide to Buying Wine.* New York: Wine Spectator Press, annual. 750 pp., photos, illus., $22.95.

LITERARY WORKS

London, Jack. *Call of the Wild and Selected Stories.* New York: Penguin Books, 1960. 176 pp., $2.50.

Stevenson, Robert Louis. *The Works of Robert Louis Stevenson.* London: Octopus Pub. Group, 1989. 687 pp., $7.98.

BIOGRAPHIES

Dreyer, Peter. *A Gardener Touched With Genius, The Life of Luther Burbank.* Berkeley: University of California Press, 1985. 230 pp., photos, index, $12.95.

London, Joan. *Jack London and His Daughters.* Berkeley: Heyday Books, 1990. 179 pp., photos, $10.95.

McGinty, Brian. *Strong Wine: The Life and Legend of Agoston Haraszthy.* Stanford: Stanford University Press, 1998. 616 pages. $65, hardbound. $24.95 paperback.

LOCAL HISTORIES

Conaway, James. *Napa, The Story of an American Eden.* Boston: Houghton Mifflin, 1990. 506 pp., photos, $24.95.

Heintz, William F. *Wine Country: A History of Napa Valley, The Early Years 1838 to 1920.* Santa Barbara, Calif.: Capra Press, 1990. 326 pp., photos, illus., $29.95.

LeBaron, Gaye, Dee Blackman, Joann Mitchell, and Harvey Hansen. *Santa Rosa: A Nineteenth Century Town.* Santa Rosa, Calif.: Historia Ltd. 210 pp., photos, sources, notes, index.

LeBaron, Gaye, and Joann Mitchell. *Santa Rosa: A Twentieth Century Town.* Santa Rosa, Calif.: Historia Ltd., 1993. 350 pp., photos, $59.95.

Lukacs, Paul. American Vintage: The Rise of American Wine. New York: Houghton Miflin, 2000. 304 pages. $28.

Wilson, Simone. *Sonoma County: The River of Time.* Chatsworth, Calif.: Windsor Publications, 1990. 121 pp., photos, illus., index, $25.95.

RECREATION

Emmery, Lena. *Wine Country Bike Rides.* San Francisco: Chronicle Books, 1997. 106 pp., illus., maps, $10.95.

Lorentzen, Bob. *The Hiker's Hip Pocket Guide to Sonoma County.* Mendocino,

Calif.: Bored Feet Publications, 1990. 201 pp., illus., maps, bibliog., index, $11.95.

Powers, Peter. *Touring California's Wine Country by Bicycle.* Eugene, Ore.: Terragraphics, 1990. 171 pp., maps, illus., $10.95.

BOOKS YOU CAN BORROW

Darlington, David. *Angel Visits: An Inquiry into the Mystery of Zinfandel.* New York: Henry Holt, 1991. 278 pages.

Dutton, Joan Parry. *They Left Their Mark: Famous Passages through the Wine Country.* Illuminations Press., 1983. 180 pp., photos, bibliog., index. A historical look at the famous people who traveled through Wine Country and the influence they had on the region.

Haynes, Irene W. *Ghost Wineries of Napa Valley.* Sally Taylor & Friends Publishing, 1980. 73 pp., photos, index. Take an eerie tour of old and abandoned wineries if you dare.

Heintz, William F. *Wine Country: A History of Napa Valley, The Early Years 1838 to 1920.* Santa Barbara: Capra Press, 1990. 326 pp., photos, illus. A study of winemakers through Napa history.

Issler, Anne Roller. *Stevenson at Silverado.* Caldwell, Id.: Caxton Printers. 1939. 247 pp., photos. Follows Stevenson as he roams through Napa Valley. The book gives insight into his work *The Silverado Squatters.*

Johnson, Rheta Grimsley. *Good Grief: The Story of Charles M. Schulz.* Pharos Books, 1989. 254 pp., drawings, cartoons, bibliography. An intimate portrait of Charles Schulz, the Santa Rosan behind the comic strip *Peanuts.*

King, Norton L. *Napa County: A Historical Overview.* Self-published, 1967. 98 pp., photos, bibliog., index. Geographic, topographic, and geologic origins of Wine Country.

Kraft, Ken and Pat. *Luther Burbank: The Wizard and the Man.* Des Moines: Meredith Press, 1967. 261 pp., bibliog., index. Burbank was as famous as Henry Ford in 1915, and this book chronicles his life in Santa Rosa.

Lundquist, James. *Jack London: Adventures, Ideas & Fiction.* Ungar, 1987. 188 pp. bibliog., index. A biography of the man who wrote *The Sea Wolf* and *The Call of the Wild.*

CHILD CARE

Child care spells relief for some parents who want to roam Wine Country without their teetotaling tots. For travelers and newcomers alike, here's a sampling of licensed child-care centers. Parents can find out more about licensed day-care providers by studying their files at Community Care

Licensing in the California State Building, 50 D. St., in Santa Rosa. The following organizations make free child care referrals:

Community Child Care Council of Sonoma County: 707-544-3077
Community Resources For Children: Napa, 707-253-0366

Here are a few specific options:

Napa County

St. Helena Corporate Child Care: Napa, 707-963-4705
Hopper Creek Montessori School: Napa, 707-252-8775
Silver Lining Child Care Center Preschool: Napa, 707-226-KIDS

Sonoma County

Alphabet Soup Pre-School and Day Care Center: Sebastopol, 707-829-9460
Happy Time Christian Pre-School & Day Care: Santa Rosa, 707-527-9135
Healdsburg Montessori School: Healdsburg, 707-431-1727

CLIMATE & WEATHER REPORTS

CLIMATE

The late Luther Burbank, known as the plant wizard, called Napa and Sonoma Counties "The chosen spot of all the earth as far as nature is concerned."

The moderate weather is a blessing for those who have suffered Midwestern blizzards. In Napa and Sonoma, the winter is cool, with temperatures dipping down to the 40s. Rainy season begins in late December and lingers until April. Of course, the droughts in recent years have made the season somewhat unpredictable, and the locals count raindrops with good cheer. Rain makes for a lush countryside and hillsides ribbed with vineyards.

TEMPERATURE AND PRECIPITATION
Average Temperatures

	Napa	Sonoma
October	62.0	62.2
January	47.6	47.2
April	56.6	56.6
July	67.4	70.0

Average Annual Total Precipitation

	Napa	Sonoma
rain	24.64	29.94
snow	0	0

WEATHER REPORTS

Napa County

Calistoga	707-942-2828

Sonoma County

Cloverdale	707-894-3545
Healdsburg	707-431-3360
Sonoma	707-938-9559

GUIDED TOURS

Looking for some packaged fun? Consider our list of tours. They will take you on a Wine Country adventure via a stretch limo, horse-drawn wagon, or even a cable car.

Getaway Adventures (707-942-0332, 800-499-2453; www.getawayadventures.com; 1117 Lincoln Ave., Calistoga, CA 94515) Day trips priced at $105 per person have bikers pedaling to five or six wineries with a gourmet lunch to boot. The company also books two- and six-day bike trips. Adventurers will find the Pedal and Paddle Tour invigorating. It features a half day of canoeing and a half day of bicycling. Rentals out of shop in Calistoga.

Wine & Dine Tours (707-963-8930, 800-946-3868; www.wineanddinetour.com; 345 La Fata St., Suite E., PO Box 513, St. Helena, CA 94574) This tour is for the discriminating traveler who would like to stop in at small boutique wineries in Napa Valley and Sonoma Valley. Most of the wineries are private or by appointment only.

HANDICAPPED SERVICES

Wine Country is accessible — even in a wheelchair. Napa and Sonoma offer a number of easy solutions to help anyone with a handicap get to and fro.

Dial-A-Ride-Services, Inter City Van-Go (707-252-2600, Greater Napa Area; 707-963-4222, Upper Valley) All vans are wheelchair accessible.

Handyvan-Calistoga (707-963-4229) The vans are wheelchair accessible.

The Vine (707-255-7631) The Valley Intracity Neighborhood Express has five routes in the city of Napa. All buses are wheelchair accessible.

Volunteer Wheels of Sonoma County (707-573-3377) Transportation for senior citizens and disabled riders.

The Hiker's Hip Pocket Guide to Sonoma County, Bored Feet Publications, includes a special section for the handicapped indicating which scenic trails are accessible.

HOSPITALS

Healdsburg General Hospital (707-431-6500; 1375 University Ave., Healdsburg) 24-hour emergency care. Physician on duty. Call the general number and ask for the Emergency Room.

Petaluma Valley Hospital (707-778-1111; 400 N. McDowell Blvd., Petaluma) 24-hour emergency care. Emergency Room, 707-778-2634.

Queen of the Valley Hospital (707-252-4411; 1000 Trancas St., Napa) 24-hour emergency services. Physician on duty. Emergency Room, 707-257-4038.

St. Helena Hospital (707-963-3611; 650 Sanitarium Road, Deer Park) Emergency Room, 707-963-6425.

Santa Rosa Memorial Hospital (707-546-3210; 1165 Montgomery Dr., Santa Rosa) 24-hour emergency services. Physician on duty. Emergency Room, 707-525-5207.

Sonoma Valley Hospital (707-935-5000; 347 Andrieux St., Sonoma) 24-hour emergency care. Emergency Room, 707-935-5105.

Sutter Medical Center of Santa Rosa (707-576-4000; 3325 Chanate Rd. Santa Rosa) 24-hour emergency care. Emergency Room, 707-576-4040.

LATE NIGHT FOOD AND FUEL

Insomnia after too much gourmet food or wine? Or perhaps you're just a weary traveler looking for a place to gas up. Whatever the case, here are some options for night birds.

Napa County

Bel Aire Shell Service: 707-226-1720; 1491 Trancas St., Napa
Albertsons: 707-255-7767; 1312 Trancas St., Napa
Safeway: 707-963-3833; 1026 Hunt Ave., St. Helena

Sonoma County

Flamingo Shell: 707-542-4456; 2799 4th St., Santa Rosa.
Ralphs: 707-545-8906; 390 Coddingtown Mall, off Hwy 101 at Steele Lane, Santa Rosa
Safeway: 707-996-0633; 477 W. Napa St., Sonoma

MEDIA: MAGAZINES, NEWSPAPERS, RADIO STATIONS AND TELEVISION

MAGAZINES AND NEWSPAPERS

The Business Journal (707-579-2900; 5510 Skylane Blvd., Suite 201, Santa Rosa, CA 95403 twice-monthly Sonoma and Marin Counties, monthly Napa and Solano Counties) The region's rendition of the Wall Street Journal, with news on the deals and the players and profiles on key business leaders.

California Visitors Review (707-938-0780; PO Box 92, El Verano, CA 95433; weekly) A good magazine for tourists, with articles on winemakers, inns, and restaurants. Helpful maps included in each issue. Free.

Healdsburg Tribune (707-433-4451; 5 Mitchell Lane, Healdsburg, CA 95448; Wed.) This Sonoma County paper, born in 1953, still has the flavor of the '50s.

Napa Valley Register (707-226-3711; 1615 2nd St., Napa, CA 94559; daily) The paper made its first run in 1865 and has proven over the years to give a good local account of Napa County.

Press Democrat (707-546-2020; 427 Mendocino Ave., Santa Rosa, CA 95401; daily) Purchased by the *New York Times* in the 1980s, the Press Democrat is the largest newspaper in the North Bay. It emphasizes Sonoma County, with newly expanded coverage of the Napa food and wine scene.

San Francisco Chronicle (415-777-7000; 901 Mission St., San Francisco, CA 94103; daily) This metro is not impressive to look at, but it's a good source for national and international news. There are often good Wine Country articles in the food and people sections.

Sonoma Business (707-575-8282; 50 Courthouse Square, Suite 105, Santa Rosa, CA 95404; monthly) Covers business and industry in Sonoma County well. It delves into the "politics" of business.

Northern California Bohemian (707-527-1200; 540 Mendocino Ave., Santa Rosa, CA 95401; weekly) Edgy alternative weekly with strong — and liberal — views on politics in Northern California.

Sonoma Index-Tribune (707-938-2111; 117 W. Napa St., Sonoma, CA 95476; twice weekly) A community paper that focuses exclusively on life in Sonoma Valley.

St. Helena Star (707-963-2731; 1328 Main St.; St. Helena, CA 94599; weekly) A folksy weekly that covers this town in the heart of Napa Valley.

RADIO STATIONS

KSXY 95.9 FM (Healdsburg, 707-588-0707) Top 40s.

KZST/100.1 FM (Santa Rosa, 707-528-4434) Adult contemporary.

KJZY 93.7 FM (Santa Rosa, 707-528-4434) Light jazz.

KRPQ 104.9 FM (Rohnert Park, 707-584-1058) Country music.

KSRO 1350 AM (Santa Rosa, 707-543-0100) News and talk.

KFGY 92.9 FM (Santa Rosa, 707-543-0100) Country music.

KMGG 97.7 FM (Santa Rosa, 707 543-0100) Oldies.

KGRP 100.9 FM (Santa Rosa, 707, 588-0707) Adult Contemporary.

KVON 1440 AM (Napa, 707-252-1440) News. Talk. Sports.

KVYN 93.3 FM (Napa, 707-258-1111) Adult contemporary.

KXFX 101.7 FM (Santa Rosa, 707-543-0100) Rock.

KRSH 98.7 FM (Middletown/Santa Rosa, 707-588-0707) Adult album alternative.

KRCB 9.9 FM and 91.1 FM (Santa Rosa, 707-585-8522) National Public Radio, and classical and eclectic music.

TELEVISION

There's only one local station in all of Wine Country. **KFTY, Channel 50,** broadcasts from 533 Mendocino Ave., Santa Rosa, CA 95401 (707-526-5050). Depending on your location, San Francisco and Oakland stations are often within range as well.

Both counties have access to cable television that offers most Bay Area and Sacramento TV channels, as well as the usual cable fare such as CNN, HBO, USA Network. **ATT Broadband** (800-482-4669) services most of the cities within Napa and Sonoma counties.

REAL ESTATE

Buying a piece of the American Dream — real estate — is downright costly for Californians. In fact, for some it is a nightmare. But if you come to Wine Country and decide to stay, here is information that may help you.

Housing costs in Sonoma and Napa are among the highest in the country. The median price for a 3-bedroom, 1.5 bath, 1,800-square-foot house in Napa County, for instance, is $195,000. Whatever the case, most natives won't dicker over price endlessly. They know they're not just purchasing real estate — they're also buying rights to the nearby ocean, the steep mountains, and a tapestry of vineyards in the countryside: a rare combination.

For information on real estate matters, consult the yellow pages of Napa and Sonoma phone books under Real Estate Agents. For insight into the real estate market, call the **Napa Chamber of Commerce** (707-226-7455), the **Napa County Association of Realtors** (707-255-1040), and the **North Bay Realtors Association** (707-542-1579). The latter two organizations compile statistics on area real estate. You can also follow the local newspapers. *The Press Democrat,* for instance, has a complete real estate section published every Sunday (see "Media" in this chapter).

RELIGIOUS SERVICES & ORGANIZATIONS

The best sources for information about church and synagogue services are the Saturday editions of the *Napa Register* and the *Press Democrat*. The Napa and Sonoma County phone books have comprehensive lists of all mainstream religious organizations along with specific church and synagogue numbers. You can also consult pamphlets put out by the Napa and Sonoma visitors bureaus. For nontraditional groups, keep an eye on community bulletin boards at colleges such as Sonoma State University and Napa Valley College.

ROAD SERVICE

Puncture your tire on a broken bottle of 1995 Rafanelli Zinfandel? Stranger things are known to have happened. For emergency road service from AAA, anywhere in Napa or Sonoma Counties, call 800-222-4357. Listed below are other 24-hour emergency road services.

Napa County

Calistoga Towing: 707-942-4445
Napa Vintage Towing: 707-226-3780
St. Helena Towing: 707-963-1869

Sonoma County

ABC Towing: Healdsburg; 707-433-1700
Sebastopol Towing: 707-823-1061
Santa Rosa Towing: 707-542-1600

SCHOOLS

PUBLIC SCHOOL DISTRICTS

Napa County

Calistoga Joint Unified School District: Calistoga; 707-942-4703
Napa County School District: Napa; 707-253-6800
St. Helena Unified School District: St. Helena; 707-967-2708

Sonoma County

Cotati-Rohnert Park Unified School District: Cotati; 707-792-4700
Healdsburg School District: Healdsburg; 707-431-3117
Piner-Olivet Union School District: Santa Rosa; 707-522-3000
Roseland School District: Santa Rosa; 707-545-0102
Santa Rosa School District: Santa Rosa; 707-528-5373
Sonoma Valley Unified School District: Sonoma; 707-935-6000

PRIVATE AND RELIGIOUS SCHOOLS

Napa County

Highlands Christian Preschool: Calistoga; 707-942-5557
Kolbe Academy: Napa; 707-255-6412
St. Helena Montessori School: St. Helena; 707-963-1527
St. John The Baptist Catholic School: Napa; 707-255-3533

Sonoma County

Brush Creek Montessori: Santa Rosa; 707-539-7980
Open Bible Christian Academy: Santa Rosa; 707-528-0546
Sebastopol Christian School: Sebastopol; 707-823-2754
St. Luke Lutheran Preschool & Day Care Center: Santa Rosa; 707-545-0512
Ursuline High School: Santa Rosa; 707-524-1130

COLLEGES

Napa County

Napa Valley College: Napa; 707-253-3000

Sonoma County

Santa Rosa Junior College: Santa Rosa; 707-527-4011
Empire College, Business School and Law School: Santa Rosa; 707-546-4000
Sonoma State University: Rohnert Park; 707-664-2880

The shady campus of Santa Rosa Junior College.

Courtesy SRJC

TOURIST INFORMATION

Napa County

Calistoga Chamber of Commerce: 707-942-6333; www.calistogafun.com; 1458 Lincoln Ave., Suite 9, Calistoga, CA 94515.

Napa Valley Conference and Visitors Bureau: 707-226-7459; www.napaval ley.com; info@napavalley.org; 1310 Napa Town Center, Napa, CA 94559.

St. Helena Chamber of Commerce: 707-963-4456; www.sthelena.com; 1010 Main St., Suite A, St. Helena, CA 94574.

Yountville Chamber of Commerce: 707-944-0904; www.yountville.com; 6516 Yount St., PO Box 2064, Yountville, CA 94599.

Sonoma County

Healdsburg Chamber of Commerce and Visitors Bureau: 707-433-6935; www. healdsburg.org; hbgchamb@pacbell.net; 217 Healdsburg Ave., Healdsburg, CA 95448.

Petaluma Area Chamber of Commerce: 707-762-2785; www.petaluma.org; pacc @petaluma.org; 800 Baywood Dr., Suite B., Petaluma, CA 94954.

Russian River Chamber of Commerce and Visitors Center: 707-869-9000; www. Russianriver.com; info@russianriver.com; 16209 1st Street, Guerneville, CA 95446

Santa Rosa Chamber of Commerce: 707-545-1414; www.gosonoma.com; kei thw@santarosachamber.com; 637 1st St., Santa Rosa, CA 95404.

Sebastopol Chamber of Commerce: 707-823-3032; www.sebastopol.org; apples@sebastopol.org; 265 S. Main St., Sebastopol, CA 95472.

Bodega Bay Area Visitors Center: 707-875-3422; www.bodegabay.org; 850 Hwy. 1, Bodega Bay, CA 94923.

Sonoma County Tourism Program: 707-565-5383; www.sonomacounty.com; info@sonomacounty.com; 520 Mendocino Ave., Suite 210, Santa Rosa, CA 95401.

Sonoma Valley Visitors Bureau: 707-996-1090; www.sonomavalley.com; svvb @verio.com; 453 1st St. E., Sonoma, CA 95476. A second office is now open below Viansa Winery: 707-935-4747; 25200 Arnold Dr., Sonoma, CA 95476.

IF TIME IS SHORT

Ideally your visit to the Wine Country should be long enough to include visits to several of the attractions in each category. But if time is of the essence, and you find yourself forced to choose just one restaurant for dining or one winery to visit, then perhaps we can help. Here are our personal favorites — with emphasis on the personal. Not everyone might pick these particular spots, but we feel confident that you will enjoy them as much as we do.

INNS

Oak Knoll Inn (707-255-2200; oakknollinn.com; 2200 E. Oak Knoll Ave., Napa, CA 94558) An intimate and luxurious inn just north of the city of Napa. The hospitality is exceptional and the breakfasts are among the best in Wine Country.

Inn at Occidental (707-874-1047, 800-522-6324; www.innatoccidental.com; 3657 Church St., Occidental, CA 95465) Well off the beaten path but worth it. Perched on a hill overlooking the quiet village of Occidental, this Victorian inn is a jewel.

CULTURAL ATTRACTIONS

The Hess Collection (707-255-1144; 4411 Redwood Dr., Napa, CA 94558) This stylish winery has one of the most impressive art collections north of San Francisco. Plus the wine is superb.

Mission San Francisco Solano (707-938-9560; corner of Spain St. & 1st St. E., Sonoma Plaza, Sonoma, CA 95476) Wine Country history doesn't get any richer than this. Built before 1841, the white adobe with a red-tile roof was the last mission built in California.

RESTAURANTS

Bouchon (707-944-8037; 6534 Washington St., Yountville, CA 94599) Bouchon has the authentic feel of an upscale brasserie in Paris, and it has a menu to match. The man behind it is Thomas Keller of The French Laundry. What a find — Paris in Napa Valley.

Deuce (707-933-3823, 691 Broadway, Sonoma, CA 95476) Deuce, set in a charming 110-year old Victorian farm house, is one of the most popular restaurants in the Sonoma Valley and rightly so. The menu offers comfort and adventure.

WINERIES

For beginners: **Korbel Champagne Cellars** (707-824-7000; 13250 River Rd., Guerneville, CA 95446) No mystery why visitors flock here. It has everything: rich history, a beautiful locale, a great tour, and lots of bubbly.

For wine buffs: **Opus One** (707-963-1979; www.opusonewines.com; 7900 St. Helena Hwy., PO Box 106, Oakville, CA 94562) This distinctive winery was largely inaccessible to the public until 1994. You'll still need an appointment. It makes one wine: a blockbuster red.

RECREATION

Lazy Fun: A spa treatment is a must. A one-hour massage with whirlpool bath is Nirvana. (Mud baths, though, aren't for everyone.) Our favorites include **Calistoga Spa Hot Springs**, **Meadowood Resort** outside St. Helena, and the unique Japanese-style spa **Osmosis** in Occidental.

Real Adventure: A **hot-air balloon ride** over Wine Country is beautiful and exhilarating. See "Ballooning" in Chapter Seven, *Recreation*, for details and suggested companies.

Index

TOURING INDEX

LODGING BY PRICE: INNS, B&BS

Price Codes
Inexpensive: Up to $100
Moderate: $100 to $150
Expensive: $150 to $250
Very Expensive: Over $250

NAPA COUNTY

INEXPENSIVE
Calistoga Inn, 47

INEXPENSIVE–MODERATE
Carlin Cottages, 47
Nance's Hot Springs, 55

INEXPENSIVE–EXPENSIVE
The Chateau, 76
El Bonita Motel, 40

MODERATE
Calistoga Country Lodge, 47
Calistoga Spa Hot Springs, 54
Discovery Inn, 76
Napa Valley Railway Inn, 35

MODERATE–EXPENSIVE
Best Western Inn at the Vines, 76
Bordeaux House, 34
Brannan Cottage Inn, 46
Brookside Vineyard, 27
Calistoga Village Inn and Spa, 54

RESTAURANTS BY PRICE

RESTAURANTS BY CUISINE

NAPA COUNTY

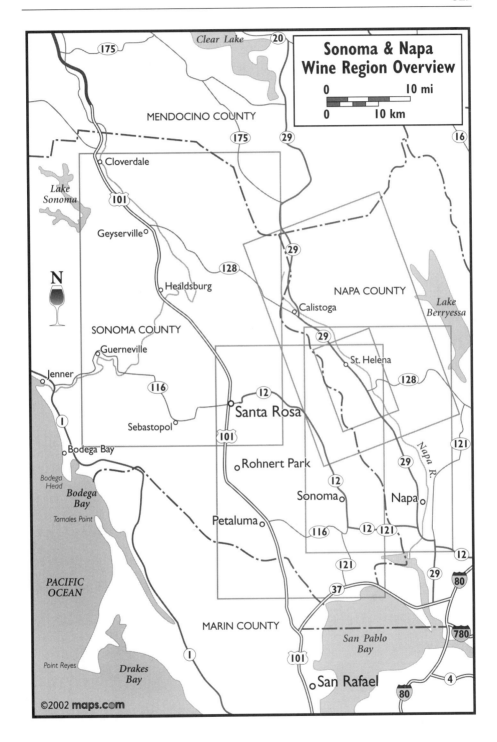

Sonoma & Napa Wine Region Overview

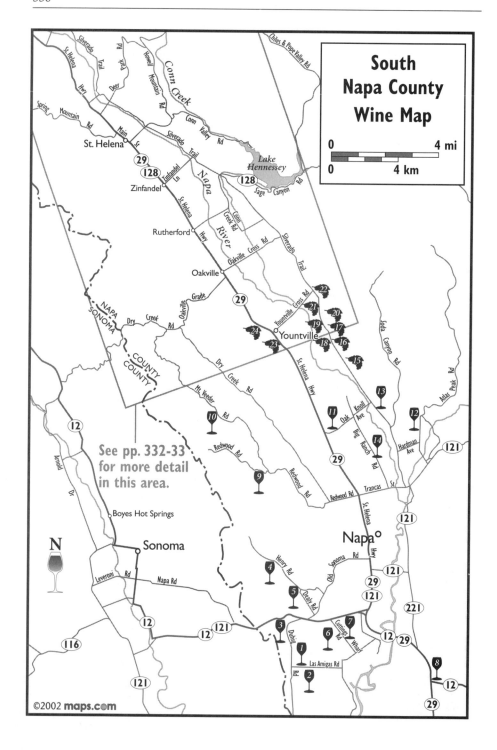

South Napa County Wine Map

0 — 4 mi
0 — 4 km

St. Helena

Zinfandel

Rutherford

Oakville

Lake Hennessey

Yountville

See pp. 332-33 for more detail in this area.

Boyes Hot Springs

Sonoma

N

Napa

Las Amigas Rd

©2002 maps.com

South Napa Wineries

🍷 Napa & Carneros Region

1. *Acacia Winery*
2. *Bouchaine Vineyards*
3. *Domaine Carneros*
4. *Artesa Vineyards & Winery*
5. *Carneros Creek Winery*
6. *Saintsbury*
7. *R.M.S. Distillery*
8. *Hakusan Sake Gardens*
9. *The Hess Collection*
10. *Mayacamus Vineyards & Winery*
11. *Trefethen Vineyards*
12. *William Hill Winery*
13. *Signorello Vineyards*
14. *Monticello Cellars*

🦃 Yountville & Stag's Leap Region

15. *Clos du Val*
16. *Chimney Rock Winery*
17. *Stag's Leap Wine Cellars*
18. *Pine Ridge Winery*
19. *Silverado Vineyards*
20. *Shafer Vineyards*
21. *S. Anderson Winery*
22. *Robert Sinskey Vineyards*
23. *Domaine Chandon*
24. *Cosentino Winery*

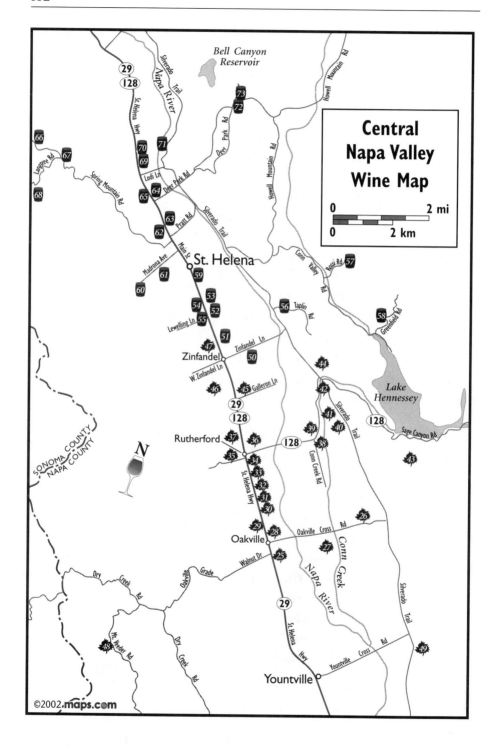

Bell Canyon Reservoir

Lake Hennessey

Central Napa Valley Wine Map

0   2 mi

0   2 km

St. Helena

Zinfandel

Rutherford

Oakville

Yountville

SONOMA COUNTY
NAPA COUNTY

N

©2002.maps.com

CENTRAL NAPA VALLEY WINERIES

Oakville &
🌸 **Rutherford Region**

25. Napa Wine Company
26. Groth Vineyards & Winery
27. Silver Oak Cellars
28. Opus One
29. Robert Mondavi
30. Turnbull Wine Cellars
31. Cakebread Cellars
32. Sequoia Grove Winery
33. St. Supéry Vineyard & Winery
34. Peju Province
35. Niebaum-Coppola Estate Winery
36. Beaulieu Vineyards
37. Grgich Hills Cellars
38. Caymus Vineyards
39. Frog's Leap Winery
40. ZD Wines
41. Mumm Napa Valley
42. Villa Mt. Eden Winery
43. Chappellet Winery
44. Rutherford Hill Winery
45. Franciscan Vineyards
46. Whitehall Lane
47. Flora Springs Wine Co.
48. Chateau Potelle
49. Miner Family Vineyards

🛢 **St. Helena Region**

50. Raymond Vineyard & Cellars
51. V. Sattui Winery
52. Heitz Wine Cellars
53. Louis Martini Winery
54. Sutter Home Winery
55. Prager Winery and Port Works
56. Joseph Phelps Vineyards
57. Anderson's Conn Valley Vineyards
58. Buehler Vineyards
59. Merryvale Vineyards
60. Newton Vineyard
61. Spottswoode Winery
62. Beringer Vineyards
63. Charles Krug Winery
64. Markham
65. St. Clement Vineyards
66. Philip Togni
67. Robert Keenan Winery
68. Cain Vineyard & Winery
69. Freemark Abbey Winery
70. Folie À Deux Winery
71. Duckhorn Vineyards
72. Burgess Cellars
73. Viader Vineyards

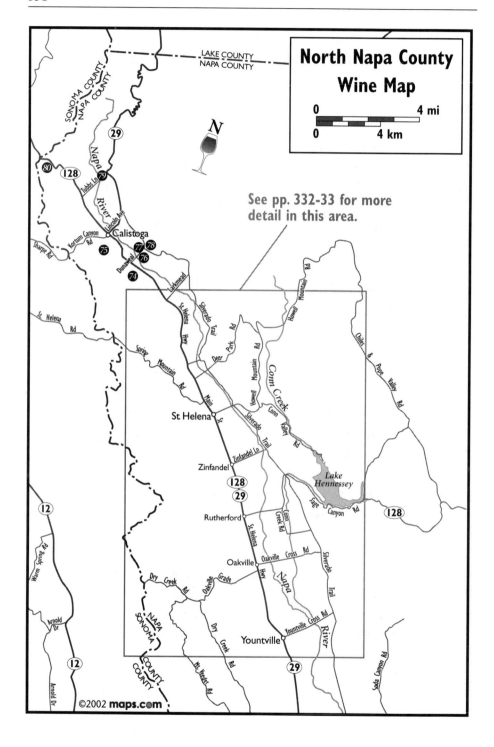

North Napa County
Wine Map

0   4 mi
0   4 km

LAKE COUNTY
NAPA COUNTY

SONOMA COUNTY
NAPA COUNTY

N

See pp. 332-33 for more
detail in this area.

Calistoga

St Helena

Zinfandel

Rutherford

Oakville

Yountville

Lake
Hennessey

Corn Creek

Napa River

St. Helena Rd

Spring Mountain Rd

Silverado Trail

Deer Park Rd

Howell Mountain Rd

Conn Valley Rd

Chiles & Pope Valley Rd

Howell Mountain Rd

Sage Canyon Rd

Conn Creek Rd

Oakville Cross Rd

Silverado Trail

Dry Creek Rd

Oakville Grade

Mt Veeder Rd

Yountville Cross Rd

Soda Canyon Rd

Warm Spring Rd

Arnold Dr

Sharpe Rd

Kortum Canyon Rd

Tubbs Ln

Lincoln Ave

Dunaweal

Larkmead

St. Helena Hwy

Main St

Silverado Trail

St. Helena Hwy

Napa River

Zinfandel Ln

Tubbs Ln

NAPA SONOMA COUNTY

29

128

80

128

79

75

77

78

76

74

12

12

128

29

128

29

©2002 maps.com

NORTH NAPA WINERIES

● Calistoga Region

74. *Schramsberg Vineyards*

75. *Von Strasser Winery*

76. *Sterling Vineyards*

77. *Clos Pegase*

78. *Cuvaison*

79. *Chateau Montelena*

80. *Storybook Mountain Vineyards*

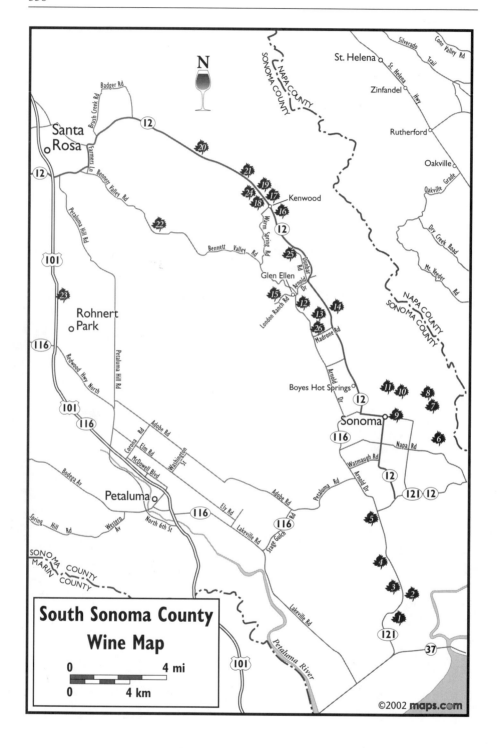

South Sonoma Wineries

🌸 Sonoma County Region

1. Roche Winery
2. Viansa Winery & Italian Market Place
3. Cline Cellars
4. Gloria Ferrer Champagne Caves
5. Schug Carneros Estate Winery
6. Gundlach-Bundschu Winery
7. Buena Vista Winery
8. Bartholomew Park Winery
9. Sebastiani Sonoma Cask Cellars
10. Ravenswood Winery
11. Hanzell Vineyards
12. Carmenet Winery
13. B.R. Cohn Winery
14. Arrowood Winery & Vineyards
15. Benziger Family Winery
16. Kunde Estate Winery
17. Kenwood Vineyards
18. The Wine Room
19. Chateau St. Jean
20. St. Francis Winery
21. Landmark Vineyards
22. Matanzas Creek Winery
23. Sonoma County Wine and Visitors Center
24. Family Wineries of Sonoma Valley
25. Wellington Vineyards
26. Valley of the Moon

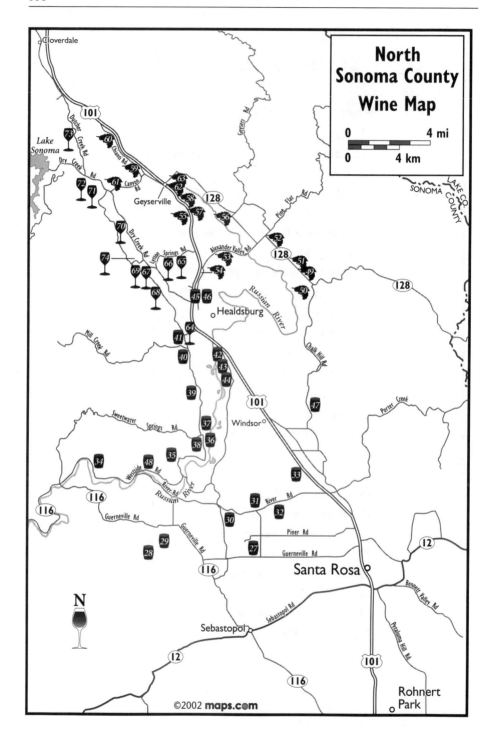

NORTH SONOMA WINERIES

▌ Russian River Region

27. *De Loach Vineyards*
28. *Iron Horse Vineyards*
29. *Topolos at Russian River*
30. *Joseph Swan Vineyards*
31. *Sonoma-Carter Vineyards*
32. *Martinelli Winery*
33. *Kendall-Jackson Wine Center*
34. *Korbel Champagne Cellars*
35. *Davis Bynum Winery*
36. *Rochioli Vineyards & Winery*
37. *Hop Kiln Winery*
38. *Williams Selyem*
39. *Belvedere Winery*
40. *Armida Winery*
41. *Mill Creek Vineyards*
42. *Foppiano Vineyards*
43. *Rodney Strong Vineyards*
44. *J Wine Co.*
45. *Kendall-Jackson Wine Country Store*
46. *Windsor Vineyards*
47. *Chalk Hill Winery*
48. *Gary Farrell Wines*

▼ Alexander Valley Region

49. *Hanna Winery*
50. *Field Stone Winery & Vineyards*
51. *Alexander Valley Vineyards*
52. *Sausal Winery*
53. *Jordan Vineyard & Winery*
54. *Simi Winery*
55. *Chateau Souverain*
56. *Muphy-Goode Estate Winery*
57. *Trentadue Winery*
58. *Clos du Bois*
59. *Geyser Peak Winery*
60. *Silver Oak Cellars*
61. *Pendroncelli Winery*
62. *Canyon Road Cellars*
63. *De Lorimier Winery*

▙ Dry Creek Region

64. *Alderbrook Winery*
65. *Ridge Vineyards*
66. *Mazzocco Vineyards*
67. *Dry Creek Vineyards*
68. *Lambert Bridge Winery*
69. *A. Rafanelli Winery*
70. *Quivira Vineyards*
71. *Preston Vineyards*
72. *Ferrari-Carano Vineyards & Winery*
73. *J. Fritz Winery*
74. *Pezzi King Vineyards*

About the Authors

Forsaking corn for grapes, Tim Fish and Peg Melnik moved from the Midwest to Sonoma County in 1989. Fish is a freelance writer and frequent guest lecturer at the Culinary Institute of America at Greystone in Napa Valley. Previously, he was the editor of *WineToday.com*, a web site published by The New York Times Company, and Food and Wine Editor for the Santa Rosa *Press Democrat*. Melnik is the wine columnist for the New York Times-owned *Press Democrat* and the editor of *TakeTwenty*, a parenting newsletter. Both Fish and Melnik have earned first-place awards from the Association of Food Journalists.

Fish was raised in Indiana and while earning his journalism degree at Western Kentucky University, he won Rolling Stone magazine's college journalism award and was an intern at Forbes magazine in New York City. He has worked at daily newspapers in Kentucky, Illinois, and Ohio.

Melnik earned a degree in English education at the University of Illinois and followed that with a masters degree in public affairs reporting. Melnik has worked for daily newspapers in Iowa and Ohio and her freelance credits include the *Los Angeles Times*, *San Francisco Chronicle*, and the *Boston Herald*.

Married since 1986, Fish and Melnik have a daughter, Sophie, born in June 1991, a week before the deadline of the first edition. Their son, Tucker, was born just before the release of the fifth edition.